# SOCIOLOGY IN FOCUS

## for OCR AS Level

### Edited by
## Michael Haralambos and Peter Langley

Michael Haw Pilkington,
John Richardsoth Viv Thompson

D0453080

**Dedication**
To our mothers from Michael and Peter

**Acknowledgements**

| | |
|---|---|
| Cover and page design | Caroline Waring-Collins (Waring-Collins Ltd) |
| Graphic origination | John A. Collins (Waring-Collins Ltd) |
| Graphics | Tim Button (Waring-Collins Ltd) |
| Author index and typing | Ingrid Hamer |
| Reader | Mike Kidson |

**Picture credits**

Advertising Archives 73(t), 81 (bl), 113 (tl), 155 (bl, bm, br), 158 (ml, bl); Allan Hutchings 17(r); Andrew Allen 21 (tl, tr), 181 (tl), 201 (mr, r), 237; Associated Press 6 (bl, br), 25 (tl), 30, 42 (b), 52 (ml), 58 (tl, ml), 64 (tr, tl), 69 (br), 84 (t), 90 (l), 109 (r), 110, 124 (l), 138 (l, r), 139, 148, 166 (bl, br), 168 (br), 173 (tr); Axel Poignant Archice 73 (b); BBC Photograph Library 6(t), 18, 161 (m, bl, br); BHS 24; Brian Smith 225 (ml, bl); Bridgeman Art Library 125 (l, r); Camera Press 182 (tl), 206 (r); Dave Gray 136, 162 (t); David Hoffman 109 (bl), 181 (tr), 184 (tr, tl), 208, 221 (r, l), 230 (tr); Equal Opportunities Commission 104; Eye Ubiquitous/James Davis Worldwide 75 (bl); Format Photographers (and Jacky Chapman) 214; Glenbow Archives 124 (r);; Hutchinson Picture Library 68; Jeff Morgan 56 (m); John Collins 28, 126, 136, 146 (mr, br), 170, 174 (tm, tr), 189; Kate Haralambos 67 (mr, bl), 84 (m), 107 (ml), 117; Lonely Planet Images/Peter Bennetts 144 (tl); North News and Pictures 42 (m); Peter Newark's Military Pictures 178; PhotoDisc 228; Photofusion (and Martin Bond) 4, (and Paula Solloway) 9 (tl, tr), 12 (tl), 52 (tl), 236, (and Jacky Chapman) 9 (br), 10 (t), 12 (bl), 18 (b), 46, 51 (br), 112 (tr), (and Julian Martin) 9 (bl), 112 (tl), (and Ulricka Preuss) 15 (br), 112 (bl), (and Don Gray) 50 (m), (and Paul Doyle) 52 (mr), (and David Townend) 64 (ml), (and Melanie Friend) 60, (and Bob Watkins) 175 (t), (and Pete Jones) 175 (tm), (and Marcella Hugard) 175 (bm), (and Liz Somerville) 175 (b); popperfoto.com 12 (tr), 25 (tr), 35, 47 (mr), 164, 181 (mr), 210, 227 (l), 230 (br); Rex Features 10 (m), 14 (tl, tr), 15 (bl), 37, 40 (br), 44 (bl), 49 (br), 50 (t, b), 52 (tr), 53, 55 (bl, br), 58 (tr), 83 (t, m), 100 (r), 119 (b), 135, 144 (tr), 158 (r), 159, 162 (b), 165 (l), 168 (tr, br), 171 (ml), 173 (tl), 182 (mr), 184 (b), 205, 206 (l), 217, 225 (r); Robert Estall Photo Agency 75 (mr); Sally and Richard Greenhill 66, 69 (tl, bl), 119 (t), 165 (r), 194, 201 (l, ml), 227 (r); Smithsonian Institution 7; Steve Bell 60 (bl); Steve Caplin 140; Topham Picturepoint 12 (br), 18 (t), 40 (bl), 41, 44 (br), 45 (m, b), 47 (ml), 49 (bl), 51 (bl), 69 (tr), 77 (tl), 92, 100 (l), 109 (tl), 112 (br), 123, 131, 146 (ml), 151, 156 (ml), 171 (br), 174 (tl), 216 (l), 234; Women's Aid 130 (l).

**Cartoons**

Unless otherwise credited, the cartoons in this book have been specially drawn by BRICK www.brickbats.co.uk

**Cover picture**
Hundertwasser
MISTER HUMUS AEROBIC, 1981
© J. Harel, Vienna

British Library Cataloguing in Publication Data
A catalogue record for this book is available from the British Library.

ISBN-13: 978-1-902796-16-1

Causeway Press Limited
PO Box 13, Ormskirk, Lancs  L39 5HP

First impression 2003, reprinted 2004, 2005, 2006, 2007
Printed and bound by Scotprint, Haddington, East Lothian.

**LEARNING ZONE
DEESIDE COLLEGE**

# Contents

# 1 The individual and society

## Introduction

Is there anybody else exactly like you? You'll probably answer 'no'. We like to think of ourselves as individuals and to see ourselves as unique.

Sociology does not deny this individuality. It does not claim that everybody is the same. However, it does argue that many of us have certain things in common. For example, members of a particular society share the same language. In this respect, we are not unique.

Most people live in social groups – in families, communities and nations – rather than as isolated individuals. As the poet John Donne said, 'No man is an island' (nowadays he would say that goes for women too). In other words, we are constantly coming into contact with other people. We are affected by them, we develop bonds with them. Indeed, we only become fully 'human' by participating in society.

Sociology has sometimes been described as the study of people in social groups. In this chapter we shall explore the fascinating story of how individuals are not isolated 'islands' but active members of society. We shall see how we learn certain values and ways of behaving, and how our membership of social groups gives meaning to our lives and shapes our identities.

Sociologists do not always agree on how and why things happen. But they help us to see more clearly how we are both 'individuals' and members of 'society'. And they help us see the connections between the two.

*Unique individuals with many things in common*

## chaptersummary

▶ **Unit 1** identifies the main components of culture.

▶ **Unit 2** identifies the main components of social structure.

▶ **Unit 3** looks at socialisation – how people learn culture and their roles in society.

▶ **Unit 4** outlines some of the ways sociologists have explained social life.

▶ **Unit 5** identifies the main changes in human societies.

▶ **Unit 6** focuses on the meaning of identity.

▶ **Unit 7** looks at the formation of gender identities.

▶ **Unit 8** looks at the formation of national identities.

▶ **Unit 9** looks at the formation of ethnic identities.

▶ **Unit 10** looks at the formation of class identities.

## Unit 1 What is culture?

### keyissues

1 Are humans ruled by instincts?

2 How does culture shape human behaviour?

3 What are the main components of culture?

## 1.1 Becoming human

### Instincts vs culture

Why do human beings behave the way they do? One view is that it is a matter of *instincts* – biological predispositions that tell us 'instinctively' what we should do. Instincts are something we are born with rather than something we learn. A great deal of animal behaviour seems to be ruled by instincts. For example, birds seem to follow fairly fixed patterns of behaviour as if they were a set part of their 'nature'.

Nowadays, a popular explanation for human behaviour is to look for the answer in our genes. People vary in their genetic make-up and this might explain why they behave differently. Some scientists claim there is a gene for crime, one for alcoholism, even a 'gay' gene. Some have offered genetic explanations for why men are unable to find butter in the fridge, or why women can't read maps!

Sociologists accept that humans have natural *reflexes* –

# *activity*1 genes or society?

There is no gene or brain pattern which makes men incapable of ironing, shopping, changing nappies or expressing their emotions. And there is none which stops women running governments or multinational corporations, flying fighter planes, abusing children or committing murder. It is culture which explains why women do more of some things and men do more of other things.

Adapted from MacInnes, 1998

## *questions*

1   What view does Item A take on the genes versus culture debate?
2   Look at Item B.
   a)   Why are the passengers reacting like this?
   b)   Is there any justification for their reaction?

**Item B  A woman's place**

THIS IS YOUR CAPTAIN JENNY ROBINSON SPEAKING...

---

for example, we automatically flinch when someone strikes us. They also accept that we have certain biological *needs* that must be met – for example, the need for food and drink. But sociologists believe human behaviour is too complex and diverse to be explained in simple biological or genetic terms. Rather, they see our actions as the result of our social and cultural environments. We *learn* to think and act in certain ways. And it is our *culture* which teaches us how we should think and act.

### Feral children

People become fully human only when they are socialised into the culture of a society – when they learn the way of life of that society. It is culture which allows them to develop their human potential. We can see this in the case of so-called feral children – children raised in the wilds or in prolonged isolation from human company. Some reported cases are pure fantasy but the few authentic cases show that when these children are discovered and enter human society they encounter serious problems. They often seem stupid, unresponsive and animal-like. Deprived of the stimulation of human company, stripped of the opportunity to acquire human language early in life, these children are sometimes barely recognisable as human.

### Cultural diversity

If human behaviour really is dictated by our genes or instincts, we would expect to find people behaving in much the same way all over the world. But what is regarded as normal behaviour varies from one culture to another. If we lived in Victorian Britain or in modern China, we would follow different customs, have different lifestyles. So human behaviour is flexible and diverse. It varies according to the culture we live in. Even the way we display our bodies in public changes over time and from place to place.

**The social body** Norbert Elias (1978) provides a detailed account of changing cultural attitudes towards the body. In sixteenth century Europe there was little sense of shame or delicacy about bodily matters. People would happily wipe snot on their sleeve or blow their nose on the tablecloth. They usually ate with their hands, and belching, farting, scratching, and even urinating or defecating in public were commonplace. But Elias describes how in the succeeding centuries people gradually became more sensitive to the 'shame' and 'disgust' of bodily functions as they developed 'good manners' and disciplined their bodies to act in a 'civilised' way.

### Becoming human – conclusion

The long-running debate over whether human behaviour is largely the result of 'nature' (genes, biology) or 'nurture' (culture, environment) shows no sign of coming to an end. Nature and nurture always interact in complex ways. Even if we have a biological inclination to behave in certain

# activity2 from monkey boy to choir boy

Walking through a Ugandan forest, a woman spotted a group of monkeys. To her astonishment, she realised that one member of the group was a small boy. Local villagers 'rescued' this 'monkey boy' and identified him as John Ssabunnya who had been abandoned as a two-year-old.

For the past three years, John had lived with a troupe of colobus monkeys. He had learned to communicate with them – with chatters, shrieks, facial expressions and body language. He shared their diet of fruit, nuts and berries, he became skilled at climbing trees and, like those who adopted him, he walked on all-fours. He was terrified of his 'rescuers' and fought to remain with his family of monkeys.

John, aged 14

John was washed and clothed – much to his disgust – and taken to an orphanage. He gradually learned to behave like a human being. Slowly but surely, he began to sing, laugh, talk, play, dress and walk like children of his age.

Today, John is a member of the Pearl of Africa Choir which has successfully toured the United Kingdom.

Adapted from the *Daily Mail*, 23.9.1999

## question

How does the case of John Ssabunnya illustrate the importance of learned behaviour for human beings?

# activity3 the body

Afghanistan

Rome

## question

What do these photographs suggest about culture and attitudes towards the body?

ways, this will be channelled by society – the aggressive individual could become a violent criminal or a successful boxer, depending on social circumstances.

Whatever our underlying nature, it is clear that culture has a huge effect on our behaviour. We saw this in the case of feral children. Also, human behaviour is enormously diverse, showing wide variations over time and between societies. Norbert Elias demonstrated how even our intimate body habits are a product of society.

Sociologists suggest that if we want to explain social behaviour, then most of the answers can be found at the social and cultural level.

## 1.2 Looking at culture

### Shared meanings and values

Sociologists usually define culture as the shared meanings, values and norms of a society or group.

**Meanings** Stuart Hall (1997) describes some of the key features of cultural meanings. First, it is largely thanks to *language* that humans are able to create meanings and make sense of the world. It is through language and other symbols, for example visual images, that people express their emotions and thoughts and communicate with one another. Second, culture is about *shared* meanings. People produce meanings together and so over time each social group builds up shared understandings of the world. Third, humans are constantly creating new meanings and revising old ones – so culture can be seen as a process or activity.

**Values** are things we regard as important, the most significant standards or principles in our lives. Love is an obvious example. Other examples are religious convictions and political loyalties. In everyday life, most people subscribe to the values of honesty, consideration towards others, justice and fairness – although we are not so good at living up to these values!

**Norms** are social expectations or rules about how people should or should not behave – for example, you should hold the door open for others, you should not grab the last biscuit. There are different rules for different situations – you can let your hair down at an end-of-term party, but the same behaviour would be frowned upon during normal class time. Norms also vary in their degree of seriousness. Committing murder will result in severe legal punishment but bad table manners might only provoke irritation in others.

## activity4 meanings, values, norms

### Item A  *Meanings*

### Item B  *Values*

The Cheyenne lived on the Great Plains of North America. This account describes their traditional culture.

The Cheyenne believe that wealth, in the form of horses and weapons, is not to be hoarded by the owner. Instead it is to be given away. Generosity is highly regarded and people who accumulate wealth and keep it for themselves are looked down upon. A person who gives does not expect an equal amount in return. The greatest gift they can receive is prestige and respect for their generous action.

Bravery on the battlefield is one of the main ways a man can achieve high standing. Killing an enemy, however, does not rank as highly as a number of other deeds. Touching or striking an enemy with the hand or a weapon, rescuing a wounded comrade or charging the enemy alone while the rest of the war party looks on are amongst the highest acts of bravery.

Adapted from Hoebel, 1960

*Cheyenne photographed in 1889*

## Item C  Norms

Culture defines appropriate distances between people when they hold a conversation. In *The Silent Language*, Edward Hall observed that these distances in North and South America are different. This can cause problems when North meets South. In Hall's words, 'The result is that when they move close, we withdraw and back away. As a consequence, they think we are distant or cold, withdrawn and unfriendly. We, on the other hand, are constantly accusing them of breathing down our necks, crowding us and spraying our faces.'

Adapted from Hall, 1973

## questions

1  What meanings does the symbol in Item A communicate?

2  a)  Identify the values of the Cheyenne described in Item B.

   b)  How do they indicate that values vary from culture to culture?

3  Norms are important. Discuss briefly with reference to Item C.

## Whole way of life

Anthropologists specialise in studying whole societies, especially small-scale, less technologically developed societies. Perhaps, as a result of this, they tend to adopt a sweeping definition of culture. Clyde Kluckhohn (1951) described culture as the distinctive 'way of life' of a group of people. This way of life includes their typical patterns of behaviour – their common lifestyles, the skills and techniques they use to make a living, and all their routines, customs and rituals.

## High and low culture

Sociologists don't usually make judgements about different cultures – they try to avoid seeing one culture as better than another. However, in everyday speech, people sometimes use the term culture to refer to classical music, opera, ballet and art. This is the idea of *high culture* – the works of people such as Mozart, Shakespeare and Van Gogh. High culture is usually seen as created by a talented few and enjoyed by a minority with refined and sophisticated tastes.

High culture is sometimes seen as superior to *low culture* or *popular culture* – the culture of the masses. Examples of popular culture include bingo, football, comics and pop music.

## Subcultures

As societies grow larger and more complex, it becomes increasingly difficult to talk about one culture which everybody shares. For example, in Britain today, there are groups who share many aspects of mainstream culture, but who also have certain beliefs, attitudes and ways of behaving of their own. In other words, they have their own *subcultures*.

Groups with distinctive subcultures include some ethnic minority groups, social class groups, regional groups and some age groups. This subcultural diversity has led to the term *multicultural society* being used to describe many large-scale industrial societies.

## The death of a princess

We can see how the different elements of culture operate by looking at the public response to the tragic death of Diana, Princess of Wales. Diana died in 1997 when her chauffeur-driven car crashed in a Paris tunnel while racing away from pursuing photographers. The reaction to Diana's death demonstrates the importance of values, symbols and norms in our lives.

**Values** Humans place high value on life and so they feel threatened and troubled by death. But they do not have to work out the meaning of life and death from scratch, alone and unaided. Their culture supplies them with ways of making sense of it all. In Diana's case, the funeral service in Westminster Abbey brought spiritual comfort to many people.

**Symbols** Many mourners used cultural symbols as a way of

# activity5 ethnic subcultures

Serving food, Pakistani wedding, Bradford

Bhangra dancing, Pakistani wedding Bradford

Steel band

Celebrating the Holi Festival, Norwood Green Nursery

## question

With reference to the pictures, identify some of the ways in which ethnic minority groups may have their own subcultures.

expressing their feelings. Some wrote poems, some hung flowers or ribbons on trees and others collected souvenirs of Diana. Music was another popular form of expression and Elton John's re-worked version of *Candle in the Wind*, played at the funeral, quickly shot to the top of the record charts.

**Norms** Cultural norms provide mourners with guidance on how to think, act and feel. In Victorian times people were expected to keep a tight control over their emotions (the 'stiff upper lip'). But cultural norms change and by the time of Diana's death it had become more acceptable to display emotions openly.

**Cultural diversity** Cultural guidelines are learned rather than innate and so there are differences between societies in their funeral customs. Nigel Barley (1995) reports that the Nyakyusa tribe ritually insult the dead and the bereaved – the relatives and close friends – who are not permitted to take offence. But in Britain, people are expected to speak respectfully of the recently dead. In Diana's case this rule was observed even by newspapers which had previously raked over her life for scandal and gossip.

**Subcultures** Various ethnic groups responded to Diana's death in terms of their own subcultures – for example, the expression of their grief was directed by their particular religions.

# activity6 the death of Diana

The reaction to the news of Princess Diana's death was immediate. A sea of flowers appeared outside the royal palaces. Crowds of mourners waited up to six hours to sign books of condolence. On the day of the funeral, as a mark of respect, the National Lottery draw was postponed, shops closed and football matches were cancelled. People appeared with sleeping bags outside Westminster Abbey days before the funeral – the vigil had begun.

At 9.08 am on September 6, 1997, the bells at Westminster Abbey began to toll for the funeral procession. Diana's coffin, draped in the Royal Standard and covered in lilies, emerged from Kensington Palace to begin its two-hour journey to the Abbey. Along the route, the procession was greeted with silence and tears. After the service, there was a minute's silence when the entire nation came to a halt in an expression of grief and loss.

Adapted from *Chronicle of the Year 1997*

Mourners created their own shrines to Diana

A floral tribute at the gates of Kensington Palace, Diana's former home

## question

Using the pictures and text, suggest how culture defines appropriate responses to death.

## Looking at culture – conclusion

Culture is essential to the operation of human society. Without shared meanings, people would be unable to communicate. Without shared values, they would be pulling in different directions. And without norms directing behaviour, there would be no order in society.

From a sociological viewpoint, human behaviour is primarily organised and directed by culture. We are not ruled by instinct, governed by our genes, or directed by biological needs and impulses. If we were, then human behaviour would be much the same in different times and in different societies. It isn't, as can be seen from the wide variation between cultures in different time periods and places.

## key terms

*Culture* The values, norms, meanings, beliefs and customs of a society; its whole way of life.
*Meanings* Things which give sense and significance to people's experiences.
*Norms* Social expectations; detailed guides to behaviour.
*Rituals* Actions regularly performed on special occasions.
*Symbols* Things – words, sounds, images – which stand for something else.
*Values* General standards or ethical principles which are highly prized.
*High culture* Culture produced by a talented few and enjoyed by a sophisticated minority.
*Low culture/popular culture* The culture of the masses.
*Subculture* Certain norms, values and meanings which are distinctive to a particular group within society.

## summary

1. Although animals sometimes learn new ways of behaving, they are largely controlled by more or less fixed biological instincts.

2. Human behaviour is too complex and too diverse to be explained solely by biologically-based instincts, needs or drives.

3. From a sociological view, human behaviour is largely directed by culture. Culture is learned rather than biologically based.

4. The example of feral children shows the importance of culture in making us fully human. Culture provides us with language, values and a sense of our human identity.

5. Culture varies from society to society.

6. Culture provides meanings, norms and values to guide our conduct and shape our emotions.

7. Sociologists try to avoid making judgements about cultures.

8. As societies become larger and more complex, there are growing numbers of groups with their own subcultures.

# Unit 2 Social structure and social control

## keyissues

1. What are the main components of social structure?
2. How are culture and structure related?
3. What are the main methods of social control?

## 2.1 Building a society

We have already seen what we mean by culture. But culture is not the only aspect of society of interest to sociologists. They also study the way societies are organised – their *social structure*.

### Lego land

It is easy to be dazzled by the sheer complexity of society. So many different things seem to be going on at once, and nothing seems to stand still for long. Yet if we follow all this activity for long enough we can detect some regular patterns. There seems to be a recognisable shape to social life. We can also see how the various parts of society are related to other parts.

These patterns and relationships are called social structure. We can think of it as like a giant Lego model, assembled by putting all the component parts together. The basic building blocks consist of *social statuses and social roles* which cluster into *social institutions* and together these make up the overall structure of society.

**Social status** A social status is a person's position in society. Examples of social statuses include teacher, student, mother, uncle, bricklayer, accountant, wife, husband.

A status can be *ascribed* or *achieved*. Ascribed statuses are largely fixed and unchangeable. Many are fixed at birth such as the statuses of male and female. However, ascribed statuses can be changed – occasionally people change their sex.

Achieved statuses involve some degree of choice – a person chooses to get married and adopt the status of wife or husband. As the term suggests, an achieved status results partly from individual achievement. To some extent, a person achieves their job as an architect, librarian, or carpenter on the basis of ability and effort.

**Social role** A role is a set of expectations that is applied to a particular social status or position in society. We expect a nun to be 'holy' and unselfish. A soldier is required to be brave and disciplined.

Each of us occupies a number of different statuses and so sometimes we have to juggle with competing expectations – this is called *role conflict*. For example, a father who is expected to put in long hours at work will find this clashes with his ability to spend time with his children.

The notion of role is borrowed from the stage. Shakespeare likened society to the theatre:

All the world's a stage
And all the men and women merely players
And one man in his time plays many parts
His acts being seven ages.

(Shakespeare – *As You Like It*)

**Social institutions** Social roles tend to arrange themselves in clusters, with each role having a strong connection with related roles. For example, the roles of patient, nurse, general practitioner and hospital consultant are interlinked. When roles group together like this they make up social institutions – economic, political, legal and other kinds of institutions. The family, too, can be considered as an institution – there are established conventions about the responsibilities and roles of parents, children and partners.

**Social structure** Just as social institutions are one level up from roles, so social structure is the next step up from social institutions – see Figure 1. The social structure of a society is the collection of social institutions in a society. These institutions are interrelated. For example, the education system trains people in literacy, numeracy and knowledge and this ensures a supply of educated workers

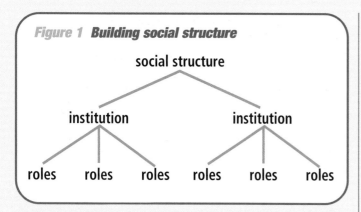

Figure 1 *Building social structure*

for the economy. The economy, in turn, creates wealth and some of this is used to finance the education system.

## Connecting culture and structure

Sociologists usually describe society as consisting of both culture and structure (see Figure 2). Certainly it is easy to separate them on a chart. However, in real life they always interact with each other. For instance, roles are both cultural (based on norms – cultural expectations) and structural (based on social statuses – structural positions). This can get confusing.

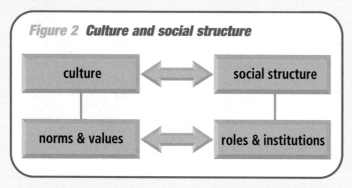

Figure 2 *Culture and social structure*

To avoid getting tied in knots, maybe it's simpler just to think of two separate spheres – culture and structure. And then think of the effect they have on each other.

Cultural norms and values shape how people behave – and this creates the roles and institutions of society. For example, a society with strong religious values will encourage religious roles (priests) and religious institutions (churches, mosques, temples). It will also ensure that religious values are reflected in other institutions (eg, media, education).

In turn, the culture of a society is shaped by that society's social structure. For example, a society with a private enterprise (market) economy is likely to promote values which support that system – values such as individualism and competition. It is unlikely to preach the values of equality and cooperation.

## Building a society – conclusion

Everyday life often seems to be a mixture of chaos and constant motion. But behind this buzz of activity it is possible to make out a shape or pattern. Sociologists call this social structure. It is a way of recognising that social

behaviour is not totally random or a matter of mere chance. Rather, there is a pattern of relationships between people, roles and institutions, and this lends some consistency and stability to social life.

Sociologists find it useful to break society into two parts – culture and structure. Each of them has an effect on the other. No society first creates culture then social structure, or the other way round. They are both essential components of society. They are always interacting.

# 2.2 Regulating social life

From the ancient Greeks to the present day, philosophers have puzzled over how societies manage to hold things together. How on earth do complex societies succeed in maintaining stability and social cohesion among their populations? This section looks at some of the more common methods of *social control*.

## Social control

Social control refers to the methods employed to ensure that people comply with society's rules and regulations. It is a way of checking that *deviance* – breaking of norms – is kept to a minimum. Peter Berger (1966) identifies some of the more common methods of social control:

**Physical violence** Sometimes people use violence against those who offend them. But it is the government and its agencies which claim the authority to exercise legitimate or lawful violence in society. The police and the military back up society's rules with the threat of physical force or imprisonment. Violence is very much a last resort – usually the mere threat of it is enough to ensure that people conform.

## key terms

*Social status* A position in society, eg father, nurse, teacher.
*Ascribed status* A status that is largely fixed and unchangeable.
*Achieved status* A status that involves some degree of choice and results partly from individual achievement.
*Social role* A set of expectations attached to a particular social status.
*Role conflict* When one role prevents the effective performance of another role.
*Social institution* A cluster of social roles; an established pattern of roles.
*Social structure* The overall network of roles and institutions in society.
*Social control* The methods used to ensure that people comply with society's rules and regulations.
*Deviance* Breaking social norms.
*Socialisation* The process by which norms and values are transmitted and learned.
*Internalise* Learning to the extent that it becomes a part of the individual's normal way of thinking. It becomes a part of them.

**Economic pressure** People may conform because it is in their economic interests to do so. Workers who misbehave may be sacked, people who refuse to take jobs can have their welfare benefits withdrawn. Strikers are often forced to return to work when they find they cannot manage without a wage.

**Social acceptance** One of the most common things that keeps us in line is the desire to be accepted by others. When we are tempted to break rules we often ask ourselves 'What will people say if I get caught?'. We fear ridicule or gossip and we dread being excluded or shunned by others.

**Socialisation** This is perhaps the main method of social control. We are taught society's rules through the process of *socialisation* – the transmission of norms and values. People are socialised into society's mainstream values by parents, schools and the media. We *internalise* cultural expectations and they become part of our own code of values. This reduces the likelihood that we will wish to break the rules.

# activity7 roles and institutions

### Item A  Roles

Policewoman

Doctors

### Item B  Institutions

School

Prison

## questions

1  What are the role expectations of the people shown in Item A?

2  In what sense can the school and prison shown in Item B be seen as institutions?

# activity8 social control

**Item A  Paedophiles out!**

**Item B  Gossip**

## question

What forms of social control are represented in Item A and Item B?

## summary

1. The various parts of society are related to each other. This forms the social structure.

2. Each social status is accompanied by a social role which provides guidelines for acting in terms of that status.

3. Roles tend to cluster together. These clusters form social institutions.

4. Social institutions are often interlinked, eg economic and educational institutions.

5. Roles and institutions form the structure of society.

6. Culture and social structure are interrelated – they interact and shape each other.

7. Society has a number of methods to maintain social control. These include physical violence, economic pressure, social acceptance and socialisation.

# Unit 3 Socialisation

## keyissues

1  What is socialisation?

2  How do people learn social roles?

3  Who are the main agents of socialisation?

## 3.1 The learning game

In this unit we turn to the question of how individuals adopt cultural values and roles. The answer is that we *learn* the culture through a process of *socialisation*. Since culture is not an innate thing, something we are born with, it has to be passed down from one generation to another.

So we have to be taught the norms and values of our society or group. Over time we *internalise* many of these – they become part of our personal set of norms and values.

But socialisation is not a simple one-sided process of instruction in which we passively accept what we are told. We are not empty vessels into which culture and customs are poured. Each of us actively participates in our own cultural learning, trying to make sense of society's values and beliefs, accepting some of them but rejecting others.

### Types of socialisation

**Primary socialisation** The early years of life are important in the learning process. This is the stage of *primary socialisation*, when we are normally in intimate and prolonged contact with parents. Our parents are *significant* *others* – they have a great influence on us and we care about their judgements of us. Significant others play a key part in teaching us basic values and norms.

**Secondary socialisation** This refers to the socialisation we receive later in life, from a wide range of people and agencies. They include peer groups, teachers, media and casual acquaintances. Sometimes they play a supportive role, adding to the primary socialisation of earlier years. But teachers also introduce us to new and more complex knowledge and skills. And friends sometimes introduce us to values and lifestyles which wouldn't win the approval of our parents!

**Re-socialisation** We usually have to learn new ways when our roles change. This may be a gradual process – for example, growing into adulthood. At other times it can be dramatic and abrupt. For example, army recruits experience the shock of basic training, when they have to abandon their civilian identity and submit to strict discipline and humiliating obedience tests.

**Anticipatory socialisation** In many cases we have already 'rehearsed' roles before we take them on. We imagine ourselves in them, we read about them, we learn something about them beforehand. For example, the young person who enters medical school already knows a bit about the life of a doctor from personal experience as a patient and from watching television shows such as *ER* or *Casualty*.

## 3.2 Agents of socialisation

The *agents of socialisation* are the people or groups who play a part in our socialisation. Sometimes they play an important role without us realising it. Sometimes we overestimate the influence they have on us. For some views on this, see Table 1.

| Table 1 **Survey of young people aged 11-21** | |
| --- | --- |
| 'From whom do you think you have learned the most about sex and growing up?' | |
| Parents | 7% |
| Teachers | 22% |
| The Internet | 7% |
| Friends | 27% |
| Brothers and sisters | 4% |
| Newspapers and magazines | 12% |
| TV and radio | 13% |
| Church/clergy | 0% |
| Don't know | 9% |
| *The Observer*, 21.07.2002 | |

### Parents

The majority of children still grow up in a family headed by both their natural parents. But over the last thirty years there has been an increase in the numbers of lone-parent and step-families. So family life has become more diverse.

# activity9 *learning the drill*

*US army recruits during basic training*

*Getting married*

## question

What kinds of socialisation apply to the people in these photographs?

But whatever the particular family set-up, parental figures remain the main agents of primary socialisation. In their first years of life children spend most of their time with their parents and are highly dependent on them. A sense of security during early childhood life is often seen as crucial for developing a stable personality and for effective learning of norms and values.

**Learning from parents** One way in which young children learn about social norms is by imitating their parents. They may copy the way adults talk, or their table manners for example. By a process of trial and error, they learn what is acceptable – asking politely – and unacceptable – rudely interrupting. As they get older they use their parents as *role models*. Girls may play with dolls 'just like mummy'. Later in life the roles might be reversed – young people sometimes have to teach their parents about things like mobile phones and computers!

For their part, parents try to instil social norms by setting an example and teaching their children how to behave. They use *sanctions* (rewards and punishments) to guide and control the learning process. If children follow the 'proper' norms, their parents will reward them with smiles, loving attention, praise and treats. But if they misbehave they are likely to be punished by frowns, reprimands, the denial of treats, and maybe even a smack.

This system of rewards and punishments does not guarantee that children will always behave 'correctly' – sometimes they will test the boundaries of acceptable behaviour, and sometimes they will show open defiance. But over a period of time they get a pretty good idea of the social norms held by their parents!

**Diversity** The socialisation process may vary according to the particular family structure. For example, an 'absent father' may find it difficult to act as a role model for his children, while a step-father may not feel entitled to control his step-children in the same way as their biological father could.

The experience of growing up within a family also varies according to its social and cultural values. For example, a devout Muslim family will ensure that religion plays a strong part in the child's upbringing.

**Class and parenting** Diane Reay (1998) made a detailed study of 33 mothers in London. All of these women put great effort into 'practical maintenance' of children – feeding, clothing and so on – as well as emotional work – reassuring and encouraging their children. All of them tried to support their children's schooling. However, Reay identified major class differences. The middle-class mothers had time and energy to spend reading to their children and were confident when talking to teachers. The working class-mothers, by contrast, had more of a struggle to make ends meet and so had less time and energy. They also had fewer cultural resources such as verbal confidence and knowledge of how the education system operates. This meant they were less effective in compensating for poor schooling and in persuading teachers to act on their complaints.

**Paranoid parents?** Frank Furedi (2001) describes a change in the role of parents in recent years. Traditionally, 'good' parents tried to care for and stimulate their children. Nowadays, they often see their main task as protecting their children from danger (accidents, paedophiles, bullies). Furedi believes parents have become paranoid. He thinks the risks of harm to children have been exaggerated and the new focus on protection is unhealthy. Children are chauffeured and shepherded from place to place by anxious parents. All sorts of risks – adventure trips with schools, even messing around in school playgrounds – are increasingly closed off to them. This may prevent children from developing a healthy sense of adventure.

## Education

Modern Western societies are too complex for young people simply to 'pick up' their culture as they go along. They are required to undergo a long period of formal education. In school they are formally taught the culture of their country – its history, language and religions. They also learn technical knowledge such as maths and science that often has practical applications in daily life.

**The hidden curriculum** School pupils also learn from the unofficial *hidden curriculum* – the background assumptions and expectations that run through the school system. For example, they learn the importance of hard work and success through the exam system. When they take part in sports they learn the value of competition and teamwork. They learn the importance of conforming to rules when they get punished for being late, misbehaving, or not handing in work on time.

School is also a setting where children's social horizons are widened. They may mix with people from different social classes, ethnic groups and cultural backgrounds. They also become more aware of the different identities of people from various ethnic, gender and social class groups.

**The importance of schools** It is difficult to judge whether schools are becoming more or less important as agents of socialisation. On the one hand, educational qualifications are now seen as essential for getting good jobs. This means that pupils are working harder than ever, with increasing numbers staying on after the minimum leaving age. On the other hand, schools often complain that they have to fight a battle over values. Some pupils may not share the values expressed by the school. Also, teachers often feel they have to compete against the attractions of mass media and youth culture for the attention of pupils.

**Schooling the boys** An example of the tough uphill task some schools face is provided by Christine Skelton's (2001) study of a primary school in the North East. This school was set in an economically deprived area with a notorious reputation for crime. The teachers regarded many of the local parents as 'inadequate' and so they felt the school had the important task of socialising children properly. When young boys came to school they brought with them the attitudes they picked up from the local 'lads' and 'hard

# activity 10 parents and socialisation

*Professor Kevin Warwick and Danielle Duval, with the chip that will be placed in her arm*

The parents of an 11 year-old girl are having her fitted with a microchip so that her movements can be traced if she is abducted. The miniature chip implanted in her arm will send a signal via a mobile phone network to a computer which will be able to pinpoint her location on an electronic map.

Some children's charities have claimed that the parents are over-reacting as the chances of a child being abducted are small.

Adapted from *The Guardian*, 3.9.02

## questions

1  What ways do parents have of 'making their children conform'?
2  In what ways does Item B support Furedi's views?

---

men' – aggression, physical toughness, dominance and hierarchy.

The school attempted to maintain social control by relying on firm measures. It created a sort of fortress (locked gates, fences, security cameras) as a defence against violence and theft. Also, the teachers (both male and female) adopted 'masculine' styles – firm eye contact, intimidatory body language – to gain 'respect', show who was 'boss' and instil some 'fear' in the troublesome pupils. Skelton points to the irony that the school's control strategies were in many ways a reflection of the 'tough' values that were prized in the local community!

## Peer group

A *peer group* is a friendship group formed by people of roughly the same age and social position. They meet each other as equals rather than being supervised by adults. In the early years of life, children like to play with one another for fun and amusement. But play is also a valuable learning experience. In play situations they learn about social norms (eg, treating others properly) and they develop social skills (eg, negotiating over toys). They can also experiment with social roles (eg, playing shop assistants and customers).

When children become teenagers, they spend increasing amounts of time away from their families and in the

# activity11 learning

*Pledging allegiance to their country*

*Playtime in a London primary school*

## question

What do you think these pupils are learning from the activities shown in the photographs?

company of their friends. Parents often worry that peer group pressures will encourage their children to steal, take drugs, or have sex. Young people themselves often worry about their popularity within the peer group. Nevertheless, these groups perform valuable functions for their members. Within them, young people begin to develop independence from their parents. This prepares them for taking on adult roles themselves.

**Peer power** Adler and Adler (1998) studied a group of white middle-class children in the United States. They found that the peer group was enormously important in the lives of these pre-adolescent children. Being popular and having friends made children feel good about themselves, but being socially isolated had the reverse effect. Adler and Adler describe how friendship groups shift and change as children move in and out. Over time a hierarchy develops, both between groups (the leading cliques have higher prestige) and within groups (some members have greater power and influence than others). Friendship cliques exercise their power by accepting some children and excluding others. Within each group, friends are expected to be loyal to the peer values, but 'weaker' members are often bullied and manipulated by the rest.

## Mass media

Mass media consume an enormous amount of our time – just think of all those teenagers locked away for hours on end in their bedroom with their own music centre, TV, game console and computer. We seem in constant danger of being overwhelmed by the sheer volume of print (newspapers, magazines, books) and electronic messages (TV, radio, the Internet). So it seems only reasonable to assume that the media have some effect on our attitudes, values and behaviour.

Admittedly, media seldom have a direct *hypodermic effect* – they do not inject their content into us and make us immediately accept what they tell us. But they help to create the cultural climate within which we live. They give us a sense of what values and behaviour are acceptable in the modern world. They provide us with role models – they hold up certain sports stars or showbiz celebrities for us to admire and copy.

**Magazines and gender stereotypes** The view of the world we get from the media is often highly stereotyped. For example, magazines such as *Cosmopolitan* seem to project an image of women as obsessed with sex and fashion. Likewise, men's magazines such as *Maxim* have been criticised for celebrating a crude 'lad culture' of lager louts, football and 'babes'. However, some people say these magazines are just escapist fun, and most people have little difficulty in separating media stereotypes from the 'real' world.

**Bollywood** Mass media can play an important role in socialisation. Marie Gillespie (1993) demonstrates this in her study of Sikhs in Southall. She shows how the videos produced by the Indian film industry (known as

# activity 12 *peer groups – the good and the bad*

### Item A  Talking

'I can talk to my friends about things I can't really talk to my parents about, because well – they seem to understand me more, and my parents don't really listen to me, and my friends do, because they've been in the same situation as me'.

Young girl, quoted in Tizard & Phoenix, 1993

### Item B  Messing up

It isn't your parents who mess you up, it's your peers. After all, it isn't your parents who ridicule your cheap trainers, or your miserable choice of music, or who force you to drink a bottle of tequila and pass out in a dog basket, or who destroy you for looking wrong or talking wrong or being interested in things that you shouldn't be interested in. It isn't your parents who give you sexually transmitted diseases or who ply you with drugs.

Adapted from Bathurst, 2002

### Item C  Friends

## questions

1  What do Items A and B reveal about peer groups?
2  Why do you think *Friends* is so popular with young people?

---

'Bollywood') are enormously popular in this community. Whole families watch them together. Gillespie found that these videos have important socialising functions – they create links between Asian communities throughout the world, they socialise younger children into Asian cultures and languages and they help to reinforce a sense of Asian identity. But Gillespie adds that Sikhs are not just a passive audience for these films. Family members respond to them in different ways: older people watch them for nostalgic reasons while younger people are more critical – they sometimes mock the films and complain that they portray India as a backward country.

## Religion

Although religions deal with spiritual matters, they also have an influence on social attitudes and behaviour. The major world religions – Christianity, Judaism, Islam, Hinduism, Buddhism – have had a deep impact on the societies in which they are dominant. This influence operates at a number of levels.

First, each religion offers a set of moral values. Over time these become part of the culture of a society. People are exposed to these values even if they do not personally attend a place of worship. Second, the rituals and ceremonies of religion have traditionally been seen as a force for social unity. Collective acts of worship such as marriages, baptisms and funerals bring people together and remind them of their common bonds and shared values. Third, religions prescribe a moral code (eg, the Ten Commandments) which guides our earthly behaviour. We can see this when people undergo a religious conversion – it usually means far-reaching changes in their behaviour and lifestyles.

**Secularisation?** The long-term decline in church attendance in Britain suggests the country is becoming more secular – non-religious. Does this mean that the influence of religion is on the decline? Not necessarily. A decline in churchgoing does not automatically mean that people have abandoned religious ideas and beliefs. Over 70% of the population still say they believe in God, while a minority are turning to New Age beliefs and practices such as the use of crystals, Tarot cards, astrology and feng shui. Religion also plays a significant role among many of Britain's minority ethnic communities.

**Muslim girls** Charlotte Butler's study (1995) of a group of teenage Muslim girls in the East Midlands shows how religious beliefs can be adapted to fit changing circumstances. These young women, born in Britain, were moving away from the traditions of their parents. They remained firmly committed to their Muslim identity but

# activity13 soaps

## Item A  Distortion?

Most parents rely on television soaps such as *EastEnders* to trigger discussion of 'difficult' personal subjects with their children, according to research by the National Family and Parenting Institution. Many parents believed the storylines help children and young people to understand family life.

But the portrayal of family life in the soaps bears little relation to real life. Eighty per cent of the parents complained that the soaps do not promote positive images of the family. They claim that soaps consistently over-represent broken families, and place too much emphasis on sex and violence, cheating on partners, and alcohol abuse.

Adapted from *The Guardian*, 17.10.2002

## Item C  Soap and society

In 2002, *The Mail on Sunday* referring to *EastEnders* declared, 'We are all tainted by this sick soap'. A *New Scientist* survey compared sex and violence in *EastEnders* over an 18 year period with figures from social surveys conducted in Britain.

## Item B  An affair

*Ricky and Natalie having an affair in EastEnders*

### Sex and violence in *Eastenders*

| Behaviour | Real life (% of pop.) | EastEnders (% of pop.) |
|---|---|---|
| Homicide | 0.0016 per year | 0.22 per year |
| Rape | 0.3 per year | 0.35 per year |
| Infidelity | women 9/men 14.6 per year | women 2/men 1.7 per year |
| Men paying for sex | 4.3 per year | 0.18 per year |
| Deceived fathers | 10 | 5.8 |

Adapted from *New Scientist*, 17.5.2003

## question

What do these items suggest about the ways in which TV soaps help children to 'understand' family life?

---

they were modifying it in certain ways. Their experience of living in Britain had led them to regard certain Pakistani and Bangladeshi customs as irrelevant to their lives. Consequently, they were rejecting customs such as arranged marriages which were not regarded as essential features of Islam.

So these young women were developing more independent lifestyles to fit more easily into the British way of life, while at the same time maintaining their commitment to Islam.

## Work

When we enter the workforce we have to be introduced to the skills, norms and values attached to the job. *Occupational socialisation* is a form of secondary socialisation as it occurs later in life, when we already have considerable cultural knowledge and skills.

It may well involve different forms of learning.

**Anticipatory socialisation** We may have learned a bit about the job beforehand, possibly by talking to people about it or taking a course in preparation.

**Re-socialisation** When we start work we have to learn new ways of behaving, such as submitting to workplace discipline (things like regular work hours and obeying the boss). This also applies when we move jobs because organisations vary in their styles and traditions.

Agents of workplace socialisation include bosses, colleagues, even customers. Some of these agents socialise us in formal ways, while others socialise us in a more informal fashion.

**Formal socialisation** The management of a firm takes formal responsibility for socialising employees. For example, they may provide training courses to develop the necessary work skills. In addition, they usually lay down norms about appearance, attitudes and behaviour. Some workplaces impose strict dress codes (eg, collar and tie for

# activity14 religion and socialisation

**Item A Former church**

Radio station, Preston

**Item B New temple**

Hindu temple, Preston

## question

What do the items tell us about the importance of religion in socialisation?

men). Behaviour may be controlled by official codes of conduct (eg, rules against private telephone calls and emails). Many firms also try to win the loyalty and motivation of their staff by encouraging them to identify with the company – some Japanese firms even have their own company song!

**Informal socialisation** This is the socialisation provided by peer groups at work. They introduce us to the informal culture of the workplace. They have their own rituals, such as playing jokes on newcomers (eg, sending them to the stores to fetch a tin of 'tartan paint'). They also have their own norms, many of which may not be approved by management.  For example, they may ignore the official rules and do things their own way. Or they may try to slow down the pace of work – any colleague who works too hard is likely to be bullied or mocked.

**Canteen culture** Canteen culture is the term given to describe the informal culture of police officers as they hang around the station or spend their off-duty hours together. Waddington's research (1999) shows how canteen culture can help socialise police officers. They learn from listening to other officers telling their 'war stories' – how they overcame tricky situations – and pick up practical advice such as 'you can't always play it by the book'.

Waddington argues that this canteen chat actually helps police officers deal with their stressful job. It boosts their

occupational self-esteem by giving them a 'heroic' identity (they are out there on the front-line bravely facing 'trouble'). It reinforces their sense of 'mission' (they are doing a valuable job by fighting crime). It also celebrates certain values that are more or less essential in police work (such as a 'macho' emphasis on physical strength and courage).

## key terms

**Primary socialisation** Intimate and influential socialisation (usually from parents) in the early years of life.

**Secondary socialisation** Socialisation that comes later in life, from various sources.

**Agents of socialisation** The individuals, groups and institutions which play a part in the socialisation process.

**Sanctions** Rewards and punishments.

**Role models** People we use to give us ideas about how to play particular social roles.

**Peer group** A friendship group formed by people in the same social situation.

**Secularisation** The view that religion is declining in importance in society.

**Occupational socialisation** A form of secondary socialisation by which people learn the skills, norms and values of the workplace.

# activity15 McJobs

## Item A  May I help you?

Young people often get their first experience of work in 'McJobs' – unskilled, low paid, part-time jobs in fast-food restaurants. They are trained to perform simple tasks in a predictable manner, doing each action in exactly the same way. They have little scope for using their initiative.

Workers are even restricted in what they can *say* on the job. Every interaction with customers is tightly scripted – 'May I help you?', 'Would you like a dessert to go with your meal?', 'Have a nice day!' They are given scripts for any situations that may arise. Workers are no longer trusted to say the right thing.

Adapted from Ritzer, 2002

## Item B  Have a nice day

## questions

1  What are the key features of socialisation into McJobs?

2  Why might these skills be less useful in other kinds of jobs?

## Socialisation – conclusion

Socialisation is an essential element in any society. There are a variety of agents who perform socialisation tasks, but experts disagree on which ones exercise the most influence. Traditionally it was thought that parents, and perhaps the church, had the greatest effect. In modern society the school, peer group and mass media seem to have growing influence.

There is also disagreement about whether these agents have a sufficiently 'responsible' attitude to their socialisation tasks. For example, parents are sometimes accused of simply putting their kids in front of the TV rather than talking to them. Peer groups offer us friendship but they also introduce us to dangerous temptations. Mass media inform us about the world, but sometimes they distort that world.

## summary

1.  Socialisation is a key feature of any society – it transmits the cultural heritage from one generation to the next. It is the way in which people learn social norms, roles and values.

2.  Socialisation is not a one-way street in which people passively accept society's norms and values. They participate in internalising, modifying or rejecting these norms and values.

3.  There are different forms of socialisation. Primary socialisation is often thought of as the most important and influential. But secondary socialisation is increasingly significant in fast-changing modern societies.

4.  Socialisation is performed by different agents – parents, school, peer group, mass media, religion and work. These agents come into play at different stages of our life, and they have different effects.

# Unit 4 *Theories of society*

## keyissues

1 What are the main sociological theories?

2 What are their strengths and weaknesses?

## 4.1 Structure and action

What shapes our behaviour? Do we control our own destiny or do social pressures determine our actions? Are we largely moulded by the wider society and forced to behave in certain ways or do we have the freedom to decide our own actions?

**Social systems** Some approaches in sociology emphasise the power of society over the individual. They are sometimes called *social systems* or *structuralist* approaches.

From this viewpoint, the individual is largely controlled by society. We are what we are because of the expectations and pressures of the social groups to which we belong. Society is in us, moulding our thoughts and directing our actions. We are socialised in terms of the culture of society, our behaviour is shaped by the social structure, we are kept in line by mechanisms of social control, we learn roles, norms and values and act accordingly.

**Social action** Other approaches emphasise the ability of individuals to direct their own actions. They are sometimes called *social action* or *interpretivist* approaches.

From this viewpoint, individuals actively create their own social world. They give meanings to social situations, interpret the behaviour of others, and they take action on the basis of these meanings and interpretations.

Social action approaches do not necessarily deny the existence of roles, norms and values. However, they tend to see them as flexible guidelines rather than inflexible directives. For example, each doctor interprets his or her role somewhat differently. Some tend to see illness as a physical problem. As a result, they are unlikely to spend much time discussing patients' personal lives. Others believe that illness often results from problems in patients' relationships. They will be more likely to discuss these problems in order to deal with the illness.

The role of doctors is also affected by interaction with patients. To some degree, it is worked out or negotiated with patients, each with their own views and expectations of behaviour appropriate for a doctor. The role of doctor is not simply acted out from a standard script.

**Systems versus action** Although we can differentiate between social systems and social action approaches, neither is quite so extreme as suggested here. Systems approaches do not see people as totally controlled by society, nor do action perspectives view people as totally

## activity 16 views of society

### question

Which of these cartoons illustrates a) a social systems approach and b) a social action approach?

Give reasons for your answer.

free agents. Rather it is a matter of emphasis.

Social systems approaches place more emphasis on the structure of society and its power to determine individual behaviour. Social action approaches place more emphasis on the freedom of individuals to direct their own actions.

## 4.2 Consensus and conflict

How would you describe society? Is it based primarily on *consensus* – agreement between people about social norms and values? Or is it based on *conflict*?

A brief glance through the newspapers, a review of family life, or a quick read through history books might well suggest that conflict prevails. But consider how we go about our daily lives. Most of us seem to agree with the rules of society, and we work together in terms of those rules. So although conflict might grab the headlines, it could be argued that social life is largely based on consensus and cooperation, not conflict.

So far, we have distinguished between social systems and social action perspectives. The distinction between consensus and conflict allows us to make a further division. Social systems approaches can be divided into those which characterise society as based on conflict and those which see society as based on consensus.

**Consensus** Consensus approaches see agreement or consensus as the basis of social life. Without it, society would collapse into chaos with its members being unable to agree on rules and norms of behaviour. Consensus provides the basis for cooperation and social unity. Unless there was general agreement about what is important and worthwhile – in other words, shared values – there would be no cooperation and unity in society. It would be replaced by conflict and division as individuals pursued their own interests which would often directly conflict with those of others. *Value consensus* provides a harmony of interests in society.

**Conflict** Conflict approaches see conflict as the main characteristic of society. This does not mean that members of society are constantly at each other's throats or on the brink of civil war. Rather it means that there are basic conflicts of interest in society with some groups gaining at the expense of others.

Some groups are more powerful than others – usually as a result of their stronger economic position. In this situation, norms and values are not freely agreed by everyone but are imposed on the weaker sections of society by the more powerful groups. What appears on the surface as consensus is in fact *coercion* – an 'agreement' based on force. What seems to be cooperation is in fact *exploitation* – one group gaining at the expense of others.

## 4.3 Functionalism and consensus theory

So far, we have distinguished between a number of broad perspectives or approaches within sociology. Social systems perspectives have been contrasted with social action perspectives. Consensus approaches have been compared with conflict approaches.

The rest of this unit looks at *sociological theories* which derive from these broader perspectives. A sociological theory is a set of ideas which claims to explain the social behaviour of human beings. This section looks at a sociological theory known as *functionalism*.

**Consensus** Functionalism sees society as a social system based on consensus. It begins from the assumption that society has certain basic needs which must be met if it is to survive. First and foremost is the need for social order – for a smooth-running, well-ordered society in which social life is predictable and people know what is expected from them.

Social order requires a certain degree of cooperation and *social solidarity* (social unity). This is made possible by shared norms and values. This in turn requires some means of socialisation to ensure that norms and values are learned, plus mechanisms of social control to ensure that norms and values are conformed to. In particular, value consensus is seen as essential since without it people would be pulling in different directions and the result would be conflict and disorder.

**Society as a system** Functionalists see society as a system – a set of parts which work together to form a whole. These parts are the institutions of society – for example, the family, the education system and the political system. Based on the assumption that society is a system, the questions now become: 'How do the various parts work together to maintain social order?' and 'What is the contribution of each part to the maintenance and wellbeing of the social system?'

# *activity*17 *contrasting views*

### Item A  **Who gains?**

**Consensus** From a consensus perspective, successful business people deserve high rewards. They have made important contributions to society by building up efficient and productive companies and providing employment. High rewards motivate them and everybody benefits from their success.

**Conflict** From a conflict perspective, the wealth and lavish lifestyles of the rich and powerful are paid for by exploiting workers. Wealth is produced by the workers but their wages are small change compared with the extremely generous salaries, bonuses and dividends which business owners pay themselves.

### Item B  **Top of the pay list**

In 2002, Philip Green paid himself over £157 million, making him the highest paid person in the UK. He is a very successful businessman with a 'hands on' approach and a reputation for turning round failing businesses. For example, he bought the ailing BHS (British Home Stores) for £200 million – it is now valued at £1 billion.

Philip Green works hard and plays hard. In 2002, he spent £5 million on his 50th birthday party, flying 200 friends in a private 747 to Cyprus where Rod Stewart and Tom Jones sang to toga-wearing guests in a Roman amphitheatre.

*Philip Green*    Adapted from the *Sunday Times Magazine*, 3.11.2002

### *question*

Explain Philip Green's wealth from a) a consensus perspective and b) a conflict perspective.

# activity18 *social solidarity*

**Item A   Golden Jubilee**

*Queen Elizabeth on her way to St Paul's Cathedral to celebrate her Golden Jubilee, June 4, 2002*

**Item B   9/11**

*Ceremony marking the first anniversary of the attack on the World Trade Center, ground zero, New York, September 11, 2002*

## question

Functionalists see celebrations, ceremonies and rituals as very important for creating social unity or social solidarity. Using the photographs in Items A and B, suggest how this is done.

Let's look at some simple answers to these questions. When looking at any part of society, functionalists often ask, 'What is its function?' By *function* they mean its contribution to the maintenance of the social system. Thus a simple answer to the question 'What is the function of the family?' is that the family socialises new members of society and teaches them the norms and values which are essential for social life. Assuming that the various parts of the social system work together for the benefit of society as a whole, the next question is: 'What is the relationship between the family and other institutions such as the education system?' Again very simply, the educational system continues the process of socialisation begun in the family. In this way, the institutions of family and education work together to maintain social order.

**Social disorder** It appears from this brief outline that society is a smooth-running, well-oiled system. What about conflict and social disorder? Functionalists obviously recognise their existence but see them as a temporary disturbance to the social system rather than inbuilt and permanent aspects of society. Functionalists accept that social groups have certain differences of interest but this usually results in competition rather than conflict. And these differences are minor compared to the values and interests they have in common.

**Criticism** Functionalists have been criticised for presenting a deterministic view of social behaviour. This refers to the tendency of some functionalists to picture human beings as shaped by the social structure, and directed by society's

norms and values. As such, they appear to lack free will, initiative and creativity. Hence Peter Berger's criticism that society is sometimes portrayed as a prison or a puppet theatre with people as prisoners of the system or puppets on the end of a string (Berger, 1966).

## 4.4 Conflict theory

This section provides a brief introduction to conflict theory and to Marxism, the best known and most influential version.

Conflict theory has a number of similarities to functionalism. It sees society as a system and human behaviour, to some extent, as a response to that system. Some of the questions asked are similar, for example: 'How is social order maintained?' However, the type of social system and the kind of social order are very different. Conflict rather than consensus is the primary characteristic of society. Social groups are in conflict since their interests are fundamentally opposed. And social order tends to be imposed by the powerful rather than based on a consensus freely agreed by all.

**Ideology** Many conflict theorists replace the idea of value consensus with the concept of *ideology*. Used in this sense, ideology is a set of beliefs and values which disguises the truth and distorts reality.

Ideology is transmitted by the agents of socialisation. For example, the mass media may present a picture of a reasonable and just society – a false view of the situation.

TV soaps and game shows may divert people's attention from the real conflicts of interest which divide them.

This lack of awareness can help to maintain social order. People will not attempt to overthrow a system if they do not recognise its injustice. In terms of conflict theory, ideology is usually seen to justify and maintain the positions of both the rich and powerful and the poor and powerless.

**Conflicts of interest** Some conflict theorists identify a range of social groups whose interests conflict. These may include economic groups such as the 'haves' and 'have nots' who compete for income and wealth; ethnic groups who are prevented from equal opportunity by the racism of the dominant group in society; gender groups in which males jealously guard their power and privilege over females; religious groups in which one group attempts to dominate another (eg, Protestants and Catholics in Northern Ireland); professional groups who go to great lengths to maintain their status and power (eg, doctors claiming that only they have the right to diagnose and treat illness and who reject the claims of so-called 'fringe' or 'alternative' medicine). In each case, groups in a stronger position seek to maintain their supremacy and subordinate those in a weaker position. In each case, someone gains at the expense of others.

The result is a conflict of interest which may or may not find direct expression. It may be suppressed by a variety of mechanisms of social control ranging from ideology through to force. Or it may find expression in a number of ways – a conflict of ideas, a war of words, industrial action, political protest, criminal behaviour, urban riots, through to revolution and civil war. Conflict may take place in the halls of government, in the classroom or workplace, on the street, in the home, on the battlefield or in the bedroom.

## Marxism

There are a number of versions of conflict theory. Marxism – named after its founder Karl Marx (1818-1883) – is the most famous and influential.

Marx saw society as a structure divided into two major parts. The first and most important part is the economic base or *infrastructure*. The second major part, known as the *superstructure*, consists of the rest of society – the political, legal and educational systems, beliefs and ideas.

Marx claimed that the infrastructure shapes the superstructure – in other words, the economic system shapes the rest of society. For example, from a Marxist viewpoint, the education system in modern industrial society has been shaped by the requirements of a capitalist economy for a literate and well-disciplined workforce.

**Social classes** Marx saw conflict between social classes as the basic characteristic of all known human societies. Every society has two main social groups, a *ruling class* and a *subject class*. The power of the ruling class comes from its ownership of what Marx called the *means of production*. This includes the land, raw materials, machinery, tools and buildings used to produce goods. Thus in Western industrial society, *capitalists* – those who own private industry – form the ruling class. The subject class – the *proletariat* in capitalist society – is made up of workers who sell their labour in return for wages.

There is a basic conflict of interest between capitalists and the proletariat. Workers produce wealth in the form of goods yet a large part of that wealth is taken in the form of profits by the capitalist class. Thus one group gains at the expense of the other.

Marx believed that this conflict could not be resolved within the framework of capitalist society. It would eventually result in the overthrow of the capitalist class. A workers' revolution would lead to a communist society in which the means of production would be owned by everyone, classes would disappear, and exploitation and oppression would end.

**Ruling class ideology** This, however, would only happen when workers became fully aware of their exploitation. But this awareness will not occur overnight because of the way society is structured. Since the infrastructure largely shapes the superstructure, the relationship of dominance and subordination between the ruling class and subject class will be reflected in the superstructure. Thus, the political and legal systems will support ruling class power – for example, laws will protect the rights of capitalists to own industry and take profits. In the same way, the beliefs and values of society will support ruling class domination. Thus, capitalism will be seen as reasonable and just, rather than exploitative and oppressive. In this way, beliefs and values will disguise and distort the true nature of society.

In Marxist terms, beliefs and values form a *ruling class ideology*. This produces a *false consciousness* which prevents people from seeing the reality of their situation. However, Marx believed that ruling class ideology can only slow down the eventual overthrow of capitalism. The conflicts of interest within the capitalist system will inevitably lead to its downfall.

**Criticisms** Like functionalism, Marxism has been criticised for portraying people as creatures of the social system, with little opportunity to direct their own actions. In addition, Marx's predictions for a workers' revolution and the end of capitalism have been rejected, especially since the downfall of communism in Eastern Europe and the former Soviet Union. Despite this, Marxist ideas continue to be influential in sociology.

## Feminist sociology

Where Marxists see the class system as the main source of conflict in society, feminist sociologists see the gender system. In other words, they see the social divisions between men and women as the main conflict of interest in society. For this reason, feminist theory is sometimes seen as an example of conflict theory.

# activity19 a picture of Marxism

This Russian cartoon from 1900 shows a social pyramid from the Tsar (monarch) at the top to the proletariat (workers and peasants) at the base. The text from the top downwards reads:

- We reign over you (the Tsar)
- We rule you (the nobles)
- We fool you (the priests)
- We shoot you (the army)
- We eat for you (the middle class)

  The banner held by members of the proletariat reads: 'To live in freedom, to die in struggle'.

## question

What aspects of Marxist theory are illustrated by the cartoon?

There are many versions of feminism. The account which follows is brief and partial. It presents some general points with which most feminist sociologists would agree.

**Gender inequality** Feminists often start from the following observations. In practically every known human society there is a division of labour based on gender – there are men's jobs and women's jobs. And in most cases, men's jobs bring higher rewards – in terms of status or prestige, in terms of power, and in terms of pay. Even when men and women have the same jobs, men still tend to receive the highest rewards.

As a result, there is a system of social inequality which benefits men at the expense of women.

**Patriarchy** This system of gender inequality tends to permeate the whole of society – it is not simply limited to occupational roles. For example, it may be reflected in religious beliefs which see men as superior to women, or in marriage vows which state that the duty of a wife is to serve her husband. It may be reflected in the education system if parents support their sons at the expense of their daughters. It may be seen in top jobs such as MPs, judges, barristers and surgeons, where despite equal opportunity laws, men still predominate. And it may be seen in family life if boys and girls are socialised to expect and accept male dominance.

The term *patriarchy* is used to describe a social system based on gender inequality. It describes a system in which male dominance is present in people's working and family lives, and is reflected in social norms and values, roles and institutions. In this sense, patriarchy has been defined as 'the combination of economic and cultural systems which ensures male supremacy' (Coote & Campbell, 1982).

**Feminist research** One of the main jobs of feminist sociologists is to reveal the extent and injustice of male domination, to show how men use their power to maintain their rewards and privileges, and to show how the major decisions in society are made by men largely for the benefit of men.

Feminist research rejects the view that male dominance is natural and inevitable. It provides evidence to support the view that gender inequalities are socially constructed rather than naturally created – they are made in society rather than made in the genes.

**Criticism** Feminists are preoccupied with gender inequality and tend to ignore other aspects of society. This is one of the standard criticisms of feminist sociology. However, without feminists, gender inequality itself would be largely ignored by the dominant 'malestream' sociology. It is now recognised as a central topic in sociology.

## 4.5 Social action theory

Social action or interpretive perspectives offer an alternative view of social life. They focus on how people interact with each other in small group settings such as the classroom, police station, hospital ward or streetcorner. They are concerned with how people define themselves, each other and their situations, and with the consequences of such definitions for their actions. There is an emphasis on *negotiation* – the meanings people give to situations are not seen as fixed but as negotiated by the actors concerned.

The difference between a social systems and a social action approach can be seen from the example of

# activity20 looking at gender

## Item A  Barbie

Every girl in America owns an average of eight Barbies. Over 500 million have been sold worldwide. And for Christmas 1995, Barbie was the bestselling girls' toy in the UK. Sun Jewel Barbie, the new fuschia-bikinied and diamond-necklaced model, is the bestselling Barbie ever. Other new models include 'Dance 'n' Twirl', a radio-controlled Barbie who flounces across the dance floor, and a horse and carriage set to take Barbie and Ken (her boyfriend) to the ball.

According to Michelle Norton, PR person for Mattel Toys who created Barbie, 'She's a wonderful role model for little girls. She does everything they want to do and dream of. She's got lovely fashions and a boyfriend. It's a friendship sort of thing.' And it has to be – sex is out as Ken lacks the appropriate parts.

Adapted from *The Observer*, 22.12.1995

## Item B  Gender and maturity

In 1972, a fascinating study was published which explored the way mental health professionals thought about men and women (Broverman et al., 1972). The researchers asked a large number of applied psychologists (both men and women) to describe the qualities of:

1  The mature, healthy, socially competent adult
2  The mature, healthy, socially competent man
3  The mature, healthy, socially competent woman.

The descriptions of the 'mentally healthy man' and the 'mentally healthy adult' were virtually identical. Both were capable, independent, objective, stable and well adjusted.

But the description of the 'mentally healthy woman' was quite different. She was characterised as more submissive, more easily influenced, as excitable in minor crises, concerned with her appearance and more likely to have her feelings hurt. She was less independent, less dominant, less aggressive, less objective and less adventurous.

Adapted from Stainton Rogers & Stainton Rogers, 2001

## question

How might a feminist sociologist analyse Items A and B?

---

marriage. A functionalist analysis looks at marriage in terms of the social system. The emphasis is on the roles of husband/father, wife/mother which are seen as largely given by the system and shaped to meet the requirements of the system. Thus, these roles are structured – for example, to provide a unit for the production and socialisation of children.

Social action theory would not reject the idea of roles. However, it would argue that when two people get married they have only a vague idea of how a husband and wife should behave. Should they share household chores, should they always go out together, should they kiss 'hello' and 'goodbye'? As a result of their day-to-day interaction, they gradually construct their own reality of married life.

They give meanings to marriage, they define and redefine what it means to be a husband and wife, and develop a shared view of their relationship.

From a social action perspective, marital roles are not prescribed by the social system, they develop from negotiated meanings during the process of interaction. This is a creative process with individuals directing their own actions rather than being constrained by the social system.

## Symbolic interactionism

*Symbolic interactionism* is an example of social action theory. It starts from the idea that people interact in terms of symbols, the most important of which is language. To understand human action it is necessary to discover the meanings which people use to guide, interpret and make sense of their own actions and those of others.

**Presentation of self** Typical of the interactionist approach is the work of Erving Goffman. In *The Presentation of Self in Everyday Life* (1969) he analyses the techniques we use in order to influence how others see us. This process, which we all employ, he calls *impression management*. As social actors, we give more-or-less continuous 'performances' in that we present an 'appearance' of 'keen student', 'hard working, professional lecturer' or 'caring parent'. Our facial movements, body language, speech content, style and so on are coordinated in an attempt to convey a particular impression. We create the proper 'setting' of office, classroom, doctor's surgery or whatever, equipping it with appropriate 'props' (desks, white coats, medical books etc) to reinforce this impression.

As everyone else is also engaged in impression management, we become very skilled in interpreting the actions of others and at watching for discrepancies in their performances. For example, when cooking a meal for a friend, their polite response of 'what a lovely meal' will be checked by looking to see how much they've eaten, whether there are any facial signals of distaste or any whispered comments of a negative nature.

**Definition of the situation** The American sociologist W.I. Thomas captured one of the main insights of symbolic interactionism when he wrote, 'If men define situations as real, they are real in their consequences'. By this he meant that people act in terms of the way they define situations. To give a rather flippant example – a person walks down a street swathed in bandages. This situation may be interpreted in a number of ways – fancy dress (the Invisible Man), a practical joke, a 'dare', a bet, someone who has serious injuries, or even a sociologist conducting an experiment. Each of these definitions is real in its consequences. People will act towards the bandaged figure depending on their interpretation of his or her behaviour. Whether or not their definition is 'really correct' is not the point. The point is that to understand their response, we have to understand their *definition of the situation*.

**Criticism** Criticisms of symbolic interactionism and social action theory as a whole are in some ways a reversal of those of systems theory. Because they focus on small-scale interaction situations, social action theorists tend to ignore the wider society. Critics argue that to some extent this wider social framework influences and even constrains interaction. They claim that social action theorists have gone too far – human action is not as free, creative, spontaneous and flexible as they appear to suggest.

## key terms

*Value consensus* An agreement about values.
*Social solidarity* Social unity.
*Function* The contribution made by a part to the maintenance of the system as a whole.
*Infrastructure* In Marxist theory, the economic base of society which shapes the superstructure.
*Superstructure* The rest of society – the political, legal and educational systems, the family, religion, beliefs and ideas.
*Ruling class* Those who own the means of production.
*Subject class* Those who do not own the means of production and are subject to the power of the ruling class.
*Means of production* This includes the land, raw materials, machinery and buildings used to produce goods.
*Ruling class ideology* A set of beliefs and values which supports the position of the ruling class by distorting reality. For example, it presents the relationship between the ruling and subject classes as just and reasonable.
*False consciousness* A false view which prevents people from seeing the reality of their situation.
*Patriarchy* A system of male domination which permeates the whole of society – from norms and values to roles and institutions.
*Negotiation* A process where the outcome is not fixed or predetermined. Instead, it is open to discussion and modification – it is negotiable.
*Impression management* A process used in social interaction designed to manage the impression others have of ourselves.
*Definition of the situation* The way people define, interpret and give meaning to situations. People then act in terms of their definition of the situation.

## summary

1. Social systems perspectives look at society as a system. They tend to see human behaviour as shaped by the system.

2. Some social systems perspectives see consensus, others see conflict, as the primary characteristic of society.

3. Social action perspectives place more emphasis on the freedom of individuals to direct their own actions.

4. Functionalism sees society as a social system based on consensus. It sees the various parts of society working together to maintain social order.

5. Marxism sees society as a social system based on conflict. It sees a basic conflict of interest between the two main classes, since one gains at the expense of the other.

6. Feminists see gender inequality as the basis of conflict in society.

7. Social action approaches focus on small-scale interaction situations. They see social life as directed by negotiated meanings. Human action is not prescribed by the social system, it is a creative process directed by individuals in interaction situations.

# activity21 negotiating justice

How is a person charged with breaking the law? The following American study of delinquency – the criminal activity of young people – shows it is not a straightforward process.

When a young person is arrested, he or she is handed over to a juvenile officer who decides whether or not to prosecute. This decision is based on a process of negotiation between the juvenile officer, the person arrested and his or her parents. Crucial to the outcome of this negotiation is the picture juvenile officers have of the 'typical delinquent'. In their eyes the 'typical delinquent' is male, from a low-income household in an inner-city area, belongs to an ethnic group, comes from a broken home, rejects authority and is a low achiever at school. If the suspect fits this picture, they are more likely to be charged with an offence.

Becoming a delinquent involves a process of negotiation between the young person, their parents and the juvenile officer.

Middle-class parents are often more skilled at negotiation than their working-class counterparts. They start with an advantage – their child does not fit the picture of a 'typical delinquent'. They present their child as coming from a stable home, as having a good background and a promising future. They promise cooperation, express remorse and define the 'offence' as a 'one-off' due to high spirits, emotional upset, or getting in with the wrong crowd, all of which tends to remove blame from the young person.

As a result, the statistics show that delinquency is mainly a working-class problem as young people from middle-class backgrounds are typically 'counselled, cautioned and released'. Thus 'what ends up being called justice is negotiable'. And what ends up as delinquency is a label attached to a person whose social characteristics are seen to fit the picture of a 'typical delinquent'.

Adapted from Cicourel, 1976

*Stop and search in Brixton, South London*

## question

In what ways does this study illustrate a social action approach?

# Unit 5 Social change

## keyissues

1 What are the main developments in human society?
2 How have they affected people's lives?

A number of sociologists have tried to identify the main developments in human society. Some distinguish between *premodern* society and today's *modern* society. Others believe we have moved beyond modernity and are now living in *postmodern society*.

These distinctions are important. They point to major changes in human society. They help to explain the behaviour typically found in each type of society.

### 5.1 Premodern society

Anthony Giddens (2001) identifies various types of society that developed in the premodern era.

**Hunting and gathering societies** Numbering between 40 and 100 people, hunting and gathering bands were the earliest form of human society. They had a simple division of labour – typically the men hunted and the women gathered nuts, roots and berries. There was little social inequality, though elders tended to have more power and status than younger members of the band.

**Pastoral societies** Developing around 20,000 years ago, pastoral societies were based on domesticated animals – cattle, sheep, goats, camels – which provided milk and meat. Like hunting and gathering bands, they were usually nomadic, moving in search of pasture for their herds and flocks. Compared to hunting and gathering bands, there was more social inequality since people could accumulate wealth in the form of animals.

**Agrarian societies** These societies were based on the cultivation of crops, often alongside domesticated animals. People usually lived in settled villages since crops needed tending over several months. Grain was often the main crop and one of the main forms of wealth. Since people could accumulate large stocks of grain, this sometimes led to considerable social inequalities.

**Non-industrial civilisations** Emerging around 6000 years ago, these civilisations were often based on the rule of kings and emperors at the head of a highly developed system of local and national government. Ultimately, they depended on an efficient agrarian economy which freed many people from food production, allowing them to specialise in a variety of roles in art, science and administration. These societies often had widespread inequalities of wealth, power and status.

Non-industrial civilisations include Ancient Greece and Rome, Ancient Egypt, the Aztecs and Mayas of Central America and the early Chinese and Indian civilisations.

# 5.2 Modern society

Although there were significant changes in premodernity, many sociologists see the move to modernity as *the* major change in human history. Here are some of the key features of modern society which sociologists have identified (Lee & Newby, 1983; Giddens, 2001).

- **Industrialism** Beginning in the 18th century in Britain, industrialism involves the production of goods using non-human sources of power (eg, electricity) and machinery (eg, conveyor belts and robots).

- **Urbanism** The movement of most of the population from rural areas to towns and cities.

- **Social classes** New social classes developed – a wealthy class whose members owned businesses and a working class whose members worked for wages.

- **Military power** The rise of professional armed services and the ever-increasing power of military technology.

- **The nation-state** This is a fairly recent development – a community with clearly defined boundaries which has power over many areas of its citizens' lives. For example, it has the right to tax them and imprison them for breaking national laws.

- **Liberal democracy** A system of government in which adult citizens have the right to elect those who govern them. This usually involves political parties and a legislature which makes laws, eg the UK Parliament.

- **Change** Compared with premodern society, the pace and scale of change is much greater in modern societies – mass movements of people from rural to urban areas, world wars, major changes in technology (eg, production by robots) and in communications (eg, the Internet).

**New ways of thinking and acting** In the premodern era, thought and action were more likely to be guided by:

- tradition – it's always been done this way
- emotion – it feels right to do it this way
- religion – the gods say it should be done this way.

In modern society, these guidelines are increasingly replaced by rational thought and action. Problems are solved by the application of reason – for example, a building is designed for a specific purpose rather than simply following tradition.

Technology and science are increasingly seen as a means of solving problems – they can be tried and tested and judged by results.

## Late modernity

Some sociologists believe that Western industrial societies are now entering *late modernity*. This is a phase rather than a new era, the development of an existing type of society rather than a new type of society. Various dates have been given for the onset of late modernity, with the early 1970s being a popular choice.

Here are some features of late modernity.

- **Risk and uncertainty** The German sociologist Ulrich Beck sees risk and uncertainty as the key features of late modernity (he calls this phase 'the second modernity') (Beck, 1992, 1997). Traditional norms and values are breaking down at an increasingly rapid rate, often leaving uncertainty in their place. And the pace and scope of social change are increasing.

  There are risks at every turn. Here are some examples.

  - **In employment** There are no longer jobs for life.
  - **In relationships** The divorce rate is approaching 50% in several societies.
  - **With new technology** Nobody really knows the risks involved with genetically-modified food.

- **Choice and individualisation** People have greater individual choice to select their own identity, construct their own roles and design their own lifestyle. For example, they have greater freedom to choose and design their relationships – to marry, to cohabit, to divorce, to live in a heterosexual or a gay or lesbian relationship and so on. People are less likely to be forced to conform to traditional marital, family and gender roles.

- **Social reflexivity** This term is used by the British sociologist Anthony Giddens (1991, 2001). In earlier phases of modernity, people were more likely to follow traditional norms and to take those norms for granted. Now they are more likely to be *reflexive* – to reflect on what they are doing, to assess and question their behaviour, to examine what was previously taken for granted.

  What was once standard is now questioned and assessed. Should I marry given the declining marriage rate and the high divorce rate? Should I cohabit given its popularity? Should I divorce and remarry? Should I call it a day and live on a desert island?!! What's best for me in my present situation?

# activity22 late modernity

## question

How do these cartoons illustrate some of the features of late modernity?

## 5.3 Postmodern society

Some sociologists disagree that the present age is simply an extension of modernity. Instead, they argue that we are moving into a brand new era – *postmodernity* – and a brand new type of society – *postmodern society*.

### Symbols and images

Postmodern society is dominated by electronic communication and media – by TV, films, DVDs, videos, websites, e-mails, chat rooms, computer games, adverts and recorded music. We are bombarded with symbols and images from around the world. They expose us to an increasingly diverse range of ideas and values, many of which have little connection with our present lives or past histories. This can cut us off from our past and make our lives feel rootless and empty.

Media symbols and images are constantly changing. TV channels multiply, new styles of music are here and gone, adverts for new perfumes, new shampoos and new drinks appear with monotonous regularity. Everything seems to be in a state of flux – nothing seems permanent or solid.

Symbols and images are enormously important in our lives. They help us build our sense of identity. For example, we buy brand name goods – Nike trainers, Levi jeans, Rayban sunglasses – for their stylish qualities and advertising image. They say something about who we are. Style is everything, and people shift from one brand or fashion to another without any great sense of commitment or loyalty. Sometimes, different styles are combined in unusual and unpredictable ways. The mood is one of novelty, irony and playfulness. Instead of a dominant or mainstream culture, there is a wide diversity of lifestyles. People choose their own values and lifestyles from the thousands on offer, rather than simply following the cultural traditions of their society.

### Postmodern identities

The drift towards postmodern culture is seen as having all sorts of consequences for people's identities.

First, the diversity of postmodern society has multiplied the *number* of social identities which people can adopt. Competing identities exist within each person's head. For example, one person can combine the identities of a forceful business executive *and* a caring mother *and* a Sikh and a British patriot *and* an enthusiastic hang-glider.

Second, postmodern identities are typically based on *choice* rather than tradition or birth.

Third, postmodern identities are becoming increasingly *decentred* – more unstable and fragile. These new identities may be exciting and offer choice but they do not provide a firm sense of roots.

### Loss of faith

Postmodernity has seen a loss of faith in science and technology. The threat of weapons of mass destruction, the risks of genetic engineering, the negative side-effects of using drugs to treat psychological problems, the dangers of global warming and the damage caused by pollution all point to science and technology gone wrong.

There has been a similar loss of faith in rational thinking. People are increasingly turning to the supernatural – to New Age religions, traditional healers and alternative therapists – in their search for answers, cures and solutions to problems.

### A new reality

Some sociologists believe that our whole view of reality in postmodern society is shaped by the flood of images from the media. Images we experience from the media become as, if not more, real and significant than things we directly experience in everyday life. For example, the death of Princess Diana resulted in an outpouring of grief across the world – but for the vast majority she existed only through the media. And, going one step further, a death, a divorce or a marriage in a soap opera glues millions to the screen and is talked about next day as if it were real.

### Postmodern society – conclusion

There are different versions of postmodern theory. Some are optimistic and welcome the new freedoms. Others are more pessimistic and point to the shallowness of postmodern life. Leaving these differences aside, what does the arrival of postmodern society mean in broad terms?

If postmodern theorists are correct, society will splinter into fleeting, unstable and fragmented cultures. And instead of a few major identities, people will move restlessly between a long list of alternative identities – and these will be superficial and give little sense of roots.

Of course, postmodernists may have greatly exaggerated current trends. They are right to point to the greater diversity of contemporary life, but many sociologists argue they over-state their case.

## key terms

*Premodern society* The society before modern society.
*Modern society* According to many sociologists, the type of society which developed during the 18th century and continues today.
*Late modern society* According to some sociologists, a development within modern society rather than a new type of society.
*Postmodern society* Some sociologists believe that a new type of society, which follows modern society, has developed.
*Social reflexivity* People reflecting on what they are doing, assessing and questioning their behaviour, and examining what was previously taken for granted.

## summary

1. A number of sociologists have tried to identify the main developments in human society.

2. Some have identified premodern and modern societies. And some believe that a new phase, late modernity, has developed within modernity.

3. Features of late modernity include:
   - Risk and uncertainty
   - Choice and individualisation
   - Social reflexivity.

4. Other sociologists claim that a new type of society – postmodern society – has emerged.

5. Features of postmodern society include:
   - Dominance of electronic communication and the media
   - The importance of symbols and images
   - Multiple identities based on choice
   - A loss of faith in rational thought, science and technology
   - A new reality largely shaped by media images.

# activity23 postmodern identity

**Item A  Identity cards**

**SUPERMODEL**

SCRATCH HERE

Dream Identity Card

**POP STAR**

**SPORTS STAR**

**FILM STAR**

Will it ever come to this? The Government is planning to sell Identity Scratch Cards. Scratch off the special square and you may win a year's worth of free identity. The winner gets to choose a dream identity, for example, a pop star or a major sports personality.

Adapted from Iannucci, 1995

## Item B  *Symbols and style*

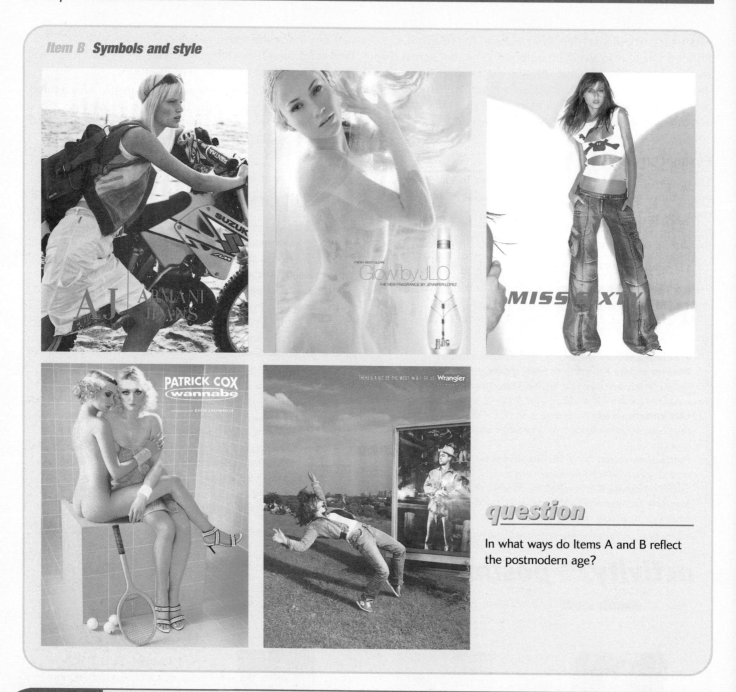

### question

In what ways do Items A and B reflect the postmodern age?

# Unit 6 *Social identities*

## keyissues

1  What is identity?
2  How are social identities formed?

## 6.1 Defining identity

Identity refers to the way we see ourselves in relation to other people – what makes us similar to some people and different from others. Identity operates at different levels.

**The inner self** At one level identity refers to the inner self, that little 'voice' inside our heads. Susan Blackmore (1999) describes this as the 'real you', the bit of yourself that feels those deep emotions like falling in love or feeling sad. It is the bit of you that thinks, dreams and has memories.  It is something which seems to persist throughout your life, giving it some kind of continuity.

**Personal identity** This kind of identity is public and visible – it can be recorded in things like birth certificates, passports, medical files and career records. Each of us is unique on account of our special combination of personal details – our date and place of birth, name, personal biography (family background) and by our history of personal relationships and life experiences.

**Social identity** Social identities are based on our membership of, or identification with, particular social groups. Sometimes these identities are given to us at birth – we are born male or female or with a white or black skin for example. But some social identities involve a greater degree of choice. We may actively choose to identify with some groups such as New Age Travellers or surfers.

We become more sharply aware of our group identities when we can contrast them with groups who are not like us. Social identities are often framed in terms of contrasts – eg, young/old.

This is illustrated by Cecil's (1993) study of Protestants and Catholics in 'Glengow', a small town in Northern Ireland. In Glengow a person's religion was regarded as the most significant way of separating 'us' from 'them'. Both sides relied heavily on stereotypes. Protestants saw themselves as hard-working, thrifty, independent, clean and tidy, but they accused Catholics of being lazy, dominated by priests, untidy and untrustworthy. Catholics saw themselves as easy-going, friendly, generous, intelligent and educated, but saw Protestants as dour, bigoted, mean and lacking in culture.

## 6.2 Constructing identities

All identities, even our 'inner' ones, are social to some extent. We would not have a sense of identity at all unless we had a language to reflect on it. And we would have little sense of group differences and similarities if we did not participate in social life.

### Symbolic interactionism and identity

One of the best ways to understand the social character of identity is to look at the ideas of symbolic interactionism (see pages 28-29). This approach to identity was pioneered by George Herbert Mead (1863-1931).

**The self** Mead argued that a basic feature of human beings is our possession of a sense of self or identity. At an early age we slowly become aware that there are people who are 'not me', in other words that each of us has a separate existence. As we grow up we also begin to form an impression of our own personal qualities and characteristics. Language enables us to reflect on ourselves ('what sort of a person am I?') and to hold little internal 'conversations' (eg, we get angry with ourselves).

**Social interaction** Interactionists argue that our identity has social origins – it emerges in the course of social interaction. We depend on other people for vital clues about who we are. Charles Cooley coined the term *looking glass* self to convey the idea that we 'see' ourselves reflected in the attitudes and behaviour of other people towards us. For example, we may be uncertain about our new haircut until we see the responses of people around us. Of course, we do not always accept what others think of us, but their opinions are hard to ignore!

## activity24 changes

### Item A  *No longer me*

The following passage was written by a journalist who had horrific operations on his tongue which altered his facial appearance and left him with severe difficulties in speech and eating.

'I found myself having depressing thoughts about who this made me. Would the people I love have loved me if this is how I was when they first met me? Would my friends have become my friends if when we first met I'd been a wounded, honking mute, unable to respond to the simplest questions without dribbling? I also knew the answer was almost certainly no. It had to be. I was not now the person my friends befriended, my wife married. The fact remained: I was not me any more. My friends seemed willing to do almost anything for me but they were responding to who I was before the operation rather than who I had become after it.'

Adapted from Diamond, 1998

### Item B  *Bar mitzvah*

*A bar mitzvah is a Jewish ceremony marking the transition of 13 year-old boys to adulthood. The picture shows a mass bar mitzvah of immigrant Russian boys in Jerusalem.*

## questions

1  How would symbolic interactionists explain the experience of the journalist in Item A?

2  In what ways are the identities of the boys in Item B likely to change?

Sometimes we take the initiative rather than waiting for others to form an opinion of us. Goffman (1969) calls this the *presentation of self*, a process where we deliberately arrange our appearance (clothes, hairstyle etc) and adopt certain mannerisms in order to make a public statement about ourselves – see page 29.

**The changing self** Interactionists challenge the idea that each of us has a fixed, stable self. Identity can change with the passage of time. The 'me' I am now is different in certain ways from the 'me' I was ten years ago. An identity may change slowly, or it may be transformed by a dramatic life event such as bereavement, mutilation, redundancy or being labelled a criminal, which forces a re-examination of one's self.

## Social identities – conclusion

Some might argue that we are 'blank sheets' and society simply writes its message on us. For example, if other people look down on us, we develop low self-esteem. If

they like us, we think of ourselves as popular. A more realistic approach is that we do not always accept the opinions of others – we interpret them and judge their value according to that interpretation.

The interactionist model certainly alerts us to the social character of identity – it is not something fixed at birth. Our identity can develop and change as we interact with others.

## key terms

*Identity* The way we see ourselves in relation to others; our self-image or group-identification.
*Looking glass self* The view of ourself revealed by listening to and watching other people respond to our actions.
*Presentation of self* The ways in which we project a desired image to others.

## summary

1. Identity can refer to the inner self, personal identity or social identity.

2. All identities are social in the sense that they depend on language and social experience. It is impossible to imagine a society where people have no sense of who they are or what makes them different from others.

3. Social identities express our similarities with others in the same social group. But they also create a divide between 'us' and 'them'.

4. Interactionists claim that the self has social origins – it emerges in the course of social interaction. Our identities may change as we move from group to group, or as a result of important changes in our lives.

5. Sometimes we have social identities imposed on us, at other times we have freedom to choose the groups with whom we identify. The 'presentation of self' is a device we use to create our own identity.

# Unit 7 *Gender identities*

## key issues

1 What is the difference between sex and gender?

2 How are gender identities formed?

3 Are gender identities changing?

## 7.1 Sex and gender

As soon as a baby is born the first question we ask is whether it is a boy or a girl. We do this because we see males and females as having different 'natures' and so we assume they will have different identities and destinies. However, sociologists challenge these commonsense assumptions. They claim that many of the differences between men and women are not natural but created by society. We can see this more clearly if we make a distinction between sex and gender.

**Sex** This refers to the physical and biological differences between males and females. They have different genes,

hormones, genitals and secondary sexual characteristics (breasts, hairiness of body and so on). Because sex is a matter of biology, it is usually regarded as something that is more or less fixed.

**Gender** This refers to the cultural expectations attached to a person's sex. In modern Britain for example, women are seen as sensitive and caring and therefore more suited to the supposedly feminine tasks of childcare. Many of these

### Table 2 *Gender stereotypes*

| Feminine | Masculine |
|---|---|
| affectionate | undemonstrative |
| tender | aggressive |
| childlike | ambitious |
| soft spoken | assertive |
| shy | confident |
| cooperative | competitive |
| gentle | dominant |

Adapted from Archer & Lloyd, 1985

gender assumptions are highly exaggerated and stereotypical – see Table 2. But they do have an influence on our expectations and perceptions.

**Sexuality** Sexual behaviour offers clear examples of different cultural expectations of males and females. It is commonly assumed that males and females have different sexual personalities (women more interested in love, men more interested in sex). Also, men and women are given different sexual 'scripts' to act out – the man does the chasing, the woman is the passive sex-object. There is also a sexual double-standard – sexual promiscuity can enhance a man's reputation but it may earn a woman an undesirable reputation as a 'slag' (Lees, 1986).

### Biology or society?

Where do gender differences come from? Are they the result of biological differences – the biological determinist view? Or are they created by society – the social constructionist view?

**Biological determinism** This approach believes gender is based on nature. The genetic differences between males and females create natural differences in their attitudes and abilities and this explains why they end up in different social roles. For example, Steven Goldberg (1979) argues that males have an inbuilt 'dominance tendency' and this is why they tend to occupy the top roles in society.

**Social constructionism** This approach argues that gender is based on 'nurture' – socialisation and social environment. Each society creates its own set of gender expectations and steers men and women in the chosen directions. Gender differences cannot be genetically programmed since there are wide variations in masculine and feminine behaviour between societies and over time.

Margaret Mead (1935) showed the cultural flexibility of gender in her famous study of three New Guinea tribes (New Guinea is a set of islands in the Pacific Ocean). Among the Arapesh both sexes were gentle and submissive ('feminine'). Among the Mundugamor both sexes were aggressive, rough and competitive ('masculine'). And among the Tchambuli the gender roles seemed the reverse of Western stereotypes (women made the sexual advances, and men enjoyed a good gossip!).

Mead perhaps over-stated her case – no other study has produced such startling results – but she certainly showed that gender differences are at least to some extent a matter of cultural *choice*.

### Sex and gender – conclusion

Reasons for the differences between men and women are a matter of dispute. It is not easy to specify the relative importance of biology and society in accounting for differences in the behaviour of men and women.

Nevertheless, the distinction between sex and gender helps us to see that biological differences do not have a direct effect on social roles. Societies have a wide degree of freedom to choose gender characteristics and gender roles. Variations from society to society show that these differences are, at least to some degree, a matter of socialisation.

# activity25 gender, biology and culture

### Item A  The Tchambuli

The women go around with shaven heads, unadorned, determinedly busy about their affairs. Adult males in Tchambuli society are skittish (highly strung and fickle), wary of each other, interested in art, in the theatre, in a thousand petty bits of insult and gossip. The men wear lovely ornaments, they do the shopping, they carve and paint and dance. Men whose hair is long enough wear curls, and the others make false curls out of rattan rings.

Adapted from Mead, 1962

### question

What do these items tell us about the nature/nurture debate?

### Item B  Looking good

*Men from New Guinea in traditional dress*

## 7.2 Gender socialisation

### Agents of socialisation

Males and females learn their gender identities and roles from a variety of agents of socialisation.

**Parents** Children are steered towards gender roles and identities by their parents. Parents use different terms of endearment for boys and girls ('my brave soldier', 'my little princess'). They dress boys and girls differently (blue for boys, pink for girls). They *channel* their children's energies in particular directions by giving them different toys – guns for boys, dolls for girls. They *manipulate* their children by encouraging different types of activity – boys can be boisterous but girls should be sweet (Oakley, 1972). Young children also observe gender differences inside the home (mother tends to do most of the housework and cooking).

**School** Studies suggest that by the time children start school they have already picked up gender stereotypes from home, peer groups and mass media. Even at this early age, they may be keenly aware of gender differences between boys and girls. Sometimes they protest when they see other children behaving out of 'character' – they will laugh at a boy who plays with dolls, or get angry when girls play with 'boys' toys'.

Some of these attitudes may be reinforced by their experiences in school. Certainly this is the view of Christine Skelton (2002), based on her study of Benwood Primary School (see Unit 3.2). She describes the various ways in which gender stereotypes were created and maintained in Benwood.

At school assembly it was the men teachers who would be called upon by the headteacher to move equipment or lead the singing. Teachers who could not recall a boy's name would refer to 'you' or 'that boy', or if it was a girl, 'darling' or 'sweetheart'. Posters and artwork on the walls of the school showed boys being active and naughty but girls being passive and good. Also, teachers read stories that encouraged boys to be 'masculine' heroes. In the school football team, boys were taught how to be 'manly' and how to use an 'acceptable' level of physical violence.

# activity 26 girls and boys

**Item A** *Dating advice*

The following advice was provided in the *Tatler* magazine

> **It is important to remember that girls and boys are not remotely alike. So here are some dating do's and don'ts to guide you:**
>
> | *For girls:* | *For boys:* |
> |---|---|
> | Never pretend to know anything about football, even if you do. Balls are strictly boys' territory. | Learn to listen to girls. They're invariably much brighter than boys. |
> | Boys are shy little creatures. Laughing at their jokes is sure to bring them out of their shells. Laughing at their dancing will not. | The words 'I love you' are taken very seriously by girls. Avoid bandying them about. |
> | Remember that girls cannot drink as much as boys. So don't try to keep up with them (it's part of their game plan). | Very few girls are funny. They probably know this, so huge guffaws every time she opens her mouth will only annoy her. |

Adapted from *Tatler*, July 1997

**Item B** *The football match*

## question

How do the items illustrate the process of gender socialisation?

## Masculinity and femininity

**Hegemonic masculinity** Boys tend to be socialised into a style of masculinity which stresses toughness, competition, hierarchy and aggression. This style is called *hegemonic* (dominant) because it crowds out other masculine styles such as artistic and gay masculine identities (Connell, 1995). Young men are put under great pressure to present themselves as hard, strong and independent. So they soon learn to conceal any 'girly' signs of gentleness, kindness and vulnerability.

**Swots** Emma Reynold (2001) demonstrated the power of hegemonic masculinity in her study of boys in their final year of primary school. She argues that some boys construct alternative masculinities – gentle, academic, artistic and non-sporting. But boys who are studious or academic find out very quickly that this conflicts with the hegemonic form of masculinity. They risk being teased and ridiculed for being swots, geeks, nerds and squares rather than 'real' boys.  So, although they continue to study hard, they learn to adopt strategies to avoid being seen as feminine. For example, they play down their academic success, they join in the teasing and bullying of other studious boys, and they sometimes behave badly in order to disguise their positive attitude towards study. They also ridicule girls who are seen as too academic, and boys with poor sporting skills.

**Looking right** One of the ways a girl expresses her feminine identity is through her appearance. The importance of appearance is described by Sue Lees (1993) in her study of female teenagers in London schools. These girls put great stress on looking right. Lees argues that this is not a natural feminine thing, neither is it a sign of vanity. Rather, it is something girls are forced into in order to show they are 'good' girls rather than 'slags'. The girls she spoke to feared that if they dressed in too 'loose' or 'sexy' a fashion their reputations would be destroyed. So they learn to dress and move in an 'appropriate' way.

According to Lees, a girl is taught that her appearance is crucial to her identity. She learns that her body must be controlled and disciplined. Girls must act modestly, sit with their legs firmly together rather than spread out, and avoid eye contact with any man they meet in the street. They are

# activity27 real women

### Item A  Snow White

I WISH SHE'D JUST GO BACK TO THE HOUSEWORK...

### Item B  Changing attitudes

Percentages disagreeing with the statement: A husband's job is to earn the money; a wife's job is to look after the home and the children

|  | 1984 | 1994 |
| --- | --- | --- |
| Men | 34 | 57 |
| Women | 41 | 61 |
| Employed women | 59 | 77 |

Adapted from British Social Attitudes surveys

## question

What do the items tell us about changes in attitudes to gender?

taught that they should not take up too much space or talk too much.

**Feminism** The basic assumption shared by feminists is that the gender divisions in society operate to the disadvantage of women. The process of gender socialisation usually encourages traditional gender roles which reinforce and justify male dominance. (See Unit 4.4 for more detail on feminism.)

But if gender differences are socially constructed then they can be changed. Feminists have shown that many of the so-called natural differences between men and women are simply not true. Women are perfectly capable of building a successful career, and men are quite capable of housework – if they try. Therefore feminists have helped transform many of our assumptions about gender. For example, young women nowadays are no longer socialised into thinking that their future consists solely of marriage and children.

### Gender socialisation – conclusion

Some experts say that gender differences are so natural that they are bound to emerge in any society. That may or may not be the case. But we can see clearly that most societies

help them on their way – they encourage gender differences. They do this through the process of socialisation.

Boys and girls are participants in this learning process and they take an active part in constructing their particular identities. But they have to do this against a background where certain forms of masculinity and femininity are dominant and others are subordinate. Hegemonic masculinity makes it difficult for boys to forge alternative masculine identities

Feminists believe that men have greater power and arrange society in a way that suits them. But feminists have challenged this male power in recent decades.

## 7.3 Changing identities

Gender roles and identities change over time. For example, in the past a woman's place was thought to be firmly in the home. But nowadays more and more women are building careers. This inevitably has an effect on how they see themselves and how they are seen by others. It also reminds us that gender identities can overlap, with men and women adopting similar attitudes and lifestyles.

## *activity*28 *lads and ladettes*

**Item A  Lad**

Liam Gallagher

**Item B  Ladette**

Sara Cox

### *question*

Are 'lads' and 'ladettes' a media creation?

Nowadays, for example, young women are sometimes accused of behaving just as 'badly' as young men.

## Behaving badly

One sign that the gender divide may be slowly disappearing is the similarity in the behaviour of 'lads' and 'ladettes'.

**Lads** Masculinity is something which varies over time. In the 1980s, for example, some claimed that 'New Men' were appearing in Britain. The New Man was a non-sexist, non-aggressive male who was sensitive and considerate, sharing and caring. But in the 1990s this sensitive type was upstaged by the rising popularity of yobbish 'lads'. It became fashionable once again for young men to have a good time through sex, lager, football and loutish behaviour. Some journalists dubbed this new style 'lad culture'. It was celebrated in television programmes such as *Men Behaving Badly* and in men's magazines such as *Loaded*. Its heroes (role models) were football stars or rock stars who behaved in outrageous ways.

**Ladettes** Today, there is a female counterpart to the lad – the 'ladette'. Following in the wake of the lads, the ladette seems equally willing to booze, swear and indulge her sexual appetites. As ladette culture has spread, new female role models have appeared in the media and they attract a huge following. They are admired for their sassy, don't-give-a-damn attitude and their readiness to compete on equal terms with the lads. Their cultural values are celebrated in magazines like *Cosmopolitan*. Judging by the similar values of lads and ladettes, the gender gap seems to be closing.

However, the extent to which lads and ladettes represent an accurate picture of young people today is open to question. Many see these terms as being used by the media to attract interest rather than accurate descriptions of social change.

## Fashion victims

Another area where gender differences seem to be converging is fashion. Traditionally, concern with fashion and personal appearance was seen as the province of women. 'Real' men, by contrast, were careless about how they looked or simply followed convention. However, this is changing.

**New masculinities** David Abbott (2000) provides a useful overview of men's growing interest in fashion and grooming. Drawing on the work of writers like Frank Mort and Sean Nixon, he describes big shifts in the fashion styles of young men over recent decades. It seems they are taking a keener interest in their clothes, hair and personal appearance. They are growing more confident about expressing themselves through the way they dress and groom (eg, use of after-shave, male perfumes, hair gel, even make-up). Nowadays, they are learning to get pleasure from what was traditionally seen as a feminine preoccupation with personal image. Their identities increasingly revolve around their dress sense, their body image and the right look.

## Crisis of masculinity

Not all men are motivated by fashion and style. Heavy manual work such as mining or shipbuilding provided some working-class men with a strong sense of male pride. Now these sorts of jobs are disappearing. New jobs tend to be based around computers and telecommunications and are often taken by women. In education, they see girls' achievement outpacing boys at every age. Mac an Ghaill (1994) describes the insecurity faced by these men as a 'crisis of masculinity'. Their traditional masculine identity is no longer relevant yet they are not comfortable with alternative male identities. Men may respond to this 'crisis' in a number of ways including becoming depressed, fatalistic (giving up), turning to crime, or by adopting new identities.

*'The Full Monty'*: redundant steelworkers practising for their new career as strippers – an unusual way of responding to the crisis of masculinity!

## Freedom's children

Helen Wilkinson (1997) refers to research she conducted on a national sample of 18-34 year-olds. This research suggests that the values of this young generation ('freedom's children') are markedly different from those of their parents. There has been a huge shift in values between the generations. Young people nowadays tend to be much more confident and assertive. Although they have to make many difficult decisions, they take it for granted that they can control their own lives and choose their own lifestyles.

Wilkinson was particularly struck by the rising power and confidence of women. They are more willing to take risks, live life 'on the edge', and seek pleasure and fun. Many of them reject the notion of separate spheres for men and women. They have discarded the stereotypes of 'male breadwinners' and 'female homemakers'. Most of them have grown up assuming that sexual equality is their birthright.

Wilkinson believes there has been a growing convergence – coming together – of the values of young men and women. Men's values are becoming more 'feminine' and women's are becoming more 'masculine'. According to her findings, young people are moving away from the old gender stereotypes and roles. Instead, they want to flirt with both their masculine and feminine sides. They value their freedom to choose and their right to express their own individuality.

## Changing gender identities – conclusion

Gender differences are becoming blurred as gender identities and lifestyles slowly converge. Many of the differences have been eroded by the impact of feminism, social change and equal opportunities legislation.

There are signs that some gender stereotypes are declining in today's British society. For example, teachers are encouraging young women to plan for a career, not just for marriage and having children.

There is greater flexibility in gender behaviour and both men and women are experimenting with a wider range of gender roles.

However, there is still a long way to go as many gender stereotypes are proving very resistant to change.

### key terms

*Hegemonic masculinity* The dominant style of masculinity which stresses toughness, competition, hierarchy and aggression.
*Gender* A set of cultural expectations about how males and females should behave.
*Sex* A classification of males and females according to their biological characteristics.
*Sexuality* The emotions, desires, attitudes and direction of our sex drive.

## activity29 gender games

**Item A   Line dancing**

Norman on Tuesdays    Norma on Wednesdays

Norman Horton enjoyed his new hobby of line dancing so much that he decided to go twice a week – once as a man and once as a woman. Mr Horton, aged 58, would set off on Tuesday nights in open-neck shirt, trousers and stetson. But on Wednesdays he transformed himself into Norma, with a frilly blouse, short skirt, gold tights and high heels. A former paratrooper and military policeman, he has been cross-dressing since the age of 12. 'My wife doesn't mind me cross-dressing as long as I don't do it too often and keep it under control.'

Adapted from *The Guardian*, 17.4.98

**Item B   Bodybuilders**

*The top three in the women's bodybuilding world championship, 2002*

### question

What do the items tell us about changing gender identities?

## summary

1. In every society, men and women are expected to behave differently from each other. Biological determinists say this is inevitable because of the biological differences between the sexes. They say men and women have different aptitudes and abilities and so they are suited for different social roles.

2. Social constructionists point out that gender expectations differ from society to society. It is hardly likely, then, that these expectations are rooted in biological differences. Rather, they are the result of socialisation. Societies have considerable choice in deciding which cultural roles they will allocate to men and women.

3. Gender socialisation operates at many levels in society. Parents and schools socialise young children into gender roles, and mass media often reinforce these distinctions.

4. Feminists believe that men benefit from the widespread view that certain tasks (like child-rearing or housework) are naturally the responsibility of women.

5. There are signs that old gender identities are breaking down. They have not vanished altogether but there is some evidence of convergence in male and female identities. At the same time, there is a new flexibility and freedom in the way people express their gender identities.

# Unit 8 National identities

## key issues

1 What are nation states?

2 How are national identities formed?

3 What forms does nationalism take?

4 How is globalisation affecting national identity?

## 8.1 Creating nations

### Nation states

The world is divided into a number of countries such as Britain, France, Nigeria and Mexico. Most of these countries can also be referred to as *nation states*. A state is an independent self-governing geographical area. The term nation state suggests that the people living within the state are a single 'nation', united by a common identity and a common culture.

However, this is not always the case. A single state might contain a number of nations (eg, the British state governs the nations of Wales, Scotland and England). On the other hand, a single nation might be scattered across different states (eg, Kurds in Iran, Iraq and Turkey). Nevertheless, states usually attempt to create an overall sense of national identity in order to secure the loyalty of their populations.

Many people assume that nation states have existed throughout history. However, Michael Mann (1986) shows that it was only in the seventeenth and eighteenth centuries that maps started to represent the world in terms of separate territories with clearly marked borders. Before then, maps of medieval Europe had only fuzzy and shifting frontiers and it was not always easy to identify a single power in control of a clear-cut territory.

### National identity

People become aware of their national identity in lots of ways. Stuart Hall (1992) points out that every nation has a collection of stories about its shared experiences, sorrows, triumphs and disasters. These stories are told in the nation's proud boasts (its democratic traditions, traditions of independence and freedom), its collective memories (the World Wars, 1966 World Cup victory) and its favourite images (England's 'green and pleasant land', cream teas). People draw on these stories in order to construct their sense of national identity.

People are constantly reminded of their national identity by symbols and rituals. Symbols include flags, coins, anthems, uniforms, monuments and ceremonies. The national flag is a powerful symbol of the identity of a nation – it separates those who belong (the 'nation') from outsiders ('foreigners'). Public rituals like Remembrance Day and royal ceremonies are occasions when people are invited to reflect on their shared history and collective identity.

Nevertheless, it is difficult to describe a particular national identity with any confidence. People may disagree on what qualifies someone for membership of the nation (see Table 3). They also disagree on the nation's chief

| Table 3 What is the basis of national identity? | |
|---|---|
| Born in country | 79 |
| Have citizenship | 86 |
| Lived most of life there | 76 |
| Able to speak language | 88 |
| Religion | 34 |
| Respect political institutions and laws | 87 |
| Feels British | 78 |
| (% of sample saying 'very' or 'fairly' important) | |

Adapted from McCrone & Surridge, 1998

features. Besides, a national identity will alter as the nation itself changes over time.

## National cultures

Each nation tends to be associated with a distinctive culture. The Japanese, for example, have a reputation for politeness and group conformity. But descriptions of national cultures are often based on crude stereotypes which seize on a few characteristics and then exaggerate them. They not only ignore the cultural similarities *between* countries, they also conceal the cultural variations which nearly always exist *within* every country.

For example, Bowie (1993) notes that outsiders generally view Wales in terms of broad stereotypes – the Eisteddfod, Welsh hats and shawls, rugby, male voice choirs. To the outsider, Wales may appear to have a firm sense of identity and a uniform culture. But in actual fact there are major cultural divisions between Welsh and non-Welsh speakers, between north and south, and between industrial and rural areas. Most so-called nations are actually cultural 'hybrids' that contain a mixture of ethnic and cultural groups.

**Traditional images** National cultures change over time. For example, the traditional image of Scotland is one of Rabbie Burns, whisky, the kilt and bagpipes. But a more up-to-date version might include oil rigs, the new Scottish Parliament,

'silicon glens' (hi-tech computer industries), and Billy Connolly. So the past is not always a reliable guide to the present. Nevertheless, the traditional images and symbols often remain real and meaningful to many people.

### Creating nations – conclusion

Most nation states actually contain a mix of cultural groups. This is true of Britain, with the Celtic nations (Scotland, Wales) claiming a different identity from the English one.

Describing a national culture or national identity is a difficult task – there are so many things to choose from, and people will have differing views on the best 'markers'. Besides, national cultures change over time and so the declared identity will be a blend of the past and the present.

## 8.2 Nationalism

*Nationalism* is a political doctrine that claims the right of every nation to have its own historical homeland and an independent state to run its own affairs. In today's world, nationalism has gained a rather nasty reputation. It can be a divisive force which pitches nations against each other, leading to conflict and violence. One example is the long

# activity30 learning national identity

### Item A  Wimbledon

Watching Tim Henman

### Item B  Golden Jubliee

Street party in Jubilee Drive, Liverpool

## question

Using the items, describe some of the ways people learn a sense of English national identity.

and violent struggle over land between Israeli Jews and Palestinians. But nationalism can also take less dramatic 'everyday' forms.

**Everyday nationalism** Nationalism penetrates into the everyday life and outlook of people in societies such as Britain. Billig (1995) calls this *banal nationalism*. It is a set of taken-for-granted assumptions (eg, that nations should be independent, that loyalty to the nation is a good thing). People are constantly reminded of their national identity in lots of subtle ways. Billig lists as examples such things as weather reports (focusing on the nation's weather) and sports coverage (the nation competing against other nations). We are gently reminded of our national identity even by minor details such as the Union flag fluttering in the forecourt of a petrol station. Politicians constantly talk about 'us', 'the nation' in their speeches.

## Nationalism and Britain

Over the last decade or so, nationalist parties have enjoyed increasing popularity in Scotland and Wales. This resurgence of nationalist feelings has led to some devolution of powers (a Parliament in Scotland, an Assembly in Wales). Some commentators fear this is a step towards the eventual break-up of Britain. However, others have welcomed the opportunity this presents for a a fuller expression of purely English nationalism. For example, the flag of St George is now rivalling the Union flag in popularity at international football matches.

Another threat to British national identity comes from membership of the European Union. Some politicians are glad that Britain is shaking off its island mentality and reaching out to other parts of Europe. But others are fearful that Britain will lose its sense of national identity as well as

# activity31 *two sides of nationalism*

### Item A  Language

The Press Complaints Commission has warned newspapers to curb their nationalistic language during the football World Cup. The Commission condemned some examples of newspaper coverage:

*Daily Star* **headline** (2.3.98): 'Frogs need a good kicking'. (Inside story – French history is littered with acts of plunder, greed and cowardice. They need a good kicking in their Gallic backsides.)

*Daily Mirror* **headline** (24.6.96): 'Achtung! Surrender – for you Fritz, ze Euro '96 Championship is over'. (Inside story – We are at soccer war with Germany.)

Adapted from *The Guardian*, 14.5.1998

### Item B  Football hooligans

*English football fans at Euro 2000 in Charleroi, Belgium*

### Item C  Wartime

*Winston Churchill giving his famous V for victory salute at the end of World War 2 in May, 1945*

## questions

1  Do you think the language in Item A is just harmless fun? Explain your answer.

2  Using the items, identify some of the advantages and disadvantages of nationalism.

its powers to make its own political and economic decisions.

## Nationalist attitudes

A survey by Dowds and Young (1996) reveals interesting variations in nationalist sentiments. The majority of their sample (English, Scots, Welsh) had a fairly well-developed attachment to a British identity. These people declared their patriotic pride in Britain's cultural heritage and national institutions and they expressed confidence in the future of the nation. But a smaller number of people seemed relatively unmoved by the symbols of nation and these were classified as having 'low' nationalist sentiments.

The survey also identified a further division between two kinds of orientation – *inclusive nationalism* and *exclusive nationalism.*

**Inclusive nationalism** People in this category had no wish to draw tight boundaries around membership of the British nation. They show a generous willingness to include certain 'marginal' groups (eg, immigrants, ethnic minorities) as part of the national community and grant them full civic rights.

**Exclusive nationalism** In contrast, people in this group place stronger emphasis on maintaining tight national boundaries by excluding immigrants and ethnic minorities. They displayed a rather mean-minded hatred of 'foreigners'

and an intense dislike for European 'interference' in British political and economic affairs. Dowds and Young's findings suggest this is a minority view.

## Nationalism – conclusion

It is difficult to escape pressures to adopt nationalist sentiments. As Billig points out, they constantly intrude into our everyday lives. In many ways this is legitimate and innocent. After all, every state is entitled to expect the loyalty of its citizens. Also, it is easy to understand why many of us develop a sense of patriotism and an affection for our country and fellow citizens.

More intense forms of nationalism – the 'exclusive' kind – are another matter. They can involve an irrational hatred of external 'foreigners' and an intense resentment of ethnic minorities living in Britain. But the research by Dowds and Young suggests only a small proportion of people take this view.

In recent years, nationalist sentiments have been re-awakened by two major developments – devolution within Britain itself (the so-called 'break-up' of Britain) and moves towards a more integrated European Union. Some commentators claim that one result of this is the strengthening of English identity. Nevertheless, in surveys many people still claim a British identity.

# activity32 views of nationalism

### Item A  Fanfare for Britain

We are blessed that we are an island. In the past the sea has protected us from rabid dogs, foreign dictatorship and our Continental neighbours, who are very different from us. We have a long and mature tradition of freedom and democracy.

Sadly, the Channel no longer protects us from Brussels' bureaucrats. The European Union is trying to merge us into a Continental culture. Even our heritage of country sports is being threatened. Also, our gentle nationalism has been threatened by large waves of immigrants who resist absorption and try to superimpose their cultures and laws upon us.

But nationality is deeply rooted in ties of blood, family, language and religion. It is time we learned to be an island again.

Adapted from N.Tebbit, 1990

### Item B  Multicultural Britain

*Christchurch Infants School*

## questions

1  State why the view expressed in Item A is an example of exclusive nationalism.

2  Explain why Item B seems to display a spirit of inclusive nationalism.

# 8.3 Globalisation

National identity may be under threat from *globalisation*. Globalisation is the term used to describe the process whereby nations are coming closer together culturally and economically. Interaction between nations becomes more frequent and intense as goods, capital, people, knowledge, culture, fashions and beliefs flow across territorial boundaries.

The process of globalisation has speeded up in recent decades with the spread of markets and the growth of global communications networks. The nation states of the world seem to be losing their independence as they become locked into global networks (eg, the world trading system) and over-arching political units (eg, the European Union).

**National cultures** Globalisation is a complex process and its impact on different regions, countries and social groups can be very different. However, it does expose people in all parts of the world to 'foreign' values, influences and goods. For example, the rest of the world has developed a huge appetite for the cultural products of the United States (Coca Cola, baseball hats, trainers, jeans). Paris EuroDisney was built in spite of fierce protests about the 'Hollywoodisation' of French life. On the other hand, most nations have a long history of cultural exchanges and this has not wiped out national differences.

Moreover, non-Western cultures have spread to the West. Examples include cuisine (Indian, Thai and Chinese dishes), music (the popularity of 'world' music), dress ('ethnic' fashions), martial arts (Tai Chi, Kung Fu) and Eastern religions (Buddhism, Transcendental Meditation).

# activity33 a small world

### Item A McDonald's

The world's largest McDonald's - Beijing, China

Jakarta, Indonesia

### Item B The American dream

My children dress like Americans, talk like Americans, behave like Americans. In their imaginations, their dreams and their souls, America is where they think they are. This is strange, because all three of my children were born in England and have lived here all their lives. Yet they dress like Harlem Blacks, with baseball caps worn backward, baggy jeans and hooded tops. They ghetto-blast rap music, breakdance, moonwalk. They watch American TV shows end-to-end and are fluent in American slang.

When we go to the local cinema, everybody in the audience seems to wear US gear and queue for popcorn, Coke, hamburgers and 26 flavours of ice cream. Afterwards we have a Big Mac with french fries.

Adapted from Hill, 1995

### question

In what ways do Items A and B reflect the influence of globalisation?

## Globalisation – conclusion

If some globalisation theorists are correct, a spreading global culture (with a heavy United States influence) may replace national cultures. Instead of national identities, people may become 'citizens of the world'.

However, globalisation theorists have been accused of exaggeration. Nation states are still important, even if they are increasingly locked into larger units such as the European Union. Most people still have a sense of national identity, even if there is greater movement between countries. Eating Chinese food is not the same thing as being Chinese.

Most experts recognise that globalisation is a complex process and it does not lead inevitably to a single world culture or identity. Differences in national cultures and identities are still clearly visible in the present-day world.

## key terms

**Nation** A population assumed to have a shared identity and culture based on their common descent and historical homeland.

**Nation state** A territory run by a sovereign government and based mainly (but not solely) on a single nation.

**Nationalism** A movement or doctrine which stresses the rights to freedom and territory of a nation.

**State** Public institutions with legal powers over a given territory and a monopoly of the legitimate use of force.

**Globalisation** The process by which the various countries and cultures of the world become more closely intertwined.

But globalisation theorists are right to point out that many of these differences have been shrinking.

## summary

1. Nation states have become an established part of the world order. Some of these so-called nation states are actually 'hybrids' and contain a mix of cultural groups within the frontiers of the state.

2. National cultures have some broad distinguishing characteristics. But they usually have a number of internal divisions (they contain different subcultures). They also have many similarities with other national cultures (eg, nations frequently exchange customs, food and dress fashions with one another). Moreover, they change over time (there are differences between the 'traditional' culture and the present-day culture).

3. National identities are created through 'official' channels (eg, flags, ceremonies) and unofficial channels (eg, stories people tell about their nation).

4. Nationalism as a political doctrine attempts to achieve sovereignty for the nation. In Britain, this has led to some devolution for Wales and Scotland.

5. In an everyday sense, nationalism expresses itself in attachment to the nation and its citizens. For many people this takes the form of inclusive nationalism but for a smaller number it leads to exclusive nationalism.

6. Globalisation theorists claim we are moving towards a more interconnected world. National cultures are not sealed off to the same extent, and ideas, values and lifestyles freely flow across frontiers.

7. Globalisation has implications for national identities. The distinctiveness of these identities is becoming eroded under the impact of global exchanges.

# Unit 9 Ethnic identities

## keyissues

1 What is an ethnic group?

2 What are the main ethnic identities in Britain?

3 In what ways are ethnic identities changing?

## 9.1 Ethnic groups and identities

In the 1950s and 1960s many thousands of people migrated from New Commonwealth countries such as Jamaica, India, Pakistan and Kenya to Britain. They brought with them the traditional customs, values, religions, diets and languages of their homelands. These cultural features set them apart from one another and from the mainstream cultures of Britain. In other words, they formed distinctive *ethnic groups* – groups with their own cultures based on a sense of shared origin.

Table 4 shows the range of ethnic groups in Britain in 2001.

### Ethnic identities

The members of an ethnic group may have varying degrees of commitment to the group's values and identities. Nevertheless, a shared cultural tradition does tend to create common identities.

### African-Caribbean identities

The identities of African-Caribbean (or 'Black') people in Britain are shaped by many things including their age and social class. They may follow lifestyles which are not much different from those of White people. However, a black skin colour is significant in a country like Britain where

| Table 4 The UK population by ethnic group | % of total population | % of minority ethnic population |
|---|---|---|
| **White** | 92.1 | n/a |
| **Mixed** | 1.2 | 14.6 |
| **Asian or Asian British** | | |
| Indian | 1.8 | 22.7 |
| Pakistani | 1.3 | 16.1 |
| Bangladeshi | 0.5 | 6.1 |
| Other Asian | 0.4 | 5.3 |
| **Black or Black British** | | |
| Black Caribbean | 1.0 | 12.2 |
| Black African | 0.8 | 10.5 |
| Black Other | 0.2 | 2.1 |
| Chinese | 0.4 | 5.3 |
| Other | 0.4 | 5.0 |
| *All minority ethnic population* | *7.9* | *100* |

Source: *National Statistics Online* (based on April 2001 Census data)

*racism* has not yet been eradicated. Black people may see themselves as the victims or survivors of racism.

African-Caribbean culture and customs have some impact on identities. For example, the use of African-Caribbean ways of speaking or dialects (patois) reinforces their sense of having a distinctive cultural identity.

**Black expressive cultures** The richness of African-Caribbean culture is celebrated every year in the Notting Hill Carnival. Paul Gilroy (1987) also notes the dazzling contributions Black people have made to mainstream popular culture in Britain – in dance, music and dress (Black youth are often seen as the cutting edge of street fashion). Gilroy believes there is no single Black culture or Black identity but he argues that there are certain common themes that run through all Black cultures. One of these is awareness of the historical experience of slavery, a bitter experience that still has an effect on the outlook of Black people.

**The art of being Black** Clare Alexander (1996) made a close study of a group of Black youths in London. She concluded that there are many different ways of being Black. Constructing a Black identity is an 'art' that needs a great deal of work and effort. The youths she studied felt there were 'symbolic markers' of being Black. They felt there is something about certain styles of dress, music, even walking and talking, that make them instantly recognisable as 'Black'.

# activity34 African-Caribbeans

**Item A  Slavery in Trinidad**

**Item B  So Solid Crew**

## questions

1  How might awareness of the history of slavery influence the values and lifestyles of Black Britons?

2  Using Item B and your own knowledge, identify symbolic markers of 'being Black'.

## Asian identities

The term Asian masks some important differences. Most of Britain's Asians have origins in Pakistan, Bangladesh and India. The first two are predominantly Muslim but India contains Sikh and Muslim minorities as well as the Hindu majority. Within these main groups there are further sub-divisions.

Britain's Muslim population is split between the Sunni and Shiah traditions and it is further broken down into various sects and territorial and language groups. However, their shared faith and identity as one nation (*ummah*) creates some bonds between these Muslim communities.

**Asian lifestyles** Each religion has its own place of worship (the Hindu temple, the Muslim mosque, the Sikh gurdwara). Also, each religious group tends to follow its own calendar of fasts (eg, the Muslim *Ramadan*) and feasts (eg, the Hindu *Diwali*). Religion affects dress codes (the Muslim veil, the Sikh turban), diet (Hindus avoid beef, Muslims avoid pork) and moral attitudes (divorce is more acceptable to Muslims than other Asian religious groups).

But there are similarities in the cultural practices of Britain's Asian populations. One example is the custom of arranged marriages where parents play a large part in choosing partners for their children. Another is the stress laid on the extended family (the wider kin group beyond the mother, father and children). Family honour is extremely important and the kin group is always anxious to protect its reputation. This is one of the reasons why the behaviour of young women is closely monitored by relatives.

## White identities

It is a mistake to think that ethnicity is something found only among minority groups. Every group has a culture and so even the White majority can be called an ethnic group. Of course, there are many different ways of being White, so it does not mean the same thing to everyone.

**Invisible culture?** Young Whites sometimes feel they inhabit an invisible culture. This was certainly true of the group studied by Roger Hewitt (1996) in a deprived working-class area of London. They felt a deep sense of unfairness because every culture seemed to be celebrated except their own. They were constantly frustrated whenever they tried to adopt symbols and emblems of White or English cultural identity. For example, the Union flag and the flag of St George were regarded with suspicion because of their association with far-right racist groups. Hewitt argues that ways must be found of allowing White people to be proud of their own cultural traditions. But this should not be done in a racist manner that excludes people from ethnic minorities from claiming an English identity too.

## Ethnic groups and identities – conclusion

Britain is a multicultural society. It contains a number of distinctive ethnic groups, each with its own identity, values

## activity 35 images of White England

**Item A   Royal Ascot**

**Item B   Fox hunting**

**Item C   Henley Regatta**

## question

Why are many people reluctant to adopt a White English identity?

and customs. People in Asian or African-Caribbean minority groups usually have a keen awareness of their cultural traditions. Of course, some people born into these groups will drift away from them, while others will remain deeply committed to their particular ethnic lifestyles. Some will regard themselves as British but British with a difference – Black British or British Asian.

Identity is not based solely on ethnicity however. For example, a Black person is not just Black but also a particular sex, age, social class – all of these will have an effect on that person's identity.

## 9.2 Changing ethnic identities

Some experts confidently predicted that ethnic minorities would slowly become *assimilated* – they would gradually abandon their ethnic cultures and adopt the culture of mainstream Britain. It was expected that this trend would affect mainly the second and third generations (those born in Britain). This has happened to some extent – the life of a Sikh is not the same in Britain as it is in the Punjab. Many male Sikhs no longer wear a turban. Yet it is equally clear that minority cultures have not vanished. This suggests that Britain might become a truly *multicultural* society in which different ethnic traditions co-exist peacefully and sometimes share customs.

Some research evidence on changes in ethnic cultures is provided by the fourth in a series of surveys by the Policy Studies Institute (Modood et al., 1997). This survey included interviews with a small sample of Caribbean and South Asian people living in Birmingham and Southall.

**Asian identities** The 4th PSI study found that cultural heritage continues to exercise an influence on behaviour and identities. Certain traditions (th[e] use of Asian languages, and arranged m[arriage] important in the lives of many Asians. But t[hey are] less true for the second generation. They are m[ore] view marriage as an individual choice, and they ex[pect to] be consulted by their parents. Religion remains of centr[al] importance for many Asians (especially Muslims) but again it is less important for the second generation (especially Sikhs). Few of the sample identified themselves as British. Likewise, few identified themselves as Asians – they were keenly aware of the many differences between Asian groups. Most of them (and especially the first generation) identified themselves in specific ethnic or religious terms (eg, Indian, Muslim).

**Black identities** Modood et al. conclude that there is no single Black identity, but Caribbean cultural traditions do still have an influence. Religious faith (mainly Christian, and especially Pentecostal) still plays an important role for the first generation but has declined among their children. Patois is not used so much now by the first generation but it has enjoyed a resurgence among some of the second generation who see it as a powerful way of asserting their cultural identity. The main identity among Caribbeans is Black although the first generation may describe themselves as West Indian and their children sometimes call themselves Afro-Caribbean. Few describe themselves as British because of the widespread racist assumption that only White people can be British.

### Between two cultures

The second generation, born or raised in this country, are sometimes portrayed as torn between two cultures – the ethnic culture of their migrant parents, and the mainstream

## *activity*36 *changing identities*

Item A **Craig David**

Item B **Primary school**

**Item E**  *Cricket fans*

**Item F**  *Notting Hill Carnival*

*Celebrating Pakistan's victory over England, June 17, 2003*

## question

How do the items illustrate that Asian and African-Caribbean identities in Britain include aspects of the traditional and the new?

culture of Britain. Some of them try to strike a compromise between the two cultures. For example, Asian parents now consult their children more than in the past and this helps to prevent conflicts over arranged marriages. Others may find that their attempts to balance the two cultures are frustrated by racism in the wider society. They may feel they are never going to be accepted by other groups and so they may turn back to their ethnic traditions. Young African-Caribbeans sometimes put on a defiant display of their ethnic identities as a way of expressing their resistance to racism.

**Cultural navigation** Roger Ballard (1994) believes the supposed conflict between Asian teenagers and their parents has been exaggerated. Ballard recognises that there are some major differences between Asian and mainstream cultures but he found that young Asians manage to navigate between them with relative ease. They simply switch codes – in their parents' home they fit in to Asian cultural expectations, but outside the home they blend into mainstream lifestyles. Few find great difficulty in handling this code switching or cultural navigation. Of course, being teenagers, sometimes there is friction with their parents. They occasionally 'act Western' at home as an expression of their independence. Outside the home, they may 'act Asian' as an act of defiance against the racist attitudes of non-Asians. But for the most part young Asians handle the two cultures with few problems.

### Hybrid identities

It is difficult to map where one culture ends and another begins. Ethnic cultures change over time and they borrow from one another. So their boundaries are always shifting. One possibility is that people combine different ethnic styles in novel ways. When they do this they create *hybrid* (mixed) lifestyles and identities.

**Youth** Les Back (1996) found that new hybrid identities were emerging among young people (Whites, Asians, Blacks) in two council estates in South London. These young people are in a transitional stage where they have a great deal of freedom and opportunity to construct new identities. Their cultures are not fixed traditions which they slavishly follow. Rather, they try out new cultural 'masks', experiment with new roles, and play with different styles, meanings and symbols in all sorts of unexpected ways. Back found a great deal of inter-racial friendship and interaction and a great deal of cultural borrowing from other groups (eg, 'cool' language and interest in reggae, soul, hip hop, rap and house). The new identities which were being forged brought Black and White people closer together and helped to blur the divisive lines of race.

## activity37 hybrid identities

### Item A  Joined up cultures

Panjabi MC. His music is a fusion of bhangra and hip hop.

### Item B  I am me

*Salima Dhalla:* I don't know how to start to describe myself. I feel identity-less but very unique. On paper I'm 'Asian' but in my head I'm a cocky little person with lots of hopes and ambitions.

My parents are East African, their parents are Indian, I was born in Wales. I went to a White middle-class girls' private school and I have brown skin, short Western hair, Western clothes, Eastern name, Western friends. So I guess I'm in an identity wasteland. Now I will only agree to being *me*.

Adapted from Kassam, 1997

### question

In what ways do Items A and B represent hybrid identities?

## Changing ethnic identities – conclusion

When members of ethnic minorities start changing their habits and values, it is not always easy to decide what this means. It may be a step towards assimilation. On the other hand, it may just be a normal development of that ethnic culture (cultures are always changing, however slowly).

The only thing that is clear at the moment is that there is a mixture of continuity and change. There is continuity in the sense that ethnic traditions still mean something to second and third generation members of minority groups. But there are also signs of change. One example is arranged marriages – now subject to much greater consultation with young people. Another example is the high rate of inter-marriage or cohabitation between African-Caribbeans and Whites, something that might be expected to modify traditional Caribbean customs.

It is young people who are at the forefront of these

changes. And it is among this group that new hybrid forms are most likely to emerge.

## key terms

**Assimilation** The process by which ethnic minorities adopt the mainstream culture.
**Black** A term sometimes applied to people of African-Caribbean descent.
**Ethnic group** A group with a shared culture based on a sense of common origin.
**Hybrid identities** Identities which draw on two or more ethnic traditions.
**Multicultural society** The co-existence of two or more distinctive ethnic groups within one society.
**Racism** Negative attitudes and discriminatory behaviour towards people of other racial or ethnic groups.

## summary

1. Ethnic minority groups in Britain were initially formed through migration from the New Commonwealth. But growing numbers (second and third generation) have been born in Britain.

2. Ethnic minority groups share many values and lifestyles with the White majority. There is a great deal of overlap. But they also have their own distinctive traditions.

3. Not everyone within an ethnic group expresses that ethnicity in exactly the same way. Besides, their identity is based not only on their ethnicity but also on other factors such as gender, age and social class.

4. Ethnic minority cultures and identities are slowly changing. This may represent a normal development of the culture rather than a step towards assimilation. Nevertheless, the divisions between cultures seem to be getting more blurred.

5. Some young people seem to be skilled at navigation between two cultures. But others find it a strain and prefer to give priority to one culture. Yet another possibility is the development of hybrid forms that mix cultural traditions in novel ways.

# Unit 10 Class identities

## key issues

1. What is social class?
2. How do classes differ in their identities and culture?
3. How is class identity changing?

## 10.1 Living in a class society

### Social class

Income and wealth are unequally distributed across the population of Britain – see Tables 5 and 6. Some groups enjoy high incomes and considerable wealth while others are condemned to poverty. Moreover, this is not a totally random lottery. Your chances of 'winning' or 'losing' depend to a large extent on your social class – your position in the social and economic structure.

**Table 5  Average weekly pay, Great Britain, 2000**

| Highest paid | (£) |
|---|---|
| General managers of large corporations | 2,079 |
| Treasurers and financial managers | 1,235 |
| Medical practitioners | 1,160 |
| **Lowest paid** | |
| Retail cash desk and checkout operators, launderers and dry cleaners, kitchen porters | 205 - 210 |

Adapted from the *New Earnings Survey*, 2002

**Occupation** Most sociologists find it convenient to use occupation as a measure of a person's social class. So a *social class* can be viewed as a cluster of occupations which share a similar economic position. Over the years

**Table 6 Marketable wealth, United Kingdom, 2000**

(stocks and shares, land, homes, savings, possessions etc)

Top 1% of population own 22% of total wealth

Top 5% of population own 42% of total wealth

Top 50% of population own 94% of total wealth

Adapted from the Inland Revenue, 2002

**Table 7 Office of National Statistics (ONS) Social Class Scheme**

| | |
|---|---|
| Class 1 | Higher managerial and professional (eg, company directors, lawyers, doctors) |
| Class 2 | Lower managerial/professional (eg, junior managers, social workers, nurses, police sergeants) |
| Class 3 | Intermediate (eg, clerical workers, secretaries, computer operators) |
| Class 4 | Small employers and self-employed (eg, taxi drivers, window cleaners, shopkeepers) |
| Class 5 | Supervisors, craft and related (eg, printers, plumbers, train drivers) |
| Class 6 | Semi-routine (eg, shop assistants, hairdressers, cooks) |
| Class 7 | Routine (eg, waiters, cleaners, labourers) |
| Class 8 | Never worked/long-term unemployed |

sociologists have used a variety of occupational classifications to identify social classes. The latest version is the Office of National Statistics (ONS) Social Class Scheme – see Table 7.

## Class cultures and identities

The narrow view of class is that it is solely a matter of occupation, income and wealth. But class is much wider than money and possessions. When we think of social class we also think of social and cultural features. We see each social class as having its own special identity, its own set of values, its own lifestyles and habits.

**Class cultures** The French sociologist Pierre Bourdieu (1984) suggests that social classes have their own cultural values, tastes and preferences. This expresses itself in things like their choice of food, music, newspapers and leisure pursuits. Social classes even develop their own ways of walking, talking and eating. They have different attitudes towards the body. For example, working-class people tend to be more tolerant of 'middle-age spread' (putting on weight as they get older) but middle-class professionals are more likely to join fitness programmes in order to keep their bodies trim.

**Class identities** From an early age we are socialised into the lifestyles and values of the class of our parents. The upbringing of a child in a wealthy detached house in a desirable suburb of London will be very different from that of the child of an unemployed single parent in the council flat half a mile away.

We learn to identify with members of our own social class ('us') and become aware of the differences that separate us from other social classes ('them'). In other words, we become *class conscious*.

# activity38 class matters

**Item A Class acts**

*Opera singer*

*Greyhound racing at Wimbledon Stadium*

### Item B  Class divisions

A bitter struggle has broken out in Gloucestershire where home owners on a private estate are objecting to an unemployed family of ten moving into a housing association property. Some residents argue they would lower the tone of the neighbourhood. They have signed a petition demanding that the local authority erect a wall to divide the private properties from the rest.

Mrs Monks flicked cigarette ash on the carpet as she said, 'It's bloody snobbery. Those people signing petitions think they're better than us because we ain't working and can't afford to buy a house.'

Mrs Smith, a home-owner, says her objection to the Monks is not personal, just business (it will affect the value of her house). 'Yes, it sounds snooty', she says, 'but I challenge anyone in our position to say they would feel differently.' She added, 'The Monks and us are different types of people. I know some people will think I'm a stuck-up cow, but I've paid for the right to live the way I want to live.'

Adapted from *The Guardian*, 22.9.95

*Tina Smith*

*The Monk family*

### questions

1 Match the pictures in Item A to the social class most closely associated with them.

2 What does Item B reveal about class identities?

## 10.2 The upper class

The upper class is not listed separately in the ONS scheme. This is partly because it is relatively small – less than 1% of the population according to Kenneth Roberts (2001). But it is also because it is defined by its enormous wealth rather than by the occupations of its members. Britain's upper class enjoys tremendous privileges of wealth and prestige.

The upper class consists of a number of interlocking groups.

- **Landowning aristocrats** These are the 'old' titled families and large landowners. The Duke of Northumberland, for example, owns about 120,000 acres of land as well as a Thames-side mansion and a medieval castle.
- **Entrepreneurs** Nowadays the 'idle rich' are a rare breed. Many of the upper class have gained their wealth from owning or running businesses. Some, such as Richard Branson, are 'self-made' rather than having inherited their wealth.
- **Jet set** The upper class includes a number of people who have made their money in the fields of sport and entertainment. It includes pop stars such as Mick Jagger and Elton John who have knighthoods and mix with aristocracy and royalty.

### Upper-class culture and identity

The upper classes share a strong sense of identity. This is because the upper class is 'closed' – its members tend to be the children of upper-class parents. Social closure in the upper class is the result of a shared culture that creates a web of links and contacts. These connections make it difficult for non-members to penetrate the upper class.

The key elements of upper-class culture involve education, family ties and social and leisure activities. According to John Scott (1982), the upper class 'is characterised by a high degree of social cohesion, the main supports of this cohesion being its system of kinship and educational experience'.

**Education** The children of upper-class families are usually educated in top public schools such as Eton and Harrow and many go on to the most prestigious universities – Oxford and Cambridge. Throughout their education, valuable social contacts are made with each other and with other young people likely to end up in positions of power and influence. These contacts can prove to be extremely helpful later in life – the 'old boy network'. Public schools also socialise their pupils into high levels of self-confidence and an acute sense of their social superiority.

**Family, marriage and kinship** The exclusive lifestyle and experiences of the upper class mean that its young members tend to socialise with other members of the same class. The result is a tendency for the upper class to intermarry. As time goes on, more and more kinship connections develop between upper-class families.

**Social and leisure activities** During their socialisation, young members of the upper class are introduced to the exclusive social events that provide a distinctive upper-class lifestyle. Often these are based on old aristocratic traditions and provide a sense of 'real class'. They also provide a circuit where further connections and contacts can be made.

These events include hunting, shooting, Wimbledon (tennis), the Henley Regatta (rowing), Cowes week (sailing), Royal Ascot (horse racing), Glyndebourne (opera) and the Chelsea Flower Show. Together, they provide a clear picture of a distinctive upper-class lifestyle (Roberts, 2001).

However, by no means all of the upper class live a life of glamorous leisure. Chris Rojek (2000) used statistics and biographical data to study the lives of three of the richest men in the world, Bill Gates (owner of Microsoft), Warren Buffett (investor in stocks and shares) and Richard Branson (owner of Virgin). He found that their lives were centred around their work. They worked long hours and, if they did attend exclusive social occasions, used them mainly to make and develop business connections.

### Upper-class values

The values of the entrepreneurial upper class centre on their work. Rojek argues that, at least for the seriously wealthy individuals he studied, work is valued as a source of pleasure, fun and excitement.

However, the values of the old aristocratic upper class are based more on the importance of tradition, authority and breeding.

**Tradition** The old upper class are conservative in their values and politics. They wish to preserve the historical traditions and customs of British society.

**Authority** A belief in social hierarchy. They think society works best when it is organised into different levels or ranks. People should show proper respect to those in positions of authority.

**Breeding and background** A 'good' background is seen as a guarantee that someone will have the appropriate attitudes, manners and values.

## 10.3 The middle classes

The term middle classes refers mainly to ONS classes 1 and 2. Sometimes the term is used in a broader way to include all non-manual workers including routine (semi-skilled) white collar workers such as secretaries and office workers. This wider definition would include ONS classes 3 and 4 although the ONS scheme now describes these classes as an 'intermediate' group (presumably somewhere between middle class and working class).

It is very difficult to make general statements about the culture and identity of the middle classes. There are two reasons for this.

# activity 39 upper-class lifestyles

## Item A  The social circuit

Strawberries and champagne at Royal Ascot

A grouse shoot in Scotland

## Item B  Richard Branson

Richard Branson in a hot-air balloon over Marrakech.

Richard Branson is said to need eight hours sleep but works for the rest of the time. He is well-known for dressing casually and has no expensive tastes in food or drink. He enjoys the excitement of potentially rewarding but risky ventures, as in air and rail transport. He owns a Caribbean island and homes in Oxfordshire and London. Branson is best known for his world record attempts at water-borne trans-Atlantic crossing and long-distance hot-air ballooning. These are extremely expensive and therefore exclusive leisure activities. For Branson, they are brief interruptions in his normal way of life.

Adapted from Roberts (2001)

## questions

1  How is attendance at the sort of events shown in Item A connected to social closure?

2  Compare the lifestyle and values of Richard Branson (Item B) with those of more traditional members of the upper class.

**The middle class come from diverse backgrounds** There has been a spectacular growth in the middle classes – from 30% of the population in 1951 to an estimated 60% by the year 2000. The 'old' middle classes (the established professions and self-employed business people) have been joined by the expanding ranks of public sector professionals (social workers, teachers, civil servants). There has also been a growth in the number of people in office work, sales and personal services.

Many members of today's middle classes have come from working-class backgrounds and many are women.

The middle classes – unlike the upper class – are thus very open to 'outsiders' who merely have to achieve reasonably well at school to join their swelling ranks. This means that the social backgrounds of the middle classes are very mixed. They may have little in common with each other, so a shared culture and identity may not be immediately visible.

**The middle class includes a wide range of jobs** There are large differences in the pay and status of the middle classes. A part-time office worker in a small engineering business has little in common with a top solicitor. A solicitor may earn up to five or six times as much. Yet, if a broad definition of social class is used, both can be placed in the middle classes as both are non-manual occupations.

The diversity of the middle classes means that people in these groups may have little in common, thus making it less likely they will develop a shared culture or identity.

## Middle-class culture and lifestyles

Most sociologists have avoided general statements about middle-class culture for the reasons given above. Roberts (2001) is an example, 'The present-day middle classes are distinguished by the fact that there are so many lifestyle variations among them, some related to age, gender, ethnicity and education'.

However, he does argue that the middle classes are characterised by a more active and diverse range of leisure activities than the working class. 'They take more holidays, play more sports, make more visits to theatres and the countryside, and eat out more frequently' (Roberts, 2001).

**Fragmentation of middle-class lifestyles** Most sociologists suggest that the middle class is broken up or 'fragmented' into different lifestyle groups.

Mike Savage et al. (1992) noted that the middle class is traditionally regarded as respectable and deeply conformist. Yet nowadays, they are often the pioneers of new cultural styles. Savage et al. used survey data to identify three distinctive (but overlapping) middle-class lifestyles.

**Postmodern** This lifestyle is adopted mainly by artists, advertising executives and 'yuppies'. It combines rather contradictory and diverse interests. They like opera and skiing as well as stock car racing and 'street culture'. They have extravagant, self-indulgent tastes (champagne, expensive restaurants, drug use), but they also follow health and fitness cults (dieting, rigorous exercise).

**Ascetic** This lifestyle is found mainly among those employed in education, health and welfare. Typically they have high cultural capital – they are confident, well-read and articulate – but modest economic capital – money, wealth, property. They are ascetic in their tastes (their consumption of alcohol is low). Their leisure pursuits tend to be intellectual (classical music) and individualistic (hill walking).

**Managerial** Managers and government officials tend to be the least distinctive group as far as cultural tastes are concerned. They follow more conventional middle-class activities such as golf or fishing. They are also keen on the countryside and on heritage (they visit National Trust houses and museums).

## Middle-class values

Again, these vary according to particular groupings in the middle classes.

**Professionals** The higher level of this group is made up of doctors, lawyers, architects, accountants and business executives. Nearly all have been to university and place a high value on education, training and independence. Most of the sons of higher professionals end up in similar jobs, suggesting that parents have been successful in passing on the values of hard work and educational achievement (McDonough, 1997).

Teachers, social workers and local government officers are among those who fit into the lower levels of the professions. Those that work in the public sector (employed by local or central government) have shown themselves willing to join with others in collective action (joining trade unions and taking strike action) to defend the welfare state or pursue a pay claim – actions typically associated with the working class.

Roberts (2001) identifies three main values (what he calls 'preoccupations') associated with the professional middle classes.

1   **Service** The middle classes expect a 'service' relationship with their employer. They value trust and responsibility in their work and want to be able to exercise discretion when and where they see fit.

2   **Career** They value the opportunity to gain promotion or to advance a career by changing job. There is a linked concern for the education of their children. The middle classes expect their children to succeed at school and are willing to take any steps necessary to make this happen (private tutors, changing schools, private education).

3   **Meritocracy** This is a belief that positions should be achieved by ability and effort. They are against any form of discrimination and believe that qualifications are very important.

**Routine white-collar workers** This group are involved in office work but have little freedom and responsibility. The work may involve sitting in front of a computer screen or using a phone all day. Many women work in these jobs and much of the work is part time. Nearly all of it is poorly paid. Some sociologists have gone so far as to suggest these workers should be in the working class and the ONS scale describes them as 'intermediate' (between the middle and working classes).

However, there is little sign that this group hold typical working-class values. Many are not in unions and they do not hold an 'us and them' view of their relationship with their bosses. They see work as a way of improving their quality of life, allowing them to take foreign holidays and buy more consumer goods (McDonough, 1997).

**Self-employed and small business owners** The middle classes also include entrepreneurs – employers with small and medium sized businesses, and the self-employed. Roberts argues that this group has a distinctive set of values. They are individualistic and proud of it. They believe that people should be independent and stand on their own feet rather than rely on the welfare state. They also place great faith in hard work and discipline – they firmly believe that success in life is a result of effort and application rather than luck.

## 10.4 The working class

The working class is composed of manual workers (ONS classes 5, 6 and 7). In 1951 this accounted for about 70% of the working population but over the years it has shrunk to under half. Like the middle class, the working class contains a range of occupations which differ in pay, status and power.

### Traditional working class

This was the dominant working class type from around the end of the nineteenth century until the 1950s or 1960s. Its culture and values have been lovingly described by writers such as Hoggart (1957) and Young and Willmott (1957). These are some of its key features.

**Male breadwinners** Men were regarded as the main breadwinners in the family. Many of them worked in heavy and dangerous industries such as mining, steel, shipbuilding and the docks. This bred a form of 'rugged masculinity' where physical strength and courage were highly valued. Bonds between men were strong and they frequently socialised outside work.

# activity40 middle-class values

### Item A Socialisation

Middle-class parents 'push' their daughters to achieve a high academic performance. These parents equate their child's happiness with educational success and they are driven by a fear of their children failing. Middle-class girls are expected to maintain high standards, to be disciplined, study hard and postpone having fun till later in life.

Working-class parents, on the other hand, are more likely to want to 'protect' their daughters from difficult school work. They want their child's happiness but they do not always equate this with academic success. So they are more 'permissive' in their socialisation styles. They tend not to push their children or place high expectations on them.

Adapted from Walkerdine et al., 2001

### Item C A middle-class revolution

### Item B Entrepreneurs

Penny and Andrew run a pest control firm. They live in a 6-bedroom Georgian house in Chiswick.

*Andrew:* We worry about our children having a decent education. We've worked very hard for our money but we don't mind spending a lot on the children's private schooling.

I'm not convinced there is real unemployment in Britain. How come our firm still has vacancies for rat-catchers?

Adapted from Phillips, 1995

## questions

1 Suggest why middle-class parents are so concerned about their children's educational success (Item A).

2 Use Items A, B and C to identify middle class values. To what extent are these values shared by all members of the middle class?

**Home** The home was often crowded and noisy but it held a special place in people's affections. The burden of housework, cooking and childcare usually fell to women. Many women were full-time housewives, unless poverty forced them to take on part-time jobs.

**Family** The traditional working class felt marriage was for life and so they disapproved of divorce. The members of the extended family often lived close to one another and there was a lot of visiting, especially among the women.

**Community** The traditional working class formed close-knit communities where they had large circles of friends and acquaintances. They valued these community bonds. They met one another frequently on the street, in shops and in the local pub, and they took a keen interest in local gossip and affairs.

**Class consciousness** The traditional working class had a strong class identity. Their identity was sharpened by the experience of working together to improve wages and working conditions. They made a distinction between 'us' (the working class) and 'them' (bosses, the middle class, anyone in authority). They sided with trade unions and the Labour Party.

## The 'new' working class

A shift away from 'smokestacks' (large factories employing lots of manual workers) towards 'high-tech' units (employing skilled technicians rather than assembly line workers) has meant that the traditional working class has declined. Sociologists have mapped the resulting changes in working-class culture over the years.

**Privatism** The working class now live a more private, home-centred life. The old ties of community have been weakened. People increasingly base their life around the home and family activities.

**Changing gender roles** Britain is hardly a 'unisex' society but the differences in gender roles are now less pronounced among the working class. The old breadwinner/home-minder distinction has largely broken down. Women are much more likely to have jobs and men are much more likely to accept at least some responsibility for housework and childcare tasks.

**Materialism** Britain's working class has benefited from the general rise in living standards over the past fifty or so years. They are more likely to own homes and cars, spend a lot on consumer goods and enjoy foreign holidays. For many it is no longer a matter of just 'getting by' – they save, plan and invest, just like the middle class.

**Social mobility** The changing occupational structure of Britain has created greater opportunities for upward mobility into the middle class. So today's working class are less likely to resign themselves or their children to their humble station in life – there is more emphasis on 'getting on' and 'getting ahead'. Social horizons have widened and they are more ambitious. One effect of this 'ladder of opportunity' may be to weaken class consciousness and class solidarity.

**Leisure** In the past working-class identity was based around work – the men in the factories or mines, the women in the home. Nowadays, they are more likely to define themselves by their hobbies and recreational activities. Leisure has become a central life interest.

# *activity*41 *spot the difference*

## question

Use the cartoons to spot the differences between the 'traditional' and 'new' working class.

## 10.5 The underclass

The underclass (ONS class 8) is located at the very bottom of the class pyramid. Its members are so poor and disadvantaged that they are 'under' the normal class structure. They suffer poverty, unemployment, bad housing, ill health and poor educational opportunities. Some sociologists see them as more or less permanently trapped at the bottom. They say children are socialised into this way of life and so the values and lifestyles of the underclass are passed on from one generation to the next (Murray, 1994).

**Underclass values** Some social scientists claim the underclass are poor or unemployed because of their values and morals – they are often seen as lazy, workshy scroungers. Charles Murray, an American writer, calls them the 'new rabble'. He claims they prefer to live off crime or welfare benefits rather than work. He also accuses them of irresponsible attitudes to parenthood – young women carelessly get pregnant and young men become 'absent fathers' and poor role models for their children. Children who grow up in a household where no-one works are likely to settle into the same lifestyle.

**Blaming the victim** Many sociologists accuse Murray of unfairly 'blaming the victim'. They say the underclass are not to blame for their social disadvantage. Rather, they have been 'socially excluded' by more powerful groups in society. These powerful groups have adopted policies that create poverty and unemployment. As a result, the underclass has been cut off from the prosperity and opportunities enjoyed by the general population.

The critics of Murray also challenge the idea that the values of the underclass are really so different from the rest of society. They say that most members of the underclass share the same mainstream social values as everyone else (Dean and Taylor-Gooby 1992).

**Cause or effect?** Even if the underclass has different values, it is not clear what this means. It is possible that their values are the cause of their problems (eg, laziness may lead to unemployment). But it is equally possible that their values are the effect of their disadvantage – if they are constantly denied employment opportunities then they may become apathetic and demoralised. Peter Saunders (1990) indicates how this might happen: 'Inactivity breeds apathy. Empty hours are filled with sleep, and days go by in a dull haze of television programmes and signing on. Sooner or later the unemployed become unemployable.'

### Living in a class society – conclusion

Class is a *complex* matter. There is no simple link between

## activity42 the underclass?

### Item A  The 'new rabble'

- Low skilled and poorly educated
- Single parent families are the norm
- Depend on welfare benefits and 'moonlighting'
- High levels of crime, child abuse and drug abuse
- Unwilling to get a job
- Children have truancy and discipline problems

Adapted from Murray, 1994

### Item B  Murray's view of the underclass

### Item C  A single parent

Judith Gardam, age 28, single mother who lives on state benefits.

I'm sure if the Government sat down and spoke to me and had a cup of tea with me they'd get to like me. I have learnt about life. I know how to love, I have got compassion, I have feelings for people. But do they have feelings for anybody but themselves? I want something better for the kids and I am attending college part time. But at the moment I feel I am lower than lower class.

Adapted from Cockburn, 1993

### questions

1 Argue the case that the behaviour in Item B is:
   a) caused by the culture and values described in Item A,
   b) creates the culture and values described in Item A.

2 Use Item C to argue that the poorest do not have separate values from the rest of society.

class and values. For example, we have seen how certain values (eg, hard work, education) are shared by most social classes. We have also seen how there are different values and lifestyles within each class.

Class is also a *contested* matter – sociologists disagree about it. For example, some sociologists think that routine white-collar workers belong to the middle class while others think they are part of the working class. Some believe a distinct underclass exists while others argue that this group is simply the lowest level of the working class.

Also, class culture and values *change* over time. For example, the values of the 'traditional' working class are not the same as those of the 'new' working class.

## 10.6 A classless society?

A number of sociologists now reject the idea that class is still the dominant force in shaping people's identities. They claim that what matters in contemporary society is no longer class and occupation. Identities are increasingly based on *lifestyle* and *consumption* (Saunders, 1990).

**Lifestyles** According to Pakulski and Waters (1996), lifestyles are becoming a central organising feature of people's lives and a major source of social and personal identity. These lifestyles are less and less likely to be based on social class.

At one time people tended to follow traditional class-based leisure pursuits. The middle class may have enjoyed golf while the working class were more likely to spend their evening greyhound racing. Nowadays, lifestyles and identities are much more diverse and flexible. They are based on individual choice rather than class background. For example, we might find it difficult to guess the class background of hang-gliders, ballroom dancers or football supporters.

**Consumption** Another threat to class identities comes from the rise of consumer culture. People may once have built their identities around work and production but nowadays their lives are more likely to be centred on their leisure and the things they spend their money on – their consumption. So identities may no longer be based on how people *earn* their money – a matter of occupation and class – but on how they *spend it* – a matter of consumer lifestyles (Clarke & Saunders, 1991).

Consumer goods are important not so much for themselves as for what they say about the tastes and style of the consumers. People are usually aware that they are making a statement about themselves through their consumption habits. They signal their lifestyles by what they choose to wear, eat, drink, listen to or collect. These consumption choices express and establish their identity.

### Answering back

Is it really true that class has become so insignificant? A number of sociologists insist that class is still an important factor in contemporary society. For example, there are still

striking inequalities between classes in many areas of life – see Table 8. And these inequalities do not appear to be declining.

---

**Table 8  Class inequalities**

**Life expectancy** People in the top two classes live five years (men) or three years (women) longer than those in the bottom two classes.

**Health** Among professionals, 17% (men) and 25% (women) report a long-standing illness. Among unskilled workers, the figures are 48% (men) and 45% (women).

**Unemployment** Unemployment rates are about four times higher among unskilled workers than among professional groups.

**Victims of crime** In 1995, 4% of affluent (well-off) suburban families were burgled, compared with 10% of families living in council and low-income estates.

**Suicide** In 1993 in England and Wales, suicide for men was four times greater in the bottom class than in the top class.

Adapted from Acheson, 1998

---

**Class identity** Is it really true that class identities have declined? A survey by Gordon Marshall et al. (1989) found that about 60% of the sample thought of themselves as belonging to a particular social class, and over 90% could place themselves in a class if prompted. These figures suggest that class identities manage to survive in spite of competition from lifestyle and consumer identities. Indeed, Marshall et al. argue that class is the most common and powerful source of social identity. Other identities may have grown in importance but they have not displaced class identities from their central position.

This view is supported by Fiona Devine (1997). After reviewing a wide range of research, she concludes that class is still the most common and significant social identity in Britain. Class identities remain much stronger than identities based on things like shopping tastes or leisure pursuits.

### Researching class identity

A survey by Mike Savage et al. (2001) presents a rather more complicated picture. They suggest that class is still an important influence on people's lives and living standards. At the same time, class identities seem to have weakened.

**Class out there** Savage et al. investigated the class identities of 178 people in the Manchester area. They found that very few of their sample believed Britain was a classless society. Most of them were quite comfortable talking about class 'out there' in society – they were familiar with class terminology and they recognised the social and political importance of class. Also, they talked freely about their own life histories in class terms (eg, some of them described how they had moved from a working-class background into the middle class).

# activity43 lifestyles and consumption

## question

How do the photographs above illustrate the importance of lifestyles and consumption in creating identity?

**Personal identity** However, Savage et al. found that most of the people they interviewed were rather hesitant about identifying *themselves* as members of any class. Most saw themselves as 'outside' classes. They preferred to describe themselves as 'ordinary' or as 'individuals' rather than see themselves as products of some class background. They felt their own individuality was under threat if they were 'labelled' in class terms.

Savage et al. conclude that class identities are generally weak. Most people recognise the relevance of class in the wider society but are not keen to express their own personal identities in class terms. So the typical attitude towards class identity is one of ambivalence – mixed feelings.

## A classless society? – conclusion

The recent emphasis on consumption and lifestyles is a response to changes in society. The old class divisions seem to be breaking down and it is not so easy to predict someone's lifestyle purely on the basis of their social class. Lifestyles appear to involve more choice than in the past.

Some sociologists say we should not be deceived by the appearance of diversity and choice in modern society. Many of the differences in lifestyles are rather superficial. When it comes to the important things – life chances, opportunities, power – class is still the most important factor governing our lives. The lone parent on the bleak housing estate has limited freedom to experiment with different lifestyles.

Nevertheless, a distinction has to be drawn between class influences and class identities. Our position in the

## key terms

**Social class** A group which occupies a particular social and economic position in society.
**Class consciousness** Awareness of being in a particular social class.
**Consumption** How people spend their money.
**Lifestyle** A distinctive set of tastes, attitudes and behaviour.
**Underclass** The poorest and most under-privileged section of society.

class structure certainly has an impact on our opportunities and living conditions. But this does not necessarily mean that we are always conscious of class, or that it is our central identity. Savage et al. show that people often have mixed feelings and are hesitant about defining themselves in class terms.

## summary

1. Sociologists allocate people to social classes according to their economic position in society. Occupation is usually selected as the most convenient indicator of class.

2. Class seems to affect many other aspects of our lives. Not just the job we do and the money we earn, but also our attitudes, lifestyles and values. You can predict quite a lot about a person's values, behaviour and identity from their social class.

3. Society can be broken down into four major classes: upper, middle, working and underclass. There are some overlaps between these classes in their values, lifestyles and identities. But there are also some broad class differences.

4. The upper class is made up of those who possess great wealth. Members of the upper class share a strong sense of identity based on public school education and family connections.

5. The middle class is made up of people in non-manual jobs. It is difficult to generalise about middle-class culture and identity as the people and jobs making up the expanding middle class are so diverse. Professionals value education highly and take part in a wide range of leisure activities. The self-employed value independence and hard work.

6. The working class consists of those in manual jobs. Traditional working-class culture emphasised class consciousness, community and the extended family. 'New' working-class culture focuses on leisure and the home.

7. Some sociologists believe that an underclass exists consisting of the unemployed and those dependent on welfare benefits. This group has developed its own norms and values. Others dispute this view and see the underclass as sharing similar values to the rest of society.

8. Some sociologists argue that lifestyles and consumption are now more important than class as sources of identity.

9. Lifestyles are much more diverse nowadays as people pursue their individual interests. These lifestyles are freely chosen rather than dictated by class positions.

10. People make statements about themselves through their consumption – the things they spend their money on.

11. It would be foolish to think that class has faded into insignificance. People's lives are still greatly affected by their class position. But class identities do seem to be weaker now than in the past.

# 2 Family

## Introduction

Picture the family. Does the image on the right come to mind – mum, dad and the kids? This is the usual picture presented by advertisers. But, for more and more of us, it no longer reflects the reality of family life.

Families are changing. Married women who devote their lives to childcare and housework are a dwindling minority. Marriage itself is declining in popularity. More and more couples are living together without getting married. And more and more marriages are ending in separation and divorce. Families have become increasingly diverse.

What do sociologists make of all this? Some believe that the family is in crisis, and that this threatens the wellbeing of society as a whole. Others welcome change. They see the diversity of family life as an opportunity for choice. No longer does the old-fashioned idea of the family restrict women to the home, keep unhappy marriages going, and maintain destructive family relationships.

This chapter looks at these different views. It investigates changes in family life and examines the causes and effects of these changes.

## chaptersummary

▶ **Unit 1** looks at definitions of household, kinship and family. It shows how families vary from society to society.

▶ **Unit 2** outlines the main sociological theories of the family.

▶ **Unit 3** looks at recent changes in marriage, divorce, births and the age of the population.

▶ **Unit 4** examines government policy towards families and children.

▶ **Unit 5** looks at recent trends in family life – cohabitation, lone-parent families, reconstituted families,

dual-career families and one-person households.

▶ **Unit 6** focuses on the following aspects of family diversity – class, ethnicity, gender, life cycle and location.

▶ **Unit 7** looks at explanations of family diversity.

▶ **Unit 8** examines the distribution of power between men and women in the family.

▶ **Unit 9** focuses on children and asks how ideas of childhood have changed.

▶ **Unit 10** looks at various aspects of 'the dark side of family life' including domestic violence and child abuse.

# Unit 1 Household, kinship and family

### keyissues

1  How have household, kinship and family been defined?

2  What are the problems with these definitions?

3  What are the main types of family?

## 1.1 Definitions

This unit begins with simple definitions of *household, kinship* and *family*. It then explores each in more depth.

**Household** A household consists of a person living alone, or two or more people who share the same residence – for

example, a house or a flat. Members of a household also share housekeeping – for example, sharing the rent and household chores. People who live together in a household may or may not be related.

**Kinship** The idea of kinship refers to relationships based on 'blood' or marriage – for example, genetic relationships such as a mother and her biological daughter and a marital relationship of wife and husband.

**Family** The Office of National Statistics provides the following definition of a family. A family is a couple and their never-married children. Families also include couples with no children or a lone parent and their never-married children (*Social Trends*, 2003).

# 1.2 Households

As noted in the above definition, people who form a household must a) live in the same dwelling and b) share a range of domestic activities. For example, they share meals, domestic chores and household expenses.

Many people who share a household have kinship ties. For example, most households consist of family members living together. However, some households consist of unrelated people – for example, student households. And, in recent years, there has been a rapid increase in *one-person households* – individuals living alone. This increase has been greatest in the younger age group (see Activity 1, Item A and pages 104-107).

Defining a household is not as simple as it appears. For example, how often does a person have to eat or sleep in a household to be a member of it? What contribution should they make to housekeeping to qualify as a household member? (Allan & Crow, 2001).

## key terms

**Household** A person living alone, or two or more people who share the same residence and share housekeeping.
**One-person household** A person living alone.

# activity1 households

## Item A Household change

| Great Britain | | | | Percentages |
|---|---|---|---|---|
| | 1971 | 1981 | 1991 | 2002 |
| **One person** | | | | |
| Under state pension age | 6 | 8 | 11 | 15 |
| Over state pension age | 12 | 14 | 16 | 14 |
| **Two or more unrelated adults** | 4 | 5 | 3 | 3 |
| **One family households** | | | | |
| Couple | | | | |
| No children | 27 | 26 | 28 | 29 |
| 1-2 dependent children | 26 | 25 | 20 | 19 |
| 3 or more dependent children | 9 | 6 | 5 | 4 |
| Non-dependent children only | 8 | 8 | 8 | 6 |
| **Lone-parent** | | | | |
| Dependent children | 3 | 5 | 6 | 6 |
| Non-dependent children | 4 | 4 | 4 | 3 |
| **Multi-family households** | 1 | 1 | 1 | 1 |
| **All households** (=100%) (millions) | 18.6 | 20.2 | 22.4 | 24.4 |

Adapted from *Social Trends*, 2003

## Item B Friends

The three young women in the pictures share a house in Manchester. They each contribute to the rent, council tax, water, gas and electricity bills, and the TV licence. They share domestic equipment – plates, cutlery and pans. They socialise and watch TV together in the lounge. They often eat together, taking turns at cooking. And they share domestic chores such as cleaning and washing up.

*Paying bills*

*Cleaning up*

## questions

1 Briefly describe the main trends shown in Item A.

2 Do the young women in Item B form a household? Give reasons for your answer.

## 1.3 Kinship

In everyday language, kinship refers to people you are related to by 'blood' or marriage. So-called 'blood' relatives are people with whom you have a biological or genetic relationship. Marital relationships include your husband or wife plus your 'in-laws' – for example, your mother-in-law and sister-in-law.

Where does kinship begin and end? How close does a genetic relationship have to be before people are counted as kin – first cousins, second cousins, or beyond? What about *fictive* or *honorary kin* such as 'Uncle' Bill and 'Auntie' Mary, longstanding family friends who despite their closeness have no actual biological or marital relationship? Does divorce end certain kinship ties and does remarriage create new kinship ties? Do people who *cohabit* – live together as a couple but are not married – have a kinship relationship?

These questions suggest that, to some extent, kinship is based on personal choice. Who counts as kin depends on *your* choice of kin. They also suggest that kinship is to some extent culturally defined – that ties of kinship are based as much on culture as on biology. This can be seen from the following activity.

### key terms

**Kinship** Relationships based on biological or marital ties.
**Fictive or honorary kin** People regarded as kin who are not linked by biology or marriage.
**Lineage** A kin group consisting of people descended from a common ancestor.

## 1.4 What is the family?

In 1949, the American anthropologist George Peter Murdock provided the following definition of the family.

'The family is a social group characterised by common residence, economic cooperation and reproduction. It includes adults of both sexes, at least two of whom maintain a socially approved sexual relationship, and one or more children, own or adopted, of the sexually cohabiting adults.'

Spelling out this definition:

- Families live together – they share the same household.
- They work together and pool their resources – to some extent they share domestic tasks and income.

# activity2 lineages

A lineage consists of people descended from a common ancestor. It is a kinship group – members see each other as relatives. Lineages are vital to people's livelihood and wellbeing. For example, lineages often own land which is farmed or used for grazing livestock by their members. And in a dispute with members of another lineage, a person can rely on their own lineage for support.

Lineages contain hundreds or even thousands of members. They are found in many small-scale, traditional societies such as the Nuer of southern Sudan and the Bunyoro of western Uganda.

People who would be seen as very distant relatives in Western

*Nuer women*

societies may be defined as close relatives within a lineage. For example, a man might call his father's father's father's brother's son's son's son 'brother' and see him as such. In the West, he would be called a third cousin, and often not even be seen as a relative.

Adapted from Beattie, 1964

## question

Kinship is culturally defined. Discuss with reference to the lineage.

- They reproduce – they have children.
- They include an adult male and female who have a sexual relationship which is approved by the wider society – for example, they have a marital relationship.
- This heterosexual couple have at least one child – either their biological offspring or an adopted child.

## The nuclear family

George Peter Murdock based his definition of the family on a sample of 250 societies ranging from hunting and gathering bands, to small-scale farming societies, to large-scale industrial societies. Although he found a variety of family forms within this sample, Murdock claimed that each contained a basic nucleus consisting of a husband and wife and one or more children, own or adopted. This is the *nuclear family*. Murdock believed that the nuclear family is 'a universal social grouping' – in other words, it is found in all societies.

# *activity*3 *defining the family*

**Item A  Lone-parent family**

*A single mother and her children*

**Item B  Extended family**

*An American extended family*

**Item C  Nuclear family**

*A heterosexual married couple and their children*

**Item D  Gay family**

*A gay married couple and their adopted childen*

## *questions*

1  Which of these 'families' fit/s Murdock's definition? Explain your answer.

2  Do you think those that do not fit should be regarded as families? Give reasons for your answer.

## Extended families

Murdock saw the other family forms in his sample as extensions of the nuclear family. These *extended families* contain kin – relatives based on 'blood' or marriage – in addition to the nuclear family. The nuclear family can be extended in various ways.

**Polygamy** Marriage in the West is *monogamous* – it involves one wife and one husband. In many societies, marriage is *polygamous* – a person is permitted additional wives or husbands. Men may have more than one wife – a system known as *polygyny*. Or, in a small number of societies, women may have more than one husband – a form of marriage known as *polyandry*.

**Other forms of extension** Apart from additional marital

# *activity*4 *polygamy*

### Item A  Polygyny

Adama is a wealthy man. He lives in a village called Sobtenga in Burkina Faso, a country in northwest Africa. Ten years ago he had two wives.

Zenabou, his first wife, thought polygyny was a good idea. It provided her with a 'sister' to share the burdens of domestic work and childcare. Now she is not so sure. Adama has taken two more wives, the youngest of whom, Bintu, is only 16. He is besotted with Bintu and she clearly enjoys the attention. Despite grumbling, his other wives accept the situation, for marriage is seen primarily as an economic affair. Adama's 12 oxen are proof that he can provide security for his wives and children.

Polygyny is much more common than polyandry. It is found in many small-scale traditional societies, particularly in Africa. As the example of Adama suggests, polygyny is a privilege of the wealthy. Not every man can afford two or more wives and in any case there aren't enough women for this. Census figures from 1911 for the Pondo of South Africa show that 10% of men had two wives and only 2% had more than two.

Adapted from Mair, 1971 and Brazier, 1995

*Adama's wives – Zenabou, Bintu, Meryan and Barkissou*

### Item B  Polyandry

The Nyinba people of Nepal practice fraternal polyandry – two or more brothers are married to one wife. They inherited this custom from their Tibetan ancestors who migrated to Nepal centuries ago. They also inherited a love for trading and herding which, together with cultivating the meagre soil, make up the traditional Nyinba economy. Polyandry suits this economy. 'With one or two husbands always on herding or trading trips, one husband will always be at home to care for the wife,' explained Maila Dai, a trader from the village of Bargaau. 'We think polyandry is just like insurance for the wife. If one husband is no good or leaves his wife, there's always another brother.'

*Polyandry among the Nyinba of Nepal. The 12 year old girl on the right is engaged to five brothers, three of whom are pictured here.*

Polyandry has been explained as a way of preventing land from being divided up into less profitable units when a family of sons inherits from the previous generation. It also concentrates the wealth of each household by maintaining a large population of working adult males under one roof.

To the Nyinbas, its advantages are obvious. 'All our brothers work together,' explained Dawa Takpa, 'so we can be wealthy people. If we all go our own way, how can we survive? We have to study, do agricultural work, take care of animals and trade, so we have to work together.' 'For me,' said Tsering Zangmo, who at 21 is the wife of three brothers (the youngest of whom is seven), 'polyandry is fine. If I had only one husband, I would be very poor.'

When asked about jealousy between her husbands, Tsering Zangmo replied, 'But they are brothers. They are never jealous.' However when pressed she giggled and blushed, admitting, 'Well, they only have a very little jealousy. If you like one husband very much, you have to be secret so the others don't know. We make love in the middle of the night, lying naked in sheepskins. We'd never do it just before going to sleep or just before waking up as the others might hear us.'

Adapted from Dunham, 1992

*questions*

1  How can polygamous families be seen as extensions of the nuclear family?

2  Judging from Items A and B, what are the advantages and disadvantages of polygyny and polyandry?

partners, families can be extended in a variety of ways. For example, a three-generation extended family may include grandparents within the family unit. Similarly, uncles and aunts (brothers and sisters of the married couple) may form part of the family unit.

## The working-class extended family

**The 19th century** Historical research by Michael Anderson (1971) suggests that the early stages of industrialisation may have encouraged the development of extended families. Anderson took a 10% sample of households from Preston in Lancashire, using data from the 1851 census. He found that 23% of households contained kin beyond the nuclear family. Most of these households were working class. This was a time of widespread poverty, high birth rates and high death rates. Without a welfare state, people tended to rely on a wide network of kin for care and support. Anderson's study suggests that the working-class

extended family operated as a mutual aid organisation, providing support in times of hardship and crisis.

**The 20th century** There is evidence that the working-class extended family continued well into the 20th century. Research indicates it was alive and well in the 1950s in a Liverpool dock area (Kerr, 1958), in a Yorkshire mining town (Dennis, Henriques & Slaughter, 1956) and in the East End of London (Young & Willmott, 1957).

In their study of Bethnal Green in the East End of London, Michael Young and Peter Willmott define an extended family as 'a combination of families who to some large degree form one domestic unit'. The extended family does not have to share the same household – ie, live under the same roof – as long as its members are in regular contact and share services such as caring for children and elderly relatives. Activity 5 is based on Young and Willmott's research in Bethnal Green.

# *activity5 Bethnal Green*

### Item A  *Mother and daughter*

The link between mother and daughter in Bethnal Green is often strong. The following example shows how much their lives are sometimes woven together. Mrs Wilkins is in and out of her mother's all day. She shops with her in the morning and goes round there for a cup of tea in the afternoon. 'Then any time during the day, if I want a bit of salt or something like that, I go round to Mum to get it and have a bit of a chat while I'm there. If the children have anything wrong with them, I usually go round to my Mum and have a little chat. If she thinks it's serious enough I'll take him to the doctor.' Her mother looked after Marilyn, the oldest child, for nearly three years. 'She's always had her when I worked; I worked from when she was just a little baby until I was past six months with Billy. Oh, she's all for our Mum. She's got her own mates over there and still plays there all the time. Mum looks after my girl pretty good. When she comes in, I say, "Have you had your tea?", and she says as often as not, "I've had it at Nan's".'

Adapted from Young & Willmott, 1957

### Item B  *Contact with kin*

**Contacts of married men and women with parents**

|  | *Fathers* | | *Mothers* | |
|---|---|---|---|---|
|  | Number with father alive | Percentage who saw father in previous 24 hours | Number with mother alive | Percentage who saw mother in previous 24 hours |
| **Men** | 116 | 30% | 163 | 31% |
| **Women** | 100 | 48% | 155 | 55% |

From Young & Willmott, 1957

*questions*

1  In view of Young and Willmott's definition, does Mrs Wilkins in Item A belong to an extended family? Give reasons for your answer.

2  Mr Sykes who lives near his mother-in-law in Bethnal Green said, 'This is the kind of family where sisters never want to leave their mother's side'. How does Item B suggest that this kind of family is widespread?

## The symmetrical family

Many sociologists have argued that there is a long-term trend towards the nuclear family. Michael Young and Peter Willmott take a similar view. In a study entitled *The Symmetrical Family* (1973), they bring together their earlier research, historical evidence, and data from a survey they conducted in London in the early 1970s. They argue that the family in Britain has developed through three stages.

**Stage 1  The pre-industrial family** The family at this stage is a *production unit* – family members work together in agriculture and cottage industries.

**Stage 2  The early industrial family** The industrial revolution disrupted the unity of the family as its economic function was taken over by large-scale industry. Men were increasingly drawn out of the home into industrial employment. The family was 'torn apart' – long working hours meant that men had little time to spend with their wives and children. Poverty was widespread. Kinship networks were extended, mainly by women, to provide mutual support. Extended families continued well into the 20th century in low-income, working-class areas such as Bethnal Green.

**Stage 3  The symmetrical family** This type of family first developed in the middle class. By the 1970s, it had spread to the working class. It has three main characteristics.

- It is nuclear.
- It is home-centred and privatised – family life is focused on the home. Husband and wife look to each other for companionship. Leisure is home-based – for example, watching TV. The family is self-contained – there is little contact with the wider kinship network.
- It is *symmetrical* – the roles of husband and wife are increasingly similar. Although wives are still mainly responsible for childcare, husbands play a greater part in domestic life.

## The modified extended family

The picture presented so far is a steady march of progress blossoming into the privatised, self-sufficient, self-centred nuclear family. Kin beyond the nuclear family appear to play a minor role. A number of sociologists argue that this process has been exaggerated. Important services are often exchanged between nuclear family members and extended kin, though the ties that bind them are not as strong as those in the traditional extended family.

The term *modified extended family* is sometimes used to describe such family groupings. Members come together for important family events and provide support in times of need. Improved communications, such as email, telephones, cars and air travel, mean that contact over long distances is easier than before.

The following evidence suggests that sociologists have tended to underestimate the importance of kinship beyond the nuclear family.

**Manchester in the 1990s** A study of Greater Manchester by Janet Finch and Jennifer Mason (1993) found that over 90% of their sample had given or received financial help from relatives, and almost 60% had shared a household with an adult relative (apart from parents) at some time in their lives. In addition, many reported giving and receiving practical assistance, emotional support, and help with children. While emphasising that family relationships are based on a sense of obligation, Finch and Mason also found that help was negotiated and not necessarily given automatically.

**Declining contact, 1986-1995** There is evidence of a decline in contact with kin. The British Social Attitudes (BSA) Survey is based on a representative sample of adults aged 18 and over. The 1986 and 1995 Surveys looked at frequency of contact with kin. They indicate a significant decline. The figures suggest that people are less likely to visit or be visited by anybody at all – relatives or friends. The data showing this is presented in Activity 6.

Why has contact declined? The average journey time between relatives has increased only very slightly since 1986. There is no evidence that friends have replaced relatives. The most likely explanation appears to be the increasing proportion of women working outside the home. The most marked fall in contact has been among women in full-time employment – for example, a drop of nearly 20% seeing their mother at least once a week (McGlone et al., 1999).

## key terms

*Nuclear family* A family consisting of an adult male and female with one or more children, own or adopted.
*Extended family* A family containing relatives in addition to the nuclear family. An extension of the nuclear family.
*Monogamy* A system of marriage involving two adults, one of each sex.
*Polygamy* A system of marriage involving two or more wives, or two or more husbands.
*Polygny* A system of marriage involving two or more wives.
*Polyandry* A system of marriage involving two or more husbands.
*Production unit* A group of people involved in the production of goods and services.
*Symmetrical family* A nuclear family in which the roles of husband and wife are increasingly similar. It is home-centred, privatised and self-contained.
*Modified extended family* A weaker version of the traditional extended family. Members don't usually share the same household. However, contact is regular and important services are often exchanged.

# activity6 declining contact

| | Frequency seeing relative/ friend at least once a week | |
| --- | --- | --- |
| | 1986 (%) | 1995 (%) |
| Mother | 59 | 49 |
| Father | 51 | 40 |
| Sibling | 33 | 29 |
| Adult child | 66 | 58 |
| Other relative | 42 | 35 |
| 'Best friend' | 65 | 59 |

Adapted from McGlone et al., 1999

| | Frequency seeing non-resident mother at least once a week | |
| --- | --- | --- |
| | 1985 (%) | 1995 (%) |
| Men in full-time work | 49 | 46 |
| Women in full-time work | 64 | 45 |

Adapted from McGlone et al., 1999

## questions

1  a)  Briefly summarise the data in Item A.

   b)  How does it indicate that friends have not taken over from family?

2  What does Item B suggest is the reason for reduced contact with relatives?

3  Items A and B refer to face-to-face contact with relatives. This may exaggerate the extent of the decline of contact. Why? Refer to Item C in your answer.

NOKIA HAS FAMILIES TALKING.

From grandson to grandpa, Nokia has a mobile phone for all the family. In fact, Nokia is a firm family favourite.

Could it be that our small and stylish phones fit so easily into the pocket? Or that they take so little out of it?

Could it be their handy memories, ease of use and crystal-clear clarity?

Is it simply that Nokia works on all national mobile phone networks? Or that Nokia manufactures one of Britain's best-selling portable phones? In a word, yes. Whether you're Mum, Dad, Aunt or Uncle, there's a Nokia phone for you. One that will get you talking.

For more details on Nokia mobile phones, call 0800 101 121 today.

NOKIA CONNECTING PEOPLE

## 1.5 Diversity in family systems

Many sociologists and anthropologists have seen the nuclear family, either in its basic or extended form, as universal, normal and natural. Others have rejected this view. For example, Felicity Edholm (1982), in an article entitled 'The unnatural family', argues that there is nothing normal and natural about the nuclear family. She claims that family and kinship relationships are *socially constructed*. They are based on culture rather than biology. The links between husband and wife, parent and child, are constructed very differently in different societies. In Edholm's words, 'Relatives are not born but made'. Here are some examples Edholm gives to support her argument. They are taken from traditional cultures and may not apply today.

**Parent-child relations – genes** Ideas about the biological relationship between parents and children vary from society to society. For example, the Lakker of Burma see no blood relationship between mother and child – the mother is simply a container in which the child grows. As a result, sexual relationships between children of the same mother are permitted – because they are non-kin, such relationships are not seen as incest.

**Parent/child relations – adoption** Most sociologists consider the tie between mother and child as basic and inevitable. However, in some societies, many children do not live with their biological parents. For example, in Tahiti, in the Pacific Ocean, young women often have one or two children before they are considered ready to settle

*A Tahitian family*

down into a stable relationship with a man. They usually give these children for adoption to their parents or other close relatives. Children see their adoptive mother and father as 'real' parents and their relationship with them as far closer than with their natural parents.

**Marriage and residence** Some sociologists argue that 'marriage' varies so much from society to society that it makes little sense to use the same word for these very different relationships. For example, the basic social group amongst the Nayar of Northern India, the lineage, is made up of men and women descended through the female line from a common ancestor. Brothers and sisters, women and children live together – children are members of their mother's group, not their father's. Nayar girls 'marry' a man before puberty and later take as many lovers as they like. Their 'husband' may or may not be one of these lovers. Children are raised in their mother's social group. 'Husbands' and fathers do not share the same residence as their 'wives' and have little to do with their children.

According to Edholm, examples such as these show that the family is socially constructed. Rather than seeing the family as a natural unit created by biological necessities, it makes more sense to see it as a social unit shaped by cultural norms. And as culture varies from society to society, so do families. In view of this diversity, Edholm rejects the claim that the nuclear family is universal.

### Family diversity today

Edholm's research focused on family diversity in non-Western societies. There is evidence that family diversity is steadily increasing in modern Western societies. In Britain, 26% of families with dependent children were headed by lone parents in 2000 (*Social Trends,* 2002). This was partly due to divorce, partly to never-married mothers, and, to a much smaller extent, to the death of one partner.

*Reconstituted families* – families in which the adult couple bring children from a previous relationship – are steadily increasing. There has also been a rapid growth in *cohabitation* – unmarried couples living together, often in a long-term relationship. And, in recent years, a small but growing number of lesbian and gay families have appeared.

This diversity in today's Western societies will be examined in later units.

## 1.6 Defining the family revisited

Where does this diversity of so-called families leave us? Is it possible to come up with a definition which covers this diversity? David Cheal (1999) summarises some of the responses to this problem.

**We don't know** Faced with the diversity of family forms, some sociologists frankly admit that no one really knows what a family is. This is not a useful state of affairs. For example, how can different family forms be compared if a 'family' cannot be identified?

**Extensions and reductions** Following Murdock, some sociologists have seen all families as extensions or reductions of one basic and elementary form – the nuclear family. So, extended families are extensions, lone-parent families are reductions. Not everybody agrees that the variety of family forms can be seen as extensions or reductions of the nuclear family. For example, if a woman decides to produce a child by *in vitro* fertilisation and rear the child herself, can this be seen as a 'reduction' of the nuclear family?

**Abandon the idea** One solution is to stop using the term family and replace it with a concept such as *primary*

### summary

1. Most households consist of family members.

2. In recent years there has been an increase in one-person households.

3. Kinship ties are based on biology, marriage, personal choice and culture.

4. According to Murdock, the nuclear family is the basic form of family. He sees all other family forms as extensions of the nuclear family.

5. Murdock claims that the nuclear family is a universal social grouping – that it is found in all societies.

6. Industrialisation may have encouraged the development of working-class extended families.

7. There is some evidence that the working-class extended family was replaced by the nuclear family in the last quarter of the 20th century.

8. Some sociologists argue that the move to nuclear families has been exaggerated. Important services are often exchanged between nuclear family members and extended kin. The term modified extended family has been used to describe such family groupings.

9. Edholm argues that the family is a social construction based on culture rather than biology. She rejects the view that the nuclear family is universal.

10. Cross-cultural evidence indicates that family forms vary considerably. Recent evidence from Western societies indicates increasing family diversity.

11. Sociologists have responded to the problem of defining the family in the following ways.

   ● By admitting that they don't really know what the family is

   ● By seeing all family forms as extensions or reductions of the nuclear family

   ● By rejecting the concept of family and replacing it with the concept of primary relationships

   ● By accepting the definitions of the family used by members of society – the family is what people say it is.

relationships (Scanzoni et al., 1989). Primary relationships are close, longlasting and special ties between people. There is no problem placing the wide diversity of 'families' under this heading. But, it does away with the whole idea of family – an idea which is vitally important to individuals, to the 'family group', and to the wider society.

**Ask people** From this point of view, families are what people say they are. If families are socially constructed, then sociologists should discover how people in society construct, define and give meaning to families. This approach may lead to a bewildering diversity of families. But, if this is the social reality within which people live, then this may well be the reality which sociologists should investigate.

# activity7 family diversity

## Item A  The Ashanti

The Ashanti of West Africa are a matrilineal society (descent is traced through the mother's line). While a child's father is important, he has no legal authority over his children. This rests with the wife's family, particularly her brother. It is from the mother's brother that children inherit, though the father is responsible for feeding, clothing and educating them. Many Ashanti men cannot afford to set up a household of their own when they first marry. Since men never live with their wife's brothers, and children are the property of the wife's family, couples often live apart. Only about a third of married women actually live with their husbands.

Adapted from Fortes, 1950

*An Ashanti puberty ritual at which a girl becomes a woman. She belongs to her mother's family.*

*Women and children in the Trobriand Islands*

## Item B  The Trobriand Islanders

Some matrilineal cultures, such as the Trobriand Islanders, think that the father's role in the conception of a child in minimal. He simply 'opens the door' or, at most, shapes the growing embryo through intercourse.

Adapted from Beattie, 1964

## question

The family is a social construction shaped by cultural norms and beliefs. Discuss with reference to Items A and B.

# Unit 2 *Perspectives on the family*

*keyissues*

1 What are the main sociological theories of the family?
2 What are their strengths and weaknesses?

## 2.1 Functionalist theories of the family

Functionalist theories see society as made up of various parts, each of which contributes to the maintenance and well-being of the system as a whole.

Some functionalist theories are based on the idea that societies need *consensus* – agreement about norms and values – in order to survive. As a result, they are also known as *consensus theories*.

Functionalists often assume that if a social institution such as the family exists, then it must have a *function* or purpose – it must do something useful. As a result, the family is usually seen to perform functions which benefit both its members and society as a whole.

### George Peter Murdock

According to Murdock (1949), the family is a universal institution with universal functions. In other words, it is found in all societies and it performs the same functions everywhere. These functions are vital for the wellbeing of society. They are:

**Sexual** In most societies, there are rules limiting or forbidding sexual relationships outside marriage. This helps to stabilise the social system. Without such rules, conflict may result.

**Economic** In many societies, the family is a unit of production – for example, a 'farming family' producing food. In the West today, the family acts as a unit of consumption – buying goods and services for the family group. These economic functions make an important contribution to the wider society.

**Reproduction** The family is the main unit for the reproduction of children. Without reproduction, society would cease to exist.

**Educational** The family is largely responsible for *primary socialisation*, the first and most important part of the socialisation process. Without socialisation, there would be no culture. And without a shared culture, there would be no consensus about society's norms and values.

Murdock believes that the nuclear family, either alone, or in its extended form, performs these 'vital functions'. He cannot imagine a substitute. In his words, 'No society has succeeded in finding an adequate substitute for the nuclear family, to which it might transfer these functions. It is highly doubtful whether any society will ever succeed in such an attempt.'

### Talcott Parsons

The American sociologist Talcott Parsons focuses on the nuclear family in modern industrial society. He argues that the family has become increasingly specialised. Functions for which families were responsible in pre-industrial societies, for example, looking after the elderly or educating children, have been taken over in industrial societies by specialised institutions such as social services and schools (Parsons & Bales, 1955).

However, Parsons claims that the family retains two 'basic and irreducible' functions. These are:

1 the *primary socialisation* of children
2 the *stabilisation of adult personalities.*

**Primary socialisation** This is the first and most important part of the socialisation process. Parsons argues that every individual must learn the shared norms and values of society. Without this there would be no consensus, and without consensus, social life would not be possible.

For the socialisation process to be really effective, shared norms and values must be 'internalised as part of the personality structure'. Children's personalities are moulded in terms of society's culture to the point where it becomes a part of them.

**The stabilisation of adult personalities** This is the second essential function of the family. Unstable personalities can threaten the stability and smooth-running of society. According to Parsons, families help to stabilise adult personalities in two ways. First, marital partners provide each other with emotional support. Second, as parents, they are able to indulge the 'childish' side of their personalities – for example, by playing with their children.

Family life provides adults with release from the strains and stresses of everyday life. It provides them with emotional security and support. This helps to stabilise their personality and, in turn, the wider society.

**Conclusion** Although the functions of the family have become fewer and more specialised, Parsons believes they are no less important. He cannot imagine an institution other than the family performing these 'basic and irreducible' functions.

### Criticism of funtionalism

The following criticisms have been made of functionalist views of the family.

- Functionalists assume that on balance families perform useful and often essential functions both for their

# activity8 functionalism and the family

**Item A** *Family shopping*

**Item B** *The 'warm bath theory'*

**Item C** *'The bottle'*

*The drunken husband – a 19th century view of domestic violence*

## questions

1 Functionalists often argue that the family's economic function as a unit of production has been replaced by its function as a unit of consumption. Explain with some reference to Item A.

2 Look at Items B and C.

   a) Parsons' theory is sometimes known as the 'warm bath theory'. Why?

   b) Critically evaluate this theory. Refer to Item C in your answer.

---

members and for society as a whole. Married couples are pictured as living in harmony, as good in bed, and as effective socialisers of the next generation. Critics argue that this does not reflect the realities of family life.

- As a result of this picture of happy families, functionalists tend to ignore the 'dark side' of family life – conflict between husband and wife, male dominance, child abuse, and so on. They give insufficient attention to the *dysfunctions* of the family – the harmful effects it may have on the wider society.

- Functionalists tend to ignore the diversity of family life in industrial society. For example, there is little reference to lone-parent families, cohabiting families and reconstituted families. Nor do they pay much attention to variations in family life based on class, ethnicity, religion and locality.

- Parsons' view of the family has been criticised as sexist since he sees the wife/mother as having the main responsibility for providing warmth and emotional support, and for de-stressing her hardworking husband.

## key terms

**Functionalism** A theory which sees society made up of various parts, each of which tends to contribute to the maintenance and wellbeing of society as a whole.

**Consensus theories** Functionalist theories based on the idea that societies need consensus or agreement about norms and values.

**Function** The contribution a part of society makes to the wellbeing of society as a whole.

**Dysfunction** The harmful effects that a part of society has on society as a whole.

**Primary socialisation** The first and most important part of the socialisation process whereby young people learn the norms and values of society.

## 2.2 New Right perspectives

Like functionalists, New Right thinkers see the family as a cornerstone of society. They also see a 'normal' family as the nuclear family unit. For example, John Redwood, a Conservative MP, stated in 1993 that the 'the natural state should be the two-adult family caring for their children'. And for him, the two adults are a male and a female.

In recent years there has been growing concern about the state of the family. It is 'in decline', 'under threat', 'fragmenting', 'breaking down'. This view of the family was put forward by New Right thinkers from the 1980s onwards.

**Evidence** They point to the following evidence to support their claims. There has been an increase in:

- Lone-parent families
- Fatherless families
- Divorce rates
- Cohabitation
- Gay and lesbian couples.

As a result of these changes, the two-parent nuclear family headed by a married couple is steadily decreasing as a proportion of all families.

# *activity*9 *New Right perspectives*

### Item A **Fatherless families**

According to the American sociologist Charles Murray, increasing numbers of 'young, healthy, low-income males choose not to take jobs'. Many turn to crime (particularly violent street crime) and regular drug abuse.

Many of these boys have grown up in a family without a father and male wage earner. As a result, they lack the male role models of mainstream society. Within a female-headed family dependent on welfare benefits, the disciplines and responsibilities of mainstream society tend to break down. Murray believes that work must become the 'centre of life' for young men. They must learn the disciplines of work and respect for work. And they must learn to become 'real fathers', accepting the responsibilities of parenthood.

Murray believes that the socialisation and role models required to develop these attitudes are often lacking in female-headed, low-income families. He claims that, 'Over the last two decades, larger and larger numbers of British children have not been socialised to norms of self-control, consideration for others, and the concept that actions have consequences'. In Murray's view, when it comes to effective socialisation, 'No alternative family structure comes close to the merits of two parents, formally married'.

Adapted from Murray, 1990, 2001

### Item B **Welfare dependency**

### Item C **A typical Victorian image**

'The abandoned mother'

## *questions*

1 Read Item A. Why does Murray see the nuclear family as superior to other family structures?

2 What points is the cartoon in Item B making?

3 How does Item C question the idea that welfare dependency has led to the breakdown of the family?

**Causes** The following have been seen as causing these changes.

- A breakdown of 'traditional family values'.
- Over-generous welfare benefits to single mothers which allow fathers to opt out of their responsibilities for raising and providing for their children.
- The influence of feminism which has devalued marriage, domesticity and childrearing, and encouraged women to seek fulfilment outside the home.
- Increased sexual permissiveness.
- Greater tolerance of gay and lesbian relationships as alternatives to heterosexual marriage.

**Consequences** According to the New Right, these changes have serious consequences. The 'fragmented family' is no longer performing its functions effectively. In particular, it is failing to provide adequate socialisation. This can result in children and young people underachieving at school and behaving in anti-social ways ranging from rudeness to crime.

Over-generous welfare benefits can lead to welfare dependency. Lone mothers become dependent on state benefits and, in effect, are 'married to the state'.

**Solutions** For the New Right, there are two main solutions to these problems. First, a return to traditional family values – life-long marriage and a recognition of the duties and responsibilities of parenthood. Second, a change in government policy – redirecting welfare benefits and social service provision to support and maintain two-parent families and penalising those who fail to live up to this ideal.

**Sociology and the New Right** New Right thinkers have tended to be journalists and politicians rather than sociologists. However, a few sociologists have developed similar arguments. For example, Norman Dennis and George Erdos make the following points in *Families Without Fathers* (2000).

Increasing numbers of children are born outside marriage and raised by single mothers. This places the children at a disadvantage. On average, they have poorer health and lower educational attainment than children from two-parent families.

Dennis and Erdos's main concern is the effect on boys. They grow up without the expectation that adulthood involves responsibilities for a wife and children. This can result in irresponsible, immature, anti-social young men.

According to Dennis and Erdos, families without fathers are not an adequate alternative to the standard nuclear family. Families are not just changing, they are 'deteriorating'.

### Criticisms of New Right views

**Blaming the victims** Critics argue that the New Right tends to 'blame the victims' for problems that are not of their own making. Many of these problems may result from low wages, inadequate state benefits, lack of jobs and other factors beyond the control of lone parents.

**Value judgements** The New Right sees the nuclear family consisting of husband, wife and children as the ideal. Other family arrangements are considered inferior. Critics argue that this reflects the values of the New Right rather than a balanced judgement of the worth of family diversity in today's society. Who is to say that families without fathers are necessarily inferior? Why should everybody be forced into the nuclear family mould?

**An idealised view of the past** New Right thinkers may be harking back to a golden age of the family which never existed. Even in Victorian times – supposedly *the* era of traditional family values – lone parenthood, cohabitation and sexual relationships outside marriage were by no means uncommon.

## 2.3 Marxist theories

Marxists reject the view that society is based on value consensus and operates for the benefit of all. Instead, they see a basic conflict of interest between a small powerful ruling class and the mass of the population, the subject class. The family is seen as one of a number of institutions which serves to maintain the position of the ruling class.

Modern industrial societies have a capitalist economic system. Capitalism is based on the private ownership of economic institutions, for example, banks and factories. In capitalist economies, investors finance the production of goods and services with the aim of producing profits. These investors form a ruling class. The subject class – the workers – produce goods and services and are paid wages for their labour. The ruling class are seen to exploit the subject class – they gain at the workers' expense since their profits come from the workers' labour.

Marxists argue that the economy largely shapes the rest of society. Thus, a capitalist economic system will produce a certain type of society. Institutions such as the family, the education system and the political system are shaped by the requirements of capitalism and serve to support and maintain it.

**Inheritance and private property** In *The Origin of the Family, Private Property and the State*, first published in 1884, Friedrich Engels argued that the modern nuclear family developed in capitalist society. Private property is at the heart of capitalism and it was largely owned by men. Before 1882 in Britain, married women could not own property – it passed to their husband on marriage.

A key concern of the capitalist was to ensure that his property passed directly to his legitimate heirs – those he had fathered. According to Engels, the monogamous nuclear family provided the answer. It gave men greater control over women – until the late 19th century wives were seen as chattels, as their husband's property. With only one husband and one wife, doubts about the paternity of children are unlikely. And with only one wife, there are no disputes about which wife's children should inherit. Within the nuclear family, a man could be fairly sure that he had legitimate children with a clear right to inherit his wealth.

**Maintaining capitalism** In some respects, Marxist views of the family are similar to those of functionalists. For example, both see the family as a unit which reproduces and socialises children. In other respects, their views are very different.

Marxists see the family as a means for:

- Reproducing 'labour power' – reproducing future generations of workers
- Consuming the products of capitalism
- Providing emotional support for workers, so helping them to cope with the harsh realities of capitalism
- Socialising children to accept the inequalities of capitalist society.

From a Marxist viewpoint, the family helps to maintain an unjust and exploitative system.

### Criticisms of Marxism

Marxist views of the family follow logically from Marxist theory. If, for example, the family provides emotional support for workers, then this helps them to accept the injustices of the capitalist system. This makes sense if capitalism is seen as essentially unjust. However, many sociologists reject this view of capitalism and, as a result, Marxist views of the family.

Sociologists generally agree that the economic system has some influence on the family. However, most would disagree with the view that the family is shaped by the needs of that system.

## key terms

**Marxism** A theory which sees a basic conflict of interest between those who own the economic institutions and those who are employed by them.

**Capitalism** A system of production in which the economic institutions, eg banks and factories, are privately owned.

## 2.4 Feminist theories

Feminists start from the view that most societies are based on patriarchy or male domination. *Radical feminists* see patriarchy as built into the structure of society. *Marxist feminists* see it as resulting from class inequalities in capitalist society. Both see the family as one of the main sites in which women are oppressed by men.

**Domestic labour** Within the family most of the unpaid work – housework and childcare – is done by women. This

## activity10 the next generation

### question

Give a Marxist interpretation of the role of the family illustrated in this cartoon.

applies even when women are working full time outside the home. Women make the main contribution to family life, men receive the main benefits (Delphy & Leonard, 1992).

Marxist feminists argue that the wife's unpaid domestic labour is invaluable to capitalism. She produces and rears future workers at no cost to the capitalist. And she keeps an adult worker – her husband – in good running order by feeding and caring for him (Benston, 1972).

**Emotional labour** The inequalities of domestic labour also apply to 'emotional labour'. Radical feminists claim that it's wives rather than husbands who provide emotional support for their partners. Wives are more likely to listen, to agree, to sympathise, to understand, to excuse and to flatter (Delphy & Leonard, 1992).

Marxist feminists take a similar view, seeing the emotional support provided by wives as soaking up the frustrations produced by working for capitalism.

**Economic dependency** Married women are often economically dependent on their husbands. In most couples, it is the wife who gives up work to care for the children. Mothers often return to part-time rather than full-time employment in order to meet their childcare and domestic responsibilities.

**Male domination** Feminists see the family as male dominated. As noted above, wives are usually economically dependent. Men often control key areas of decision-making such as moving house and important financial decisions. And they sometimes use force to maintain control. Domestic violence is widespread and the majority of those on the receiving end are women. Around 570,000 cases are reported each year in the UK and probably a far larger number go unreported (Hopkins, 2000; see pages 128-131).

## Criticisms of feminism

**Ignores positive aspects of family life** Critics argue that

## activity 11 housewives

Magazine cover from 1955

Magazine cover from 2003

### question

How might a feminist analyse these magazine covers?

feminists are preoccupied with the negative side of family life. They ignore the possibility that many women enjoy running a home and raising children.

**Ignores trend to gender equality** There is evidence of a trend towards greater equality between partners (see Section 8.2). Critics argue that rather than celebrating this trend, feminists remain focused on the remaining inequalities.

## key terms

**Feminism** A view which challenges the power of men over women.
**Patriarchy** A social system based on male domination.
**Radical feminists** Feminists who see patriarchy as the main form of inequality in society.
**Marxist feminists** Feminists who see patriarchy as resulting from class inequalities.
**Domestic labour** Unpaid work such as housework and childcare, within the home and family.

## summary

1. Functionalists argue that the family is a universal institution. It performs functions which are essential for the maintenance and wellbeing of society.

2. Parsons argues that the family performs two 'basic and irreducible' functions in modern industrial society – primary socialisation and the stabilisation of adult personalities.

3. The New Right sees the nuclear family as the ideal family form. They believe the nuclear family is under threat. Alternative family forms, particularly lone mother families, fail to provide adequate socialisation.

4. Marxists argue that the modern family has been shaped to fit the needs of capitalism. It helps to maintain an economic system based on exploitation.

5. Feminists see the family as patriarchal – it is dominated by men and serves the needs of men.

# Unit 3 Recent social and demographic change

## key issues

1. What are the main changes in marriage, divorce, births and the age of the population?
2. What reasons have been given for these changes?

## 3.1 Marriage

Apart from a few ups and downs, the number of marriages per year in the UK increased steadily from 1838 (when they were first recorded) until the early 1970s. Since then there has been a significant decline, from 480,000 marriages in 1972 to 306,000 in 2000.

These figures refer both to *first marriages*, in which neither partner has been married before, and to *remarriages* in which one or both partners have been married before. The number of first marriages peaked in 1970 at almost 390,000 and steadily decreased to 180,000 in 2000 (*Social Trends*, 2003 – unless mentioned, the figures in this unit are taken from various issues of *Social Trends*).

**Remarriage** Remarriages increased from 57,000 in 1961 (14% of all marriages) to 126,000 in 2000 (41% of all marriages). Most remarriages involve divorced persons rather than widows and widowers. The largest increase occurred between 1971 and 1972 following the introduction of the Divorce Reform Act of 1969.

**Age at marriage** Over the past 30 years, people have tended to marry later. In 1971, the average age for first marriages was 24 for men and 22 for women. By 2000, it was 30 for men and 28 for women. The increase in cohabitation – living together as a couple – partly accounts for this. Many couples see cohabitation as a prelude to marriage.

**Reasons for decline in marriage** Part of the fall in marriage is because people are marrying at a later age. A major part, however, is due to people choosing *not* to marry. Instead, they are choosing to remain single or to cohabit – live together as a couple.

Today, most people cohabit before marriage. They see cohabitation as a stepping-stone to marriage. However, increasing numbers see cohabitation as an alternative to marriage. Judging from a study of cohabiting mothers, the main reasons for rejecting marriage are as follows.

● Marriage limits personal freedom and independence. 'I feel more independent not being married. I do not feel tied, but am here by choice in this relationship.'

● There's no advantage to marriage. 'I've been married before and it's no different than living together.'

● Fear of divorce – the experience of a previous divorce or seeing others going through a divorce has led some to reject marriage (McRae, 1999).

Over the past 50 years, attitudes have changed towards alternatives to marriage. As a result, remaining single and cohabiting have become increasingly attractive options. Reasons for these changes in attitudes are given below.

# activity12 *patterns of marriage*

## Item A  *Marriages and divorces*

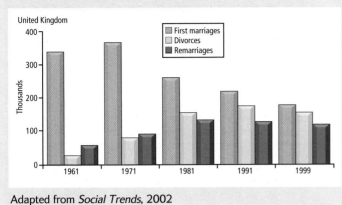

United Kingdom

Legend: ■ First marriages □ Divorces ■ Remarriages

(Vertical axis: Thousands, 0–400; horizontal axis years: 1961, 1971, 1981, 1991, 1999)

Adapted from *Social Trends*, 2002

## Item C  *Wary of marriage*

Sue Sharpe studied working-class girls in London schools in the early 1970s. She found their main concerns were 'love, marriage, husbands, children, jobs, and careers, more or less in that order'. A third wanted to be married by 20 and three-quarters by 25.

When she returned to the same schools in the early 1990s, she found the girls' priorities had changed to 'job, career and being able to support themselves'. In her words, 'Young people had witnessed adult relationships breaking up and being reconstituted all around them. Girls in particular were far more wary of marriage. Now, only 4 per cent wanted to be married by 20, although there was still a feeling of "A wedding day – that sounds good fun".'

Adapted from Sharpe, 1976 and 1994

## Item B  *Keep on marrying*

*Patsy Kensit with husband number three, Liam Gallagher. The marriage is now over.*

*Joan Collins with husband number five, Percy Gibson.*

## questions

1  a)  Describe the trends shown in Item A.
   b)  What does Item A suggest about the relationship between divorce and remarriage?

2  Why does the term serial monogamy fit Patsy Kensit's and Joan Collins's marital history?

3  How might Item C help to explain
   a)  the decline in marriage
   b)  the later age of marriage?

## key terms

*First marriage* A marriage in which neither partner has been married before.
*Remarriage* A marriage in which one or both partners have been married before.

## Singlehood

Some people never marry. They either choose to remain single or fail to find a suitable marriage partner. There are increasing numbers of 'never-married' people. For example, in England and Wales only 7% of women born between 1946 and 1950 remained unmarried by the age of 32, compared with 28% of those born between 1961 and 1965. There is a similar trend for men.

Many 'never-married' people cohabit – they live with a partner as a couple. There has been a steady increase in cohabitation in recent years as the following section indicates. There has also been a steady increase in singlehood – living without a partner.

**Living alone** Growing numbers of people are living alone. The largest increase is in the 25 to 29 age group in social class 1 – people in professional occupations, particularly women. In England and Wales in 1971, 6% of this group lived alone, in 1991 just under 20%.

# activity13 singlehood

### Item A  Creative singlehood

Never-married people who live alone tend to see their situation in positive terms. They have chosen to remain single. They emphasise the importance of independence and freedom. As one single woman in her 30s put it, 'It was the freedom of it really, come and go when I like'.

Others emphasise the importance of work. One woman said, 'Until the age of 30 there was always a man in my life, but around the age of 30, it all started to change and work took over. By the age of 35, I had come to the conclusion that I should knock it on the head and concentrate on work'.

Adapted from Hall et al., 1999

Singles night in a supermarket

### Item B  Single women

Women are choosing to live alone because they have the capacity to do so. New opportunities in education and employment over the past few decades mean there is now a third way for women between living with and looking after their aged parents, or getting married. Single women tend to have much more developed and intense social networks and are involved in a wide range of social and other activities. Single men, by contrast, tend to be lonely and isolated. The signs are that living alone is good for women but bad for men.

Adapted from Scase, 2000

Girls' night out

## questions

1  How does the term creative singlehood apply to Item A?

2  Why are more women choosing to remain single? Refer to both items in your answer.

---

In 1991, 90% of the under 30 age group who lived alone were never-married, over 50% of the 30-39 age group and 30% of the 40-59 age group. In many cases, remaining single and living alone was the 'desired' option (Hall et al., 1999).

**Creative singlehood** In the past, being single was seen as a negative status, particularly for women. They had 'failed' to find a marriage partner, their situation was 'unfortunate', they were 'spinsters' and 'old maids' – terms with negative overtones.

Today, views are changing. The term *creative singlehood* is sometimes used to describe a positive view of singlehood whereby people choose to remain single as a lifestyle option.

## 3.2 Divorce and separation

This section looks at the breakup of partnerships. It is mainly concerned with divorce.

### Trends in divorce

In the UK, as in other Western societies, there has been a dramatic rise in divorce during the 20th century. This can be seen from the actual number of divorces each year and from the increase in the *divorce rate* – the number of divorces per thousand married people.

Table 1 shows both these measures for *decrees absolute* (final divorces) in England and Wales from 1931 to 2000. Both the number and rate of divorce peaked in 1993. Since then, there has been a gradual decline. If the divorce rate continues at its present level, around 40% of marriages will end in divorce.

### Interpreting divorce statistics

Divorce statistics provide an accurate measure of one type of marital breakdown – the legal termination of marriages. However, marriages can end in other ways.

**Separation** The married couple end their marriage by separating – living in separate residences. However, they

## Table 1 Divorce: decrees absolute (England and Wales)

| Year | Numbers | Rate per 1,000 married population |
|------|---------|-----------------------------------|
| 1931 | 3,668 | 0.4 |
| 1951 | 28,265 | 2.6 |
| 1964 | 34,868 | 2.9 |
| 1969 | 51,310 | 4.1 |
| 1972 | 119,025 | 9.5 |
| 1981 | 145,713 | 11.9 |
| 1991 | 158,745 | 13.4 |
| 1993 | 165,018 | 14.2 |
| 1996 | 157,107 | 13.9 |
| 1998 | 145,214 | 12.9 |
| 2000 | 141,135 | 12.7 |

From various issues of *Population Trends*

remain legally married. Some couples obtain separation orders granted by magistrates' courts.

**Empty-shell marriages** The couple live together, remain legally married, but their marriage exists in name only. Love, sex and companionship are things of the past.

As the divorce rate increased, there may have been a decrease in separations and empty-shell marriages. From 1897-1906, around 8,000 separation orders were granted each year compared to 700 divorces. By 1971, only 94 separation orders were granted compared to over 74,000 divorces. There are no figures on informal ('unofficial') separations. Nor are there any figures on the extent of empty-shell marriages. Such marriages were often maintained in order to 'keep up appearances' and avoid the stigma (shame) of divorce. This stigma considerably reduced during the last half of the 20th century.

As the next section indicates, divorce has become easier and cheaper throughout the last century. In view of this, people who previously separated or endured empty-shell marriages are probably more likely to choose divorce.

**Cohabitation** Marriage is only one form of partnership. As noted earlier, cohabitation is an increasingly popular form of partnership. Available evidence suggests that, in any

## key terms

**Divorce** The legal termination of a marriage.
**Divorce rate** The number of divorces per thousand married people.
**Separation** A married couple who end their relationship and live in separate residences but remain legally married.
**Empty-shell marriage** The couple share the same residence, remain legally married, but their marriage exists in name only.

given period, a significantly higher number of cohabitations are terminated than marriages (Allan & Crow, 2001).

**Conclusion** Are partnerships becoming more unstable, more likely to break up? In view of the evidence outlined above, it is not possible to answer this question. However, one sociologist, Robert Chester (1984), believes that the increase in divorce rates probably reflects an increase in marital breakdown – though he admits this cannot be proved.

### Explaining changing divorce rates

**Changes in the law** Before 1857 a private Act of Parliament was required to obtain a divorce in Britain. This was an expensive and complicated procedure beyond the means of all but the most wealthy. In 1857 the Matrimonial Causes Act set up a new court for divorce. The grounds for divorce included adultery, cruelty and desertion. At least one partner had to be proven guilty of one of these 'matrimonial offences'. Although the costs of obtaining a divorce were now reduced, they were still beyond the reach of most people.

Throughout the first half of the 20th century a series of Acts simplified divorce proceedings, reduced the costs involved and widened the grounds for divorce. The financial burden of divorce was eased for the less well-off by the Legal Aid and Advice Act of 1949 which provided free legal advice and paid solicitors' fees for those who could not afford them.

The Divorce Reform Act of 1969 involved a major change in the grounds for divorce. Before this Act, a 'matrimonial offence' had to be proven, a 'guilty party' had to be found. However, many people who wanted a divorce had not committed adultery, been guilty of cruelty, and so on. The 1969 Act defined the grounds for divorce as 'the irretrievable breakdown of the marriage'. It was no longer necessary to prove guilt but simply to show that the marriage was beyond repair. The Act came into force in January 1971.

The Matrimonial Family Proceedings Act of 1984 came into effect in 1985. This Act reduced from three years to one the time a couple had to be married before they could petition for a divorce.

Changes in the law have made divorce a lot easier. The grounds for divorce have been widened, the procedure has been simplified and the expense reduced. Changes in the law have provided greater opportunities for divorce. However, this doesn't explain why more and more people are taking advantage of these opportunities.

**Changing expectations of love and marriage** Since the 1950s, a number of sociologists have argued that changes in people's expectations of love and marriage have resulted in increasingly unstable relationships. Functionalists such as Ronald Fletcher and Talcott Parsons claim that people expect and demand more from marriage. Because of this, they are less likely to put up with an unhappy marriage and more likely to end it with divorce. Ronald Fletcher (1966) argues that a higher divorce rate reflects a higher

# activity14 divorce and the law

Divorce rates (England and Wales)

| Year | Rate |
| --- | --- |
| 1931 | 0.4 |
| 1951 | 2.6 |
| 1964 | 2.9 |
| 1972 | 9.5 |
| 1981 | 11.9 |
| 1991 | 13.4 |
| 2000 | 12.7 |

From various issues of *Population Trends*

## question

How have changes in the law affected the divorce rate?

value placed on marriage. In terms of this argument, the fact that a large proportion of divorcees remarry suggests that they are not rejecting the institution of marriage but simply expecting more from the relationship.

More recently, the British sociologist Anthony Giddens (1992) has seen a trend towards what he calls *confluent love*. This form of love focuses on intimacy, closeness and emotion. It forms the basis of relationships rather than the feelings of duty and obligation reflected in the traditional marriage vows of 'for better or worse, for richer or poorer, 'til death do us part'. Intimate relationships based on confluent love tend to last as long as partners find satisfaction and fulfilment.

The decision to marry is increasingly based on confluent love. When marriage ceases to provide the intimacy demanded by confluent love, individuals are likely to end it. If Giddens is correct, then marriage is an increasingly unstable and fragile institution, and divorce will become more frequent.

**Changing social values** Throughout the 20th century divorce became more socially acceptable. Couples were less likely to stay together in order to 'keep up

appearances' and to avoid the stigma and shame formerly associated with divorce.

The rising divorce rate has led to the 'normalisation' of divorce. This, in itself, has made divorce more acceptable as a means of dealing with a failed marriage (Cockett & Tripp, 1994).

**The economic position of women** Women have often been 'trapped' in unhappy marriages because they cannot support themselves and their children without their husband's income. Unless they can become economically independent, their opportunities to divorce are severely restricted (Kurz, 1995).

Over the past 50 years, married women's chances of economic independence have improved significantly. Increasing numbers of women have entered the labour market, divorce settlements have taken more account of the financial needs of women, and welfare benefits for women with dependent children have improved (Allan & Crow, 2001). Although most women find themselves financially worse off after divorce, they are able to live independently from their former husband.

**Women and marriage** Feminists have seen rising divorce rates as a reflection of all that is wrong with traditional patriarchal marriage – male dominance and the unequal division of domestic labour, with women still largely responsible for housework and childcare even when they are employed outside the home (see page 103). It is women rather than men who are increasingly dissatisfied with marriage.

There is some evidence for this view. Divorced men are more likely to remarry than divorced women. According to Diana Gittins (1993), this is because women are more disillusioned with marriage. In the 1940s, around two-thirds of divorce petitions (the legal starting of divorce) were brought by husbands. By 2000, the situation was reversed with 70% of petitions brought by wives (*Population Trends, 109*, 2002). This may indicate that women are more dissatisfied with marriage than men. Or, it may reflect a greater need to settle financial and housing arrangements, particularly for women with dependent children (Allen & Crow, 2001).

## key term

**Confluent love** A term used by Giddens to describe a form of intimate relationship which is dependent on both partners finding fulfilment and satisfaction in the relationship.

## Who divorces?

So far, this section has been concerned with the rise in divorce rates. The focus now is on the social distribution of divorce – on the variation in divorce rates between different social groups. This variation is particularly apparent for age and social class groups.

**Age** In general, the earlier the age of marriage, the more

# activity 15 case studies

## Item A  Sarah

Sarah, 39, runs a public relations consultancy. During her marriage she was largely responsible for caring for the children – two girls – and running the home – 'all the washing, the cleaning and the cooking' – as well as working full time. She found that, as the children grew older, 'I started to resent what I saw as the inequality in our lives'. Her husband Adam 'could not see what I thought was glaringly obvious'. She felt that she couldn't be herself because 'he used to put me down and was so controlling'.

She decided to divorce Adam. She notes, 'Economic independence played a big part. I knew I could afford to run my own life because I had a successful business, and it made it possible for me to initiate the breakup. I feel so much more myself, being in control of my life. I think it's hard for women to stay married today. We have high expectations, but men and women are still not equal and so many women are resentful about being expected to do it all.'

Adapted from Appleyard, 2002

## Item B  Jan

Jan, 43, is a writer. She has four children, three with her former husband and one with her new partner Mike. 'I met Mike four years ago, and happy as we are, I have no desire to marry. I want to be in control of my life – and the majority of women today feel the same.'

'The reason so many are initiating divorce is because we don't have to be dependent  on – or controlled by – a man. We want to lead our lives in a way that makes us happy, without being answerable to men. When I was married, I was expected not only to bring money into the house, but to do all the domestic chores as well. The big issue between us was always money. He was earning £30,000 a year, which was a big salary, but I wasn't allowed to buy as much as a magazine without asking him first.'

Adapted from Appleyard, 2002

## Item C  Domestic labour

## question

To what extent do Items A, B and C support the explanations given for divorce?

---

likely it is to end in divorce. For women who were under 20 when they married in the late 1980s, 24% had separated within 5 years compared with 8% who married between the ages of 25 and 29. Reasons suggested for the high divorce rate of young marrieds include:

- The bride is more likely to be pregnant which places a strain on the marriage.
- Money problems – young people are more likely to be low paid or unemployed.
- Lack of experience in choosing a suitable partner.
- Lack of awareness of the demands of marriage.
- More likely to 'grow apart' as their attitudes and beliefs are still developing.

**Social class** In general, the lower the class position of the husband, the more likely the couple are to divorce. Financial problems appear to be the main cause. Unemployment, reliance on state benefits and low income are all associated with high divorce rates (Kiernan & Mueller, 1999).

**Other factors** A number of other factors are associated with high divorce rates. They include:

- Experience of parents' divorce – this may cause psychological problems which are carried forward to the child's marriage. Or, it may simply make divorce more acceptable.
- Remarriages are more likely to end in divorce than first

marriages. Maybe the problems which caused the first divorce are carried through into the second marriage.

- Differences in class, ethnicity and religion between the couple are associated with higher divorce rates. They will have less in common, they may have different expectations about marriage, and these differences may result in conflict.

## The consequences of divorce

Divorce has a variety of consequences – for the couple involved, for their children, their relatives and friends, and for the wider society. This section looks at the effects of divorce on children and on the wider society.

**Divorce and children** Opinions about the effects of divorce on children abound. Some see it as uniformly harmful and argue that parents should go to great lengths to stay together for the sake of the children. Others argue that if divorce frees children from a bitter and hostile family environment then, on balance, it is beneficial. In these circumstances parents should divorce for the sake of the children.

In a study entitled *Divorce and Separation: The Outcomes for Children*, Rodgers and Pryor (1998) reviewed some 200 studies. They attempted to find out whether claims about the harmful effects of divorce on children were supported by research evidence.

The review confirmed that children of divorced or separated parents have a higher probability of experiencing a range of problems such as poverty, poor housing, behavioural problems (eg, bedwetting and anti-social behaviour), teenage pregnancy and educational under-achievement. Although children of divorced and separated parents have around twice the chance of experiencing these sorts of problems, only a minority actually do so. A key question is why a minority of children appear to suffer from divorce while most do not.

Rodgers and Pryor suggest that it is not divorce alone which causes these problems, but the association of divorce with other factors. These include:

- Financial hardship – which may have an effect on educational achievement.
- Family conflict – which may create behavioural problems for children.
- Parental ability to cope with the changes that divorce brings – if parents cannot cope, then children are less likely to do so.
- Multiple changes in family structure – if divorce is accompanied by other changes, such as moving in with a step-family, children are more likely to experience problems.
- Quality and degree of contact with the parent who has left – children who have regular contact appear to cope better.

According to Rodgers and Pryor, these findings help to explain why some children experience problems with divorce, while the majority, at least in the long term, do not.

A large-scale research project conducted by Mavis Hetherington (2002) in the USA reached similar conclusions. Her findings are based on a longitudinal study over 25 years of 2500 people from childhood in 1400 families. Her evidence includes tens of thousands of hours of videotapes of families at dinner, at play, relaxing and having rows. Hetherington concludes that three out of four children experience little long-term damage from divorce. She admits that 25% have serious emotional or social problems which compares with 10% from families that stay together. In her view, the negative effects on children have been exaggerated and we must accept that 'divorce is a reasonable solution to an unhappy, acrimonious, destructive marital relationship' (Hetherington, 2002).

**Divorce and society** From a New Right perspective (see pages 77-79) high divorce rates, and the lone-parent families that often result from divorce, are a serious threat to society. Most lone-parent families are headed by women. They lack a father-figure – a male role model who can provide discipline and an example for the future. This can lead to inadequate socialisation, particularly for boys, which can result in anti-social behaviour. Some New Right thinkers see a direct relationship between rising divorce rates and rising crime rates. In Patricia Morgan's (1999) words, 'large numbers of fatherless youths represent a high risk factor for crime'. A return to 'traditional family values' is needed to strengthen marriage, and 'tougher' laws are required because divorce has become 'too easy'. These measures will lower the divorce rate and so reduce the threat to social stability.

In contrast, many feminists strongly object to any barriers to divorce. Compared to the past, the present divorce laws provide freedom and choice, particularly for women. Restrictions on divorce may force them to endure unhappy marriages, and in some cases, physical and sexual abuse of themselves and their children. Liberal divorce laws offer greater independence for women and represent a positive step towards gender equality.

## 3.3 Childbearing and fertility

Women are having fewer children. And fewer women are having any children. This section looks at the decline in *fertility*.

**The fertility rate** Fertility is measured by the fertility rate – the number of live births per 1,000 women aged 15 to 44. In 1900, the UK fertility rate was 115, in 1961 it was 91, and in 2001 it had fallen to 54.5. This is the lowest rate since records began (*Annual Abstract of Statistics*, 2003).

**Childless women** Part of the decline in fertility in recent years is due to an increase in childless women. About 11% of women born in 1943 in England and Wales were childless by age 45, this rose to 16% for those born in 1953, and projections suggest that 23% of women born in 1973 will be childless at 45.

Probably all of the increase in childlessness since the

1950s is voluntary – it is chosen. Involuntary childlessness affects between 5% and 8% of couples – there is no reason to suppose this is increasing (Coleman & Chandola, 1999).

**Age and fertility** Women are having children later in life. In England and Wales, the average age at childbirth increased from 26.1 years in the early 1970s to 29.1 in 2000.

While the fertility rates of women under 30 have steadily fallen, the rates for those 30 years and older have risen since the mid-1970s (Ghee, 2001).

**Births outside marriage** An increasing proportion of births occur outside marriage. In 1900, the proportion was 4% compared with almost 10 times that a century later. The greatest increase has occurred in recent years – from 8% in England and Wales in 1971 to 39% in 2000.

Most of this increase in births outside marriage has been to cohabiting couples – to parents living at the same address. In 2000, about four-fifths of births outside marriage were jointly registered by both parents – three-quarters of these births were to parents living at the same address.

The proportion of births outside marriage registered by the mother alone has remained more or less the same at 7% to 8% since the late 1980s.

### Explaining the trends

The following explanations have been suggested for the changes in childbearing outlined above.

**Changing attitudes** There is far greater tolerance of births outside marriage than in the past. In the early 1950s, unmarried mothers were sometimes seen as 'psychologically disturbed' (McRae, 1999). Births outside marriage were defined as 'illegitimate' which literally means 'unlawful' and implies that such births were improper and immoral.

Attitudes to childlessness have also changed. The word 'childless' suggests a loss. Now many women who *choose* not to have children see themselves as 'childfree' – they emphasise liberation from children rather than loss of children.

**Control of births** Reliable contraception was made available on the National Health Service in 1967 to all women, both married and unmarried. It was now possible for women to control the number of births they wanted.

**Changing opportunities** Researchers often point to expanding educational opportunities and the increase in women's participation in the labour market as reasons for the decline in fertility. As noted earlier, the numbers of female undergraduates increased more than threefold between 1970/71 and 2000/01. And during those same years the numbers of women in paid employment in the UK increased from 10 to 14.1 million.

These changes provided alternatives to women's traditional role as mothers and child-raisers.

**Changing values** Some researchers claim that in recent years there has been increasing emphasis on individual freedom, on the individual's right to choose, and on personal fulfilment. As a result, people are increasingly concerned with constructing their own lifestyle. Some researchers see this concern reflected in *choosing* to cohabit rather than marry and in *choosing* to have fewer children or none at all.

## key terms

*Fertility rate* The number of live births per 1000 women aged 15 to 44.
*Childless women* Women who, for whatever reason, do not produce children.
*Childfree women* Women who choose not to have children as a lifestyle option.

## activity16 childbearing

### Item A Fertility rates

| United Kingdom | | | Live births per 1,000 women | | |
| --- | --- | --- | --- | --- | --- |
| | **1961** | **1971** | **1981** | **1991** | **2000** |
| Under 20 | 37 | 50 | 28 | 33 | 29 |
| 20-24 | 173 | 154 | 107 | 89 | 69 |
| 25-29 | 178 | 155 | 130 | 120 | 95 |
| 30-34 | 106 | 79 | 70 | 87 | 88 |
| 35-39 | 51 | 34 | 22 | 32 | 40 |
| 40 and over | 16 | 9 | 5 | 5 | 8 |
| All ages | 91 | 84 | 62 | 64 | 55 |

This table shows fertility rates by age of mother at childbirth.
Adapted from *Social Trends*, 2002

### Item B Births outside marriage

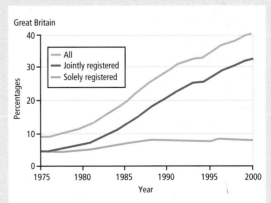

This graph shows births outside marriage as a percentage of all live births.
Adapted from *Social Trends*, 2002

## Item C Childless women

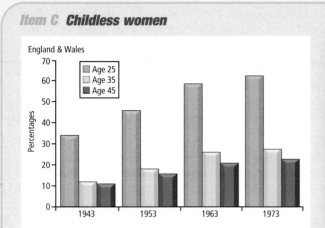

England & Wales

This chart shows the percentage of childless women at age 25, 35 and 45, by year of birth. Data for women age 35 and 45 in 1973, and those aged 45 in 1963 are projections.

Adapted from *Social Trends*, 2000

## questions

1 Outline the trends shown in Items A, B and C.

2 Being childfree is a lifestyle choice. Discuss with reference to Item D.

## Item D Childfree couples

*Famous childfree women – actress Helen Mirren and novelist Iris Murdoch.*

Eighteen years ago, Barry Butler proposed to Lysette. They decided to have a childfree marriage. Now 42, Lysette Butler is a ward nurse in her local general hospital in Essex. She says, 'My life is about me and my husband; it's not about anybody else. I've been told so often that that makes me selfish but I don't understand why that is so. I just don't have any maternal feelings. I don't dislike children, they are just not a way of life for me.'

It was the freedom of not having children that led Catherine James, a 52-year-old writer in Edinburgh, to decide to be childfree. 'I can stay awake with my husband until the early hours, just talking. We can have sex at three in the afternoon without worrying that the children will walk in. We can go away for the weekend at the drop of a hat – and yes we do all of those things!'

Adapted from Hill, 2002

## 3.4 An ageing population

The United Kingdom, like most industrial societies, has an ageing population. This means that an increasing proportion of the population are elderly – aged 65 and over.

In 1961, just under 12% of the population were aged 65 and over, by 2001 this had risen to 16%. At the other end of the scale, children under 16 made up 23% of the UK population in 1961 compared to 20% in 2001 (*Social Trends*, 2003).

There are two main reasons for an ageing population – a decline in *fertility* and an increase in *life expectancy*.

### Declining fertility

As outlined in the previous section, the fertility rate in the UK declined from 115 in 1900, to 91 in 1961, to 54.5 in 2001 – the lowest rate since records began.

This trend is reflected in the *birth rate* – the number of live births per thousand of the population per year. In 1900 the UK birth rate was 29, by 1961 it was 18, and by 2001 it was 11.4. Again, this is the lowest rate since records began (*Annual Abstract of Statistics*, 2003).

Women are now having fewer children and increasing numbers are choosing to have no children. Reasons for these trends are given in the previous section.

### Increasing life expectancy

An increase in life expectancy is the second reason for an ageing population. Life expectancy refers to the average number of years a person can expect to live.

Table 2 shows life expectancy at birth from 1901 to 2001. It shows that by 2001, both males and females could expect to live over 30 years longer than their counterparts in 1901.

### Table 2 Life expectancy at birth, UK 1901-2001

| Gender | 1901 | 1971 | 1981 | 1991 | 2001 |
|--------|------|------|------|------|------|
| **Males** | 45 | 69 | 71 | 73 | 76 |
| **Females** | 49 | 75 | 77 | 79 | 80 |

From various issues of *Social Trends*

People in every age group are living longer. Table 3 shows expectation of life at age 65. It shows that men at this age can expect to live a further 6 years in 2001 compared with 1901, and women a further 8 years.

| Table 3 *Expectation of life at age 65, UK 1901-2001* | | | |
|---|---|---|---|
| Gender | 1901 | 1971 | 2001 |
| **Males** | 75 | 77 | 81 |
| **Females** | 76 | 81 | 84 |

Adapted from *Social Trends*, 2003

The trends shown in Table 3 are reflected in the *death rate* – the number of deaths per 1,000 people per year in a particular age group. Table 4 shows death rates for older age groups from 1971 to 2001. In each case there is a marked decline.

### Table 4
### Death rate of older age groups, UK 1971-2001

| Gender | Age 65-74 | Age 75 and over |
|---|---|---|
| **Males** | | |
| 1971 | 51.1 | 131.4 |
| 1981 | 46.4 | 122.2 |
| 1991 | 38.7 | 110.7 |
| 2001 | 28.8 | 96.7 |
| **Females** | | |
| 1971 | 26.6 | 96.6 |
| 1981 | 24.7 | 90.2 |
| 1991 | 22.3 | 84.1 |
| 2001 | 17.9 | 81.7 |

Adapted from *Social Trends*, 2003

## Why are people living longer?

The following reasons have been suggested for the increase in life expectancy and the decline in death rates.

- Improvements in diet, sanitation and hygiene
- Advances in medical practice, technology and drugs
- Higher social protection benefits – eg, direct cash payments and pensions
- Rising living standards generally – eg, improved heating and housing
- Better care facilities – eg, residential homes and home improvements provided by social services designed to help the elderly
- Changing occupational structure – fewer dangerous and physically demanding manual jobs.

## The dependency ratio

One consequence of an ageing population is an increase in the *dependency ratio*. Children under 16 and older people aged 65 and over are known as *dependent age groups*, since they typically do not work to support themselves. Those aged 16-64 are known as the *working population*, even though many are not employed – eg, students and the unemployed.

The dependency ratio is the ratio of the dependent population to the working population. Since the 1970s, the increase in the dependency ratio is due to older people living longer. This is illustrated in Figure 1, which also shows projections – estimates for the future – based on 2001 data.

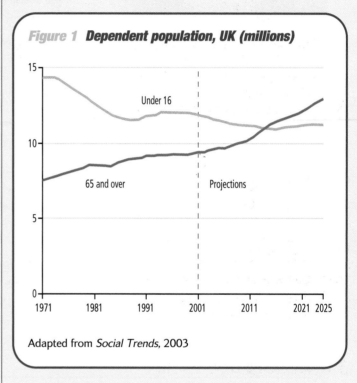

Figure 1 *Dependent population, UK (millions)*

Adapted from *Social Trends*, 2003

## Consequences of an ageing population

An ageing population is often seen as a problem. More older people means more pressure on those who may be caring for them – their families and the welfare state. This can be seen from the following quotation from *Social Trends* (2003).

'The increase in the number of pensioners places greater demands on health, social services and social security arrangements. As a response to this, the state pension age (currently 65 for men and 60 for women) will be increased between 2010 and 2020 to 65 for both sexes.'

The view of an ageing population as a problem is one-sided. The majority of older people are fit and healthy. A survey of older people in the European Union found that most have a fairly active life. Their most common pastime – as for the population as a whole – was watching TV, closely followed by seeing and looking after relatives and friends. 70% liked shopping, 40% enjoyed gardening and DIY and 50% took a regular walk or exercise (Help the Aged, 1995).

# activity17 two views of old age

**Item A  Fit and healthy**

**Item B  Benefits**

Alma Kent, aged 85, the oldest woman in the 2003 London Marathon

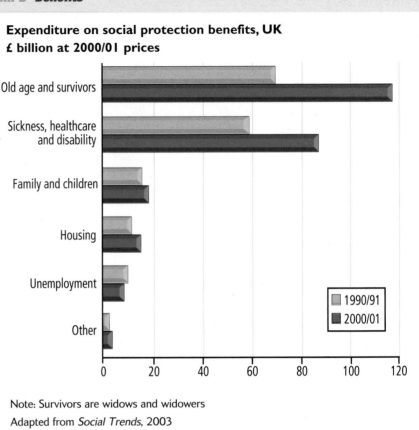

**Expenditure on social protection benefits, UK £ billion at 2000/01 prices**

- Old age and survivors
- Sickness, healthcare and disability
- Family and children
- Housing
- Unemployment
- Other

1990/91
2000/01

Note: Survivors are widows and widowers

Adapted from *Social Trends*, 2003

## question

How can Items A and B be used to support positive and negative views of an ageing population?

## The family life of older people

**Households** The older people get, the more likely they are to live alone. This is usually because of the death of their spouse – husband or wife. Women over 65 are more likely to live alone than men – on average, women live longer than men and they usually marry men who are older than themselves. These points are illustrated in Table 5.

**Family ties** Even when living alone, the majority of older people have regular contact with kin, particularly their adult children. The birth of grandchildren often increases the number of contacts and gives the relationship between parents and their adult children a new lease of life (Allan & Crow, 2001). Older people who are isolated from kin are usually those without children.

Many older people are extremely independent and determined to stand on their own two feet. However, when they become weak and infirm, support is usually provided by their spouse or adult children. Clearly, support is more

**Table 5**

### Households of older people, UK 1996 *(Percentages)*

| Household type | Males | | Females | |
|---|---|---|---|---|
| | 65-74 | 75 and over | 65-74 | 75 and over |
| One-person household | 21 | 34 | 40 | 68 |
| With spouse only | 68 | 59 | 50 | 25 |
| With spouse and child(ren) | 9 | 4 | 5 | 1 |
| With someone other than spouse and child(ren) | 2 | 3 | 4 | 5 |

Adapted from *Social Trends*, 1997

easily provided if their children live nearby. Most older people still live fairly near to at least one of their children (Phillipson et al., 1999).

In recent years, there is some evidence of a decline in face-to-face contact between older people and their adult children. This may be partly due to increasing distances between kin. However, this may be made up for by communication via telephone and email, which can provide 'intimacy at a distance' (McCrae, 1999).

## Family structure in an ageing population

In an ageing population, families tend to become longer and thinner. With fewer children being born, there are fewer brothers, sisters and cousins. In this sense, families are thinner, they are not so spread out horizontally. With life expectancy increasing, families are becoming longer, they are stretched out vertically to include three or four generations. The result is the so-called *'beanpole' family* – a multigenerational family.

Research in the Netherlands found that 54.6% of old people were grandparents, belonging to three-generation families, and 17.8% were great-grandparents, belonging to four-generation families. The researchers called this process the *verticalisation of family life* (Dykstra & Knipscheer, 1995).

The decline in fertility and the increase in life expectancy are leading to an increase in beanpole families. This is a further example of the trend towards family diversity.

### key terms

**Ageing population** A population in which an increasing proportion are aged 65 and over.
**Birth rate** The number of live births per thousand of the population per year.
**Life expectancy** The average number of years a person can expect to live.
**Death rate** The number of deaths per thousand people per year in a particular age group.
**Dependent age groups** Children under 16 and older people age 65 and over. They are seen to be dependent on the working population – those aged 16-64.
**Dependency ratio** The ratio of the dependent population to the working population.
**Beanpole family** A multigenerational family with few members in each generation.
**Verticalisation of family life** The tendency for the number of generations in families to increase.

## *activity* 18 *the beanpole family*

### question

Use the cartoon to explain what a beanpole family is.

## summary

1. There has been a significant decline in first marriages and in the overall total of marriages since the early 1970s. Within this total, there has been an increase in the numbers and proportion of remarriages.

2. There has been an increase in singlehood – living without a partner.

3. There has been a significant decline in fertility during the 20th century, particularly since the 1960s. This is due to increasing numbers of women deciding to have either fewer children or none at all.

4. An increasing proportion of births are occurring outside marriage.

5. There has been a dramatic rise in the divorce rate during the 20th century. In England and Wales the rate peaked in 1993.

6. Reasons for the rise in divorce include changes in:
   - the law, leading to cheaper and easier divorce
   - expectations of love and marriage
   - attitudes towards divorce
   - the economic position of women and their view of marriage.

7. Divorce is not spread evenly throughout the population – eg, there are age and class variations in divorce rates.

8. Most children appear to experience no long-term harm from their parents' divorce.

9. While the New Right sees the rise in divorce as a threat to society, feminists tend to see it as an expression of women's right to choose.

10. The United Kingdom, like most industrial societies, has an ageing population.

11. This is due to a decline in fertility and an increase in life expectancy.

12. In the UK, an ageing population has led to greater demands on the health system, social services and social security provision.

13. Most older people are fit and healthy and have a fairly active lifestyle.

14. Most older people are in regular contact with kin, especially their adult children.

15. The decline in fertility and the increase in life expectancy have led to the verticalisation of family life and an increase in beanpole families.

# Unit 4 Social policy and the family

## keyissues

1 What are the main government policies towards families and children?

2 How have they changed in recent years?

In recent years, governments have been increasingly concerned about families. And government policies have reflected this concern.

These policies are influenced by values. Should government policies be shaped by 'traditional family values' which see the nuclear family as the ideal? Or, should they recognise the increasing diversity of family life and support *all* family types?

### The New Right

The New Right comes down firmly on the side of the nuclear family (see Section 2.2). It's the best kind of family and should be encouraged. The rest are second-best and should be discouraged. How does this translate into social policy?

**Encouraging nuclear families** Governments should 'explicitly *favour* married parenthood over all other choices for raising children' (Saunders, 2000). Taxes and welfare benefits should be directed to this end. The marriage contract should be strengthened and married couples should have special legal rights and safeguards.

**Discouraging family diversity** According to the New Right, over-generous welfare benefits have supported the rapid increase in lone-parent families. These benefits should be reduced so lone-parenthood becomes a less attractive option. Cohabitation should be discouraged by denying unmarried couples the legal rights and privileges given to married couples. And divorce should be made more difficult to discourage marital break-up (Morgan, 1999; Saunders, 2000).

### Supporting all families

Critics of the New Right argue that governments should not attempt to impose one type of family and force everybody into the same mould. Instead, they should recognise that families are diverse and the trend is towards increasing diversity. Government policy should therefore support *all* families (Bernardes, 1997).

It is not the job of government to force couples to stay together by making divorce more difficult. Nor should rights and privileges be denied to those who cohabit simply because they aren't married. Governments should not make judgements about which form of family is best and base policy on such judgements. They should accept the decisions people have made about *their* form of family life and develop policies to support all families.

## Family policy in the UK

**Conservative policy** This section looks at family policy from 1990. The Conservative Party under John Major was in government from 1990 to 1997. It showed a clear preference for the married, two-parent nuclear family. Lone parents were denounced in what one writer described as 'an orgy of lone-parent bashing' (Lister, 1996). John Major himself heralded the virtues of 'traditional family values' in his Back to Basics campaign. However, this campaign was quietly brushed under the carpet, not least because many Cabinet members were divorced – hardly a reflection of traditional family values.

Talk rather than action characterised the Major years. There were only two major pieces of legislation directed at the family. In 1991, The Child Support Act was passed which led to the formation of the Child Support Agency. The main aim was to force absent fathers to pay maintenance for their children in the hope of reducing welfare payments to lone mothers. Although the government claimed this would help lone mothers, any money received from the fathers was deducted from the mothers' benefits.

# activity 19 party manifestos 2001

**Item A** *The Labour Party*

**Item B** *The Conservative Party*

Strong and stable family life offers the best possible start to children. And marriage provides a strong foundation for stable relationships. The government supports marriage. But it has to do more than that. It must support families, above all families with children. Our vision of the tax and benefits system for families with children is to provide help for all families; to give most help at the time families need it most; and to give more help to those families most in need.

We will create an integrated Child Credit of cash support for children, built on the foundation of universal child benefit.

Conservatives will help families bringing up children. We will let families keep more of what they earn. We will support marriage.

Despite all the evidence that marriage provides the best environment for bringing up children, married couples do not fit into Labour's politically correct agenda. That is why they have penalised millions of families by abolishing the Married Couple's Tax Allowance.

The arrival of children often puts a family under particular pressure. One parent may give up work for a while, reducing the couple's income just when their expenses are greatest.

A Conservative government will support families coping with these pressures. We will introduce a new Married Couple's Allowance which will give a tax cut worth £1,000 to many families when they need help most.

**Item C** *The Liberal Democrats*

We will establish a scheme for the civil registration of partnerships. This will give two unrelated adults who wish to register a settled personal relationship legal rights which are at present only available to married couples.

## questions

To what extent do these manifesto statements support

a) the traditional nuclear family

b) family diversity?

The Family Law Act of 1996 introduced a one year waiting period before a couple could divorce. The intention of the act was to support the institution of marriage. Couples were encouraged to take every possible step to save their marriage. However, the act was never implemented as judges saw it as unworkable.

**Labour policy** The tone of Labour's words on family policy was milder than those of the Conservatives. There was an attempt to steer a middle course between supporting both marriage and the nuclear family and providing help for other forms of family. There was no 'back to basics' but no 'anything goes' either. Labour has been careful not to condemn alternatives to the nuclear family (Lewis, 2001).

This can be seen from *Supporting Families* (1998) – a discussion document which suggested ways of providing 'better services and support for parents'. The emphasis is on *all* families. The government doesn't want to 'interfere' in family life, to 'pressure people' into a preferred family form, or to 'force' married couples to stay together. It accepts that many lone parents and unmarried couples raise children successfully. But, at the end of the day, 'marriage is still the surest foundation for raising children'.

This is what Labour said. What have they done?

Labour's family policy has formed part of its welfare policy. Summed up in Tony Blair's statement, 'Work for those that can, security for those that can't', this policy seeks to move those who can work from welfare into work and to improve benefits for those who can't.

Labour's New Deal schemes are designed to help people find paid employment. One of these schemes is aimed at lone parents, most of whom are lone mothers. Since April 2001, all lone parents are required to attend an annual interview about job opportunities. The Working Families Tax Credit tops up the wages of parents moving from benefits to low paid jobs.

Various childcare schemes have been introduced. For example, the Sure Start programme provides health and support services for low-income families with young children.

One of Labour's stated aims is to take all children out of poverty. Various benefits have been increased with this in mind. For example, Child Benefit has been increased by 26% in real terms from 1997 to 2001 (Page, 2002).

Labour's policies focus on money and work – children need money, parents have a responsibility to work (Lewis, 2001).

**Conclusion** Government policies are increasingly recognising the realities of family life – that family diversity is here to stay. Politicians are realising that the clock can't be turned back, that they have a responsibility to support all families. Alternative family forms are no longer condemned. But despite this, both Labour and Conservative Parties see marriage and the nuclear family as the ideal.

This can be seen clearly from David Willetts' speech at the Conservative (Tory) Party Conference in October 2002. He announced, 'Let me make it absolutely clear: the Tory war on lone parents is over'. He admitted that families come in all shapes and sizes, and that the state had a duty to support them all. Talking about lone parents, he said, 'We'll support them and value them and, above all, we'll back them'. Yet, despite this, Willetts claimed that the evidence was 'overwhelming' that it was better for children to be brought up by two parents in a stable marriage.

## summary

1. According to the New Right, government policy should favour marriage and the nuclear family.

2. Others argue that governments should recognise family diversity and support all family forms.

3. In practice, governments have seen the nuclear family as the preferred family form. However, there is increasing acceptance of family diversity and a recognition that government should support all families.

# Unit 5 Recent trends in family life

## keyissues

1 What are the recent trends in family life?
2 How have they been explained?

## 5.1 Cohabitation

**Definition** Cohabitation is living together as a couple without being married. It involves a shared residence in which a couple set up home together. Love is the most

common reason people give for cohabiting (McRae, 1999).

**Extent and age** From 1976 to 1998, the proportion of women under 50 who were cohabiting more than trebled – from 9% to over 27%. Cohabiting couples tend to be young – nearly 40% of non-married women aged 25 to 29 were cohabiting in 1998. The picture is similar for men (Haskey, 2001).

**Cohabitation and marriage** Cohabitation before marriage has now become the norm. Figure 2 shows the proportions of first and second marriages in which the couple lived together before marriage. For first marriages in the 1950s

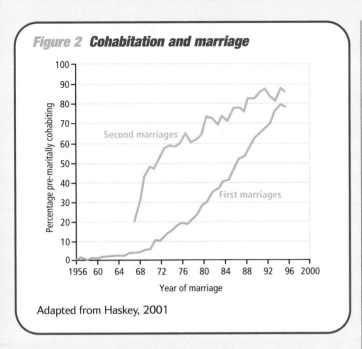

**Figure 2** *Cohabitation and marriage*

Adapted from Haskey, 2001

- For most people, cohabitation is part of the process of getting married – it is a prelude to marriage, *not* an alternative to marriage.
- Over half saw cohabitation as a trial marriage – it provided an opportunity to test the relationship before making it legally binding.
- Around 40% saw cohabitation as an alternative to marriage – they saw advantages to living together rather than marrying.
- Some mentioned the absence of legal ties – this gave them more freedom to end the relationship (*Social Trends*, 2002).

## Causes

Over the past 50 years, cohabitation has increased rapidly. What accounts for this increase?

**Changing attitudes** Attitudes towards sexual relationships and living arrangements outside marriage have changed. Cohabitation is no longer seen as 'living in sin' or described with negative phrases such as 'living over the brush'.

Evidence for change can be seen from the 1996 British Household Panel Survey. Asked whether they thought 'living together outside marriage was always wrong', a third of those aged 60 and over thought it was wrong compared with less than a tenth of those under 30 (*Social Trends*, 2002).

the figure was less than 2%, by 1996 it was 77%. For second marriages, the figure rose from less than 20% in 1967 to 84% in 1996 (Haskey, 2001).

**Reasons for cohabitation** The 1998 British Household Panel Survey asked people why they chose to cohabit. These are the reasons they gave.

# activity20 cohabitation

**Cohabitation by marital status**

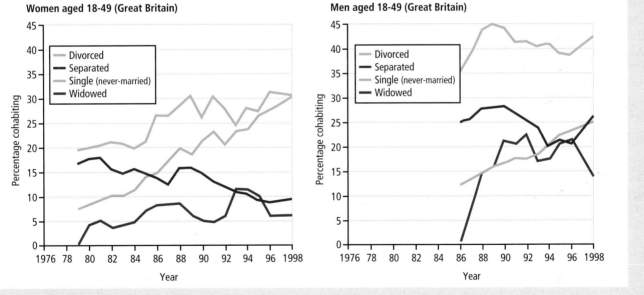

Adapted from Haskey, 2001

## questions

1 Describe the trends shown in the graphs.
2 Suggest a reason for the different percentages of divorced women and men cohabiting.

**Effective contraception** From 1967, reliable contraception was made readily available to unmarried women with the passing of the NHS (Family Planning) Act. For the first time, the possibility of unwanted pregnancy was no longer a factor in the decision to have sexual intercourse. Effective contraception made it possible for couples to cohabit with little fear of pregnancy (Allan & Crow, 2001).

**Changes in parental control, education and housing** There is some evidence that parental control over children has decreased over the past 50 years. The 1960s are often seen as the decade when young people revolted against the authority of their parents and the 'older generation'.

The expansion of higher education means that increasing numbers of young people are leaving home at an earlier age for reasons other than marriage. For example, there were 173,000 female undergraduates in the UK in 1970/71 compared with 602,000 in 2000/01. As a result, many young people have more freedom from parental authority at an earlier age, and they are able to live in their own housing. This makes it easier for couples to cohabit. In addition, building societies are now more likely to lend money to unmarried couples – at one time they were very unlikely to lend to those 'living in sin' (Allan & Crow, 2001).

**Changes in divorce** The divorce rate has increased rapidly over the past 50 years. Couples in which one or both partners are divorced are the most likely to cohabit. Having already achieved independence from their parents, they are less likely to be affected by parental control. Also, if their divorce has not gone through, cohabitation is their only option if they want to live as a couple.

The rise in divorce means that the view of marriage as a 'union for life' has less power. This may lead many people to see cohabitation, without its binding legal ties, as an attractive alternative to marriage. Some people actually give 'fear of divorce' as a reason for cohabiting (McCrae, 1999; Allan & Crow, 2001).

## 5.2 Lone-parent families

### Definition

The official definition of a lone-parent family goes as follows. A mother or father living without a partner, with their dependent child or children. The child must be never-married and aged either under 16 or 16 to under 19 and undertaking full-time education. Partner in this definition refers to either a marriage or cohabitation partner (Haskey, 2002).

The above definition is not as straightforward as it seems. What about a father who does not live with the mother and child but is in regular contact, takes part in 'family' decisions and provides for the family in various ways – from income support to helping the child with homework? Is he still a member of the family?

A number of separated and divorced couples attempt to share the responsibility for raising their children. This is known as *co-parenting* or *joint parenting*. It is difficult to

see such arrangements as simply lone-parent families (Neale & Smart, 1997).

Faced with this kind of problem, some sociologists have argued that the term *lone-parent household* is more precise. It simply states that the 'absent parent' is not part of the household – ie, does not live under the same roof (Crow & Hardy, 1992).

### Types of lone parents

Lone parents are a diverse group. This can be seen from the ways they became lone parents. The various routes into lone parenthood are summarised below.

- The ending of a marriage either by separation or divorce (separated and divorced lone parents)
- The ending of cohabitation where the partners separate (single lone parents)
- Birth to a never-married, non-cohabiting woman (single lone parents)
- Death of a partner – for example, a husband dies leaving his wife with dependent children (widowed lone parents).

Despite these diverse routes into lone parenthood, most lone-parent families have one thing in common, they are headed by women – over 90% in 2001.

### Trends in lone-parenthood

In Britain, since the early 1970s, lone-parent families, as a proportion of all families with dependent children, have increased nearly threefold – from 8% in 1971 to 22% in 2001.

During the 1960s, divorce overtook death as the main source of lone-parent families. From then until the mid-1980s, a large part of the increase was due to marital breakup – the separation or divorce of a married couple. After 1986, the number of *single lone mothers* grew at a faster rate. This group is made up of 1) never-married cohabiting women whose partnership ended after their child was born and 2) never-married women who were not cohabiting when their child was born. Each group accounts for around half of single lone mothers.

Table 6 illustrates these trends. It shows various types of lone parent families as a percentage of all families with dependent children.

The above statistics are snapshots at particular points in time. Families move in and out of lone parenthood. It is estimated that the average length of time spent as a lone parent is a little over 5 years (Allan & Crow, 2001). The routes in and out of lone parenthood are summarised in Activity 21.

### Explaining the trends

Why has lone parenthood increased so rapidly over the past 30 years?

**Divorce** As Table 6 shows, a large part of the increase from 1971 to 1991 was due to marital breakup. The divorce rate

Table 6 *Lone-parent families*

| **Great Britain** | | | | *Percentages* |
|---|---|---|---|---|
| | 1971 | 1981 | 1991 | 2001 |
| **Lone mothers** | | | | |
| Single | 1 | 2 | 6 | 9 |
| Widowed | 2 | 2 | 1 | 1 |
| Divorced | 2 | 4 | 6 | 6 |
| Separated | 2 | 2 | 4 | 4 |
| All lone mothers | 7 | 11 | 18 | 20 |
| **Lone fathers** | 1 | 2 | 1 | 2 |
| **All lone parents** | 8 | 13 | 19 | 22 |

Adapted from *Social Trends*, 2002

rose rapidly after the Divorce Reform Act came into force in 1971. Reasons for the rise in divorce are outlined on pages 85-86.

**Cohabitation breakup** Since the mid-1970s, the proportion of women under 50 who were cohabiting more than trebled – from 9% to over 27%. Nearly 40% of non-married women aged 25 to 29 were cohabiting in 1998 (Haskey, 2001). Over the same period, the number of marriages was steadily declining. Reasons for the increase in cohabitation are outlined on pages 97-98.

Since 1986 the number of single lone mothers has grown at a faster rate than any other category of lone parent. By 2001, they accounted for 45% of all lone mothers in Britain. Roughly half became lone mothers as a result of a breakup of their cohabitation. Cohabiting couples with children are twice as likely to end their relationship than married couples with children (Haskey, 2001).

**Non-cohabiting never-married mothers** This group form the other half of single lone mothers. Their children were born outside marriage and cohabitation. Their numbers have increased rapidly since the mid-1980s.

**Choice** Very few women give lone parenthood as their first option. In other words, the vast majority would prefer to raise their children with a partner. For example, in one study only one out of 44 lone mothers had deliberately decided to become a lone mother from the outset (Berthoud et al., 1999).

However, this does not rule out choice. Many women choose to end a marriage or cohabitation. They see this decision as a solution to a problem. It ends a relationship which is unhappy, which may be violent and abusive, and destructive for themselves and their children (Bernardes, 1997). In this sense, they are choosing to become a lone parent.

Similarly, many non-cohabiting never-married mothers choose lone parenthood from the options available to them. These options are:

- An abortion
- Give the baby up for adoption

# *activity21 moving in and out of lone parenthood*

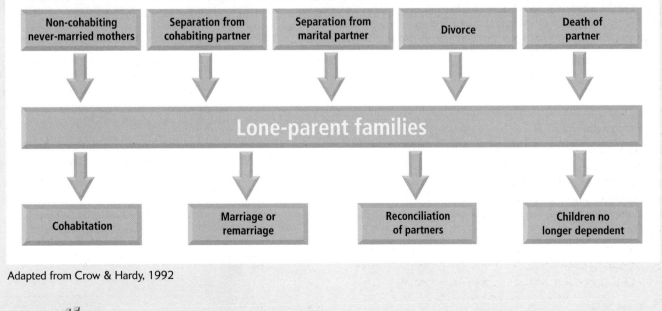

Adapted from Crow & Hardy, 1992

## question

Lone parenthood is not a permanent status. Explain with reference to the above diagram.

- In some cases, the opportunity to cohabit with or marry the father.

Many women decide against these options and choose lone parenthood. To some extent, this choice reflects changing attitudes.

**Changing attitudes** As outlined in the previous unit, there is greater tolerance of births outside marriage (see page 89). The stigma attached to children of unmarried mothers has reduced considerably. The term 'bastard' is rarely heard, and the less offensive 'illegitimate', which implies improper or immoral, is passing out of common usage.

There is far less pressure for single mothers to get married. The term 'shotgun wedding', frequently used in the 1950s and 60s, is not often heard today.

Lone-parent families are becoming increasingly acceptable. They are less likely to be described with negative phrases such as 'broken families' and 'incomplete families'.

Changing attitudes towards lone parenthood reflect a growing acceptance of the diversity of family life. This makes lone parenthood a more likely choice.

However, it is important not to exaggerate changing attitudes. As the following quotation shows, lone parents and their children are often still seen as second-class families. 'I think single parents have a lot to prove because we're constantly being told that we're not a correct family; that we can't look after our children the same as a two-parent family' (quoted in Beresford et al., 1999).

# activity22 lone parents

### Item A   Divorced lone mother

Sarah Ferguson, formerly married to Prince Andrew, with her daughters at the première of Harry Potter and the Philosopher's Stone in London

### Item B   Single lone mother

Film star Michelle Pfeiffer with her baby. 'I really wanted a child but I didn't want some guy around to drive me nuts.'

### Item C   Household income

| Families with dependent children | | | | | | Great Britain: 2000 |
|---|---|---|---|---|---|---|
| Family type | | Usual gross weekly household income | | | | |
| | | Under £150 | £150-£250 | £250-£350 | £350-£450 | Over £450 |
| Married couple | % | 10 | 6 | 8 | 11 | 64 |
| Cohabiting couple | % | 15 | 11 | 12 | 12 | 51 |
| Lone mother | % | 46 | 21 | 12 | 8 | 12 |
| Single | % | 58 | 21 | 8 | 5 | 8 |
| Divorced | % | 35 | 20 | 20 | 7 | 18 |
| Separated | % | 39 | 23 | 10 | 16 | 12 |
| Lone father | % | 34 | 7 | 13 | 18 | 29 |
| All lone parents | % | 45 | 19 | 12 | 9 | 14 |

Adapted from *Living in Britain*, 2002 (General Household Survey, 2000)

## questions

1   Why are the lone mothers in Items A and B untypical?

2   Outline the key points revealed by Item C.

**Economic independence** Lone parenthood is only possible if individuals are able to support themselves and their children. However, for the majority, economic independence from a partner means barely making ends meet.

Most lone-mother families live in poverty – defined as living below 50% of average income after housing costs have been met. Often, the low pay levels of many 'women's jobs' plus the costs of childcare mean that lone mothers are better off on state benefit than in paid employment. However, there is some evidence that government New Deal schemes are helping some lone parents and their children out of poverty (see page 96).

### Views of lone parenthood

**The parents' views** As noted earlier, becoming a lone parent was not usually the lone mother's or father's first choice option. The vast majority would rather raise their children with a partner in a happy relationship. Failing this, most choose to become lone parents. Many decide to separate from their partners, believing that it is better to become a lone parent rather than endure an unhappy and destructive relationship. Many decide to keep their child and raise it themselves, seeing this as preferable to abortion, to adoption, or to cohabiting with or marrying the child's other parent.

And, although being a lone parent is far from easy, many see benefits. In the words of one lone mother, 'I'm a bloody sight better off than many women who are married and have to run around after the husband as well as the kids' (Sharpe, 1984).

**New Right views** These views are outlined on pages 77-79. To recap, lone-parent families fail to provide adequate socialisation. In lone-mother families, there is no father present to discipline the children and provide a male role model. This can lead to underachievement at school, and anti-social behaviour ranging from rudeness to crime. Boys grow up with little awareness of the traditional responsibilities and duties of a father. Lone mothers become dependent on state benefits. Their children lack examples of the disciplines and responsibilities of paid employment.

As noted earlier, if the children of lone parents do have more problems, this may have little to do with lone parenthood as such. It may well result from the poverty that most lone parents experience (Allan & Crow, 2001).

**Feminist views** Lone parenthood usually means lone mothers. From a feminist viewpoint, this indicates that women have the freedom to choose. Rather than seeing the lone-parent family as a malfunctioning unit, some see it as an alternative family form in which women are free from male domination. And there is evidence that many single mothers welcome this independence and the opportunity it provides to take control of their own lives (Graham, 1987).

## 5.3 Reconstituted families

Many lone parents find new partners and form new families. These *reconstituted families* or *stepfamilies* are defined as a married or cohabiting couple with dependent children, at least one of whom is not the biological offspring of both partners (Haskey, 1994).

Compared to lone-parent families, there has been little research, public debate or government policy directed towards reconstituted families. This may be because such families tend to present themselves as 'normal' family groupings. And it may be because they are sometimes seen as a 'solution' to the so-called 'problem' of lone parenthood (Allan & Crow, 2001).

There has been a rapid increase in the number of reconstituted families. In 1998-99, they accounted for around 6% of all families with dependent children in Britain. According to one estimate, by 2010 they will outnumber families with two birth parents (Bedell, 2002).

### Diversity and reconstituted families

Reconstituted families are a diverse group. Parentline Plus, formerly the National Stepfamily Association, has identified 72 different ways in which stepfamilies can be formed. For example, some are formed by first marriage, some by remarriage, some by cohabitation. And once formed, this diversity continues. For example, some children may have close and regular relationships with their absent biological parent, other children may hardly see them.

Children are likely to stay with their mother after the break-up of a partnership. This can be seen from Table 7 – nearly 9 out of 10 stepfamilies contain at least one child from the female partner's previous relationship.

### Table 7 Stepfamilies

| Type of stepfamily | Great Britain: 2000 % |
|---|---|
| Couple with child(ren) from the woman's previous marriage/cohabitation | 88 |
| Couple with child(ren) from the man's previous marriage/cohabitation | 9 |
| Couple with child(ren) from both partners' previous marriage/cohabitation | 3 |

Adapted from *Living in Britain*, 2002

## Tensions within reconstituted families

Reconstituted families tend to present themselves as 'normal', 'ordinary' families. And, if estimates are correct, they may well become 'the norm'. Many reject labels such as stepfamilies, step-parents and stepchildren. Despite this desire to present themselves simply as a family, reconstituted families experience particular problems.

Families are social groups with boundaries. These boundaries include some people (these are my family members) and exclude others (these are not). Clear boundaries give families a definite sense of identity and unity. Sometimes the boundaries of reconstituted families are not clearly drawn. They may become fuzzy when partners from the couple's previous relationships become involved in the new family, especially if the children maintain a close relationship with the non-residential 'natural' parent. This may weaken the boundaries of the reconstituted family and threaten its unity (Allan & Crow, 2001).

Being a step-parent can be a difficult and delicate relationship. There are no clearly stated norms defining this role. For example, to what degree should a step-parent be involved in disciplining the child? Things are made more difficult if the child resents sharing their biological parent with a new partner and, in some cases, with other children. The role of the stepfather is often shifting and uncertain – a sort of uncle, father, big brother, friend or companion depending on the time and place (Bedell, 2002).

The additional strains of reconstituted families may help to explain their high level of breakup. A quarter of stepfamilies break up during their first year. And half of all remarriages which form a stepfamily end in divorce. But, as Peter Eldrid of Parentline Plus warns, 'It's important not to assume that every difficulty you face is to do with being a stepfamily. All families have upheavals' (quoted in Bedell, 2002). And, as reconstituted families become increasingly common, norms will probably develop to clarify the roles of those involved, so reducing the tension that lack of clarity brings.

## New opportunities

Research has tended to focus on the problems of reconstituted families. There is another side to the coin. For the adults, they offer the chance of a successful partnership after an earlier one has failed. And, if the parents are happy and committed to making the new family work, then the children are likely to be happy too (Bedell, 2002).

Reconstituted families can provide new and rewarding relationships for all concerned. The family expands overnight with step-brothers and sisters, step-cousins, step-parents and uncles, and step-grandparents. An expanded family network can lead to arguments, jealousy and conflict. But, it can also lead to a wider support network and enriched relationships.

# activity23 the 'new extended families'

## questions

Reconstituted families have been described as the new extended families.

a) What does this mean?

b) What advantages does it suggest?

# 5.4 Dual-earner families

Over the past 50 years there has been a steady rise in the number of married women in employment. This means that an ever-increasing proportion of couples combine paid work with family life. In other words, they are *dual-earner families*. At one extreme is the *dual-career family*. Here both partners 'possess a high degree of commitment to a career', typically working full time and gaining a strong and positive sense of identity from their employment (Rapoport & Rapoport, 1971). At the other extreme, one partner (the wife in the vast majority of cases), is involved in a small amount of part-time work which is arranged so as to interfere as little as possible with family responsibilities (Gowler & Legge, 1978).

## Trends in dual-earner families

According to the British Household Panel Study, 'Double work is now the majority option for couples (although many of the second jobs held by parents are part time)'. In 1973, 43% of couples with children and 61% of those without had two jobs. By 1996, the figures had increased to 60% of couples with children and 68% of those without (Berthoud & Gershuny, 2000).

So most couples – whether or not they have children – combine family life and employment. What is less clear however, is the number who are genuinely dual career – pursuing career and family life with equal commitment.

**The double shift** Many women in dual-earner families experience what has been referred to as a *double shift* (Hochschild, 1990). One 'shift' consists of their paid employment, the second is their responsibility for managing and organising family life.

The extent to which women build their jobs around family responsibilities is indicated by the numbers of each sex in part-time work. 60% of women with dependent children are in part-time work compared with 4% of men with dependent children (Labour Force Survey, Spring 2002).

Women's careers are far more likely to be disrupted by having children than men's. Fathers' work is rarely affected by the birth of children. Women, however, are more likely to drop out of employment or move to part-time work. However, this trend is becoming less pronounced with successive generations – an increasing proportion of women with young children are staying in full-time work (Moss, Brannen & Mooney, 2001).

An influential study by Robert and Rhona Rapoport (1971) focused on case studies of five dual-career families. They found that the couples had negotiated ground rules about managing family and work commitments – for example, neither partner should accept promotion involving a change of geographical location. But social pressures from friends, family and the media kept reasserting conventional gender stereotypes. As a result, the female partner ended up with primary responsibility for the childcare and household arrangements needed to sustain work and family life.

## Balancing employment and family life

Dual-earner families are faced with the problem of balancing the demands of a job with the needs of a family. David Cheal (2002) identifies six main strategies. Couples are likely to adopt one or more of these depending on their particular circumstances.

**Employment at home** Developments in computer technology and telecommunications make it possible for those with the appropriate skills and contacts to work from home. This means that parents can organise their work around the demands of their children. Some parents enjoy the flexibility and freedom of homeworking but others experience tensions because they feel they can never really escape from work (Perrons, 2003).

Most homework, however, is in low-skill, low-pay work such as finishing and packing. These jobs rarely have pension schemes and medical benefits and are not attractive, particularly to those with good educational qualifications.

**Working non-standard hours** Shift work can allow one parent to be in the home at any one time. This strategy may be appealing to women who like the idea of being a full-time mother and housekeeper but who have a financial need for full-time work (Garey, 1995). In reality, the arrangement is likely to create stress which can lead to relationship problems.

**Altering work practices** Rapid increases in the numbers of dual-earner families have created pressure on employers and governments to adopt 'family-friendly' policies. These may include extended maternity and paternity leave, discretionary days off for family emergencies and flexible working hours. In 2000, the government launched a 'Work Life Balance' campaign and from April 2003, employees can request a 'flexible working pattern' which their employer has to consider 'seriously'. Such practices are helpful, but a substantial commitment to work is still expected by most employers.

**Employment reduction** Moving to part-time work is one of the most common strategies for families with young children in contemporary Western societies, as the figures above indicate. It tends to be the choice of those with more traditional attitudes to the sexual division of labour (Tam, 1997).

**Reallocation of domestic labour** A more radical approach is for male partners to take an equal share of housework and childcare, so eliminating the problem of the 'double shift'. Evidence indicates that men are slow to adapt. This is discussed at length on pages 116-122.

Alternatively, other relations (particularly grandparents), friends and older children may help out. Money rarely changes hands, especially in the case of support from kin since family members feel strong obligations towards each other. However, favours may be expected in return (Folk, 1994).

**Paid childcare services** If relatives are unable to help, families may well turn to paid childcare services in the form of nurseries, nannies or au pairs. They may also employ cleaners to ease the burden of domestic work. Once again, it is women who take most of the responsibility for organising care for their children, and women who take the low pay, low status jobs in childcare and domestic work, jobs with little security and few fringe benefits (Leonard, 2000).

## The future

The increase in dual-earner families is likely to continue. Two sources of income are essential for many families in order to maintain what they see as an acceptable standard of living.

However, managing a family, home and paid work is a complex juggling act. The adoption of 'family-friendly' policies by employers can make the 'work-life' balance more manageable. But despite some signs of change – men are participating rather more in housework and childcare – it is still the women in dual-earner families who bear most of the domestic responsibilities. The 'double-shift' is still very much alive.

## 5.5 One-person households

More and more people in Western societies are living alone. They are living in one-person households. Table 8 shows the growth of one-person households in Britain from 1971 to 2002. They are shown as a percentage of all households.

### Who lives alone?

**Age** Most people picture one-person households as older people living alone. As Table 8 shows, until the 1990s,

## activity24 working couples

### Item A *I can't carry on*

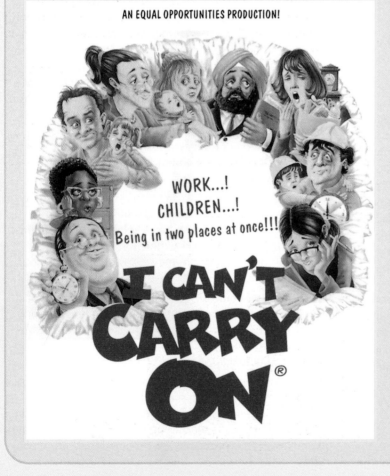

AN EQUAL OPPORTUNITIES PRODUCTION!

WORK...!
CHILDREN...!
Being in two places at once!!!

I CAN'T CARRY ON®

### Item B *A dual-career family*

Typical weekdays start with Mrs Harris getting the children up before 7.30 am. The au pair comes in at 7.30. Mrs Harris sees that the family have breakfast together. Mr Harris leaves for work at 8.15. Their daughter walks to school with a friend, their son is taken by Mrs Harris or the au pair. When the little boy was at nursery school, the au pair fetched him home for lunch. Mrs Harris would prepare his lunch in advance or the au pair would provide a snack.

Mr and Mrs Harris have dinner together when the children are in bed, at about 7.30 pm. Normally, Mrs Harris cooks on Sundays, not only for that day but for several days in advance. Mr Harris is relatively active with family and household activities at the weekend. In addition, he helps by not being too demanding, for example, he does not expect an elaborate dinner in the evening.

Adapted from Rapoport & Rapoport, 1971

## questions

1  What problems faced by dual-earner families are illustrated by the poster in Item A?

2  How does Item B illustrate the 'double shift'?

**Table 8  *One-person households***

| Great Britain | | | | Percentages |
| --- | --- | --- | --- | --- |
| | 1971 | 1981 | 1991 | 2001 |
| Under state pension age | 6 | 8 | 11 | 15 |
| Over state pension age | 12 | 14 | 16 | 14 |

Adapted from *Social Trends*, 2003

there was evidence to support this view. However, by 2001, people below state pension age formed the majority of one-person households.

The largest increase is in the 25 to 29 age group in social class 1 – people in professional and managerial occupations. In England and Wales in 1971, 6% of this group lived alone, in 1991 just under 20% (Hall et al., 1999).

**Gender** Most people picture one-person households as older women living alone. As with age, evidence from 1971 supports this view. However, by 2000, as Figure 3 shows, men aged under 65 formed the largest group of one-person households.

**Marital status** For the under 30 age group living alone, 90% are never-married. For age groups under 60, increasing numbers who live alone are divorced – 23% of the 30-39 age group and 36% of the 50-59 age group. For the 60 plus age group, the death of a spouse – usually the husband – accounts for their living alone – 73% of this age group are widowed (Hall et al., 1999).

**Location and occupation** Younger one-person households are concentrated in large cities – Manchester, Newcastle-upon-Tyne, Liverpool, Sheffield, Nottingham and particularly London. Many are young professionals who migrate to cities to find employment. Of the young, professional migrants to London, 62% of men and 53% of women live alone (Hall et al., 1999).

## Explaining the trends

Why do people live alone? Why are increasing numbers of people living alone?

**Possibilities** There are three possible reasons why people live alone.

- For some, living alone is a deliberate choice. They want to live alone, at least for part of their lives.
- For others, living alone is seen as a temporary arrangement due to particular circumstances – for example, a partnership break-up.
- For others, they have no choice in the matter – for example, their partner has died and they have nowhere else to go (McRae, 1999).

**Singlehood, marriage and divorce** There has been a decline in marriage and an increase in singlehood. The age at which people first marry has increased. There has been a rise in separation and divorce. These factors help to account for the rise of one-person households resulting from deliberate choice (eg, a desire to be single), or from particular circumstances (eg, a divorce).

**Jobs, money and geographical mobility** Over the past 30 years there has been a steady growth in professional, managerial and technical occupations. These jobs are concentrated in large urban centres – they often involve people moving to a different location. For a single person moving to a new job in an area where they have no friends, a one-person household makes sense.

One-person households are expensive. Two people together can live more cheaply than two people separately. Professional and managerial jobs are well paid. As a result, people in these jobs can afford to live alone.

The above factors help to explain the rapid growth of young professionals and managers in one-person households.

**Age and gender** In younger age groups, men are more likely than women to live alone. In general, men earn more

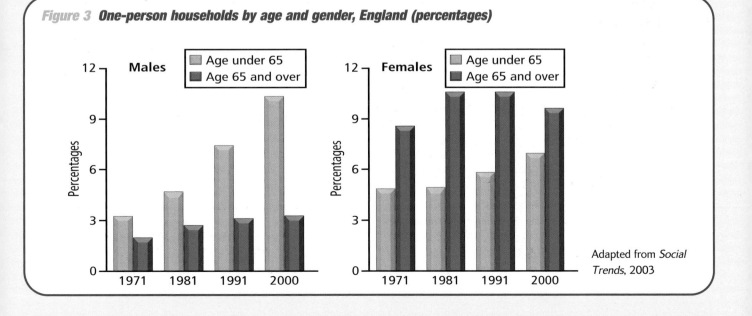

**Figure 3  *One-person households by age and gender, England (percentages)***

Adapted from *Social Trends*, 2003

than women and are therefore more likely to be able to afford to live alone. And men are far more likely than women to be in the professional and managerial class.

After separation or divorce, women are more likely to be living with dependent children. 90% of lone-parent families are headed by women.

In older age groups, women are more likely than men to live alone. This is mainly due to the death of their partner. Women tend to be younger than their partners. And, on average, women live longer than men – in 2001, life expectancy for women was 80 years, for men 76 years (*Social Trends*, 2003).

**Changing attitudes** At one time, people felt sorry for those living alone. In particular, an unmarried woman living on her own was described in negative terms as a 'spinster' or an 'old maid'. Today, attitudes are changing. Many now see living alone as a positive lifestyle option.

Some sociologists see this change in attitude as a reflection of the 'rise in non-family living' (Goldscheider & Waite, 1991). They argue that the family has become less central to people's lives.

**Choice** Available evidence indicates that many people who live alone do so by choice. They value the freedom and independence which living in a one-person household provides. Most have active social lives and many are involved in a close relationship. The following quotations from interviews illustrate these points.

- 'I wanted my own thing and freedom to do exactly what I wanted.'
- 'I find I do need the time and space on my own. I thoroughly enjoy it.'
- 'I love it. It's rather like going on holiday.' (Hall et al., 1999).

## Consequences

The rise in one-person households is projected to continue, at least until 2021 (*Social Trends*, 2003). This has a number of implications for housing, land use and resource use.

Around 80% of new housing demand in the UK is for one-person households. One estimate puts the figure at over 4 million homes. The land needed for this massive building programme has been described by the Campaign for the Protection of Rural England as a 'nightmare scenario'.

Compared to multi-person households, one-person households consume more gas, electricity and water per person, they generate more waste and more greenhouse gases (Morgan, 2003).

On the positive side, most people who choose to live alone are happy – they feel they have made the right choice (Hall et al., 1999).

## summary

1. There has been a large increase in cohabitation from the 1970s onwards. Cohabitation before marriage is now the norm. While most people see it as a prelude to marriage, some see it as an alternative to marriage.

2. The following reasons have been suggested for the increase in cohabitation.
   - Changing attitudes
   - Availability of reliable contraception
   - Reduction of parental control
   - Expansion of higher education
   - Increased availability of housing for non-married people
   - Increase in divorce rate.

3. In Britain since the early 1970s, lone-parent families have increased from 8% to 22% of all families with dependent children.

4. Lone parents are a diverse group – eg, some were previously married, some cohabiting, some neither.

5. Although very few women choose lone parenthood as their first option, choices are involved – eg, whether to keep, abort, or give the baby up for adoption.

6. Lone parenthood has become increasingly acceptable.

7. There has been a rapid increase in reconstituted families. They are a diverse group – eg, some are formed by cohabitation, some by first marriage, others by remarriage.

8. There are particular tensions in reconstituted families, partly because the roles of family members often lack clear definition.

9. Reconstituted families offer new opportunities – they can lead to a wider support network and enriched relationships.

10. There has been a steady rise in dual-earner families. Most couples now combine family life and employment.

11. Many women experience a double shift – paid employment and primary responsibility for childcare and housework.

12. Dual-earner families adopt various strategies for balancing the demands of a job and the needs of a family. These include flexible working and moving from full to part-time work.

13. There has been a rapid growth in one-person households since the 1970s. People under 65 account for most of this increase.

14. Men under 65 form the largest group of one-person households followed by women over 65.

15. Reasons for the growth of one-person households include:
    - Rise in singlehood and divorce, and decline in marriage.
    - Increase in professional and managerial jobs, which are well paid and often demand geographical mobility.
    - Changing attitudes – many now see living alone as a positive lifestyle option.

# *activity***25** *one-person households*

**Item A** *Two views of living alone*

**Item B** *Peter*

Peter is a solicitor. He is 28, single, and has recently moved to Liverpool to join a law firm. He lives alone in an expensive waterfront apartment at the Albert Docks. He didn't know anyone in Liverpool so he decided on a one-person household. He had shared a house with friends in his hometown of Leeds. To his surprise, he really enjoys living alone and intends to do so for the foreseeable future.

## questions

1 Which of the two cartoons best describes the experience of living alone?

2 How typical is Peter of younger one-person households?

# Unit 6 Dimensions of diversity

*keyissue*

How do class, ethnicity, gender, life cycle and location affect family diversity?

## 6.1 Social class and family diversity

Many sociologists argue that social class has an important influence on family life. They make the following points.

**Income inequality** In general, the lower a person's class position, the lower their income. Income inequality leads to variations in living standards, housing quality and lifestyles. For example, low-income families are more likely to live in overcrowded and substandard housing, and less likely to own a car or afford a family holiday.

**Life chances** These refer to a person's chances of obtaining things defined as desirable – eg, good health – and avoiding things defined as undesirable – eg, unemployment. Often, there is a fairly close relationship between social class and life chances. For example, the higher the class position of a child's parents, the more likely the child is to attain high educational qualifications and a well paid, high status job.

**Family breakup** As noted earlier, the lower the class position of a married couple, the more likely they are to divorce – see page 87. High divorce rates are related to poverty – to low income and reliance on state benefits (Kiernan & Mueller, 1999).

**Family structure** In the past, class had an important influence on family structure. Working-class families tended to be extended, particularly in low-income urban areas. The traditional working-class extended family operated as a mutual aid organisation, providing support for its members particularly in times of hardship and crisis. Today, there is little difference in the structure of working and middle-class families (see pages 71-72).

## 6.2 Ethnicity and family diversity

To some degree, ethnic groups have their own subcultures – norms and values which differ from those of mainstream culture. And to some degree, these subcultures influence family life. This section takes a brief look at ethnic minority groups and family diversity in the UK.

**Diversity within ethnic groups** There is a danger in talking about 'typical ethnic families'. Often there is as much family diversity within ethnic groups as there is within white society.

And there is a danger of ignoring cultural variation *within* ethnic groups. For example, within the South Asian community there are variations in religion – Sikhs, Muslims and Hindus – in countries of origin – India, Pakistan and Bangladesh – and in regions within those countries – for example, Goa and Bengal.

Finally, there is a danger of exaggerating differences between ethnic and White families and of creating stereotypes in the process – for example, Asians live in extended families and their marriages are arranged.

**Asian families** Most Asian households are based on nuclear families. However, around 20% are extended families, a higher proportion than other groups. Although there is a trend towards nuclear families, wider kinship ties remain strong (Westwood & Bhachu, 1988).

Asians are more likely to marry and to marry earlier than their White counterparts. Cohabitation and divorce are rare (Berthoud & Beishon, 1997). Marriages are sometimes arranged, but there is little research on this subject. There is some evidence which suggests that the couple have more say in arranged marriages as Western ideas about love and romance become more influential (Allan & Crow, 2001).

**African-Caribbean families** In 2000, nearly 50% of African-Caribbean families with dependent children were lone-parent families compared to around 22% for Britain as a whole (*Social Trends*, 2002). African-Caribbeans have the lowest marriage rate, the highest proportion of single (never-married) lone mothers, and the highest divorce rate (Berthoud et al., 1999).

Statistics such as these have led some researchers to talk about the 'problem' of the 'African-Caribbean family'. However, this ignores the strength of wider kinship networks – in particular, the support provided for lone mothers by female relatives. This support can cross national boundaries with family members in the UK and West Indies providing support for each other (Goulborne, 1999).

**Multicultural families** Recent statistics suggest an increase in the number of partnerships between people from different ethnic groups. Elisabeth Beck-Gernsheim (2002) uses the term *multicultural families* for families in which the partners come from different ethnic backgrounds. She recognises that such couples may face prejudice from their ethnic groups of origin, and conflict because they bring differing expectations of family life to the relationship. However, she is cautiously optimistic about the promise of multicultural families. They may help to break down barriers between ethnic groups. And they reflect a growing opportunity for individual choice – people are now choosing partners who fulfil their personal needs rather than being directed by the concerns of their parents or the norms of their ethnic group.

*key terms*

**Life chances** A person's chances of obtaining things defined as desirable and avoiding things defined as undesirable.

**Multicultural families** Families in which the partners are from different ethnic groups.

# activity26 class, ethnicity and family d...

*Outside the family home*

*Outside the family home*

*This couple have a business specialising in wedding accessories for multicultural couples*

## questions

1 With reference to Item A, suggest how class differences might affect family life.

2 Look at Item B.

   a) What problems might this couple experience?

   b) How can an increase in multicultural families be seen as a positive development?

## 6.3 Gay and lesbian families

Until recently, there was little research on gay and lesbian families. This began to change in the 1990s.

**Families of choice** Judging from a series of in-depth interviews conducted in the mid-1990s, many gays and lesbians are developing new ways of understanding the idea of family (Weeks et al., 1999a). Many believe they are *choosing* their own family members and creating their own families.

These *families of choice* are based on partnerships, close friends and members of their family of origin. This network provides mutual support, loving relationships and a sense of identity. It feels like a family. As one interviewee put it, 'I think the friendships I have are family' (Weeks et al., 1999b).

**Same-sex partnerships** In recent years, increasing numbers of gays and lesbians have formed households based on same-sex partnerships. And many are demanding the same rights as heterosexual partnerships – for example, the right to marry and adopt children. This does not mean they wish to copy heterosexual relationships, they simply want the same rights as everybody else.

In practice, same-sex partnerships tend to be more democratic than heterosexual partnerships. Many gay and lesbian couples strive for a relationship based on negotiation and equality (Weeks et al., 1999a).

**Same-sex parents** A growing number of lesbians are choosing to have children and to raise them with a female partner. Many use artificial insemination with sperm donated by friends or anonymous donors. In the traditional sense of the word, they are choosing to have a 'family'.

# activity 27 families of choice

Noah and Mackenlie pose with their parents, Hazel, left and Donna, right. Hazel is the biological parent of Noah, and Donna is the biological parent of Mackenlie. The two lesbians cross-adopted each other's child to legally form their family.

### Item C  A neighbour's response

We (a lesbian couple) live together in a stable unit with a child. It sometimes feels like a marriage. But I only have to walk out into the street to know that it's not. There's one neighbour next door that just won't speak to us. She spoke to us before we had the baby, and now she won't speak to us.

Adapted from Weeks et al., 1999b

### Item B  Our family

Amanda and her partner Ruth decided to have children – they each had a son. The father is a close friend. He is now seen as part of the family. Amanda writes:

'Our children love having two mummies. They know they are different. They are proud of being special. At this young age, mummies are still hot property, and to have two is twice as nice. They see their dad regularly, and ring him when they want. And having three parents, they get all the extra grandparents, aunties, uncles, and cousins too. All our families have been fantastic. Some of them had their doubts when we first told them that we were having children, but since our boys first came into the world they have been cherished by an extended family that goes beyond a basic biology.

I'm excited about our future. I know things will not always be easy. I know that as our children get older, and learn about sexuality and the pressures of conformity, they will have many questions. They may face prejudice themselves. I hate that thought, but I know that as a family we have the strength to help them deal with it.'

Adapted from *The Independent*, 4.2.02

## question

There's no particular problem with gay or lesbian families – apart from some heterosexuals! Discuss.

---

Gay men have more limited options. Either they must find a surrogate mother to bear their children, or else adopt. In the UK, the adoption route was closed until 2002 when an Act of Parliament made it legal for gays and lesbians to adopt children.

**Children** Concerns about children's gender identity and sexual orientation have been the main focus of research on gay and lesbian parenting. Most studies show that children raised by gay and lesbian parents are no different from those raised by heterosexuals (Fitzgerald, 1999). The evidence suggests that what matters is the parent-child relationship rather than the sexual orientation of the parents.

## key term

*Family of choice* A family whose members have been chosen, rather than given by birth and marriage.

## 6.4  Family life cycles

At one time, sociologists attempted to map out the 'typical' life cycle of the 'normal' family. They tried to identify a set of stages through which most families pass. Here is a simple example.

- Marriage
- Birth of children
- Children grow up within family
- Children leave home
- Old age and death of parents.

This model may have fitted many families in 1950s Britain – a time of stable marriages and high fertility. But it hardly fits the diversity of family life today (Cheal, 1999).

Modern family life is a lot less standardised and predictable than in the 1950s. Fewer people marry and increasing numbers cohabit. The rates of divorce and

## activity28 Bill

When Bill was ten his parents divorced. He lived with his mother and saw his father every Saturday. Four years later, his mother remarried, and Bill added a stepfather to his family. At eighteen, Bill left home to attend college and after graduation he and his girlfriend moved in together. A year and a half later, they married and soon afterwards they had a child. After several years, the marriage began to turn sour. Bill and his wife eventually separated and she retained custody of the child. Three years later, Bill married a woman who had a child from a previous marriage and together they had another child. Bill's second marriage lasted 35 years until his death.

Adapted from Cherlin, 1992

### question

Why doesn't Bill fit the 'standard' family life cycle?

remarriage have risen dramatically, along with lone-parent and reconstituted families.

Faced with this diversity, sociologists have largely abandoned the idea of a standard family life cycle.

Activity 28 looks at the diversity of family life cycles in terms of the experience of a single individual.

## 6.5 Locality and families

David Eversley and Lucy Bonnerjea (1982) claim that there is a relationship between locality and family type. They identify six kinds of areas in England and Wales, each of which is associated with characteristic types of families and households.

1 **The sun belt** This includes many of the better-off areas in south and south-eastern England. It is characterised by two-parent households, by 'family builders' who often own their own home.

2 **The geriatric wards** These include many of the coastal areas in England and Wales, particularly the south coast of England. They have large numbers of retired people in one and two-person households, often living some distance from their nearest relatives.

3 **Older declining industrial areas** These are founded on industries such as coal, iron and steel, shipbuilding and textiles. They tend to be characterised by older populations and stable family households with traditional patriarchal family structures and strong family and neighbourhood loyalties.

4 **Newly declining industrial areas** These are found mainly in the Midlands – for example, Coventry. Such areas were prosperous, with high rates of female employment, but now face higher unemployment, particularly among older workers. As many people are relatively recent arrivals, they may have little support from extended family networks. Family types are varied.

5 **Truly rural areas** Few of these survive as commuters and wealthy retired people have moved in to many rural villages. Where family-based farms and businesses continue to exist, there is a high proportion of two-parent families, and often strong extended family networks.

6 **The inner cities** They have a high proportion of lone-parent families, multi-adult households and ethnic minority families. Many people in inner city areas are isolated from family networks – for example, single young people and older people whose children have migrated to more prosperous areas.

Eversley's and Bonnerjea's research was conducted over 20 years ago. The economic and social characteristics of the localities may have changed. Nevertheless, their research shows how regional differences may affect families and households. And it points to the danger of generalising about the 'typical British family'

### summary

1. Social class can have an important impact on families. It can affect their members' standard of living and life chances. And it can affect a couples' chances of staying together.
2. Ethnic differences add diversity to family life.
3. Gay and lesbian couples are adding further diversity to family life.
4. Most studies show that children raised by gay and lesbian parents are no different to those raised by heterosexuals.
5. Sociologists have abandoned the idea of a standard family life cycle – it does not fit the diversity of family life today.
6. There is some evidence of a link between locality and family type.

# activity29 regional diversity

**Item A  Southwark, London**

**Item B  Detached housing**

**Item C  Family farm**

**Item D  Eastbourne, Sussex**

## question

Match each of the pictures to one of the six areas identified by Eversley and Bonnerjea.

# Unit 7 Explaining family diversity

## keyissues

1  How diverse are families?

2  What are the main explanations for family diversity?

## 7.1 Introduction

**Family diversity as a theme** This unit is entitled *Explaining family diversity*. Read any recent introductory textbook on the sociology of the family and one statement rings out loud and clear – families and households in today's

# activity30 pictures of the family

**Item B  Book covers**

## questions

1  How can ads portraying the nuclear family be seen as ideological?

2  How do the book covers in Item B picture the family today?

society are more complex and diverse than ever before. Here is a typical statement by Susan McRae in the introduction to her edited book, *Changing Britain: Families and Households in the 1990s* (1999). 'Britain today is a much more complex society than in past times, with great diversity in the types of household within which people live: one-person; cohabiting; families with children and families without; stepfamilies; lone parents – whether divorced or never-married; gay and lesbian couples; pensioners.'

**Family diversity as a cause for concern** Alongside this recognition of family and household diversity is concern. For some, particularly the New Right, increasing diversity means increasing breakdown. A picture is presented of the family in crisis. Alternatives to the 'traditional family' are poor substitutes for the real thing. So, the families formed by cohabiting couples, the reconstituted families created by remarriage, and families headed by lone parents or by gay or lesbian couples are at best, second best. For some, they represent a disintegration of traditional family values, a breakdown of the traditional family.

**The ideology of the nuclear family** What is this wonderful family compared to which all others fall short? It is the nuclear family of mum, dad and the kids. For some, it was found in its ideal form in the 1950s with mum as a full-time mother and housewife and dad as the breadwinner. The couple are male and female rather than same-sex, they are married rather than cohabiting, and married for the first rather than the second or third time.

This image of the nuclear family is fostered by advertisers. Called the *cereal packet image of the family* by

Edmund Leach (1967), it portrays happy, smiling nuclear families consuming family products from Corn Flakes to Oxo.

This picture can be seen as ideological. An ideology is a misleading view, based on value judgements, which obscures reality. Diana Gittins (1993) argues that the idealised picture of the nuclear family acts as a powerful ideology, defining what is normal and desirable and labelling alternative family forms as abnormal and undesirable.

It creates the impression that the nuclear family headed by a married, heterosexual couple is the only family unit that can effectively raise the next generation.

## key terms

***Cereal packet image of the family*** Stereotypical view of the family common in advertising. The family is presented as nuclear with a traditional division of labour.
***Ideology*** A misleading view based on value judgements which obscures reality.

## 7.2  Changing households

This section looks at changes in household composition in Britain over the past 40 years. Looking at household composition provides one way of assessing the extent of family diversity. And it gives an indication about what might be happening to the nuclear family.

Table 9 shows the changing proportions of each type of household from 1961 to 2001. During this period the proportion of households made up of a couple with dependent children has declined from 38% to 23%. During this same period, the proportion of lone-parent with dependent children households has risen from 2% to 6%. These figures have sometimes been used to indicate a decline in nuclear families. They have also been used to argue that the nuclear family is no longer the dominant family type.

### Table 9 Households: by type of household and family

| Great Britain | | | | | Percentages |
|---|---|---|---|---|---|
| | 1961 | 1971 | 1981 | 1991 | 2001 |
| **One Person** | | | | | |
| Under state pension age | 4 | 6 | 8 | 11 | 14 |
| Over state pension age | 7 | 12 | 14 | 16 | 15 |
| **Two or more unrelated adults** | 5 | 4 | 5 | 3 | 3 |
| **One family households** | | | | | |
| Couple | | | | | |
| No children | 26 | 27 | 26 | 28 | 29 |
| 1-2 dependent children | 30 | 26 | 25 | 20 | 19 |
| 3 or more dependent children | 8 | 9 | 6 | 5 | 4 |
| Non-dependent children only | 10 | 8 | 8 | 8 | 6 |
| Lone parent | | | | | |
| Dependent children | 2 | 3 | 5 | 6 | 6 |
| Non-dependent children only | 4 | 4 | 4 | 4 | 3 |
| **Multi-family households** | 3 | 1 | 1 | 1 | 1 |
| **All households** | | | | | |
| (=100%) (millions) | 16.3 | 18.6 | 20.2 | 22.4 | 24.1 |

Adapted from *Social Trends*, 2002

Table 10 provides a somewhat different picture. It looks at the percentage of people living in each type of household. It shows that in 1961, 52% of people lived in households made up of a couple with dependent children. By 2001, this figure had dropped to 39%. Even so, there are still a lot of people living in nuclear family households.

Figures for one year are just a snapshot of one part of a family's life cycle. Many households contain people who have been, or will be, members of nuclear family households – for example, couples with no children and people living alone. And the majority of British children still live in couple-headed households – 70% in 2001. This suggests that living in a nuclear family is a phase that most people, as children and adults, go through in the course of their life (O'Brien, 2000).

### Family diversity assessed

The extent of family diversity should not be exaggerated. Most people, as children and adults, live parts of their lives

### Table 10 People in households: by type of household and family in which they live

| Great Britain | | | | | Percentages |
|---|---|---|---|---|---|
| | 1961 | 1971 | 1981 | 1991 | 2001 |
| **One family households** | | | | | |
| Living alone | 4 | 6 | 8 | 11 | 12 |
| Couple | | | | | |
| No children | 18 | 19 | 20 | 23 | 24 |
| Dependent children | 52 | 52 | 47 | 41 | 39 |
| Non-dependent children only | 12 | 10 | 10 | 11 | 9 |
| Lone parent | 3 | 4 | 6 | 10 | 10 |
| **Other households** | 12 | 9 | 9 | 4 | 5 |
| **Total population** (millions) | 51.4 | 54.4 | 54.8 | 56.2 | 57.2 |

Adapted from *Social Trends*, 2002

in nuclear families. Even so, the trend is towards family diversity as the figures in Tables 9 and 10 indicate. There has been a significant decline in:

● the proportion of households made up of a couple with dependent children
● the proportion of people in such households
● the proportion of dependent children living in couple families.

This decrease in nuclear families has been matched by an increase in lone-parent families. This indicates an increase in family diversity.

The terms nuclear family and couple family conceal further diversity. The couple may be:

● married for the first time
● remarried
● cohabiting
● opposite sex
● same sex.

Over the past 30 years there has been a significant increase in remarriage, reconstituted families, cohabitation and same-sex couples. Again, this can be seen as indicating an increase in family diversity.

## 7.3 Family diversity and society

Explanations of various instances of family diversity – for example, lone-parent families and reconstituted families – have been examined in previous units.

This section examines family diversity in the context of the wider society. It looks at views which see increasing family diversity as a reflection of broader changes in society as a whole.

## Giddens and late modernity

According to the British sociologist Anthony Giddens, we live in an era known as *late modernity*. This era is characterised by choice and change. Opportunities to choose an identity and select a lifestyle are increasingly available. In the pre-modern era, tradition defined who people were and what they should do. Today, people have far more freedom to try on different identities and to try out different lifestyles (Giddens, 1991; 1992).

Where does the family fit into late modernity? If Giddens is correct, family diversity is a reflection of the opportunities and priorities of late modernity. People have greater freedom to construct their own domestic arrangements. They are not bound by existing family forms and family roles. There are more choices available and more opportunities to experiment, create and change.

Within limits, people can tailor their partnerships and their families to meet their individual needs and to reflect their own identities. They can choose to cohabit or to marry, to end one partnership and to begin another. The emphasis is on building and constructing family units, on creating and defining family relationships. People build reconstituted families. They enter uncharted territory constructing gay and lesbian families with no clear patterns to work from. They choose to become lone parents rather than accept an unsatisfactory relationship.

According to Giddens (1992), relationships in late modernity are increasingly based on *confluent love* – deep emotional intimacy in which partners reveal their needs and concerns to each other. Commitment to the relationship lasts as long as the individual receives sufficient satisfaction and pleasure from it. Failure to experience this is justification, in itself, for ending the relationship. If Giddens is correct, this helps to explain the fragility of partnerships in late modernity, as seen in the high rates of separation and divorce.

**Evaluation** Giddens's views of late modernity help to explain the trend towards family diversity. However, he may have exaggerated people's freedom to choose. Take lone-parent families. In one sense they are *not* based on choice – at least not first choice. Most single (never-married) mothers did *not* choose to become pregnant. However, they did choose to have the baby and raise it themselves (Allen & Dowling, 1999). Similarly, divorced lone mothers did not set out to become lone parents. This

was a second-best choice after the failure of their marriage.

Even so, there is evidence to support Giddens' claim of increased choice in late modernity. People can choose between marriage and cohabitation, they can choose to remain married or to divorce, they can choose to become a lone parent or to maintain a partnership, they can choose to remain a lone parent or to form a reconstituted family. There is far greater freedom to make these choices than there was 50 years ago.

## Postmodernity

Some sociologists believe that the modern age has ended and that we now live in the *postmodern* era. They describe this era as a time of change, of flux, of fluidity and uncertainty. Gone is the consensus or agreement about norms and values which characterised most of the modern age.

The American sociologist Judith Stacey (1996) sees family diversity as a reflection of postmodern society. There is no one family form to which everyone aspires. There are no generally agreed norms and values directing family life. In her words, 'Like postmodern culture, contemporary family arrangements are diverse, fluid and unresolved'.

Stacey welcomes this diversity, seeing it as an opportunity for people to develop family forms which suit their particular needs and situations. She looks forward to the possibility of more equal and democratic relationships which she sees in many gay and lesbian families.

**Evaluation** Stacey's research was conducted in Silicon Valley in California, home to many of the world's most advanced electronics companies. This is hardly typical of American society in general. She also studied research findings on gay and lesbian families. Again, these groups are hardly typical. Despite this, Stacey may well have identified those at the forefront of a trend which is spreading to the wider society.

### key terms

*Late modernity* The term used by Giddens to describe the contemporary period, which is characterised by choice and change.
*Postmodernity* The era after modernity which is characterised by fluidity, uncertainty and a lack of consensus.
*Confluent love* Deep emotional intimacy which individuals expect from their partnerships.

### summary

1. Many sociologists see families and households in today's society as more diverse than ever before.

2. In Britain, nuclear family households have declined as a proportion of all households. The proportion of people living in these households has also declined. Despite this, living in a nuclear family is a phase that most people go through.

3. There is diversity within nuclear families – eg, the couple may be married or cohabiting.

4. According to Anthony Giddens, family diversity results from broader changes in late-modern society. In particular, family diversity reflects the growing freedom to choose identities and select lifestyles.

5. According to Judith Stacey, family diversity reflects the lack of consensus, the uncertainty and the fluidity of postmodern society.

# activity31 choice and creativity

'With no script to follow, we are making up our own story and hoping that we'll live happily ever after.'

Amanda Boulter referring to her lesbian partner and their two boys. Quoted in *The Independent*, 4.2.2002.

'I don't necessarily think we should be wanting to mimic everything, kind of anything that heterosexual couples or heterosexual relationships have. I don't see that we need to be mimicking them. I think it's about having choice and about being able to be creative and decide what we want for ourselves.'

From Weeks et al., 1999a

## questions

1  How does Item A reflect Giddens' picture of late modernity?

2  Look at Item B. To what extent are reconstituted families based on choice?

---

# Unit 8  Gender, power and domestic labour

## keyissues

1  To what extent is the division of domestic labour linked to gender?

2  To what extent is this division unequal?

3  What does this indicate about the distribution of power?

4  What changes have taken place in these areas?

## 8.1 Introduction

This unit examines the distribution of power between men and women in the family. It looks at *domestic labour* – work conducted by people as members of a household. It looks, for example, at housework and childcare and asks who does what.

Most of the research in this area focuses on the contribution of husband and wife to domestic tasks. It asks four main questions.

- First, to what extent is the division of domestic labour based on gender? For example, are certain household tasks done by men and others by women?
- Second, is the division of domestic labour equal – do partners pull their own weight, is the division of labour fair?
- Third, what does this indicate about the distribution of

power within the family? Is power shared equally between husband and wife or do men dominate the domestic scene?

- Fourth, what changes have taken place in these areas? For example, is there a move towards a more equal distribution of power?

## 8.2 Gender and the domestic division of labour

In 1973, Michael Young and Peter Willmott announced the arrival of the *symmetrical family* (see page 72). They claimed that *conjugal roles*, the roles of husband and wife, were becoming increasingly similar. In the home, the couple 'shared their work; they shared their time'. Husbands increasingly helped with domestic chores such as washing up and cleaning. They also helped more with raising children, though this still remained the main responsibility of the wife. Decisions about family life were largely shared. It appeared that the division of labour based on gender was breaking down.

In 1974, Ann Oakley dismissed this view of the sharing caring husband. Young and Willmott had claimed that 72% of husbands 'help in the house'. To be included in this figure, husbands only had to perform one household chore a week. In Oakley's words, this is hardly convincing evidence of 'male domestication' (Oakley, 1974). Oakley's own research conducted in the early 1970s shows a clear division of labour along gender lines. Based on interviews with 40 women with one or more children under 5, it shows clearly that wives saw housework and childcare as their responsibility and received little help from their husbands.

Since these early studies, there has been considerable research on gender and the division of domestic labour.

This research shows that most women:

- still become mothers and housewives
- experience a period of full-time housework, though this is becoming shorter
- return to work part time when their youngest child is at school.

# activity32 gender and domestic labour

## Item A  Gender divisions

| Great Britain | Allocation of tasks (percentages) | | | | | |
| --- | --- | --- | --- | --- | --- | --- |
| | 1983 | | | 1991 | | |
| | Mainly man | Mainly woman | Shared equally | Mainly man | Mainly woman | Shared equally |
| Household shopping | 5 | 51 | 44 | 8 | 45 | 47 |
| Makes evening meal | 5 | 77 | 17 | 9 | 70 | 20 |
| Does evening dishes | 17 | 40 | 40 | 28 | 33 | 37 |
| Does household cleaning | 3 | 72 | 24 | 4 | 68 | 27 |
| Does washing and ironing | 1 | 89 | 10 | 3 | 84 | 12 |
| Repairs household equipment | 82 | 6 | 10 | 82 | 6 | 10 |
| Organises household money and bills | 29 | 39 | 32 | 31 | 40 | 28 |
| Looks after sick children | 1 | 63 | 35 | 1 | 60 | 39 |
| Teaches children discipline | 10 | 12 | 77 | 9 | 17 | 73 |

Adapted from *Social Trends*, 1995

## Item B  Lagged adaptation

**Changes in couples' work patterns, 1974/5 to 1987**

Minutes per average day

Husbands Wives (1974/5)  Husbands Wives (1987)

☐ Paid work
■ Unpaid work

Adapted from Gershuny, 1992

## Item C  Household tasks

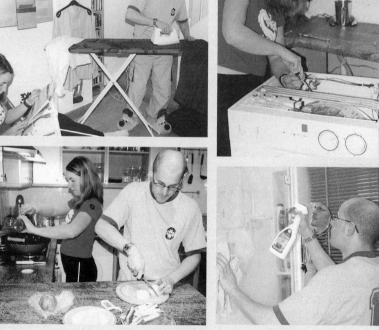

# questions

1  Look at Item A.

a)  To what extent are tasks allocated on the basis of gender?

b)  To what extent did this change from 1983 to 1991?

2  a)  Summarise the changes shown in Item B.

b)  Suggest a reason for these changes.

3  Look at Item C. Judging from Item A, which of these pictures are untypical?

This early period of full-time housework sets the pattern for the future, as the following findings indicate.

- Housework and childcare remain the primary responsibility of women.
- As women enter the labour market in increasing numbers, there is some evidence of men making a greater contribution to domestic tasks.
- However, this increased contribution is not significant. As a result, most working wives have a *dual burden* or a *double shift* – paid employment and domestic labour (Allan & Crow, 2001).

The findings summarised above are taken from small-scale studies often based on interviews, and large-scale surveys usually based on questionnaires. For example, Fiona Devine's small-scale study of car workers' families in Luton indicated that men's contribution to domestic labour increased when their wives re-entered paid employment. But the man's role is secondary – 'Above all women remain responsible for childcare and housework and their husbands help them' (Devine, 1992). This picture is reflected in large-scale surveys such as the British Social Attitudes Survey and the British Household Panel Survey. These surveys show a clear gender division of labour in most household tasks. However, they do indicate a slight trend towards sharing tasks as shown in Activity 32.

Further evidence of a trend towards greater equality in the domestic division of labour is provided by Jonathan Gershuny's (1992) analysis of data from 1974/5 to 1987. It shows a gradual increase in the amount of domestic labour performed by men. This increase is greatest when wives are in full-time employment. From 1974/5 to 1987, husbands whose wives worked full time doubled the amount of time they spent cooking and cleaning.

Gershuny concludes that though women still bear the main burden of domestic labour, there is a gradual trend towards greater equality. He suggests there is a process of *lagged adaptation* – a time lag between women taking up paid employment and men making a greater contribution to domestic labour. At this rate, he reckons it may take a generation or more before men 'catch up' and make an equal contribution.

### Gender and domestic tasks – evaluation

Much of the research into gender divisions of domestic labour is based on *time-use studies*. This research asks who does what and how long does it take them. There are problems with this method.

**Time** Women tend to underestimate time spent on domestic labour. This often happens when several tasks are performed at the same time. For example, women often combine childcare with tasks such as cleaning and preparing meals. As a result, they underestimate the amount of time spent on childcare (Leonard, 2000).

Men tend to overestimate time spent on domestic labour. For example, in one study, men estimated they spent an average of 11.3 hours a week on childcare. However, their diary entries showed only 1.7 hours a week (Pleck, 1985).

**Urgency** Time-use studies say little about the urgency of tasks. Women's domestic tasks, such as cooking and washing clothes, are more urgent than typical male tasks such as gardening and household maintenance (McMahon, 1999).

**Responsibility vs help** There is a big difference between being responsible for a task and helping with a task. For example, being responsible for cooking and cleaning is not the same as helping with those tasks. Being responsible requires more thought and effort, it can be more tiring and more stressful (McMahon, 1999). Again, this aspect of gender divisions and domestic tasks is not revealed by time-use studies.

**Job satisfaction** Time-use studies tell us little about the amount of satisfaction women and men derive from domestic labour. Typical female tasks are often experienced as tedious, boring and monotonous. Typical male tasks are more likely to be experienced as interesting and creative. For example, some men regard DIY and gardening as hobbies rather than chores (Allan, 1985).

## key terms

*Conjugal roles* Marital roles, the roles of husband and wife.
*Symmetrical family* A family in which the roles of husband and wife are similar.
*Dual burden/double shift* The double burden/shift of paid employment and domestic labour.
*Lagged adaptation* A time lag between women taking up paid employment and men adapting to this by increasing their contribution to domestic labour.
*Time-use studies* Studies which examine how people use their time – how long they spend on various activities.

## 8.3 Gender and the division of emotion work

So far domestic labour has been defined as household tasks such as ironing and cooking, and time spent looking after children. Little has been said about the emotional side of domestic labour. Partnerships and families are kept together as much if not more by *emotion work* than by the more practical household tasks. Emotion work refers to the love, sympathy, understanding, praise, reassurance and attention which are involved in maintaining relationships.

According to many women, it is they rather than their male partners who are responsible for most of the emotion work. In other words, emotion work is gendered. A study conducted by Jean Duncombe and Dennis Marsden (1993, 1995) based on interviews with 40 couples found that most women complained of men's 'emotional distance'. They felt they were the ones who provided reassurance, tenderness and sympathy, while their partners had problems expressing intimate emotions. Men showed little awareness or understanding of their 'shortcomings', seeing their main role as a breadwinner – providing money rather than emotional support.

These findings are reflected in other studies. For example, research into family meals shows that women give priority to their partner's and children's tastes, often at the expense of their own. They do their best to make mealtime a happy family occasion (Charles & Kerr, 1988).

According to Duncombe and Marsden (1995), many women have to cope with a *triple shift* – 1) paid work 2) housework and childcare and 3) emotion work.

## key terms

*Emotion work* The emotional support which members of a social group – in this case the family – provide for each other.
*Triple shift* The three areas of responsibility which many women have – 1) paid work, 2) housework and childcare, 3) emotion work.

## 8.4 Family finances

So far, this unit has outlined evidence which indicates that domestic tasks, childcare, and emotion work are divided along gender lines. This section looks at money management within families. It reaches a similar conclusion – access to and control over money are gendered. And this division of labour along gender lines tends to favour men.

**Systems of money management** Jan Pahl's *Money and Marriage* (1989) identified various systems of money management used by the 102 couples in her study. They ranged from a *housekeeping allowance system* whereby the husbands give their wives a fixed sum of money for housekeeping expenses and control the remaining money, to a *pooling system* where both partners see themselves as equally responsible for and jointly controlling money management. A later study by Carolyn Vogler and Jan Pahl (1994), based on interviews with over 1200 British couples, showed that whatever money management system was used, men tended to come out on top.

**Inequalities in money management** Vogler and Pahl report the following results. When asked who gets most personal spending money, 58% of couples said it was equally distributed, 12% said the husband, 4% the wife, and the rest disagreed amongst themselves. When asked who suffers cutbacks when money is tight, it was wives who reported most hardship. They were more likely to cut back on their own food and clothing, and shield their children and husband from hard times. And when asked who has the final say in important financial decisions, 70% say both, 23% the husband and 7% the wife.

**Trends** Vogler and Pahl see a trend towards greater equality in access to and control of family finances. They argue that greater equality depends in part on women's full-time participation in the labour market. There is a large body of research which indicates that the partner with the largest income has the biggest say in family decision-making.

*activity*33 **emotion work**

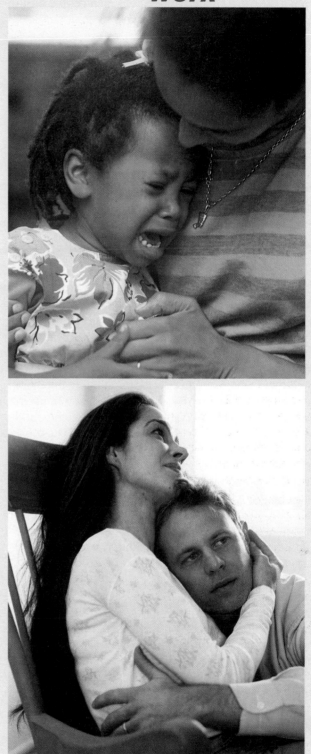

## questions

1 How do the pictures illustrate emotion work?
2 Why do you think women are primarily responsible for emotion work in the family?

# 8.5 Domestic labour, power and gender

Are families *patriarchal* or male dominated? Are women exploited by their male partners? Do men get the best deal in the home? Do they get their own way in domestic situations?

Are these questions still relevant today? Aren't partnerships rapidly moving towards equality? Haven't many already reached the stage where the domestic division of labour is equal?

These questions are about *power*. This section looks at various ways of defining and measuring power and applies them to family life.

## Decision making

The decision-making model measures power in terms of who makes the decisions. For example, if wives made most of the decisions concerning the home then, in this context, they would have most power. However, this fails to take account of the importance of the decisions. For example, the wife may make more decisions but those decisions are minor and trivial. The really important decisions are made by her husband.

The following study uses the decision-making approach and takes the importance of decisions into account. Stephen Edgell (1980) interviewed 38 middle-class couples. He asked them who made the decisions and how important those decisions were. Wives dominated decision making in three areas – interior decoration, children's clothes, and spending on food and other household items. These decisions were frequent and seen as not very important. Men had the main say when it came to moving house, buying a car and other major financial decisions. These decisions were infrequent and seen as important. Other decisions, such as holidays and children's education were made by both husband and wife (see Item A, Activity 34).

Based on decision making and the importance of the areas of decision, it appears that husbands have more power than their wives.

**Evaluation** This study is over 20 years old and is based on a small, unrepresentative sample – 38 middle-class couples. It uses the decision-making approach. There are a number of problems with this approach. For example, it ignores agenda-setting – which issues should be placed on the agenda to be decided upon. The person who sets the agenda may use this power to their own advantage.

## Non-decisions

The decision-making approach fails to take account of non-decisions. Many actions do not involve conscious decisions – as such, they can be seen as 'non-decisions'. They are based on taken-for-granted assumptions – for example, women should take primary responsibility for childcare. Often there is little or no discussion because those involved are simply following social norms which are largely unquestioned.

In terms of domestic labour, there are a number of non-

decisions. The following are traditionally seen as women's work.

- Washing, cleaning, ironing
- Childcare
- Emotion work.

It is often taken for granted that the man's job is more important than his partner's, since she will probably give up paid employment when the couple have children.

**Who benefits?** Those who gain from non-decisions can be seen as more powerful than those who don't. Take the assumption that men's jobs are more important than their female partner's jobs. This assumption lies behind the following behaviour of newly-wed couples.

- Around 1/3 of men changed jobs at or near their wedding. Typically, this change advanced their careers.
- Over 2/3 of women changed jobs at or near their wedding. Typically, this resulted in lower pay and lower job status (Mansfield & Collard, 1988).

Judging by this study, men gain and women lose from the taken-for-granted assumption that men's jobs should take priority over women's jobs. In terms of the consequences of this non-decision, men have more power than women.

At some time in their lives, most women are full-time mothers and housewives. Who benefits from following these traditional social roles? According to many feminist writers, men are the beneficiaries. First, they gain from avoiding the negative aspects of these roles. Second, they directly benefit from much of their partner's domestic labour.

Full-time domestic labour means that the wife is economically dependent on the male breadwinner. This reduces her power in the household. There is a tendency to see housework as low status, as different from 'real' work (Oakley, 1974). Typical women's jobs – washing, ironing and cleaning – are often experienced as boring, monotonous and unfulfilling. And these are the very jobs which directly benefit their partner, providing him with clean clothes and a clean home. Similarly, women's responsibility for emotion work can be seen as an example of 'he gains, she loses'.

Allocating housework and emotion work to women is often based on a non-decision – it is 'normal' and 'natural' for women to perform such tasks therefore there is no decision to make. In terms of this view of power, men gain at the expense of women therefore men have more power than women.

**Evaluation** Choosing winners and losers is based on judgements. What's wrong with being a housewife and a mother? Housework might be boring and monotonous but so are many jobs outside the home. Today, many women have the freedom to choose between a career and becoming a full-time mother and housewife. This is hardly a non-decision. And many women who give up paid employment feel they've gained from the decision (see Activity 34).

There is, however, plenty of evidence to support the view that in general men gain and women lose. Take the triple shift – women combining paid work, domestic labour and emotion work. The clear winner here is the man.

## Shaping desires

Power can be seen as the ability to shape the wishes and desires of others in order to further one's own interests. In this way, a dominant group can persuade others to accept, or actually desire, their subordinate position. In terms of this argument, men have power over women because many women accept and even desire their traditional roles as mothers and housewives, and accept their subordinate status. For example, women often put their partners and children's preferences first when shopping for food. And they usually put 'the family' first when spending on clothes and entertainment (Charles, 1990).

Women get satisfaction from self-sacrifice. Her loved ones gain pleasure from her actions. This confirms her identity as a good mother and wife (Allan & Crow, 2001). The fact that she wants to serve and sacrifice can be seen as an indication of male power.

# activity34 gender, power and domestic labour

**Item A  Making decisions**

| Decision area | Perceived importance | Frequency | Decision maker |
|---|---|---|---|
| Moving | Very important | Infrequent | Husband |
| Finance | Very important | Infrequent | Husband |
| Car | Important | Infrequent | Husband |
| House | Very important | Infrequent | Husband and wife |
| Children's education | Very important | Infrequent | Husband and wife |
| Holidays | Important | Infrequent | Husband and wife |
| Weekends | Not important | Frequent | Husband and wife |
| Other leisure activities | Not important | Frequent | Husband and wife |
| Furniture | Not important | Infrequent | Husband and wife |
| Interior decorations | Not important | Infrequent | Wife |
| Food and other domestic spending | Not important | Frequent | Wife |
| Children's clothes | Not important | Frequent | Wife |

Adapted from Edgell, 1980

**Item B  Satisfaction**

Many women appear to be satisfied with the domestic division of labour. They recognise that they do most of the work, but only 14% said they were dissatisfied with their partner's contribution.

Adapted from Baxter & Western, 1998

**Item C  Choice**

In recent years, there has been a string of newspaper articles about successful and powerful career women who gave up highly-paid jobs in order to take care of their children. They include:

- Lisa Gordon, corporate affairs director of Chrysalis Records who earned £336,000 a year.
- Penny Hughes, formerly in charge of Coca-Cola UK, who gave up £250,000 a year.
- Tina Gaudoin, former editor of the glossy women's magazine Frank.

Adapted from Weale, 2002

**Item D  The triple shift**

# questions

1  Judging from Item A, who has most power – husbands or wives? Give reasons for your answer.

2  a)  Use Items B, C and D to argue that men have more power than women.

   b)  Using the same information, criticise this view.

**Evaluation** This view of power is based on the assumption that it is not in women's interests to accept or desire their traditional roles as housewife and mother. Any pleasure they experience from their 'subordination' is 'false pleasure' because it disguises their exploitation and makes it more bearable.

But who is to say that women in the family are exploited and oppressed? As noted earlier, it's a matter of weighing the evidence and making a judgement.

## Power and same-sex households

So far, this section has looked at the distribution of power in heterosexual families – families in which the partners are male and female. The focus now moves to power in same-sex families where both partners are either male or female.

**Equality as an ideal** Most studies of gay and lesbian partnerships are based on interviews. Bearing in mind that people don't always do what they say, this is what the interviews reveal. Same-sex couples emphasise equality and strive to remove power differences from their relationship. They see issues like the division of domestic labour as a matter for discussion and negotiation. They feel that being lesbian or gay offers more opportunities for equality. As one woman put it, 'It's much easier to have equal relations if you're the same sex' (Weeks et al., 1999a).

Women focus on alternatives to the unequal division of domestic labour which they see in heterosexual relationships. Men focus on alternatives to the macho male and the passive female which they see in heterosexual relationships. In both cases the emphasis is on equality (Weeks et al., 1992a).

**Lesbian households** A study of 37 cohabiting lesbian couples by Gillian Dunne (1997) indicates how far these ideals are translated into reality. Some of the couples have children, and in most cases childcare was shared. Similarly, time spent on housework tended to be shared equally. However, when one partner was in full-time employment, she did less housework than her partner in part-time work.

**Explanations** Why are same-sex relationships more equal than heterosexual relationships? Gillian Dunne (1997) suggests the following reasons.

- Gender inequalities in the labour market shape gender inequalities in partnerships. Men generally have jobs with higher status and pay than their partners and this tends to shape their relationships at home.
- Gay and lesbian partnerships are free from the social norms and conventions which surround and direct heterosexual relationships. They are not weighed down by this cultural baggage. As a result, they have more freedom to construct 'families of choice' (see pages 109-110).

## key terms

**Decision-making approach** A method for measuring power in terms of who makes the decisions.
**Agenda-setting** Deciding which issues will be placed on the agenda to be decided upon.
**Non-decisions** Issues which never reach the point of decision making.

## summary

1. The division of domestic labour is gendered – household tasks are divided along gender lines.

2. Housework and childcare remain the primary responsibility of women.

3. There is evidence of a gradual increase in men's contribution to domestic labour, especially where their partners are in full-time employment.

4. There are problems with time-use studies of domestic labour. For example, women tend to underestimate and men to overestimate time spent on household tasks.

5. Emotion work is mainly performed by women. As a result, many women have a triple shift – 1) paid work, 2) housework and childcare, 3) emotion work.

6. Research into money management within families indicates that control over money is gendered – men tend to have greater control.

7. There is evidence of a trend to greater equality in access to and control of family finances, especially where women are in full-time employment.

8. Research indicates that power is unequally distributed in families, with male partners having the largest share.

9. Decision-making studies indicate that in general husbands have more power than their wives.

10. Non-decisions – issues that do not reach the point of decision-making – tend to favour men. They are likely to gain at the expense of their partners.

11. There is a tendency for many women to accept their subordinate position. From this, it can be argued that men have power over women.

12. Studies of lesbian and gay households suggest that there is a more equal division of domestic labour between partners.

# *activity*35 *same-sex relationships*

## Item A **Talking about relationships**

'Everything has to be discussed, everything is negotiable.'

'There are no assumptions about how you will relate, what you will do, who does what.'

Lesbian women quoted in Weeks et al., 1999a

## *question*

With some reference to Items A and B, suggest why the domestic division of labour in lesbian families may be more equal than in heterosexual families.

## Item B **Partners and mothers**

*Lesbian couple sharing childcare*

# Unit 9 *Childhood and children*

## *keyissues*

1 How have views of childhood changed?
2 How have children been affected by these changes?

## The social construction of childhood

Childhood can be seen as a *social construction*. From this point of view, it is not a natural state or a biological stage. Instead, it is shaped and given meaning by culture and society. As a result, the idea of childhood, the types of behaviour considered appropriate for children, the way children should be treated, and the length of time that childhood should last, are socially constructed.

**Cross-cultural evidence** Evidence from different cultures provides support for the view that childhood is a social construction. If childhood were simply a 'natural' state, then it would be similar across all cultures. This is not the case.

Anthropological studies show that other cultures treat children in ways which might seem unusual or even unnatural in contemporary Britain. Raymond Firth (1963), in his study of the Pacific island of Tikopia, found that children carried out dangerous tasks such as using sharp tools and fishing in the open sea. They were allowed to carry out these tasks when they themselves felt ready rather than when adults decided they were competent or safe to do so.

## A brief history of childhood

In *Centuries of Childhood* (1962), the French historian Philippe Ariès argued that the concept of childhood did not exist in medieval Europe. He based his argument on contemporary letters, diaries and other documents, plus the way children were depicted in paintings of the time. Ariès claimed that soon after children were weaned, they were regarded as little adults and treated as such. From an early age, they worked alongside adults in the fields or in cottage industries, they dressed like adults and in many ways behaved like adults.

**The emergence of modern childhood** Ariès sees the modern concept of childhood developing from the separation of children from the world of adults. This process began in the 16th century when the upper classes sent their children to schools to be educated. In the early years of the industrial revolution, child labour was widespread – children and adults worked side by side. Throughout the 19th century, a series of factory acts banned the employment of children in mines and factories. By the end of the 19th century, elementary state education was compulsory in most European countries. Children were now physically separated from adult settings and had a separate legal status.

This process was accompanied by the development of experts specialising in children – child psychologists, paediatricians (doctors who specialise in children), educationalists and parenting experts. According to Ariès, 'Our world is obsessed by the physical, moral and sexual problems of childhood'. Children are seen as different from adults. As a result, they have special needs. Because of this they require treatment, training and guidance from an army of specially trained adults. This is very different from the

Middle Ages when 'the child became the natural companion of the adult'.

**Evaluation** Ariès has been criticised for overstating his case. In certain respects, children in medieval Europe were seen as different from adults. For example, there were laws prohibiting the marriage of children under 12 (Bukatko & Daehler, 2001). However, many historians agree with the broad outline of Ariès's history of childhood in Western Europe.

### key term

**Social construction** Something that is created by society, constructed from social meanings and definitions.

### Images of childhood

Wendy Stainton Rogers (2001) looks at the social construction of childhood in 20th century Europe. She identifies two 'images' of childhood – 'the innocent and wholesome child' and 'the wicked and sinful child'. Both images coexist – they exist together. Both have a long history and continue to the present day. They can be seen in a variety of forms – for example, in novels such as Arthur Ransome's *Swallows and Amazons* with its charming and wholesome children and William Golding's *Lord of the Flies* where children descend to their 'natural' savage and barbaric selves.

Each image suggests a particular way of acting towards children. The image of the innocent and wholesome child

## activity36 childhood across cultures

**Item A** *Child soldier*

*A member of a local militia in Zaire*

**Item B** *Blackfoot boys*

The Blackfoot Indians lived on the Plains of Western Canada. Children were taught the skills of horse riding at an early age. One of Long Lance's earliest recollections was falling off a horse. He was picked up by his eldest brother and planted firmly on the horse's back. His brother said, 'Now, you stay there! You are four years old, and if you cannot ride a horse, we will put girls' clothing on you and let you grow up a woman.'

Fathers were responsible for the physical training of the Blackfoot boys. They wanted to harden their bodies and make them brave and strong. Fathers used to whip their sons each morning with fir branches. Far from disliking this treatment, the youngsters proudly displayed the welts produced by whipping. Sometimes they were whipped in public and they competed to see who could stand the most pain.

Adapted from Long Lance, 1956

### question

How do Items A and B indicate that childhood is socially constructed?

# activity37 little adults

### Item A  Medieval Europe

In medieval society the idea of childhood did not exist. This is not to suggest that children were neglected, forsaken or despised. The idea of childhood is not to be confused with affection for children: it corresponds to an awareness of the particular nature of childhood, that particular nature which distinguishes the child from the adult, even the young adult. In medieval society, this awareness was lacking. That is why, as soon as the child could live without the constant solicitude (care) of his mother, his nanny or his cradle-rocker, he belonged to adult society.

Adapted from Ariès, 1962

### Item B  Paintings

Family saying grace before a meal (1585)

### question

What evidence do the paintings in Item B provide to support Ariès' statement in Item A?

Group of doctors (right) and men, women and children (left), 15th century

suggests that children should be protected from everything that is nasty about the adult world, from violence and from the worries and concerns of adults. Childhood should be a happy, joyous and carefree time. By contrast, the idea of an essentially sinful child suggests that children should be restrained, regulated and disciplined.

Both these views of childhood imply that adults should be concerned about children and take responsibility for their upbringing.

**The welfare view** The first view suggests that children are vulnerable and need protection. This 'welfare view' forms the basis of social policy towards children in the UK today. For example, the Children Act of 1989 states that 'When a court determines any question with respect to the upbringing of a child … the child's welfare shall be the court's paramount consideration'.

**The control view** The second view assumes that children are unable to control their anti-social tendencies. As a

result, they need regulation and discipline. This 'control view' is reflected in education policy – children must submit to education and the form and content of their education must be strictly controlled from above.

According to Wendy Stainton Rogers, these images of childhood are social constructions. She argues that 'there is no *natural* distinction that marks off children as a certain category of person'. Seeing children as innocent and wholesome or wicked and sinful or a mixture of both is not right or wrong, it is simply a meaning given to childhood at a particular time and place (Stainton Rogers, 2001).

### Childhood in an age of uncertainty

Nick Lee (2001) sees a change in the social construction of childhood towards the end of the 20th century. He claims that for most of the century adults and children were seen as 'fundamentally different kinds of humans'. Adults were stable and complete, children were unstable and incomplete. Adults had become, children were becoming. Adults were self-controlling, children were in need of control.

In the early 21st century, 'growing up' is no longer seen as a journey towards personal completion and stability. This is because adulthood is no longer complete and stable. Adult relationships are increasingly unstable as indicated by high divorce rates. The labour market is changing rapidly and 'jobs for life' are a thing of the past. With new partners and new jobs, adults are in a constant state of becoming. They are living in an 'age of uncertainty'.

Where does this leave children? For much of the 20th century, childhood was defined in relation to adulthood. Adults and children were very different. Children had yet to become full human beings. They were not fully rational, they were not seen as 'persons in their own right', they had to be guided along the path to adulthood by child experts and child trainers such as teachers and social workers.

By the 21st century, adults were becoming more like children. Both were in a continual state of becoming, both were defining and redefining their identities, both were unstable and incomplete.

This growing similarity between adults and children is leading to a new social construction of childhood. Children are seen increasingly as 'beings in their own right'. As such, they have their own concerns, their own interests, and should have their own rights, just like adult members of society. This is reflected in the UN Convention on the Rights of the Child (1989). Article 3 states:

> 'In all actions concerning children, whether undertaken by public or private social welfare institutions, courts of law, administrative authorities or legislative bodies, the best interests of the child shall be a primary consideration.'

Changes in the social construction of childhood result in changes in the way adults treat children. This can be seen from the 1989 Children Act which stated that in court proceedings, 'the child's welfare must be paramount'. In cases of divorce, the court used to decide which parent had custody of the children. Since 1989, the child's view is taken into account – children have a say in decisions about who they will live with. This is a long way from the traditional view that children should be seen and not heard.

### The end of childhood?

Will the 21st century see the end of childhood? Will new social constructions end up abolishing the whole idea of childhood?

According to Neil Postman (1983) in *The Disappearance of Childhood*, this process is well underway. Postman argues that childhood is only possible if children can be separated, and therefore protected from, the adult world. In his words, 'Without secrets, of course, there can be no such thing as childhood'. The mass media, and television in particular, have brought the adult world into the lives of children. Secrecy has been wiped out by television. As a

## *activity38 ambiguities of childhood*

### Item A  'Pester-power'

Children can influence what adults buy through 'pester-power'. In the UK, the take-up of satellite and cable television, video, camcorders and home computers is much higher in households with children: 35% of households with children now subscribe to cable or satellite television, for example, as compared with 25% overall; while 90% of households with children have access to a video cassette recorder as compared with 75% overall.

Adapted from Buckingham, 2000

### Item B  Young and sophisticated

Aged 11

### question

Why is childhood in the 21st century seen as 'ambiguous'? Make some reference to Items A and B in your answer.

result, the boundaries between the worlds of children and adults are breaking down. Postman believes that in the long run, this means the end of childhood.

**Dual status** Postman has been criticised for overstating his case. Clearly television and the media in general have brought adult priorities and concerns into the lives of children. But childhood is a long way from disappearing. For example, children in late 20th century Western societies have become a major economic force. Their tastes and preferences, not just in toys and games, but also in information and communication technologies such as personal computers and mobile phones, have a major effect on what is produced and purchased (Buckingham, 2000).

According to Nick Lee (2001), childhood has not disappeared, it has become more complex and ambiguous. Children are dependent on their parents, but in another sense they are independent. There is a mass children's market which children influence – they make choices, they decide which products succeed and fail, though at the end of the day, they depend on their parents' purchasing power.

This is one of the ambiguities of childhood in the 21st century. Things are not clearcut. Children are both dependent and independent.

## summary

1. Many sociologists see childhood as a social construction rather than a natural state. Ideas about childhood vary between different societies and different times.

2. According to Philippe Ariès,
   - The concept of childhood did not exist in medieval Europe. Children were seen as little adults.
   - Modern ideas of childhood as a separate state began with the onset of formal education and the gradual withdrawal of children from the workplace.

3. Wendy Stainton Rogers identifies two images of childhood in modern Western society – 'the innocent and wholesome child' and 'the wicked and sinful child'. The first image suggests that children are vulnerable and need protection – the welfare view. The second image suggests children need regulation and discipline – the control view.

4. According to Nick Lee, adulthood has become less stable and more uncertain. In these respects, it has become more like childhood. This similarity has led to a change in the social construction of childhood in the 21st century. Children are increasingly seen as having their own rights and interests.

5. Neil Postman argues that the media is breaking down the boundaries between the worlds of children and adults, leading to the 'disappearance of childhood'.

6. Postman has been criticised for overstating his case. Childhood is a long way from disappearing. For example, children remain a distinct group – they are a major force in the market place. And they remain dependent on their parents.

# Unit 10 *The dark side of family life*

## keyissues

1. What are the harmful effects of family life?
2. How have they been explained?

Until the 1960s, the sociology of the family was dominated by the functionalist perspective which focused on the positive side of family life (see pages 76-77). The family was seen as beneficial to individuals – providing them with 'a haven from a heartless world' – and as functional for society – ensuring that children were socialised into well-adjusted adults.

This rosy view of the family was challenged from the 1960s onwards. There was a growing awareness of problems in family life – for example, domestic violence and child abuse. As a result, both sociologists and policy makers became increasingly aware of the *dark side of family life*.

## 10.1 The psychology of family life

### R.D. Laing

In the 1960s, a number of psychiatrists (people who treat mental disorders), focused on the harmful effects of family life. For example, the British psychiatrist R.D. Laing (1976) argued that many so-called 'mental illnesses' are normal responses to the pressures of family life. For example, he claimed that mental disorders such as schizophrenia can be seen as reasonable and rational responses to destructive family relationships. An example of Laing's approach is given in Activity 39.

**Evaluation** Many psychiatrists have rejected Laing's views, arguing that there is a lot more to the causes of mental disorders than family relationships. Others argue that Laing has overstated his case, but agree that the family can play a major part in the development of certain mental disorders.

# activity39 Jane and her family

Jane has been diagnosed as schizophrenic. She lives in her own little dreamworld which consists of a game of tennis. It is a mixed doubles and she is the ball.

Most of the time Jane sits motionless and silent. The adults in her family are in a state of conflict – her father and his mother against her mother and her mother's father. The two halves of the family communicate only through Jane – she is the go-between.

Eventually, the strain becomes too much for Jane and she escapes into her dreamworld. However, even here she cannot escape from the clutches of her family.

Adapted from Laing, 1976

## question

How can Jane's 'disorder' be seen as a response to relationships in her family?

## Oliver James

In a book entitled *They F*** You Up : How To Survive Family Life*, Oliver James (2003) claims that many of the problems we experience in adult life can be traced to our infant years. If we lack confidence, if we are over-competitive, if we are constantly jealous of other people, then those problems are largely due to the type of care provided by our parents during infancy.

James's approach is illustrated by his views on relationships. Relationship problems in later life tend to result from *unempathic care* during infancy and disturbed relationships with parents as children grow older. Unempathic care means ignoring or misunderstanding infants' needs – for example, not feeding them when they're hungry or forcing food on them when they're not hungry. This can create fears of abandonment or rejection which can lead to feelings of insecurity and mistrust. This, in turn, can lead to relationship problems in adult life.

These problems can cross generations. Parents who divorce are more likely to have received unempathic care as infants. And the children of divorced parents are more likely to divorce themselves. They are also more likely to experience depression in later life.

**Evaluation** Although there is evidence to support James's

views, many researchers would object to the priority he gives to parental care during infancy. For example, sociologists would point to influences such as peer groups, gender and social class when explaining adult behaviour.

## 10.2 Domestic violence

### Definitions

*Domestic violence* is any form of violence which takes place in the home. However, the term is often used to refer to *partnership violence*, that is violence between partners who live together as a married or cohabiting couple. It will be used in this way in this section.

Domestic violence is not easy to define. Should it include both actual violence and the threat of violence? Should a distinction be made between violence which is intended to injure and violence used in self-defence? As this section will show, these are important questions.

### Measuring domestic violence

Drawing on a variety of sources, Elizabeth Stanko (2003) provides the following estimate of the extent of domestic violence in the UK.

- One in four women and one in seven men report a physical assault by a partner during their lifetime.
- Around 10% of women experience domestic violence in any given year.
- The form of violence is largely male offenders against female victims.

## Men, women and domestic violence

An understanding of domestic violence requires information about the severity, the meaning and the effects of violent acts. James Nazroo (1999) attempted to discover this information in a small-scale study of couples. Members of each couple were interviewed separately. The results are as follows.

**Levels of violence** Men's violence is far more likely to result in physical injury. Only 1% of men had been severely injured by their partner compared to 10% of women.

Men often seemed intent on harming their partner – for example, by repeatedly kicking and punching her or banging her head against the wall.

Women rarely seemed intent on causing harm. When they did, it was usually in self-defence after years of physical abuse. Even then, they stopped when they gained the upper hand, unlike many violent males.

**Threat and intimidation** Men's violence is far more likely to be experienced as threatening and intimidating. Many women were terrified by their partner's attacks.

Most men were able to defend themselves quite easily by holding their partner off, pushing her away, or simply by shouting at her. They often laughed at her 'attacks'. Men were unlikely to experience fear or feel threatened.

**Psychological consequences** Women who have experienced domestic violence often have anxiety symptoms. Men do not. This suggests that domestic violence is experienced differently by women and men.

**Conclusion** James Nazroo's research suggests that domestic violence has different meanings and different consequences for women and men. This is important both for explaining domestic violence and for developing policies to deal with domestic violence.

## Explaining domestic violence

**Psychological theories** These theories suggest that men who abuse their partners are suffering from some kind of psychological disorder. A long list of possible disorders has been compiled. Suggestions range from organic or biochemical brain abnormalities, to insecure childhoods, to uncontrollable anger due to family conflicts during childhood and adolescence. These problems are seen to express themselves in domestic violence (Mullender, 1996).

Sociologists have criticised psychological theories for the following reasons.

- Domestic violence is widespread. It is not limited to a minority who are psychologically disturbed.

- Psychological theories tend to ignore the wider society and its values – for example, they ignore the possibility that we live in a patriarchal society in which men seek to dominate women.

**Dysfunctional partnerships** Explanations based on the idea of *dysfunctional partnerships* state that the couple don't get on, that they rub each other up the wrong way, that they are basically incompatible. This leads to stress in the relationship which results in occasional outbursts of violence (Sclater, 2001).

Supporters of this view claim that there are two distinct forms of domestic violence. The first, *common couple violence* involves:

- Occasional outbursts rather than systematic, ongoing violence
- Violence of both genders – of men and women
- Violent rows rather than a deliberate attempt to dominate.

This type of domestic violence is seen to result from dysfunctional partnerships.

The second type of domestic violence, *patriarchal terrorism*, is systematic and ongoing rather than occasional, is conducted by men against women and is designed to dominate (Johnson, 1995).

**Male domination** A number of researchers see domestic violence as a form of social control – in this case, the control of women by men. And like all forms of social control, it is based on force and the threat of force.

Feminists, in particular, see domestic violence as an expression of patriarchy – of a society in which women are controlled and subordinated for the benefit of men. From this point of view, men use patriarchal terrorism to dominate women.

As outlined above, there is evidence to support this point of view. Nazroo's research and a number of other studies document example after example of male violence, of women living under threat and intimidation, of men seeking to harm and causing serious injury to their wives and partners.

## Victims' response

Researchers have outlined the following responses to domestic violence.

**Keep it hidden** Women often attempt to hide the violence they have suffered. This is due to shame and embarrassment and/or fear that their partner will become even more violent if his behaviour becomes public. However, some will confide in a relative or close friend.

**Blame themselves** Many women blame themselves for the violence they suffer. This is partly due to a lack of confidence that results from the humiliation of physical and verbal abuse. And it is partly due to a sense of failure – women are seen as primarily responsible for family care. Domestic violence suggests they have failed in this area (Allan & Crow, 2001).

**Social isolation** Women feel socially isolated, they feel alone with nobody to turn to. The key to this isolation is fear – they fear their partner's response if they turn to others for help.

**Economic dependency** Many women stay with their partners and live with domestic violence because they feel they have no alternative. They may lose their home and their means of support, especially if they have young children. They feel imprisoned in the family.

**Seeking help** Some victims of domestic violence seek help – from charities set up to aid them, from social services, from friends and relatives and from the police. Sources of help are examined in the next section.

## Dealing with domestic violence

**The police** The police have been accused of seeing domestic violence as less serious than other forms of violence, of giving 'domestics' low priority and regarding them as something the couple should sort out for

themselves. In 1987, the Metropolitan Police responded to this criticism by issuing new guidelines and informing all officers that 'an assault which occurs within the home is as much a criminal act as one which may occur in the street'. Most police services have now established Domestic Violence Units specialising in domestic violence (Mullender, 1996).

Despite these initiatives, only a minority of victims turn to the police for help. The British Crime Survey, based on a large national sample, asks people what crimes they have experienced during the last year. The 2001 survey found that only one in three victims of domestic violence reported the incident to the police. A desire for privacy was the main reason given for non-reporting (BCS, 2003).

Even when women do report incidents to the police, only a small minority agree to prosecute their partners.

**Government policy** Over the past 20 years, governments have become increasingly aware of the problem of domestic violence. In 1995, the Labour Party's Peace at

# *activity* 40 *domestic violence*

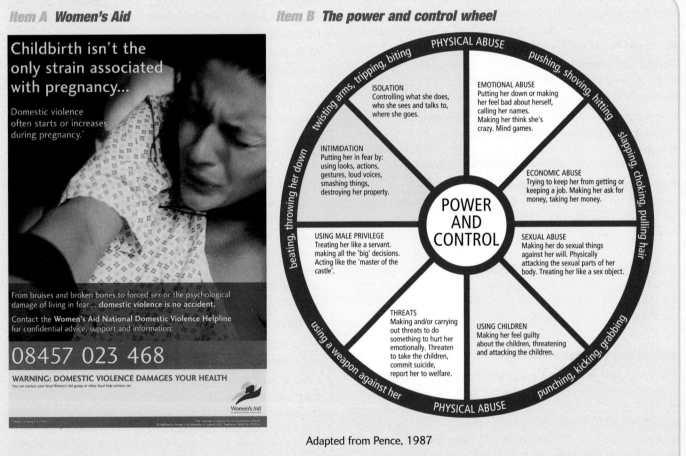

**Item A** *Women's Aid*

Childbirth isn't the only strain associated with pregnancy...

Domestic violence often starts or increases during pregnancy.'

From bruises and broken bones to forced sex or the psychological damage of living in fear ... **domestic violence is no accident.**

Contact the **Women's Aid National Domestic Violence Helpline** for confidential advice, support and information:

## 08457 023 468

**WARNING: DOMESTIC VIOLENCE DAMAGES YOUR HEALTH**
You can contact your local Women's Aid group or other local help services on:

Women's Aid

**Item B** *The power and control wheel*

**PHYSICAL ABUSE**

twisting arms, tripping, biting / pushing, shoving, hitting / slapping, choking, pulling hair / punching, kicking, grabbing / using a weapon against her / beating, throwing her down

**POWER AND CONTROL**

**ISOLATION** Controlling what she does, who she sees and talks to, where she goes.

**EMOTIONAL ABUSE** Putting her down or making her feel bad about herself, calling her names. Making her think she's crazy. Mind games.

**INTIMIDATION** Putting her in fear by: using looks, actions, gestures, loud voices, smashing things, destroying her property.

**ECONOMIC ABUSE** Trying to keep her from getting or keeping a job. Making her ask for money, taking her money.

**USING MALE PRIVILEGE** Treating her like a servant. making all the 'big' decisions. Acting like the 'master of the castle'.

**SEXUAL ABUSE** Making her do sexual things against her will. Physically attacking the sexual parts of her body. Treating her like a sex object.

**THREATS** Making and/or carrying out threats to do something to hurt her emotionally. Threaten to take the children, commit suicide, report her to welfare.

**USING CHILDREN** Making her feel guilty about the children, threatening and attacking the children.

**PHYSICAL ABUSE**

Adapted from Pence, 1987

## *questions*

1 Look at Item A. Why are organisations such as Women's Aid so important?

2 a) There's more to domestic violence than physical abuse. Discuss with reference to Item B.

b) How does Item B provide a summary of patriarchal terrorism?

Home initiative put forward a national strategy on domestic violence which included better funding for refuges for 'battered women', housing provision, more effective policing and improved public education.

In June 2003, the Labour Party's White Paper on domestic violence announced that there will be better coordination between agencies such as the police, the courts, social services and the NHS in order to protect victims. One possibility raised to improve the prosecution and conviction rates of violent partners is the granting of anonymity to victims in court (*Observer*, 15 June 2003).

**Aid organisations** These are charitable organisations set up to help the victims of domestic violence. The two main charities are Women's Aid and Refuge.

Women's Aid offers 'support and a place of safety to abused women and children by providing refuges and other services'. In 2000, 54,000 women and children stayed in their refuges and over 35,000 people called their National Domestic Violence Helpline (Women's Aid, 2001).

Refuges have a vital function. According to Dobash and Dobash (1992), they provide women with 'safety, an end to isolation, companionship, solidarity, independence and mutual assistance'. And they help women regain their self-respect.

Aid organisations also put pressure on governments to improve their policies on domestic violence. Sandra Horley is chief executive of Refuge. Here is an extract from her

## key terms

**The dark side of family life** Damaging aspects of family life often hidden from view.
**Domestic violence** Any form of violence which occurs in the home. Often used to refer to partnership violence.
**Partnership violence** Violence between partners who live together as a married or cohabiting couple.
**Dysfunctional partnership** A partnership in which the couple are incompatible – they don't get on.
**Common couple violence** Occasional outbursts of domestic violence.
**Patriarchal terrorism** Systematic and ongoing violence in which men seek to dominate and control women.

criticism of government policy published in *The Guardian*, (March 12, 2001).

'To date the response to domestic violence has been piecemeal and patchy. The key element to achieving a consistent approach is funding. Domestic violence is an issue which has been woefully under-funded for decades and there is still a reliance on the voluntary sector to provide vital, life-saving services.'

## 10.3 Child abuse

### Definitions

*Child abuse* is the abuse of young people under the age of 16.

# activity41 culture and child abuse

*Azande boys from Sudan in Africa during their initiation ceremony. They are pictured here in the circumcision camp.*

What counts as child abuse varies from culture to culture. And as cultures change, so do definitions of child abuse. For example, some small-scale, traditional societies mark the passage from adolescence to adulthood with initiation ceremonies. These ceremonies sometimes include beatings, genital operations and depriving the young person of food and sleep. In the West today, such practices would probably be seen as child abuse.

However, the reverse is sometimes true. In some societies, Western practices such as isolating infants and small children in rooms or beds of their own and feeding them at specific times, rather than when they're hungry, may well be seen as child abuse.

Adapted from Korbin, 1981

## questions

1 Child abuse is culturally defined. Briefly explain this statement.

2 Suggest ways in which views of child abuse in the UK might change in years to come.

**Table 11  Children on child protection registers**

| Category Of abuse | 1978 | 1984 | 1986 | 1988 | 1991 | 1995 | 1999 |
|---|---|---|---|---|---|---|---|
| Physical abuse | 7,944 | 7,856 | 10,422 | 11,100 | 9,000 | 12,300 | 6,500 |
| Physical neglect | 289 | 933 | 1,888 | 4,900 | 5,600 | 9,200 | 11,100 |
| Sexual abuse | 89 | 1.088 | 5,922 | 5,800 | 5,600 | 7,200 | 4,800 |
| Emotional abuse | 0 | 200 | 455 | 1,700 | 2,600 | 3,800 | 5,400 |
| Grave concern | 3,522 | 2,312 | 5,133 | 14,400 | 21,100 | ------ | ------ |
| Total | 11,844 | 12,389 | 23,820 | 39,200 | 45,200 | 35,000 | 31,900 |

Adapted from Corby, 2000

The Department of Health (2000) identifies four main forms of abuse – physical, physical neglect, sexual and emotional.

**Physical abuse** This is deliberately causing physical harm to a child. It must be fairly serious – a minor bruise wouldn't count.

**Physical neglect** This refers to neglect which is likely to result in serious damage to the child's health and development. Examples include failure to provide adequate clothing or access to medical treatment.

**Sexual abuse** This involves forcing or enticing the child to take part in sexual activities. It need not involve physical contact. An adult encouraging a child to view pornographic material would count as sexual abuse.

**Emotional abuse** This involves harming the child's emotional development – for example, making the child feel worthless and inadequate.

Table 11 shows a sharp reduction in the number of children registered after 1991, mainly because of the ending of the 'grave concern' category. Emotional abuse did not officially exist in 1978. Since its introduction, the numbers registered as emotionally abused have steadily increased. Cases of abuse are reported by the public, police, social workers, teachers and others. These cases are then investigated by social workers who decide whether or not to place children on the child protection register. There are two main problems with the figures.

- First, they seriously underestimate the extent of child abuse. Surveys suggest that most cases go unreported.
- Second, they reflect the concerns and priorities of governments, local authorities and the public. For example, in 1978 little was known about sexual abuse – it was not a matter for official or public concern. By the mid-1980s, priorities had changed and registrations for sexual abuse rose dramatically. The figures in Table 11 probably say more about changes in child protection concerns than the actual extent of child abuse (Corby, 2000).

**Survey research** There are no large-scale studies of the extent of physical abuse in the UK. There are some studies of physical punishment of children. For example, Newson and Newson (1989) in a longitudinal study (a study over time) of 700 families in Nottingham, found that 41% of seven-year-old children were smacked at least once a week and 22% of mothers used a variety of implements including straps, canes and slippers. However, this says little or nothing about actual physical abuse as defined by the Department of Health.

Table 12 shows the results of a survey of sexual abuse in Britain. The study was based on a representative sample of 2019 adults. The researchers used a fairly broad definition of sexual abuse – it 'might involve intercourse, touching, exposure of the sexual organs, showing pornographic material or talking about sexual things in an erotic way' (Baker & Duncan, 1985). Of those questioned, 105 said they had been sexually abused. Their experiences are shown in Table 12.

**Table 12  Sexually abused children**

| Type of abuse | % of those abused |
|---|---|
| Abuse by a stranger | 51 |
| Abuse by a known person | 49 |
| Abuse by a family member | 14 |
| Non-contact abuse | 51 |
| Contact abuse not involving intercourse | 44 |
| Abuse involving intercourse | 5 |
| One incident involving one person | 63 |
| Repeated abuse | 23 |
| Multiple abuse | 14 |

Adapted from Baker & Duncan, 1985

Figures vary considerably depending on the definition of sexual abuse. For example, one study using a very broad definition found that 59% of female students and 27% of male students at colleges of further education reported at least one experience of sexual abuse as children (Kelly et al., 1991).

## Who abuses?

This section looks at some of the attempts to identify the typical gender, social position and family situation of those who abuse children.

**Gender** An analysis of abuses reported to the NSPCC from 1983 to 1987 found that in cases of physical abuse, fathers were involved in 61% of cases, mothers in 36%. Mothers were more likely to be involved in neglect and emotional abuse (Creighton & Noyes, 1989).

Males were much more likely than females to be involved in sexual abuse. In a study of sexually abused children referred to Great Ormond Street Hospital between 1980 and 1986, only 8 out of 411 (2%) had been abused by females (Ben-Tovin et al., 1988).

**Poverty** People who physically abuse children appear to be concentrated in low-income groups. Statistics from the Department of Health (1995) show that 95% of children on child protection registers are from families living in poverty.

Is there really a link between child abuse and poverty? Or, is abuse in low income groups more likely to be spotted since these groups have greater contact with local authority officials, such as social workers? Or, do these officials picture people living in poverty as more likely to abuse children? (Corby, 2000).

Survey data indicates that sexual abuse is spread fairly evenly throughout all social classes. However, *reported* cases tend to come from low-income groups. For example, in the Great Ormond Street study, 92% of the sexual abuse cases came from manual working-class backgrounds. Again, this may reflect contact with care professionals.

**Family structure** Official statistics and survey data suggest that children from lone-parent families are more at risk of all forms of abuse than those from two-parent families. This may have nothing to do with lone-parents as such. Lone-parent families are more likely to live in poverty, and more likely to be in regular contact with care professionals.

Children living in reconstituted families are also more at risk of all forms of abuse than those from two-parent families. Again, this may have nothing to do with reconstituted families as such.

## Explaining child abuse

This section looks at the main theories which claim to explain child abuse.

**Psychological theories** These theories assume that child abuse is due to the psychological defects or inadequacies of the abuser. A whole catalogue of psychological problems have been linked to parents who abuse their children. They include chronic depression, extreme guilt, inability to control impulses, excessive anxiety, extreme aggression and rigid, cold and detached personalities (Elliot, 1996).

Some psychologists look for the origin of abuse in family relationships. The family is seen as disturbed, family relationships are destructive, and this leads to child abuse.

Criticisms of psychological explanations include the following.

● They are often based on very small samples.

● The personality characteristics attributed to abusers are sometimes contradictory.

● Since child abuse is widespread it cannot be explained in terms of abnormal personality characteristics.

**Sociological explanations** These theories look for explanations of child abuse in society rather than the individual. For example, one theory states that poverty creates a sense of frustration which leads to aggression. This makes those in low-income groups more prone to child abuse. However, as noted earlier, the apparent link between poverty and abuse may be due to the increased presence of care professionals, their views of likely abusers, and a tendency to see working-class families as more prone to abuse than middle-class families.

**Feminist explanations** These are also sociological explanations – they look for the cause of child abuse in society. Feminists start from the position that child sexual abuse is overwhelmingly committed by males. They see men's sexual and physical abuse as a result of a patriarchal society based on male dominance. Child abuse is seen as an extreme form of male sexual aggression. Physical abuse of children reflects a system of male domination based ultimately on force and on a culture which defines aggression as a valued male characteristic.

Feminists have often been criticised for failing to explain physical abuse and neglect by women. Some have responded by seeing female abuse as a response to the stresses created by the mother role. In a patriarchal society, women are defined as having the prime responsibility for childcare. Often they receive little support from men (Corby, 2000).

## The effects of child abuse

**Physical abuse and neglect** There is evidence that physical abuse and neglect can have serious effects on children's emotional, intellectual and social development. Abused children often lack self-esteem, they are fearful and wary of other people and withdrawn. Sometimes they act aggressively as a result of their experience (Corby, 2000).

A study of physical abuse looked at children four years after the abuse and compared them with their brothers and sisters. The abused children made less progress at school, had fewer friends, and appeared anxious and extremely shy (Lynch & Roberts, 1982).

**Sexual abuse** Depression, guilt, shame, low self-esteem, hostility, aggression and suicide have all been linked to sexual abuse. In a study of 144 cases of child sexual abuse in Liverpool, 36% were suffering from depression and anxiety nine months after help was provided, and nearly as many after two years (Calam et al., 1998).

The effects of child sexual abuse often continue into adulthood.

## Government policy

In 1995, the Department of Health published a report entitled *Child Protection – Messages from Research*. The report argued that the child protection services tended to focus on actual incidents of child abuse, rather than family problems and neglect. Research indicated that many of the negative effects of physical and sexual abuse were experienced by children who were neglected and raised in poverty. The report recommended a shift in emphasis to working with families and reducing poverty. One of the present government's aims is to end child poverty.

This approach to child abuse has placed more emphasis on prevention. Supporting families and reducing poverty are seen as important steps to prevent child abuse. However, critics argue that this change of focus may endanger children. They point to cases of abuse and neglect which have led to children dying. They believe that child protection professionals should pay more attention to the danger signs, to detecting and recording those signs, and taking action where necessary (Corby, 2000).

## summary

1. Some psychiatrists argue that mental disorders can develop from destructive family relationships.

2. Oliver James claims that many of the problems people face in later life stem from parental care during infancy.

3. In cases of domestic violence, there are important differences between men's and women's violence. Men's violence is far more likely to:
   - result in physical injury
   - be experienced as threatening
   - result in psychological problems.

4. Domestic violence has been explained in terms of:
   - psychological disorders of the abuser
   - dysfunctional partnerships
   - patriarchy and male dominance.

5. There is a tendency for victims to hide the violence they have suffered.

6. Police services and governments now take domestic violence more seriously.

7. Aid organisations, and the refuges they set up, provide vital help for women who have experienced domestic violence.

8. Estimates of the extent of child abuse come from government statistics and survey research. Both probably underestimate its extent.

9. Child abuse has been explained in terms of:
   - psychological disorders of the abusers
   - poverty and the frustration it produces
   - patriarchy and male dominance.

10. Abuse can have significant effects on children's emotional and social development.

11. Recent government policy has placed more emphasis on prevention – on working with families and reducing poverty.

# 3 Mass media

## Introduction

Can you imagine a day going by without watching a television programme or a film on video or DVD; listening to music on the radio, CD or the Internet; or reading a newspaper, magazine or book? If your answer is yes then you're a pretty unusual person! We live in a world where we are surrounded by print and electronic media and depend upon them for information and entertainment.

Use of the media is huge and still growing. In 2001, 55% of adults in the United Kingdom read a daily newspaper and the average person spent nearly three hours a day watching television. In addition to these well-established communications media, more and more people have access to new media products. In 2001, 80% of households owned CD players and 40% had access to the Internet. At the same time, the proportion of adults, especially those aged between 15 and 24, attending the cinema at least once a month has grown in the last few years. And the purchase of Video Cassette Recorders (VCRs) and Digital Versatile Discs (DVDs) has increased rapidly (*Social Trends*, 2003).

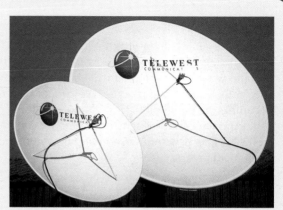

*Telewest satellite dishes*

Television programmes and other media products are produced by organisations. Does it matter who owns and controls these organisations?

We rely upon the media for much of our information and entertainment. Are the media giving us an accurate picture of the world? What images of men and women, for example, are being presented?

We watch, listen to and read media messages. How do audiences respond to these? Do the media have significant effects upon us?

## chaptersummary

▷ **Unit 1** examines trends in the ownership and control of media institutions and assesses the influence of media owners and journalists.

▷ **Unit 2** examines the content of the mass media and the portrayal of particular groups and issues.

▷ **Unit 3** investigates the effects of the media on its audiences.

# Unit 1  Media institutions

## keyissues

1 What are the key characteristics of the media? Who owns and controls media institutions?

2 What role do owners and professionals play in the production of media messages? In particular, how is the news constructed?

3 How significant is the development of new media? What is the impact of the Internet?

### 1.1 Defining the media

**What are the mass media?** The term *media* describes different means of communication. Some media – such as

the telephone – enable communication between two people. However, others allow communication with a *mass* audience. These include newspapers, television, radio, and the Internet.

For much of human history, social relations have been face to face. People communicated by talking and through body language. Now technological developments have made it possible to communicate with large numbers of people at one time. It is these forms of communication that have come to be known as the *mass media*.

'The mass media are simply the means through which content, whether fact or fiction, is produced by organisations and transmitted to and received by an audience' (McCullagh, 2002).

This definition identifies three key aspects of the mass media.

- The production of messages by media institutions
- The content of media messages
- The reception of messages by audiences.

While these three dimensions are interrelated, it is important that each is examined separately. We cannot understand what factors shape media content without looking at the production process. We cannot understand the meanings of media messages without analysing their content. And we cannot reach an informed judgement about media effects without examining how audiences interpret media messages.

We shall examine each of these processes in turn, beginning with media organisations.

## 1.2 Ownership and control of media institutions

**Types of media organisation** There are three forms of media organisation.

- Community-based media organisations, eg a radio station in a local hospital
- Public/state owned media organisations, eg the BBC
- Privately owned media organisations, eg News Corporation (Devereux, 2003).

While all three forms still survive, privately-owned media organisations are by far the most significant. Community-based media continue to play a minor role, usually appealing to limited local audiences. Public/state owned

# *activity1 defining the mass media*

## question

Why is each picture an example of the mass media?

media organisations, although in an earlier media age often enjoying a national monopoly, have steadily lost their dominance. They have either been privatised or face significant competition from a limited number of privately-owned global media institutions.

## Trends in media ownership

**Increasing media choice?** In the last fifteen years there has been a rapid increase in the range of media outlets. 'In 1988 there were four TV channels; today over 70; there were sixty commercial radio stations, today 260; 14 cinema multiplexes, today 143; zero web pages, today a billion' (Peake, 2002). These changes indicate a much wider range of choice. However, the source of these 'choices' is an increasingly small number of extremely large and powerful media institutions.

**Increasing concentration of media organisations** 'Fewer and fewer large companies increasingly own what we see, hear and read' (Williams, 2003). This process is known as the *concentration of media organisations*.

The increasing concentration of media organisations is the result of three major developments:

● Vertical integration
● Horizontal integration and multi-media ownership
● The expansion of transnational organisations.

Let's take each in turn.

**Vertical integration** This refers to 'the process by which one owner acquires all aspects of production and distribution of a single type of media product' (Croteau & Hoynes, 1997). Vertical integration is not new. Production and distribution of movies were concentrated in the hands of the big five Hollywood companies in the early part of the twentieth century. This enabled them to build a dominant position in world film production. Although film industries subsequently developed elsewhere, Hollywood still retains its dominance. 'The most comprehensive survey of cinema-going in Britain…by the Film Council reveals that although younger people are flocking to the cinema in ever increasing numbers, they are overwhelmingly watching films made by the big US studios' (Kennedy, 2003).

**Horizontal integration** This refers to 'the process by which one company buys different kinds of media, concentrating ownership across different kinds of media' (Croteau & Hoynes, 1997). Horizontal integration has developed rapidly in recent years. The largest media groups own a range of media. Take News Corporation whose top executive is Rupert Murdoch. Although this company initially produced newspapers, it now has interests in a range of other media, including book and magazine publishing (eg, Harper Collins), television (eg, BSKYB), radio (eg, SKY), film (eg, 20th Century Fox), as well as sports franchises (eg, the Los Angeles Dodgers baseball team).

**Transnational ownership** The major media organisations operate across national boundaries. Take News Corporation again. Although this company originated in Australia, it now operates on a global scale. It produces over 175 newspapers in Australia, Britain, the USA and Asia; it owns 37 television stations; and it is able to beam programmes into homes through its control of cable programming and satellite operations across Europe, Asia, Australia, Latin America and the USA.

## Explaining increasing concentration

Media products such as newspapers and films are costly to produce. They require a large upfront investment. But while producing the first newspaper or film is expensive, the cost of reproducing copies is cheap. This encourages media organisations to maximise their audiences. Hence the three developments outlined above – all of which have led to increasing concentration.

Vertical integration has enabled Hollywood companies to sell their films more easily. Horizontal integration has allowed organisations to promote their products across a range of media. 'Batman was developed into a film publicised by Time Warner through its magazines and promoted via its cable and television networks, the soundtrack of which was released on its record labels and whose merchandising included children's toys produced through its manufacturing interests' (Williams, 2003).

What is more, the development of multi-media organisations operating across the world enables them to search for markets on a global scale. 'The marketing of *The Lion King, Pocahontas*, and many other animated characters, by Walt Disney (the film, the dolls, the books, the jigsaw puzzles, lunchboxes and so on) is but one of many examples of this (worldwide) exploitation of one product in as many markets as possible' (Newbold et al., 2002).

## Liberal and radical approaches to media concentration

Does media concentration matter? Are we, the audience, well served by the concentration of ownership in the hands of a few, extremely powerful media magnates?

**In defence of the market: The liberal approach** This approach argues that private ownership of the media is the most effective way to ensure that audiences have a wide range of media products to choose from. Publicly-owned media and state regulation are dangerous since they concentrate too much power in the hands of the government and are not responsive to what audiences demand. By contrast, privately-owned media organisations compete with each other to give audiences what they want.

Increasing concentration of ownership 'should be positively welcomed rather than resisted since it encourages investment' (Curran & Seaton, 1997). Concentration is essential for economic success in a global market and competition enables consumers to have a wider choice of a greater range of media products at affordable prices.

From this point of view, laws which limit the concentration of media ownership should be reduced or abolished. This is known as *media deregulation*. In many countries, laws prevent organisations from dominating large sections of the media.

**Criticising media concentration: The radical approach**
This approach takes a very different view. Media organisations have a responsibility to provide a public service. For example, we depend upon the media for a range of information about the world. Publicly-owned

# *activity2 media concentration*

### Item A  National newspaper ownership

| Group name | Market share (%) | Title control | Executive |
|---|---|---|---|
| News International (part of News Corporation) | 37.2 | *Sun* *Times* *Sunday Times* *News of the World* | Rupert Murdoch |
| Trinity Mirror | 20.5 | *Daily Mirror* *Sunday Mirror* *People* | Victor Blank |
| Daily Mail and General Trust | 18.7 | *Daily Mail* *Mail on Sunday* | Lord Rothermere |
| Northern and Shell | 9.6 | *Daily Express* *Daily Star* *Sunday Express* | Richard Desmond |
| Hollinger International | 7.0 | *Daily Telegraph* *Sunday Telegraph* | Conrad Black |
| Guardian Media Group | 3.3 | *Guardian* *Observer* | The Scott Trust |
| Pearson | 1.9 | *Financial Times* | Pearson Board |
| Independent News and Media | 1.8 | *Independent* *Independent on Sunday* | Tony O'Reilly |

Adapted from Peake, 2002

### Item B  Transnationals
Transnationals dominate the market in the United States, the UK, Canada, Germany, Italy, Australia, Sweden, Japan, France and the Netherlands. There were 5 countries (UK, Italy, Japan, Sweden, France) where transnationals had between 60 and 80% of total market share. In the rest, transnationals controlled over 80% of market share.

Adapted from Burnett, 1996

### Item C  The Top Ten

| | Media group | Revenue, 2002 ($ billion) |
|---|---|---|
| 1 | AOL Time Warner | 41.0 |
| 2 | Walt Disney | 25.3 |
| 3 | Viacom | 24.6 |
| 4 | Comcast | 21.1 |
| 5 | Sony | 20.0 |
| 6 | Vivendi Universal | 19.7 |
| 7 | News Corporation | 15.2 |
| 8 | Cox Enterprises | 9.9 |
| 9 | Hughes Electronics | 8.9 |
| 10 | Clear Channel | 8.4 |

Adapted from *Broadcasting and Cable*, 2003

### Item D  Media merger

Viacom chairman Sumner Redstone announces the merger between CBS and Viacom in 1999. Viacom, the owner of MTV and Paramount Studios, bought CBS for $36 billion – the most expensive media merger in history.

AOL Time Warner headquarters under construction in Manhattan, New York, 2003

## *question*

How does each of the items indicate media concentration?

# *activity3* media deregulation

## Item A  *The USA*

The US is intending to relax media ownership laws further, allowing the largest media companies to deepen their presence in established markets and expand into new ones.

Adapted from *The Guardian*, 16.5.2003

## Item C  *Italy*

The Italian senate has been debating a controversial bill that critics say would enable the prime minister, Silvio Berlusconi, to extend his already formidable influence over the country's media.

The bill would allow Mr Berlusconi's Mediaset television group to keep all three of its channels, enable it to increase substantially its advertising revenue and to buy into the newspaper market.

Directly through Mediaset, in which Mr Berlusconi has a 48.6% stake, and indirectly by way of the state broadcaster, Rai, Italy's prime minister is in a position to influence more than 90% of the country's television output.

The dangers posed by his grip on the media were highlighted last week when the main Rai evening news bulletin failed to broadcast remarks by him that caused uproar across Europe.

During an appearance before the European parliament, Mr Berlusconi told a German MEP (Member of the European parliament), he would be ideal for the part of a concentration camp guard in a film being produced in Italy.

Adapted from *The Guardian*, 9.7.2003

## Item B  *Britain*

The British media market is to be opened to all-comers. The government has proposed to sweep aside ownership rules that have kept out US and other non-European buyers.

AOL Time Warner, Viacom and Disney – the world's biggest media groups – are effectively being invited to move into the biggest English-speaking market outside the USA.

Adapted from *The Financial Times*, 8.5.2003

*Silvio Berlusconi, centre*

## *question*

Discuss the items in terms of a) the liberal approach and b) the radical approach.

---

media, like the BBC, and regulations that oblige both the BBC and ITV to provide impartial news and current affairs help to ensure that this need is met. Unregulated privately-owned media organisations are driven by commercial considerations and often ignore their public service responsibilities.

Increasing concentration is dangerous since it gives too much power to a small number of *oligopolies* (large organisations dominating the market). Competition between these oligopolies has resulted in more television channels for example, but these all broadcast the same kind of programmes. This means that the concentration of media organisations actually limits audience choice (Mosco, 1996).

## The influence of proprietors

Supporters of the radical approach differ in their view of the influence of media *proprietors* – the owners of large media organisations. Views can be divided into two broad positions: the *instrumental* and the *structural* approach.

**The instrumental approach** This approach argues that the

proprietors of media organisations directly influence the content of the media they own. Between the two world wars, press barons such as Lord Rothermere and Lord Beaverbrook used their newspapers to put across conservative political views. Miliband (1973), claims that the press has always put forward conservative views and represented the interests of the ruling class. Indeed, in the view of some commentators, the growing concentration of the media has increased the power of proprietors who frequently mount propaganda campaigns 'to defend the economic, social and political agenda of privileged groups' (Herman & Chomsky, 1988).

**The structural approach** The structural approach also recognises that top executives, like Rupert Murdoch, exercise considerable power. However, those who favour this approach argue that it is impossible for one individual to control the day-to-day output of a huge media organisation. Murdoch's power within News Corporation is better described as *allocative control* – the power to set the goals of the organisation and to make key financial decisions (Williams, 2003). In his case, key decisions relating to the press have involved:

- Relocating the production of his British newspapers in 1986 from Fleet Street to Wapping, where new technology could be employed to destroy the power of the print unions
- Sacking editors who did not share his views
- Reducing the price of his newspapers to drive out competitors (Eldridge et al., 1997).

**The drive for profits** The structural view also believes that the power of media owners is limited by the need for their companies to make profits. In other words, the profit motive is the key influence on media content.

The influence of the drive for profits can be seen in the following two examples.

1. The need to make more money by increasing

# activity4 the influence of proprietors

## Item A  Rupert Murdoch

Rupert Murdoch is chairman and chief executive of News Corporation which owns more than 175 newspapers on three continents. It publishes 40 million papers a week and dominates the newspaper markets in Britain, Australia and New Zealand. In an interview in his own *Sydney Daily Telegraph*, Murdoch backed President Bush's stance against Saddam Hussein and called for war against Iraq. And the editors of his 175 newspapers around the world mirrored his views, supporting military action against Saddam.

Adapted from *The Guardian*, 17.2.2003

## Item B  Conducting his campaign

This graphic by Steve Caplin gives one view of Murdoch's campaign for war against Iraq.

## Item C  What his papers say

**The tyranny of Saddam and the danger to innocent lives demand the world responds.**

*Sydney Daily Telegraph*

**There comes a time when evil must be stopped, and it is better to do that sooner rather than later.**

*Brisbane Courier-Mail*

**The doubters must say how much more time they would give Saddam to play his delaying games.**

*Wellington Dominion-Post*

**Stick with the friend you can trust through and through – America.**

*The Sun*

**Item D  Sun versus Mirror**

US Secretary of State Colin Powell presented evidence to the United Nations which he claimed justified war against Iraq. Murdoch's Sun supported his claim. The Mirror took a different view.

## questions

1  How do Items A, B and C support the claim that proprietors directly influence the content of the news media?

2  How does Item D support the claim that the free market gives audiences the opportunity to hear different viewpoints?

readership of newspapers has led to the growth of the 'human interest' story. This has largely replaced political coverage in the tabloid press (McCullagh, 2002). Now news has become 'infotainment' – part of the entertainment industry. Investigative journalists have been replaced by celebrity columnists and presenters (Franklin, 1997).

2. The importance of advertising as a major source of revenue has encouraged media organisations to focus on audiences with significant purchasing power. This has led to a decline in the number of newspapers and minority interest programmes whose audiences are relatively poor (Curran & Seaton, 1997). At the same time, the boundary between media content and advertising is being broken down (Murdock, 1992).  For example, companies pay for products to be 'placed' in films.

## key terms

**Mass media** Means of communication through which content – news, sport, music, drama, writing, advertising – are transmitted to large audiences.

**Media concentration** The concentration of mass media ownership into fewer and fewer organisations.

**Vertical integration** One company acquiring all aspects of the production and distribution of a single type of media product.

**Horizontal integration** One organisation buying up companies from different media, concentrating ownership across different kinds of media.

**Transnational ownership** The ownership by a single company of media organisations which operate in two or more countries.

**Media deregulation** The reduction or abolition of laws limiting media ownership and regulating media output.

**Oligopoly** A situation where a few very large companies dominate a market.

**Proprietor** The owner – in this case of a large media organisation.

**Allocative control** The power of a proprietor to set the goals of the organisation and to make key financial decisions.

# activity5 the drive for profits

Adapted from Glasgow Media Group, 1982

## question

How does this cartoon suggest that the drive for profits influences media content?

## 1.3 The influence of media professionals: the production of news

So far, we have concentrated on the economic pressures which shape the production of media messages. But there may be other important influences. Williams (2003) identifies the following three.

- The power of those who actually work in the media – people like journalists

- The day-to-day organisation and routine of media companies

- The culture of society – its wider norms and values.

We shall examine each of these factors by taking a specific example: the production of news.

### The influence of media workers

An influential study conducted by White in 1950 argued that particular individuals play a significant role in determining which items make news. This study was based on the decisions made by one news editor on what should appear as national and international news in a small American newspaper. White's study suggested that the editor's individual prejudices played a significant role in the selection process. He acted as a *gatekeeper,* only allowing his preferred stories to pass through the 'gate' into the news.

Later research has challenged this view. An investigation of the selections made by a number of news editors did not find any significant variation in the news items they chose (Williams, 2003). This suggests that individual media workers are influenced in their decision-making by the organisations in which they work rather than their own preferences. Such a suggestion is reinforced when we realise that the selection of news involves many people – no one individual can be held responsible for the final product.

### The influence of organisational structures

Watch the 10 o'clock news on ITV and BBC. While there is some variation in the events reported, there is also a noticeable similarity between the two news broadcasts on any day. This agreement over what counts as 'news' is the starting point for sociologists who highlight the importance of organisational structures in shaping the news. They believe that the routines of news organisations and the occupational socialisation of journalists are vital in explaining the content of the news.

**Routines** A daily newspaper works on a 24 hour cycle. To ensure that the news is fresh, one routine adopted is to focus on events that occur within that cycle. A train crash occurring since the previous day's newspaper is more likely to be reported as news than a famine that unfolds over time.

To make the reporting of events manageable, newspapers are divided up into sections (foreign news, crime news, sports news etc) and specialist correspondents are allocated to report on different kinds of news. Events happening in the real world are squeezed into these sections, with those occurring in locations where journalists are placed the most likely to be reported. So we know more about what is happening in North America and Europe than in South America and Africa.

**News values** Journalists learn the kind of events seen as newsworthy in the course of their professional socialisation. They pick up a set of informal rules or *news values* which enable them to identify what is newsworthy. A former editor of *The Guardian* identifies these news values as follows:

> **Significance**: social, economic, political, human.
> **Drama**: the excitement, action and entertainment in the event.
> **Surprise**: the freshness, newness, unpredictability.
> **Personalities**: royal, political, 'showbiz', others.
> **Sex, scandal, crime**: popular ingredients.
> **Numbers**: the scale of the event, numbers of people affected.
> **Proximity**: on our doorsteps, or 10,000 miles away?
> (Hetherington, 1985).

Events that correspond to these values are more likely to be identified as newsworthy than others. What's more, in reporting these events journalists will present them in dramatic and personalised terms. 'Surprises' become 'shocks'; 'disagreements' become 'open conflicts'; and political debates are translated into choices between rival personalities (McCullagh, 2002).

News values have to be interpreted on a daily basis, with newspapers differing in the priority they give to some news values over others. However, there is often a remarkable similarity across the British news media when it comes to the main story of the day (Allan, 1999).

**Objectivity** Journalists often claim to be objective – to provide balanced and neutral accounts of events. Tuchman (1978) argues that the desire for objectivity means that the news media adopt a number of conventions in reporting the news. Facts are distinguished from opinions, with hard news, for example, being separated from editorial comment. The most important elements of the story are presented first, with the background outlined later. Different sides of the story are given; supporting evidence is produced for the claims made; and reliable sources are quoted.

However, in practice these conventions mean that the voices of powerful organisations such as the government are often given prominence as they tend to be seen by the media as credible and authoritative.

**Frameworks** To enable newsworthy events to be understood by audiences, the news media place them within familiar frameworks. Take the coverage of two seemingly similar tragedies, the shooting down of a Korean civilian airliner by the Soviet Union in 1983 and the shooting down of an Iranian airbus by the USA in 1986. Both events took place during the 'cold war' when communism was seen as a threat to Western societies. In this context, a common way of interpreting events involved a contrast between the civilised West and the uncivilised East. In both the American and British news media, this familiar framework was employed to interpret what happened in 1983 and 1986. The first event was presented as 'a barbaric, terrorist, heinous act', while the second was presented as 'an understandable accident' (McNair, 1996).

This framework was of course not the only one that could have been used. The Soviet (Russian communist) news media reversed the Western view and interpreted the first event as an unfortunate accident and the second as a terrorist act.

In Britain and America the same framework was used across the news media and reflected how both governments saw these incidents. Hall et al., (1978) argue that this is not uncommon and that powerful groups are able to act as *primary definers.* Less powerful voices may be heard, but these voices are often drowned out. And when they are not drowned out, they are often ridiculed.

**Evaluation** Sociologists agree that we need to take account of the influence of both media owners and organisational factors in order to understand the production of media messages. In many cases, these influences mean that media coverage reflects the interests of powerful groups. However, this is not always the case.

Powerful groups do not always speak with one voice. This means that there can be conflict over how events are to be interpreted. Powerful groups disagreed about war with Iraq in 2003. And they are bitterly divided over Britain's adoption of the euro as its currency. In these instances, it is not possible to identify one primary definition of the issues.

The media sometimes challenge powerful groups. Some investigative journalists can become the primary definers, with powerful groups being obliged to respond to the way the media define the issues. Two journalists on the *Washington Post,* for example, uncovered a range of illegal activities by the US government that culminated in the resignation of the President in 1974 (Schlesinger,1991).

## The influence of wider culture

What counts as news and the way it is reported will, to some extent, reflect the wider culture – the shared norms, values, concerns and beliefs of society. To take an obvious example, baseball, ice hockey, basketball and American football dominate sports reporting in newspapers in the USA. They are rarely found in British newspapers.

News often reflects strongly held values. For example,

murder is regularly reported and condemned. This reflects the value placed on human life.

News reporting often draws on widely held cultural stereotypes. For example, Schudson (2000) argues that news reports which represent young Black people as a problem and women as sex objects reflect shared cultural stereotypes.

We live in an age where organisations attempt to manage the news, to 'spin' information in order to present themselves in the best possible light. They try to ensure

# activity6 news values

### Item A  Islanders consider exodus as sea levels rise

*Tuvaluan children playing in the sea which threatens to swamp their island.*

Faced with the prospect of being swamped by rising sea levels, the Pacific island nation of Tuvalu is considering evacuating its 9,300 residents.

With sea levels predicted to rise by more than 80 cms over the next century due to global warming, Tuvaluans are living on borrowed time. The most recent figures suggest that Tuvalu's sea levels have risen nearly three times as fast as the world average over the past decade, and are now 5cms higher than in 1993.

Adapted from *The Guardian*, 19.7.2003

### Item B  Harry is 'out of control'

Prince Harry's late-night drinking and wild behaviour have forced one of his royal protection officers to quit. Sergeant Ieuan Jones was transferred to other duties after telling colleagues he could not cope with the tearaway Prince.

One Buckingham Palace worker said: 'He won't do what he is told and when you are dealing with the safety of someone like him that is a dangerous situation. They get totally fed up sitting around in pub after pub while Harry knocks back drink after drink. They can only have tonic water or coke and it gets very boring indeed for them.'

Adapted from *Sunday Express*, 20.7.2003

### Item C  A balanced discussion

"AND TO ENSURE A BALANCED AND IMPARTIAL DISCUSSION OF THE LATEST GOVERNMENT MEASURES, I HAVE WITH ME A GOVERNMENT SPOKESMAN AND A WILD-EYED MILITANT FROM THE LUNATIC FRINGE."

Adapted from Glasgow Media Group, 1982

## questions

1  Assess the 'newsworthiness' of the news stories in Items A and B using the list of news values.

2  What point is being made by the cartoon in Item C? What does it suggest about the influence of the powerful?

that their actions are seen to be in line with society's norms and values. For example, Tony Blair's Labour government has been accused of exaggerating the threat of weapons of mass destruction in order to justify the war against Iraq and the deaths of British soldiers and Iraqi civilians.

However, governments and powerful organisations are not always able to portray their actions as fitting the norms and values of society. For example, it is difficult for

## activity7 news frameworks

### THE SUN SAYS

*Pig headed*
*WATCH out, bigots about.*

That's the sign that should go up in Leicester.

Racial and religious intolerance are rearing their ugly heads.

*Not among the whites – among the local Asian Muslims.*

They complain that a collection of ceramic pigs in a house window is racially offensive.

That's daft. But not as ridiculous as the police going round to the house and seizing the pottery pigs as 'evidence'.

**Culture**
What will the Pig Squad do next: shut down Tescos for selling bacon?

*The unbending attitude of militant Muslims who think they have a right to impose their culture in a Christian country is frightening.*

There has to be give and take if we are all to get on together.

But it seems **WE** give and **THEY** take.

This does nothing for racial harmony. It just makes Muslims look mean-minded – which the vast majority are not.

This country is very easy-going and accepting of its new citizens.

*But pigs will fly before we put up with this kind of nonsense.*

From *The Sun*, 25.5.1995

### questions

1  What framework can be identified in this editorial?
2  Who are 'we'?
3  Who are 'they'?

governments and business organisations to control media coverage when accidents such as oil spills and explosions at nuclear plants occur (McCullagh, 2002).

### key terms

**Gatekeeping** Making decisions about what will and will not become 'news'.
**News values** A set of informal rules used by journalists to identify what is newsworthy.
**Primary definers** Individuals and groups who are able to influence what events become news and how they are reported.

## 1.4 Trends in production and consumption of the mass media

Many sociologists believe that we are in the middle of a communications revolution which is transforming the way images, text and sounds are communicated. Three technological developments are seen as particularly important in bringing about this revolution.

- The development of relatively cheap personal computers allowing access to the Internet for millions of people at home and at work
- The emergence of new ways of sending audio-visual signals to individual households
- The growth of digital technology causing changes in the way information (images, texts and sounds) is stored and transmitted.

### New media

The Internet, along with cable television and satellite broadcasting, are examples of *new media*. The new media share three characteristics:

- 'They are screen based', with information being displayed on a television screen, PC monitor or a mobile telephone.
- 'They can offer images, text and sounds.'
- 'They allow some form of interaction.'
  (Collins & Murroni, 1996)

**The Internet** The Internet is a global system of interconnected computers. It is not owned by any individual or company, but comprises a network that stretches across the world. The best known part of the Internet is the World Wide Web (WWW), effectively a global multi-media library.

The Internet was created in 1969 by the American military to enable scientists working on military contracts across the US to share resources and information. It developed further in the 1980s within universities, but it was not until the second half of that decade, with the increased availability of PCs in the home, that the Internet really took off (Gorman & McLean, 2003). The proportion of households in the UK who owned computers increased from 18 to 34 per cent between 1988 and 1998 and the proportion who have access to the Internet has jumped from under 10 per cent in 1998 to 47 per cent in 2003 (ONS, 2003).

**Cable television and satellite broadcasting** Terrestrial broadcasting by the BBC and ITV operates by sending audio-visual signals through the air which are picked up by ordinary television aerials. By contrast, cable television relies on a physical cable link and satellite broadcasting on dishes to pick up signals (Negrine, 1994).

In contrast to the US and the rest of Europe, cable television in the UK is less popular than satellite broadcasting. In 2002, only 14.7 per cent of homes in the UK where cable is available had taken out a television subscription. By contrast, a quarter of UK homes have satellite dishes, with the number of subscribers to BSkyB topping 6 million in July 2002 (Peake, 2002). The development of cable television and satellite broadcasting enables people to choose from a much larger number of television channels.

# *activity8 the new media*

### Item A  *Big Brother*

Cameron winning Big Brother. Using a remote, viewers with digital television were able to vote on screen.

### Item B  *The Internet*

Buying a book online

### Item C  *Playstation*

## question

What characteristics of the new media do each of these items illustrate?

**Digitalisation** Of central importance to recent technological developments in the media is digitalisation – the shift from analogue to digital coding of information. Digital systems translate all information – images, texts, sounds – into a universal computer language. The use of this common language reduces the boundaries between different media sectors. 'Digital transmission technology has a broadcasting capacity many times bigger than analogue, opening the door on a new era: many more TV channels and radio stations; higher quality pictures and sound; multimedia facilities; and interactivity (home shopping, games, video on demand)' (Peake, 2003).

## The impact of the new media

There is disagreement about the impact of the new media. Some believe that the new media widen consumer choice and help citizens engage in public debate. Others are less optimistic. They believe that commercial pressures lead to lower quality and a dumbed-down version of the same old thing rather than increased diversity. They also highlight inequality of access to the new media.

**Diversity and choice** There is no doubt that the new media have led to more consumer choice. For example, cable television and satellite broadcasting have increased the number of television channels. While many of these are entertainment channels, the number of news channels has also increased. Sometimes these provide views of world affairs that are very different from British and American sources. During the war in Iraq in 2003, the Arab news channel Al Jazeera provided an alternative source of news for viewers in the Arab world. In addition, new media

products such as the video cassette recorder (VCR) have provided opportunities for audiences to design their own programme schedules.

**Quality and inequality** The government exercises some control over the quality and range of programmes on the BBC and ITV. However, the main providers of cable and satellite broadcasting – NTL, Telewest and BSkyB – face 'no regulatory directives on either the range or the sources of programme material' (Negrine, 1994). Anxious to make as much profit as possible on their massive investments, cable and satellite broadcasters fill their channels with cheap imported material, films, or sport.

Other broadcasting organisations are tempted to follow suit as they too search for large audiences to generate advertising revenue or, in the case of the BBC, to justify the license fee. According to many commentators, 'there is a consequent loss in both the quality, and the range, of programmes produced' (Negrine, 1994). Increased choice does not therefore mean increased diversity.

There is also inequality of access to the new media. As subscription channels and pay-per-view become more popular, poorer people become excluded from key world events, especially in entertainment and sport.

## The public sphere

**The media as a public sphere** The idea of a *public sphere* refers to a space where people can freely debate issues that are of importance to them as citizens. Habermas (1992) argues that the public sphere emerged in eighteenth

# *activity9 regulation of the new media*

### Regulations, duties and obligations of different media (1992)

| | BBC/ ITV | Satellite services | Cable systems |
|---|---|---|---|
| High quality/standard | YES | NO | NO |
| Information, education, entertainment | YES | NO | NO |
| Proper balance and wide range in subject matter | YES | NO | NO |
| Secure showing for programmes of merit | YES | NO | NO |
| Programmes must not offend good taste and decency | YES | YES | YES |
| There must be sufficient time for news and current affairs | YES | NO | NO |
| News programmes must be impartial and accurate | YES | NO | YES for UK news |
| 'Due impartiality' in matters of controversy | YES | NO | YES |
| There must be suitable material for the regions | YES | NO | NO |
| Independent producers must provide 25% of output | YES | NO | NO |
| Programmes covered by Obscene Publications Act | NO | NO | YES |
| Control of operations must be in British hands | YES | NO | NO |
| Must carry a majority of programmes of European origin | YES | NO | NO |

Adapted from Negrine, 1994

*question*

What are the differences in regulations and duties between terrestrial television and cable/satellite systems?

century coffee houses where individuals could meet to discuss the issues of the day. This sphere was independent of both commerce and the government. The mass media in Habermas's view threaten this space because they are cultural industries concerned to make profits. This means they seek to manipulate our thoughts and behaviour in order to make money.

This picture of the mass media has been criticised because it ignores the pressures on the news media to be 'objective' and does not take account of public service broadcasting. In Britain, for example, the BBC was established as a public service organisation funded by the license fee and obliged to present news and current affairs in an impartial way. While increased competition for readers and viewers has, in the view of many sociologists, led to more 'infotainment', public service broadcasting survives.

**The Internet as a public sphere** The spectacular growth of the Internet has suggested to some people that the public sphere is being given a new lease of life. There are two main reasons for this.

- In contrast to conventional news media, where editors and journalists act as gatekeepers, the Internet provides individuals with the opportunity to access a wider range of information and interpretations. Any point of view, no matter how extreme, can be found on the Internet.

- The Internet provides individuals with the opportunity to engage in online discussions and debates across the globe. In contrast to conventional news media, where communication is predominantly one way, the Internet provides a means through which people can interact with others.

# activity10 the Internet as a public sphere?

### Item A  *Internet use around the world*

| Internet use by continent 1996-9 (millions) | | | |
|---|---|---|---|
| | 1996 | 1997 | 1999 |
| Africa | -- | 1 | 1.14 |
| Asia | 6 | 14 | 26.55 |
| Europe | 9 | 20 | 35.11 |
| Middle East | -- | 0.5 | 0.78 |
| US/Canada | 30 | 64 | 94.2 |
| South America | -- | 1.3 | 4.5 |

Adapted from Campbell & Breen, 2001

### Item C  *ISP Top Five*

| The top 5 Internet service providers, March 1999 | | |
|---|---|---|
| Rank | Site | Visitors per month |
| 1 | yahoo.com | 26,480,000 |
| 2 | aol.com | 23,321,000 |
| 3 | microsoft.com | 20,243,000 |
| 4 | netscape.com | 15,892,000 |
| 5 | geocities.com | 15,238,000 |

Adapted from Campbell & Breen, 2001

### Item B  *Sex.com*

In 1994 a young computer engineer registered the domain name 'sex.com'. Now, after a decade of legal battles, he has finally won the right to regain control of the world's most valuable web address.

Gary Kremen realised the potential of the Internet in 1994 and applied for the domain 'sex.com'. At the time, the Internet was only known to academics and computer students. Kremen couldn't believe it when he was awarded – for free – a piece of Internet property now worth $500,000 a month just in advertising space.

Adapted from *The Guardian*, 26.6.2003

Millions of men log on to adult sex sites every day. One estimate puts their annual revenue at £70-100 million. (*Observer*, 30.3.2003)

# questions

1  What does Item A tell us about access to the Internet?

2  How do Items B and C demonstrate the commercialisation of the Internet?

**The Internet: media giants and global inequality** Not all commentators are so optimistic about the potential of the Internet to aid freedom and democracy. They point to the domination of the Internet by a small number of huge corporations and to global inequality of access to the Internet.

The Internet is dominated by a few major media organisations. Microsoft is the best known. It not only developed the software for personal computers that was essential for the widespread take-up of the Internet, but has also become a major Internet service provider (ISP). A few oligopolies, including the biggest media organisation, America Online (AOL) Time Warner, own and control the most widely used Internet service providers. These ISPs enable us to log on in the first place, direct users to particular commercial services and play a key role in online advertising. Since the mid-1990s, the Internet has become much more commercialised. E-commerce has taken off and there has been 'a shift from educational to commercial use' (Gorman & McLean, 2003).

There is considerable inequality in Internet access. Castells (1996) argues that Internet use remains 'the domain of an educated segment of the population of the most advanced societies'. In many countries, the technology needed for widespread Internet use is undeveloped, and in other countries people do not have the income or skills to use the Internet.

## Evaluation

The freedom and lack of regulation of the Internet is both its strength and its weakness.

On the positive side, a vast range of information is available and a wide variety of views can be heard. Public debate can take place across the world.

On the negative side, lack of control of the Internet means that information can be inaccurate, one-sided or simply not true. Extreme views (racist, sexist, homophobic and political) are freely available.

Some people have called for greater regulation of the Internet by governments. At present, information can only be controlled if it breaks the laws of a particular country – for example, the clamp down on use of the Internet by paedophiles. Others believe that irresponsible use of the Internet is a price worth paying for the free expression and exchange of information it provides.

## key terms

*Gatekeeping* Making decisions about what will and will not become 'news'.
*News values* A set of informal rules used by journalists to identify what is newsworthy.
*Primary definers* Individuals and groups who are able to influence what events become news and how they are reported.

## summary

1. The mass media are the means of communication through which messages are produced by organisations and received by audiences.

2. Most people use the mass media extensively for information and entertainment.

3. Ownership and control of the mass media has become increasingly concentrated in recent years due to vertical integration, horizontal integration and transnational ownership.

4. There are different views of the impact of media concentration. The liberal approach argues that concentration of ownership creates greater efficiency and more choice for the public.

5. Other sociologists take a more radical approach. They believe that increasing concentration is dangerous since it concentrates too much power in the hands of a few media organisations that are driven by commercial considerations.

6. Proprietors may influence the content of the mass media directly by using the media to put their own views across. They also exert an indirect influence by setting the goals of the organisation and making key financial decisions.

7. The production of media content is also influenced by professionals such as editors and journalists.

8. The work of professionals in the news media is influenced by organisational factors such as the routines of news reporting and by ideas about what is newsworthy (news values).

9. The wider cultural environment also influences media content. Powerful organisations usually have the ability to become primary definers of the news. And journalists are influenced by dominant cultural values and assumptions.

10. Technological developments are creating new media. These include cable television, satellite broadcasting, and the Internet.

11. Optimists argue that these increase consumer choice and provide new opportunities for people to engage in public debate.

12. Pessimists argue that the quality of media content is declining and that inequality of access and commercialisation prevent the opportunities offered by the new media from being realised.

# Unit 2 Media content and representation

## keyissues

1 How important are the media in identifying social problems? What role do they play in creating moral panics?

2 How do the media represent different groups? Do they present biased and stereotypical pictures of gender, ethnicity and class?

3 Why does media content take the form that it does? How do different sociological theories approach the media?

## 2.1 The news and moral panics

Journalists often claim that the news represents a 'mirror on the world' (Allen, 1999). They believe that the news gives an accurate and impartial reflection of events. Research evidence gives a somewhat different picture. Section 1.3 showed that the news media not only select certain events as newsworthy, but also place a particular interpretation on those events. From this point of view, the media construct news rather than mirror the world.

**Mods and rockers** It is not unusual for the news media – especially the tabloid press – to sensationalise the events they report. This can be seen from the following research. In a groundbreaking study conducted in the 1960s, Stanley Cohen looked at media coverage of the activities of two youth subcultures – mods and rockers. On Easter bank holiday in 1964, large numbers of young people, including mods on their scooters and rockers on their motor cycles went to Clacton for a day out at the seaside. Cohen was interested in how the media reported their behaviour and the consequences of that reporting.

The media presented a picture of two rival gangs 'hell bent on destruction'. Fighting, vandalism and anti-social behaviour were reported as widespread and those responsible were identified as mods and rockers.

On closer inspection, Cohen found little evidence of serious violence and vandalism. True, there were large crowds of often noisy young people. And there were mods and rockers baiting each other and sometimes getting into scuffles. But most young people did not identify with either group, and were not involved in any disturbances.

The mass media had presented a distorted and sensationalised picture of events. And this media picture created public fears and concerns about mods and rockers. The police responded to these concerns by increasing their presence at seaside resorts on future bank holidays and by making more and more arrests. Young people resented what they saw as heavy-handed and unjustified police

behaviour and were more likely to identify with mods and rockers. There were further disturbances followed by yet more sensationalised reporting, and increased police activity in response to public demands to deal with the 'problem'.

**Moral panics** Cohen argued that the reaction of the media created what he called a *moral panic*. A moral panic exists when 'a condition, episode, person or group of persons emerges to become defined as a threat to societal values and interests' (Cohen, 1987). In this particular case, mods and rockers were singled out as *folk devils* whose behaviour was seen as a threat to social order.

**Creating a moral panic** Moral panics occur on a regular basis. Newspapers (especially tabloid newspapers) often play a key role in their creation. They sensationalise issues by using emotive headlines, language and pictures. They present groups as stereotypes. They associate those groups with stereotypical behaviour – for example, New Age Travellers with drugs; Black youth with street crime; English football supporters abroad with violence. Contrasts are drawn between a rosy image of the past and a decline in modern-day morals. Finally, the media clamour for a clampdown on the group, and/or the behaviour identified as a threat.

**Young people and moral panics** Young people continue to be the focus of moral panics. Their behaviour has frequently been identified as a problem. Examples include youth subcultures such as hippies, skinheads and punks, and behaviour associated with young people such as street crime, football hooliganism and drug taking.

Young people are sometimes seen as the victims in moral panics. Critcher (2003) argues that moral panics increasingly focus on threats to children. Concern over child abuse, paedophilia and the influence of violent films on young viewers are examples of these kinds of moral panics.

**Features of a moral panic** The term moral panic has been taken up widely and is now regularly used by politicians and journalists. Often the term is used quite loosely. Goode and Ben-Yehuda (1994) try to define moral panic precisely. They argue that moral panics have five distinguishing features.

- Increased public concern over the behaviour of a certain group
- Increased hostility towards the group
- A certain level of public agreement that there is a real threat and that it is caused by the group
- Public concern is out of proportion to the real harm caused by the group
- Moral panics appear and disappear very quickly.

(Goode and Ben-Yehuda, 1994)

# activity11 paedophilia: a moral panic?

## Item A  Tabloid headline

### WE TRAP INTERNET CHILD SEX SICKO

**Shocking Internet peril that all concerned parents should be aware of**

Adapted from *The People*, 20.7.2003

*Mothers of four murdered children lead a march through central London demanding more action to protect youngsters from paedophiles.*

With references to the items, explain how media concern over paedophilia can be described as a moral panic.

## Item B  Public reaction

Eight-year-old Sarah Payne was abducted while playing near her grandparents' house in West Sussex on July 1st 2000. Her half-buried body was found by a farm labourer on July 17th. On December 12th 2001, a 42-year-old local man and convicted sex offender, Roy Whiting, was found guilty of her 'sexually-motivated' murder and sentenced to life imprisonment.

When Sarah Payne's body was discovered, the *News of the World* launched a campaign: How do you know if there's a paedophile in your midst? The paper published the names and photographs of 50 people it claimed had committed child sex offences, and promised: 'We pledge we will pursue our campaign until we have publicly named and shamed every paedophile in Britain'.

The paper produced figures suggesting 88% of Britons believed parents should be told if a child sex offender was living in their area. It provided a website on which parents could use an interactive map to find their local paedophiles. It asked readers to report any convicted child abusers living in their area. And it published an endorsement of the campaign from Sarah's parents, Sarah and Michael Payne, who later spoke of their unease at being press-ganged into giving the campaign their support.

From Plymouth to Portsmouth, Manchester to London, wrongly identified men and known paedophiles found themselves being hounded by mobs up to 300 strong. The vigilante action was most severe on the Paulsgrove estate in Portsmouth, where protesters circulated a list of 20 alleged sex offenders in the community and proceeded to target them.

The crowds – 40 of whom were later charged with offences – smashed windows, torched cars and forced five families, wrongly identified as harbouring sex offenders, out of their homes. A suspected paedophile in nearby Southampton shot himself dead and a female registrar was hounded from her South Wales home because neighbours confused 'paediatrician' with 'paedophile.'

Adapted from *The Guardian*, 13.12.2001

**Evaluation** Critcher (2003) examined five case studies – Aids, ecstasy and raves, video 'nasties', child abuse in families, and paedophilia. In his view, only two of these cases were full moral panics – video 'nasties' and paedophilia. In these cases an issue was seen as a threat; the media defined the 'problem' in the same way; organised groups generally supported the panic; and the state eventually responded by bringing in new legislation to combat the apparent threat.

Critcher challenges the view that moral panics are always triggered by a concern over identifiable folk devils. What triggered concern in the cases he examined was the death of children or young people. These events were seen to reflect major social problems. In only one of the cases was there an indisputable folk devil – the paedophile.

Critcher argues that a consensus (agreement) is necessary for a moral panic to develop. Some newspapers tried to create a moral panic over Aids by identifying it as 'a gay plague'. They were unsuccessful because experts challenged this view and Aids was eventually seen as a health risk to the population as a whole.

Critcher disagrees with the last feature of moral panics identified by Goode and Ben-Yehuda – that they appear and disappear very quickly. He gives examples of moral panics that last for years.

## activity 12 video 'nasties'

### Item A The Video Recording Bill

The Video Recording Bill was passed by the Conservative government in 1984. Its aim was to place strict controls on video 'nasties' – videos with high levels of violence and sex which were seen as harmful to children.

Adapted from Harris, 1984

### Item B Child's Play

In November 1993, two 11-year-old boys from Merseyside were found guilty of murdering a two-year-old child. The 'horror' video *Child's Play 3* had been rented by the father of one of the boys shortly before the murder. There were certain similarities between scenes in the video and the killing of the child. But there was no evidence that either boy had seen the video. Despite this, the judge at the trial stated, 'I suspect that exposure to violent films may in part be an explanation'.

Adapted from *The Guardian*, 26.11.1993

### Item C The police view

Merseyside police detectives who had interviewed the boys for several weeks before the trial rejected any suggestions that 'horror' videos had influenced the boys' behaviour. One detective said, 'I don't know where the judge got that idea from. I couldn't believe it when I heard him. We went through something like 200 titles rented by the family. There were some you or I wouldn't want to see, but nothing – no scene, or plot, or dialogue – where you could put your finger on the freeze button and say that influenced a boy to go out and commit murder.'

Quoted in *The Independent*, 26.11.1993

### Item D Reaction in Parliament

In the Commons, the Conservative MP Sir Ivan Lawrence QC called for action to curb 'the constant diet of violence and depravity' fed to youngsters through television, videos and computer pornography. Sir Ivan, chairman of the Home Affairs Select Committee, said it was becoming 'daily more obvious' that this was a major reason for the rise in juvenile crime.

Quoted in *The Independent*, 26.11.1993

### Item E Burning videos

Azad Video, Scotland's largest video renting chain, burned its *Child's Play* videos including 300 copies of *Child's Play 3*. Xtra-Vision, the Irish Republic's biggest video chain, withdrew *Child's Play* from its shelves.

Adapted from *The Sun*, 26.11.93

### Item F The Sun's reaction

The Sun, 26.11.1993

### Item G Moral panics

At the turn of the century, there was great concern about violent images in Penny Dreadful comics. In the 1950s, panic that horror comics would lead to children copying the things they saw, led to the Children and Young Persons (Harmful Publications) Act 1955. In the 1980s, there was the huge panic about films such as *Drillerkiller*, which also led to a new law. There's been a recurrent moral panic about violent images which looks to a mythical golden age of tranquil behaviour.

T. Newburn, Policy Studies Institute, quoted in *The Guardian*, 26.11.1993

### Item H  Press editorials, 26.11.1993

The uncanny resemblance between the film *Child's Play 3* and the murder must be of concern. A link between the film and the crime would not prove that the former caused the latter. Yet it seems quite possible that exposure to images of brutality could turn an already disturbed child towards violence.
*(Independent)*

More and more children are growing up in a moral vacuum, which for so many is being filled with fetid (stinking) junk from the lower depths of our popular culture – video nasties, crude comics and violent television.
*(Daily Express)*

Instead of urging legislation to ban violent films, it would surely be more to the point if we took it upon ourselves as adults to ensure their prohibition in our own homes.
*(Daily Telegraph)*

### questions

1 Read Items A, B, C and D. What justification is there for the views of the judge and Ivan Lawrence? Why do you think they reacted in this way?

2 Do you think the reactions in Items B, D, E, F and H can be described as a moral panic? With some reference to Item G, give reasons for your answer.

## 2.2  Media representations

### Representations and stereotypes

**Representations** We experience many events first hand. We meet other people, go to school or college, visit different areas and so on. The judgements we make about these people, events and places are based on our own direct impressions.

However, we directly experience only a tiny proportion of the world. We rely on the media for knowledge about unfamiliar places, people and events. The sort of information we gain from the media is indirect – the media actually re-present the world to us. In providing these *representations* of the world, the media will highlight some aspects and neglect others. The language they use and the pictures they choose will give particular impressions.

In general, the media do not have very long to provide background detail. For example, news broadcasts are made up of a number of short items. This means that 'shorthand' methods are often used to describe people and events. The media rely on the images of particular groups that are already in the heads of their audience. In other words, they rely on *stereotypes*.

**Stereotypes** The term stereotype was introduced by the journalist Walter Lippman in his book *Public Opinion*, published in 1922. He described stereotypes as 'the little pictures we carry around our heads'. Stereotypes are widely-held beliefs about the characteristics of members of social groups. Simply because they belong to a particular group, people are seen to have certain attitudes and behaviour.

Stereotypes are generalisations – they are applied to all members of a group. For example, Germans may be seen as efficient, Black people as good athletes and students as layabouts. Stereotypes can be positive or negative, they can offer a favourable or unfavourable image of a group. Nurses are usually pictured as kind and caring, whereas dealers in stocks and shares are often portrayed as money-grabbing and selfish.

### Representations of gender, ethnicity and class

Representations are important because we depend on the media for much of our information about society. Even when we have direct experience of different social groups, media representations will still be in our heads. This will affect the way we think about and interact with others.

This section looks at representations of gender, ethnicity and social class.

### Representations of gender

**Gender stereotypes: the 1950s to 1970s** What is a woman? Judging from media representations of women from the 1950s to the 1970s, a woman is a:

- housewife and mother
- domestic servant
- domestic consumer
- sex object.

This stereotypical view of women was particularly apparent in advertising where the roles of housewife, domestic servant and domestic consumer were often combined. For example, women were regularly presented as cleaners, consuming particular brands of washing powder, washing-up liquid, furniture polish, toilet cleansers, air fresheners, disinfectants and the like. At other times, they were presented as sex objects selling products to women to make them appear more attractive to men, or using their sex-appeal to sell products to men.

When the media portrayed women outside this narrow stereotype, it was often in negative terms. A study of gender representations in the American media from the 1950s to the 1970s found that women shown in paid employment on TV programmes often had unstable or unsatisfactory relationships with male partners. Married women with jobs, particularly more demanding, higher-status jobs, were much more likely than full-time housewives to be portrayed as unhappily married in television drama and comedy (Tuchman, 1981).

# activity 13 stereotyping

### Item A  Racial stereotypes

A number of experiments were conducted in the USA using the following procedure. After being shown this picture, one participant described it to a second participant, who then described it to a third, and so on. After six descriptions, over half the final participants reported that the Black person, not the White person, was holding the razor. Some even had the Black person waving the razor in a threatening manner.

Adapted from Allport & Postman, 1947

A response by an American cartoonist to the torture and execution of American airmen who had bailed out from damaged planes during a bombing raid over Japan. (Tojo was the Japanese Prime Minister during World War II.)

### Item B  American stereotypes of Japanese

| 1932 | 1950 | 1967 |
|------|------|------|
| intelligent | treacherous | industrious |
| industrious | sly | ambitious |
| progressive | extremely nationalistic | efficient |

Adapted from Katz & Braly, 1933; Gilbert, 1951; Karlins, Coffman & Walters, 1969

The cover of an American magazine published five days after the Japanese bombed the American fleet at Pearl Harbour in 1941.

## questions

1  Explain the results of the experiment in Item A, using the idea of stereotypes.

2  Look at Item B.

   a)  Describe the changes in American stereotypes of Japanese.

   b)  Suggest reasons for these changes.

The following quotation by Tunstall (1983) provides a summary of the main findings of research into gender representation in the media from the 1960s and 70s.

'The presentation of women in the media is biased because it emphasises women's domestic, sexual, consumer and marital activities to the exclusion of all else. Women are depicted as busy housewives, as contented mothers, as eager consumers and as sex objects. This does indeed indicate bias because, although similar numbers of men are fathers and husbands, the media has much less to say about these male roles. Just as men's domestic and marital roles are ignored, the media also ignore that well over half of British adult women go out to paid employment, and that many of both their interests and problems are employment-related' (Tunstall, 1983).

**Patriarchy** From a feminist perspective, the gender representations outlined above are an aspect of patriarchy – a social system based on male domination. Women are portrayed either as domestic servants providing comfort and support for men, or as sex objects to service men's sexual needs. In both cases, women play subordinate and subservient roles.

Such media representations suggest that these roles are natural and normal. Feminists see this as an example of patriarchal ideology – a set of beliefs which distorts reality and supports male dominance.

## Changes in media representations of gender

There is some evidence that the representation of gender roles has become more equal and less stereotyped. Drawing upon two content analysis studies of gender representations on prime-time TV shows, Gauntlett (2002) identifies the following changes.

- A significant increase in the proportion of main female characters, from 18% in 1992-93, to 43% in 1995-96.
- A massive decrease since the 1970s in the proportion of women whose main occupation was represented as housewife – now only 3%.
- A marked shift towards equality within the last two decades. 'Female and male characters are likely to be as intelligent, talented and resourceful – or stupid – as each other' (Gauntlett, 2002).

## Films, soaps and sit-coms

Further evidence that gender representations are changing comes from analysis of films, soap operas and situation comedies. Gauntlett (2002) argues that women and men tend to have similar skills and abilities in films today. While a film like *Charlie's Angels* does focus on women as physically attractive, they are also presented as 'amazingly multi-skilled'.

Strong female characters are central to British soap

# *activity 14 gender stereotypes*

## questions

1   What stereotypes are illustrated in these representations of women?

2   How can they be seen as examples of patriarchal ideology?

operas and many actually drive the stories, for example Peggy Mitchell of *EastEnders* (Abercrombie, 1996).

In situation comedies, women are no longer portrayed in traditional 'feminine' roles. For example, both *Roseanne* and *Absolutely Fabulous* show 'unruly women who refuse the straightjacket of femininity' (Newbold et al., 2002).

**Women's magazines** Evidence of changes in gender representations are also evident in magazines targeted at young women. Ferguson (1983) conducted a study of young women's magazines from 1949 to 1980 and found that they promoted a traditional idea of femininity. The dominant assumption was that girls should aspire to be beautiful in order to get a husband and once married

should become home-makers and carers.

By contrast, the focus of magazines since the 1980s is on young women seeking to control their own lives rather than being dependent on men. There is now more emphasis on sexuality and less on romance. Articles such as 'The hottest sex you'll ever have' (*MORE!* May, 2003) illustrate this shift. The traditional idea of femininity is challenged, with women no longer portrayed as the weaker sex. Instead, young women are encouraged 'to be assertive, confident, and supportive of each other' (McRobbie, 1999). In some ways, these magazines turn the tables on men by encouraging women to be sexual aggressors rather than sexual objects (Gauntlett, 2002).

# activity15 *changing representations of women*

Angelina Jolie as Lara Croft in Tomb Raider.

## questions

1   How do the items illustrate changes in media representations of women?

2   To what extent do you think the items accurately represent media representation of women today?

**Evaluation** Are the changes in media representations of women as significant as the above studies suggest? Think about the following evidence. A study of gender representations on American TV in 1995-96 found that men took 63% of the speaking roles compared to women's 37% (Gauntlett, 2002). Research on television sports coverage reveals that sportswomen continue to be under-represented. What little coverage there is 'tends to sexualise, trivialise and devalue women's sporting accomplishments' (Newbold et al., 2002).

While accepting the above points, available evidence indicates that media representations of women are now less likely to rely on traditional stereotypes and less likely to portray women in a narrow range of subordinate roles.

## Representations of ethnicity

Research into the media treatment of ethnicity has emphasised the way in which minority ethnic groups are almost always represented as a 'problem'. They tend to be reported as the cause of social disorder (eg, riots) and crime (eg, 'mugging'). While Black youths *are* involved in these actions, so are large numbers of White youths. The negative representation of minority ethnic groups was particularly noticeable in earlier decades, as the following example from the 1980s illustrates.

**Racism and the press** In a detailed examination of racism and the press, Van Dijk (1991) focused on the reporting of ethnic relations in the 1980s. He studied a sample of British newspapers from 1985 and 1989. His main finding was a positive presentation of White British citizens and a negative presentation of non-White British citizens. Minority group members were quoted less often and less fully than majority group members – even when minority 'experts' were available for comment. White authorities – especially the police and politicians – were the major speakers.

Van Dijk showed that the voice of the British press was predominantly 'white' in both 1985 and 1989, although some improvement was noticeable in the later sample.

**Racial stereotypes** Most recent studies argue that minority ethnic groups continue to be represented in a stereotypical way. The research, almost without exception, has emphasised the large proportion of negative images in the portrayal of Black and Asian people (Cottle, 2000). Complex differences – for example, those between different minority ethnic groups – are ignored. The point of view is virtually always a White one: that 'of the dominant looking at the subordinate: how *they* are different from us rather than how *we* are different from them (Ross, 1996).

**Overt and inferential racism** Both press and television news are often seen by these studies as racist. However, there is a difference between what Hall (1995) calls 'overt' and 'inferential' racism. Overt racism is apparent when racist arguments are presented favourably. Sometimes overt racism does occur but more often what is at issue is inferential racism.

Inferential racism occurs when coverage seems balanced but is based on racist assumptions. Television news and current affairs programmes make an effort to be balanced yet debates are often based on the assumption that Black people are the 'source of the problem' (Hall, 1995).

## Changes in media representations of ethnicity

Much of the research on racism and the media relates to the 1970s and early 1980s. In recent years there has been a growth in both the number and range of representations of minority ethnic groups.

**Film and television drama and comedy** In Britain the ideal of public service broadcasting has allowed Black programming to develop on Channel 4 and BBC2 (Daniels, 1996). This has led to the emergence of Black British cinema through films such as *My Beautiful Launderette* (Higson, 1998).

In recent years, programmes and films developed primarily for minority audiences have become popular with White audiences, for example, the Black sit-com, *Desmond's* and the Asian comedy, *Goodness Gracious Me*. Although integrated casting is still exceptional, Black and Asian actors 'are now playing "ordinary" characters...and the new way of presenting Black [and Asian] people effectively says to the audience that Black [and Asian] people are just like White people' (Abercrombie, 1996). This is apparent in popular programmes such as *The Bill* and *EastEnders* in Britain and *The Cosby Show* in America.

It is still rare for Black or Asian actors to receive star billing but even this has become more common. In some cases this has resulted in the production of positive images of minority communities as in the representation of the Black middle-class family the Huxtables in *The Cosby Show*. The overall result has been an expansion in 'the *range* of racial representations and the *complexity* of what it means to be Black [or Asian]' (Hall, 1997).

**Advertising** Changing representations are also evident in advertising. 'Colonial images and crudely nationalistic emblems are relatively rare in the current period' (Solomos & Back, 1996) and the under-representation of non-Whites in advertising is no longer evident (Glasgow Media Group, 1997). Instead, some multinational corporations now acknowledge and celebrate difference. A classic example is the 'United Colours of Benetton' advertising series in which the message of human unity is based on an acceptance of ethnic and cultural differences (see Activity 16, Item A). While this campaign and others have been criticised for reinforcing ethnic stereotypes, shifts towards a positive valuation of difference 'can unsettle...racism within popular culture' (Solomos & Back, 1996).

Even more unsettling to racist beliefs are the attempts by some artists to challenge our traditional ways of looking through the development of new forms of representation. An example is the presentation by Toscani, the photographer responsible for the Benetton campaign, of a series of well known people with transformed racial characteristics. The picture of the 'Black Queen', for example, reveals and challenges our taken-for-granted assumptions about the necessary whiteness of British identity (see Activity 16, Item C).

**The news** A study from the 1990s of news reporting on TV, radio and in newspapers presents an optimistic picture. The content analysis, conducted over a six month period from November 1996 to May 1997, revealed that most news items that dealt with racial issues put across an anti-racist message.

No explicit racist messages in cartoons could be found. Extensive coverage was given to instances of racism. Immigration was treated in a sympathetic way and press silence on racist attacks was no longer evident. Multiculturalism and Islam were more likely to be valued than attacked. And minority voices were more likely to be heard.

However, the extent of progress should not be exaggerated. While deliberate bias against minorities was found to be rare, about a quarter of news items still conveyed a negative message about minority groups. And

the old framework depicting minority ethnic groups as a social problem was at times all too evident, especially in the tabloid newspapers (Law, 1997).

**Evaluation** Research indicates that media representations of ethnicity do change. They are not simply based on the same old negative stereotypes. While old stereotypes do persist, for example in coverage of Islam after September 11th, media representations of ethnicity are becoming more diverse and more positive.

## Representations of class

It is not difficult to think of stereotypes of social classes. The upper class with their posh accents, country estates and fondness for hunting; the eternal search for status and security of the paranoid middle class; and the cloth cap and close communities of the working class. The media have had a lot to do with the creation of these stereotypes and frequently use them as 'shorthand' ways for recognising characters and situations.

Media representations of social class have received less attention from researchers than those of gender or ethnicity

# activity 16 *changing representations of ethnicity*

**Item A** *Benetton ads*

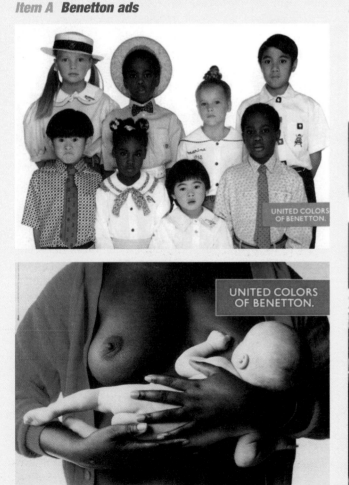

**Item B** *Michael Jackson*

## Item C  Queen Elizabeth II

## Item D  Goodness, Gracious Me

The following dialogue is from the comedy programme *Goodness, Gracious Me*.

The setting is late on a Friday night at an English restaurant in downtown Bombay. Several drunken Indians stagger in. A White waiter helps them into their seats.

I'm totally off my face. How come every Friday night we end up in a Berni Inn?

Cos that's what you do innit? You go out, you get tanked up and you go for an English.

*They peer bleary-eyed at the menu.*

Could I just have a chicken curry?

Oh no, Nina, it's an English restaurant, you've got to have something English – no spices.

But I don't like it, it's too bland.

Jam-mess (*mispronouncing James – the waiter*) What've you got that's not totally tasteless?

Steak and kidney pie sir?

There you are, steak and kidney pee.

No, no. It blocks me up. I won't go to the toilet for a week.

That's the whole point of having an English.

Adapted from Gillespie, 2002

## question

How does each of the items demonstrate that media representations of ethnicity are changing?

---

(Devereux, 2003). What attention there has been has focused primarily on representations of the working class.

British soap operas continue to present the working class as a close-knit community. However, this community is increasingly presented as multi-ethnic and threatened by outside criminal and racist forces (Dodd & Dodd, 1992).

There is some evidence that the media have represented the poor in negative terms. One study showed that welfare issues only became newsworthy when associated with crime and fraud. By focusing on cases of welfare abuse, the media have portrayed the underclass as the undeserving poor, sponging off the welfare state (Golding & Middleton, 1982).

### How important are representations?

The previous sections have demonstrated continuity and change in media representations of different social groups. But how important are these representations? Do they actually influence viewers, listeners and readers?

Their impact cannot be assessed without looking carefully at how audiences respond to the media. The problem here is that people do not respond in a simple and straightforward way to what they see, hear or read. The

effects of the mass media on audiences are discussed at length in Unit 3.

## key terms

**Representations** The way the mass media portray particular social groups, individuals or events.

**Stereotypes** Widely held beliefs about the characteristics of members of social groups.

**Content analysis** A method of analysing the content of the mass media by counting the number of occurrences of particular words, phrases or images.

**Patriarchal ideology** The idea that traditional gender roles are natural and inevitable.

## 2.3 Theories of media content

### Pluralism

Pluralism is also known as the liberal approach – see page 138. It states that the content of the mass media reflects what the public, or a section of the public, wants. In other words, the media simply respond to the demands of the market.

Those who own and control the media usually adopt a pluralist view, arguing that they must satisfy public demand to stay in business. If they failed to do this, nobody would buy their newspapers or watch their TV programmes.

**Diverse society, diverse media** The media presents a range of views which reflect the diversity of opinions in society. The pluralist theory of power states that no one group dominates the whole of society – power is shared among a range of groups. The mass media reflect this diversity. They present a wide range of views, which allows the audience freedom to choose between them. Minority views and tastes are catered for because of the choice of newspapers, magazines, films, radio and TV channels available in a free market.

The media may be biased in certain ways but this is simply because the views they broadcast are those that most people sympathise with and want to hear. If asylum seekers are represented as a 'problem' it is because this reflects the majority view; if women are portrayed in domestic roles, this reflects the reality of most people's lives.

## Marxism

Marxists reject the pluralist view that power is widely distributed throughout society. They believe that power in society is in the hands of a ruling class. For more detail on Marxist views see page 26.

The Marxist approach emphasises the way in which the media support the interests of the rich and powerful. As part of the ruling class, those who own the media and have a vested interest in portraying capitalist society in a positive light. As a result, the media transmit a conservative, conformist view, promote established attitudes and values, and reinforce the position of the powerful.

**Ideology** Ralph Miliband's study *The State in Capitalist Society* (1973) provides an example of a Marxist approach. The ruling class have to convince the rest of the population to accept the widespread inequalities which are inevitable in capitalist societies. Miliband points to the power of the dominant classes to control the way people think through *ideology* – a false view of reality. This control is exercised through the mass media, as well as through other institutions, such as education and the law.

Miliband rejects the idea of pluralist diversity. He sees the choice of alternative options and ideas presented by the media as very limited. The content of the media reflects the viewpoint of the dominant group in society – the White, male, ruling class. It is not just political reporting that supports the system, the content of entertainment programmes is also seen as supporting the way things are by portraying the capitalist system in a favourable light.

**The new 'opium of the people'** Miliband describes the media as the new 'opium of the people', adapting Marx's famous phrase, 'religion is the opium of the people'. He sees the media acting like opium, a hallucinatory drug which creates illusions and produces a feeling of well-being. This keeps the working class quiet and encourages them to accept a system which, in reality, exploits them.

In a similar vein, Marcuse (1964) suggests that programmes which simply entertain, plus the promise of consumer satisfaction that advertisements and game shows provide, help to remove any doubts people may have about the organisation of society. Programmes such as *Neighbours* and *Coronation Street* divert attention from the unfair nature of society, give the impression that nothing is radically wrong with the world we live in, and provide enjoyment and a sense of well-being for millions.

From a Marxist viewpoint, the media's message is simple – accept the way things are!

## Postmodernism

Some observers believe that we are living in a postmodern society, a society that comes after and is different from modern society. More detail about postmodern society can be found on pages 32-33.

This section looks at some views on the nature and content of the mass media in postmodern society. It is largely based on a summary of postmodernism and the media by Dominic Strinati (1992).

**Media realities** We live in a media-saturated society. The media bombard us with images which increasingly dominate the way we define ourselves and the world around us. Media images, it is argued, do not reflect or even distort social reality. They are themselves realities. Our consciousness is invaded by the multiple realities provided by news, documentaries, pop music, advertisements, soaps and movies set in the past, present and future, on this world and other worlds.

Stereotypes still exist but are often used in a playful and ironic way to confuse and amuse us and to attack the very stereotypes on which they are based. For example, the film *Me, Myself and Irene* plays with the idea of racial stereotypes. Jim Carrey plays a White policeman whose three Black sons have been fathered by a midget who ran off with his wife on their wedding day. The sons' behaviour reflects the stereotype of young, ghetto-wise African Americans, apart from the fact they turn out to be geniuses, live in a rural area on Long Island and are devoted to their White policeman father.

**Style and image** Postmodern society is based on style and image. This can be seen in the priority given to designer clothes and their identifying labels. The media plays a central part in this process. Adverts sell images and style rather than content and substance. Jeans are not marketed as hard wearing and value for money but rather as style in the context of rock, R&B or rap music. Drinks like Tango, Bacardi and Smirnoff Ice are sold on style and image rather than taste or quality.

## key term

**Ideology** A false view of reality which supports the interests of the ruling class.

**Time and space** The media allow us to criss-cross time and space. *Romeo and Juliet* was written by Shakespeare in the 16th century but the film starring Leonardo di Caprio takes place in the present day. Watching TV news we can go round the world in 30 minutes from Iraq to the USA, from Afghanistan to Northern Ireland. Adverts use music from the 1950s, 60s and 70s to sell beer, washing powder and jeans. 'Time and space become less stable and comprehensible, more confused, more incoherent, more disunified' (Strinati, 1992).

**A media culture** The mass media increasingly dominate our sense of reality. To a large extent our world now consists of sounds and images from TV, advertisements, computer games, videos, DVDs and CDs. This collage of disjointed and disconnected sounds and images presents not one but many realities. Certainty and fixed standards have been replaced by uncertainty and scepticism.

# activity**17** Pluralism and Marxism

**Item A  EastEnders**

## questions

1  How might a pluralist interpret the items?
2  How might a Marxist interpret the items?

**Item B  BBC News**

**Item C  The National Lottery**

# activity18 postmodernism and the media

**Item A** *The Truman Show*

In the film *The Truman Show* a man discovers that his life has been constructed as a soap opera. His family, friends and neighbours are all actors and he is the central character. Everything around him is an illusion, created by the media.

**Item B** *Saving Private Lynch*

Jessica Lynch has become an All-American heroine. During the Iraq conflict of 2003, the Americans claimed she was injured – suffering from stab and bullet wounds, captured by the Iraqis, slapped and interrogated while on her hospital bed, and then rescued from an Iraqi hospital bed by US Special Forces. The news footage of her rescue became one of the great patriotic moments of the conflict. It couldn't have happened at a more crucial moment, with coalition forces bogged down and little sign of victory.

It now appears that the event was stage-managed by the US propaganda machine. The doctors that cared for her now say that they provided the best treatment they could, gave her their own blood and the only specialist bed in the hospital. The only nurse on the floor was assigned to her. There was no bullet wound, only signs of a road traffic accident. What is more, the Iraqi military had fled from the hospital the day before the US Special Forces arrived – there was no opposition.

An Iraqi doctor said: 'It was like a Hollywood film. They cried, "Go, go, go", with guns and the sound of explosives. They made a show – an action movie like Sylvester Stallone or Jackie Chan, with jumping and shouting, breaking down doors.' All the time the cameras were rolling.

The cult status of Jessica Lynch herself is now stronger than ever. On the Internet oil paintings of her are available at $200 and fridge magnets at $5.

Adapted from *The Guardian*, 15.5.2003

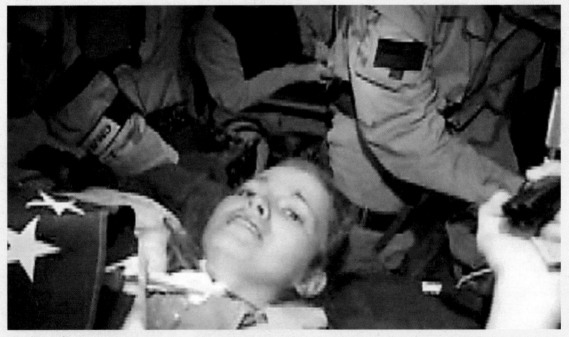

The 'rescue'

## question

How do the items illustrate a postmodern view of the media?

## summary

1. The mass media select certain events as newsworthy and place a particular interpretation on those events. In this way, the media construct news rather than mirror the world.

2. At times, the media sensationalise the events they report. This can lead to moral panics.

3. Certain groups of young people are seen as a threat to social order and a cause for public concern. Sensationalised reporting of their activities can result in a moral panic.

4. Moral panics sometimes view young people as victims – for example, as victims of paedophiles.

5. The mass media represent the world. The representations they use are often based on stereotypes.

6. Studies of gender representations from the 1950s to 1970s showed that the media presented a stereotype of women as domestic servants and sex objects.

7. More recent evidence indicates that media representations of women are now less likely to be based on traditional stereotypes.

8. Media representations of ethnicity have tended to rely on negative stereotypes. Black people were routinely presented as a 'threat' and a 'problem'. Ethnic issues were seen from a White point of view.

9. Recent research indicates more positive representations of minority ethnic groups and a growth in the number and range of representations. However, old stereotypes persist.

10. Media representations of social classes are often based on stereotypes.

11. People do not respond in a straightforward way to what they see, hear and read. As a result, it is difficult to assess the effect of media representations.

12. Pluralist theories see the mass media responding to public demand. Media content reflects what the public want.

13. Marxist theories see the media as an instrument of ideological domination. Their content reflects the interests of the powerful and controls the thinking of the rest of the population.

14. The media in postmodern societies are seen as a major source of our reality.

# Unit 3 *Media effects*

## keyissues

1   What effects do the mass media have on audiences?

2   Do the media make us more violent? Should media output be censored?

3   Media organisations now operate on a global scale. What are the consequences of this?

## 3.1 The media and audiences

How do the mass media affect their audiences? Are audiences vulnerable to media manipulation – do they believe everything they see, hear and read? Or are they sceptical, placing their own interpretations on media messages and making their own judgements?

### Hypodermic syringe theory

Early theories of media effects claimed that the mass media have a direct and immediate effect on behaviour. *Hypodermic syringe theory* likened the effect of the media to the injection of a drug into a vein. The media were seen to have an immediate effect on people's moods and actions. For example, violence in a movie produces feelings of aggression which can lead to violent behaviour.

This view pictured a powerful media which could manipulate and control audiences. Much of the evidence used to support hypodermic syringe theory came from laboratory experiments. But they way people behave in laboratories is often very different from their behaviour in real life situations.

### Two-step flow theory

Hypodermic syringe theory largely ignores the fact that people are social beings, that they have families, friends and work colleagues. Katz and Lazarsfeld's influential *two-step flow theory* (1955) emphasised the importance of social relationships in shaping people's response to the media. They argued that opinions are formed in a social context.

Within this context certain people – *opinion leaders* – are influential in shaping the views of others. These individuals are more likely to be exposed to the media, for example to read more newspapers and magazines. As a result, they are more likely to be influenced by the media and, as opinion leaders, to transmit media messages to others. Hence the idea of a two-step flow – attitudes and ideas 'flow *from* radio and print to opinion leaders and *from them* to the less active sections of the population' (Katz and Lazarsfeld, 1955).

Two-step flow theory was largely based on research into short-term changes in attitudes and opinions. For example, media presentations of election campaigns were examined in order to discover to what extent they changed people's voting intentions. Often, such studies showed that the media had little effect on people's opinions.

# activity 19 the Martians are coming

Orson Welles broadcasting War of the Worlds

'The girls huddled around their radios trembling and weeping in each other's arms. They separated themselves from their friends only to take their turn at the telephone to make long distance calls to their parents, saying goodbye for what they thought might be the last time. Terror-stricken girls, hoping to escape from the Mars invaders, rushed to the basement of the dormitory.'

With these words, an American college student recalls the reaction of herself and her friends to a radio broadcast in 1938. The broadcast was a radio play by Orson Welles based on H.G. Wells' *War of the Worlds*, a novel about an invasion from Mars. It was so realistic that hundreds of thousands of people, who missed the announcement that it was only a play, were convinced the Martians had invaded. There was widespread panic at the news that millions had been killed by Martian death rays.

Many people just didn't know how to respond. They turned to family and friends to see whether they should believe what they'd heard. They interpreted what they saw in terms of the radio programme. One person looked out of his window and saw that Wyoming Avenue was 'black with cars. People were rushing away, I figured'. Another recounted, 'No cars came down my street. Traffic is jammed on account of the roads being destroyed, I thought.'

Thousands fled towns and cities and took to the hills.

Adapted from Cantril, 1940

## question

To what extent does the behaviour of the radio audience support the hypodermic syringe theory?

## Cultural effects theory

This theory assumes that the media does have important effects on its audience. These effects are not as immediate and dramatic as those indicated by the hypodermic syringe theory. Nor are they relatively insignificant as suggested by research into two-step flow theory. Rather they can be seen as a slow, steady, long term build-up of ideas and attitudes.

Cultural effects theory assumes that if similar images, ideas and interpretations are broadcast over periods of time, then they may well affect the way we see and understand the world. Thus if television and radio broadcasts, newspapers and magazines all present, for example, a certain image of women, then slowly but surely this will filter into the public consciousness.

Like the two-step flow theory, cultural effects theory recognises the importance of social relationships. It argues that media effects will depend on the social position of members of the audience, for example, their age, gender, class and ethnicity.

Researchers who attempt to examine the effects of the mass media on attitudes and behaviour have a basic problem to solve. How can these effects be measured? How can they be separated from the range of other factors which influence people's attitudes and behaviour? Some of these problems are examined in Activity 20.

## Audience research

Researchers are increasingly turning to the audience in order to understand and explain media effects. Early theories tended to see media effects as a one-way process with a powerful media shaping audience response. Audience research shows that people interact with the media and interpret media output in various ways. They draw on their beliefs, values, knowledge and experience when making decisions to accept or reject media messages.

This can be seen clearly from Activity 20. It is taken from an article by Greg Philo (1993), a member of the Glasgow Media Group – an important centre for research into British media. Philo's study examined audience response to television news coverage of the 1984/5 miners strike.

**Audience understandings** In more recent research, Greg Philo and David Miller (2002) looked at news reports of the Israeli/Palestinian conflict. They analysed 89 TV news bulletins on BBC1 and ITV from September 28 to October 16, 2002. Their audience sample included 300 young people, aged 17-22. The researchers argued that both the content of the media and audience understandings of that

# activity20 *audience interpretation*

### Item A *The strike*

### Item B *The research*

One hundred and sixty-nine people were interviewed a year after the miners strike of 1984/5. Television news programmes had focused on violent incidents during the strike – clashes between picketing miners and police. Those selected for interview included miners and police who had been involved in the strike, plus a range of people from different parts of the country and with different social backgrounds.

The researchers found that people interpreted the media's version of the strike in terms of their experiences and previously held attitudes and beliefs. 54% of those interviewed believed that the picketing was mostly violent. This reflected media coverage of the strike. However, none of those who had direct knowledge of the strike – the miners and police – believed that picketing was mostly violent. They rejected the impression given by the media. According to them, strikers and police spent most of their time standing round doing nothing.

Studies like this show that media effects are not simple and direct. They are interpreted in various ways in terms of people's experiences and beliefs.

Adapted from Philo, 1993

### questions

1  a)  Which picture is typical of the strike?

   b)  Why do you think TV news focused on violent confrontations?

2  Judging from this study, why is audience research valuable?

content, must be studied together in order to analyse media effects.

Transcripts of reports on the Israeli/Palestinian conflict ran to 3536 lines of text. Of those only 17 lines explained the history of the conflict. The news focused on violent events, on the tragic loss of life and on the bleak prospects for peace.

Over 80% of the sample relied on TV news for information about the conflict. Most had little understanding of the reasons for the conflict, and at times completely misunderstood what was going on. They had insufficient background knowledge to make sense of news broadcasts. For example, 80% of the sample did not know where Palestinian refugees came from and why they were refugees. When TV journalists talked about 'occupied territories', 71% of the sample did not know that it was Palestinian territory occupied by Israelis, 11% thought it was Palestinians who were doing the occupying, and only 9% knew it was Israelis. When images of Palestinians burning an American flag were shown on the news, 66% did not know why Palestinians might be critical of the USA, 24% thought America 'supported' Israel, and only 10% knew that America supplied Israel with money and weapons.

As noted earlier, the researchers argue that media effects can only be understood by looking at media content and audience response together. Only a minority of the sample had a clear understanding of what was going on. This was because they already had sufficient background knowledge to make sense of what they saw and heard. Most members of the sample did not have this knowledge *and* it was not supplied in the news reports (Philo & Miller, 2002).

**Asking the audience** Audience research is based on the view that audiences must be studied in order to understand and explain media effects. For example, one study showed that many young British Asians enjoyed soap operas such as *Neighbours* (Gillespie, 1995). Why should they be drawn to a soap about White middle-class suburban Australians?

Research amongst young Punjabis suggested that they saw parallels in the role that gossip plays as a mechanism of social control in their own community and in *Neighbours*. And they used the programme as a reference point in discussions about their own identity.

This explanation of media effects is only possible if researchers 'ask the audience'.

### Media effects – conclusion

Some studies focus on media content, analyse that content

# *activity21 audience understandings*

### Item A  Burning the President

*Palestinians chant anti-Israeli slogans while burning an effigy of US President George Bush on a mock-up of an Israeli tank in Rafah refugee camp, Gaza Strip.*

### Item B  Running for cover

*Palestinian youths run for cover as an Israeli armoured personnel carrier opens fire to disperse them in Massader village. Mortar bombs had been fired from the village at nearby Jewish settlements in the Gaza Strip.*

## question

What background knowledge would an audience need to make sense of the images in Items A and B?

and assume it is having a particular effect on audiences. For example, a researcher may analyse media representations of women, see them as stereotypes portraying women as domestic servants and sex objects, and assume that this affects how women are seen in the wider society. In terms of cultural effects theory, the constant repetition of these images will lead to a slow, steady build-up of ideas and attitudes about women.

Other studies focus on the audience, arguing that media effects can only be understood and explained by studying audience response to the media. Researchers cannot assume that audiences will respond in a particular way to a particular news bulletin, movie, advertisement or novel, or to the constant repetition of particular images.

Today, many researchers argue that both approaches are necessary to understand media effects – both media content and audience response must be studied.

## 3.2 Media effects, violence and censorship

Does media violence – on TV, video and DVD, in newspapers, magazines and books – lead people to commit violent acts? The idea of a link between media violence and violent behaviour has a long history stretching back to the 19th century. Comics, radio, movies and more recently TV, video, DVD and video games, have all been accused of causing violence in the wider society.

The primary concern of research has been the effects of media violence on the more 'vulnerable' and 'impressionable' members of society, particularly children. Despite the large amount of research, usually by psychologists, surprisingly little is known about the effects of media violence. It becomes a hot political topic at regular intervals, usually following the publication of a new study or the reporting of a 'copycat' crime which appears to mirror a media portrayal of violence.

### A word of warning

**Defining violence** Why has so little progress been made in understanding the effects of media violence? One of the main problems is defining and measuring violence. First the term 'violence' can cover a vast range of very different acts. For example, in one study of television violence, violent acts included using physical force against oneself or others, threatening to hurt or kill others, and accidents and natural disasters involving injury or death (Gerbner & Gross, 1976).

These are very different actions and events which involve a range of very different meanings, intentions and motives. This can be seen from the following examples: a 'cold-blooded' murder, a fatal skiing accident, bombing an enemy position, killing somebody in self-defence.

Many studies simply count the number of violent actions that appear on television over a given time period and lump them together in a grand total. This ignores the many different forms that 'violence' can take.

**Context and meaning** Second, the context in which so-called violent acts are portrayed can be very different and affect the meaning given to such acts. For example, physical violence is portrayed in cartoons such as *Tom and Jerry*, in soaps such as *Coronation Street*, in series such as *The Bill*, in films such as *The Matrix* and *Scary Movie* and in news and documentary programmes.

Clearly the context will affect the meaning and therefore the effect. 'Real' violence on the news can hardly be compared to the 'fun' – and for many funny – violence in *Scary Movie*. Again, simply adding up the acts of violence ignores the variety of meanings that may be given to apparently similar acts in different contexts.

**Audience response** Studies based on counting produce data that, on the face of it, are alarming. For example, British viewers watch an average of 1.68 acts of violence on TV every hour (Cumberbatch, 1987). American children see 8,000 murders and more than 100,000 other acts of violence on TV by the time they finish elementary (primary) school (DeAngelis, 1993).

Such studies tend to picture viewers as sponges, passively soaking up what they see. They suggest that this vast output of 'violence' must have an effect on the viewer. Often, however, little attempt is made to say how that effect actually occurs – ie the psychological processes involved – and how it might be translated into behaviour.

Sometimes conclusions can be extremely simplistic – a diet of TV violence will increase aggressive and violent behaviour. However, research has indicated that things are not nearly so simple. Viewers are not merely a mass of identical and passive sponges. Their response to the media is influenced by a range of factors including their personal experiences, age, gender, sexual orientation, ethnicity, social class and culture. They actively and creatively engage with and think about the programmes they watch. Different viewers may interpret the same programmes in very different ways (Livingstone, 1997).

### Studies of television violence

Most studies on the effects of media violence have investigated violence on television. These studies have used a variety of methods including laboratory and field experiments.

**Laboratory experiments** Laboratory experiments into television violence usually take two groups of participants and expose one group to violent programmes, whilst showing the other group non-violent programmes. Aggressive behaviour is then measured in both groups at a later point. Laboratory studies have generally shown that exposure to violent programmes does result in an increase in aggressive behaviour.

For example, Liebert and Baron (1972) showed one group of children an episode of a TV police drama featuring high levels of violence. They showed a second group of children an equally exciting TV sporting event,

# activity22 defining media violence

**Item A**

From a Tom and Jerry comic

**Item B**

From the movie Reservoir Dogs

**Item C**

Las Vegas, 2003

**Item D**

Irish Guards in Iraq, 2003

## question

How do these items illustrate the difficulty of defining media violence and measuring its effects?

which did not feature violence. After the viewing session, the children were allowed to play with a further group of children, who had seen neither programme. Children who had seen the violent programme tended to behave more aggressively than those who watched the non-violent programme.

**Evaluation** Laboratory studies of TV violence have been criticised for the following reasons.

- They tend to be unrealistic and artificial. Often the programmes are specially made and quite unlike typical television programmes which depict violence – for example, there is often no plot, no character development, no moral theme.

- Laboratory studies are limited to studying short-term effects. They are unable to assess the effects of long-term exposure to media violence.

- Sample sizes are often small. This makes generalisation difficult.

**Field experiments** These experiments are conducted in real-world settings such as the workplace, home, or school. They can avoid some of the artificiality of the laboratory. In a famous experiment, Feshbach and Singer (1971) studied 652 boys, aged 8-18, living in residential institutions – three private schools and two boys' homes. The boys were randomly divided into two groups. The first group watched only violent programmes for 6 weeks, the second group only non-violent programmes.

Surprisingly, the boys who watched non-violent programmes showed more aggression towards others than those who watched violent programmes. This result was interpreted as evidence for a *catharsis* view of aggression – those who watched violent programmes could 'let off steam' safely by empathising with the violence. Those who watched non-violent programmes did not have this opportunity, leading them to express their feelings in actual physical aggression.

Other field experiments have produced different findings. For example, American and British teenage delinquents in residential institutions were shown violent and non-violent films. Those who watched the non-violent films appeared to behave less aggressively. The violent films appeared to increase aggression, but *only* in boys who had a record of violent behaviour (Parke et al., 1977).

**Evaluation** The findings of field experiments are inconclusive – they are not clear-cut. In general, field experiments indicate that exposure to violent films appears to produce an increase in aggressive behaviour, at least in the short term. However, the effect is usually weaker in the more natural surroundings of the field experiment than in the laboratory (Wood et al., 1991).

**Correlation studies** These studies collect information on viewing patterns and measures of aggression from large samples of participants. They then compare the two sets of information to assess whether there is any correlation, that is a significant statistical relationship, between the two. For example, Belson (1978) organised interviews with over 1,500 boys aged 12-17 in London to assess their television viewing habits and to measure their aggressiveness. It was found that those who tended to watch more violent programmes also committed more violent acts. This may mean that television violence encourages violent behaviour. Or it may simply mean that violent people prefer to watch violent programmes.

**Evaluation** Correlational studies simply show a statistical relationship. They do not necessarily indicate a cause and effect relationship. In other words, just because two variables correlate does not mean that one causes the other.

Many correlational studies of the possible effects of TV violence are very simplistic. Often, they fail to consider a range of variables such as age, gender, class and ethnicity. When these variables are taken into account, they usually have a stronger relationship to aggressive behaviour than viewing habits (Newburn & Hagell, 1995).

## Possible effects of media violence

How might violence on the screen lead to heightened aggression and an increase in violent behaviour? The following processes have been suggested.

**Arousal** Psychological arousal can result from viewing violent imagery. This arousal may be carried over into a new situation where it can encourage the aroused individual to react aggressively if they are provoked. Zillmann and Bryant (1984) found that individuals who viewed high levels of violent pornography tended to react with aggression when they were then subjected to a frustrating experience. However, the link between television violence and emotional arousal does not appear to be particularly strong (Bryant & Zillmann, 1994).

**Desensitisation** Many studies of television violence claim that watching violent programmes may *desensitise* viewers to actual violence. Individuals desensitised to violence will not find aggressive acts particularly disturbing or unusual. They are therefore less likely to be restrained by social norms against aggression. Although this claim is often made in the popular reporting of research, there is little hard evidence to support it. Belson (1978) found that teenage boys who had been exposed to violent programmes were not desensitised in their reactions to either directly experienced violence or news reports of violent events.

**The 'zombie' effect** Another effect often claimed is that widespread exposure to television can make viewers – particularly children – into 'mindless', uncritical individuals who are unable to distinguish fantasy from reality. Gauntlett (1995) calls this the 'zombie' effect. As with desensitisation, there is little evidence to support the claim. Neumann (1991) presented evidence that television neither reduces children's attention spans nor blurs their ability to think clearly. Buckingham (1996) found that children could make clear and confident distinctions between what happens on television and what happens in the real world.

**Imitation** Some researchers claim that children often imitate adult behaviour – in this case, adult violence (see Chapter 4, Activity 7, page 188).

It is imitation of a particular form of media violence that is most often reported. For example, when John Hinckley shot US President Reagan, he appeared to imitate a scene from the film *Taxi Driver.* Some press reports claimed that the two children who murdered the toddler James Bulger imitated certain aspects of the violence in the horror film *Child's Play 3* (see Activity 12).

However, it cannot be proved that viewing a portrayal of a violent act on television directly causes a re-enactment of that act in real life. Even when a violent act closely mirrors a media depiction, this may have little significance. For example, three gunmen behaving like characters in the movie *Scream* held up two restaurants in Omaha, Nebraska. They may well have robbed the restaurants without seeing the film – behaving like characters in *Scream* may simply have added spice to their venture.

**Catharsis** This refers to the release of tension and anxiety resulting in a calming effect. The idea of catharsis was used by Feshbach and Singer (1971) to explain their finding that the boys who watched violent films behaved less aggressively than those who watched non-violent films. In terms of catharsis theory, images of violence can serve as a release for pent-up aggression and therefore have a positive effect on behaviour.

### Media violence – conclusion

The results of research on the effects of media violence are inconclusive – no firm conclusion can be reached. Despite this uncertainty, many so-called experts claim that media violence does lead to violent behaviour.

It's easy to blame the media for a range of social problems. The media are highly visible and provide a convenient scapegoat for the ills of society.

Inconclusive results do not mean that years of research have been a waste of time. They question the views of those who demand the removal of violence from our TV screens. And they raise doubts about the claim that TV violence has no effect at all.

## key terms

**Arousal** A heightened state of mental and physical alertness.
**Desensitisation** A decrease in sensitivity. In the context of the media, a failure to be disturbed by violent behaviour. Desensitisation is seen to result from high levels of exposure to images of violence.
**The 'zombie' effect** The claim that widespread exposure to television can make viewers, particularly children, into 'mindless', uncritical individuals who have difficulty distinguishing fantasy from reality.
**Catharsis** The release of tension and anxiety resulting in a calming effect.

### Censorship

Censorship of the media refers to the prevention or removal of material from films, newspapers, radio, television, advertisements, and so on. A variety of reasons are given for censorship. For example, the material in question may be seen as a danger to the public or a threat to national security.

**Censorship in Britain** In Britain, films, videos and DVDs are censored in two ways. First, material may be removed – because, for example, it is judged to be too violent or too sexually explicit. Second, by restricting certain age groups from viewing material regarded as unsuitable for them.

## *activity23 copycat murders*

### Item A  *The Matrix*

One of the attractions of the film *The Matrix* is its blend of fantasy and reality.

A series of murders in the United States suggests some people have been unable to distinguish between the two.

Josh Cooke, a 19-year-old in Oakton, Virginia, owned a trenchcoat like the one worn by Neo, the character played by Keanu Reeves in the movie, and kept a poster of his hero on his bedroom wall. Then he bought a gun similar to the one used by Neo to fight evil.

In February 2003, he shot his father and mother in the basement of their home and then called the police. His lawyers say he believed that he was living inside the Matrix.

In May 1993, a woman in Ohio was found not guilty of killing the professor whose house she rented, on the grounds of insanity. Tonda Lynn Ansley, 37, said she had had dreams which turned out not to be dreams. The local prosecutor said that, 'in her warped perception', *The Matrix* played a part in the killing.

Adapted from *The Guardian*, 19.5.2003

### Item B  'Scream' killings

A number of murders apparently linked to the *Scream* horror film trilogy have heightened fears about the impact of screen violence on the young.

#### ENGLAND

**1999** Thirty-four violent films, including *Scream*, found in the rooms of two male college students at Hadlow, Kent, who stabbed a friend to death, dismembered his body and burnt it.

**1999** Two boys, who stabbed a friend and left him for dead after watching *Scream*, were convicted of attempted murder in Hull.

**2000** Man shot dead in Liverpool after two men, one wearing a *Scream*-type mask, burst into his house.

#### FRANCE

**2000** A 15-year-old, who said he was obsessed by *Scream*, wore the mask while stabbing his sleeping parents to death.

**2002** 14-year-old girl tortured and left for dead by two friends who had watched *Scream*, near Mulhouse in eastern France.

**2002** A 17-year-old, arrested for the murder of a 15-year-old stabbed at Saint-Sébastien-sur-Loire, western France, admitted he was obsessed by *Scream*.

#### UNITED STATES

**1997** Three male teenagers who had repeatedly watched *Scream* murdered two girls in Salem, Massachusetts.

**1999** With the help of two cousins, a youth from Lynwood, California, stabbed his mother to death after watching *Scream*.

**2000** A woman and two men wearing *Scream* masks robbed a store in Lowell, Massachusetts, and shot a man dead.

**2002** Man accused of shooting two men dead in a bar in Pennsylvania wore a *Scream* mask.

#### BELGIUM

**2001** A lorry driver put on a *Scream* costume before killing a 15-year-old girl with two enormous kitchen knives, in the town of Gerpinnes.

Adapted from *The Observer*, 9.6.2002

A still from Scream 2 showing the Scream mask

### Item C  Video games

The Columbine High School shootings in Colorado in 1999 drew widespread attention to graphic violence in video games. Teenagers Dylan Klebold and Eric Harris shot dead 12 classmates and a teacher before killing themselves. A recording they left behind describes how the slaughter would be just like their favourite video game, *Doom*. This is an extremely violent game used in the training of US marines.

A study led by Dr Craig Anderson looked at the effect of violent video games on people already prone to aggression. He states that, 'Our study reveals that young men who are habitually aggressive may be especially vulnerable to the aggression-enhancing effects of repeated exposure to violent games'.

Violent video games are sometimes seen as more harmful than television violence because they are interactive, they are realistic, they are particularly engrossing and they often require the player to identify with the aggressor.

Adapted from McVeigh, 2001

*James Lewis, 12, playing Duke Nukem, a violent video game which allows the player to shoot and kill. James does not show aggressive behaviour and is an excellent student with high grades.*

## question

Do you believe that watching *The Matrix* and *Scream* films and playing violent video games such as *Doom* resulted in the murders described in Items A, B and C? Give reasons for your answer.

Television is also subject to rules about the portrayal of violence and sex. For example, the Independent Television Commission provides a list of guidelines for broadcasting scenes of violence.

**Views of censorship** There are two main views of censorship – the liberal view and the conservative view. Liberals argue 'that no human expression should be suppressed unless it can be proved that it will result in harming someone' (Carter & Weaver, 2003). Although media violence may be deeply offensive to many people, liberals believe it should not be banned unless it can be proved to be harmful. The difficulty here is that the issue is not clear-cut. As noted earlier, research on the effects of media violence is inconclusive.

The conservative view is more sympathetic to censorship. It argues that in certain cases material should be banned if it offends good taste – for example, swearing and explicit sex – or undermines strongly held values – for example, gratuitous violence, that is violence for no good reason or just for the fun of it.

**The Internet** Some writers argue that the development of the Internet means censorship has had its day. Extreme violence and explicit sex are widely available. Attempts at censorship are difficult as users can gain access by direct satellite links or Internet service providers in other countries (Gorman & McLean, 2003). International cooperation has led to some success in removing images of child abuse from the Internet and prosecuting those who download them. However, plenty of sites specialising in child abuse are still available.

It remains to be seen whether international cooperation will result in effective censorship of the Internet.

# 3.3 Mass communications and globalisation

## What is globalisation?

Many sociologists believe that a process known as *globalisation* is occurring. Communication is often on a global scale. As a result, we are increasingly aware of events occurring across the globe. The world appears to be shrinking.

A key feature of globalisation is *time-space compression* – time seems to be quickening up and space seems to be getting smaller. This is partly due to the development of information and communications technology. For example, the computerisation of financial markets enables vast amounts of money to be transferred rapidly from one side of the world to the other. And communication satellites allow instant communication across the globe. As a result, events occurring thousands of miles away can have an immediate impact as time and space are increasingly compressed.

**Global village** The Live Aid movement of the mid-1980s provides a good example of the way that the world has come to seem more like a village. The movement, founded by the singer Bob Geldof, emerged in order to raise money to relieve an appalling famine in Ethiopia. Its highlight was a day-long concert, held at venues in Britain and America 3,000 miles apart, and linked by satellite into one programme. The mass media were central. It was television which allowed people in Britain and America to become aware of a famine thousands of miles away. And it was television which broadcast the concert around the world.

**Spaceship earth** The explosion in 1986 at the Chernobyl nuclear plant in the former Soviet Republic of Ukraine provides a dramatic example of our ecological interdependence on spaceship earth. The consequences of the explosion were felt as far away as Cumbria. The explosion provides an example of the way in which the very survival of the planet is threatened by the use of certain technological developments. Media coverage across the world made many people realise that they shared their fate with everyone else on the planet.

**The medium as the message** The media played a key role in both Live Aid and Chernobyl. Live Aid would not have happened without the media and we might not have heard about Chernobyl without media coverage. Media technologies are crucial in creating a shrinking world.

Some writers go further and argue that the content of media messages has always been less important than the media technologies used for conveying messages (McLuhan, 1994). Take, for example, the invention in the fifteenth century of a printing process using movable metal type. This enabled books to be produced more cheaply. Publishers initially produced books in Latin but the market for such works was limited. Keen to expand their market, publishers produced translations in local languages. The increased availability of books, along with the establishment of newspapers in the eighteenth century, helped to standardise and spread these languages. 'For the first time, it was possible for the mass of people within a particular state to understand each other through a common print language' (Barker, 1999). In this way, the print media enabled people to develop a common national identity.

For McLuhan and his followers, the significance of the new media, like satellite broadcasting and the Internet, is that they bring people closer together and enable people to see themselves as members of a 'global village'. While an earlier print technology encouraged identification with the nation, the new technologies encourage identification with the global village.

**Evaluation** McLuhan's emphasis on media technology – the medium is the message – has been criticised. New technologies don't operate in a vacuum. What sociologists stress is the need to examine the social context within which they operate. Which technologies are developed and how they are used depends upon economic and political factors. The private and increasingly concentrated ownership of media industries, coupled with increasing reliance on the market, are now the key economic and political factors shaping the development of the media.

# *activity*24 *a shrinking world*

### Item A  9-11

Attack on the World Trade Center, New York, September 11, 2001

### Item B  David Beckham

*David Beckham escorted through a cheering crowd in China. It is estimated that a billion Chinese watched his debut for Real Madrid against the all-star Chinese Dragons in Beijing on August 3, 2003.*

### question

How do these items suggest that we are living in a shrinking world?

---

New technologies create a range of opportunities. The new media *may* encourage people to see themselves as members of a global village, but whether this happens will depend upon other factors. The Internet provides opportunities across the globe for both commercial gain and public debate. The context within which the Internet has recently developed means, however, that the 'trend towards the commercialisation of the web is becoming the dominant one' (McCullagh, 2002).

**Globalisation and the media** The global context has the following characteristics.

- Across the world, a small number of transnational media organisations have emerged. Organisations such as AOL Time Warner, Disney, Viacom and News Corporation operate at a global level in terms of the production, distribution and sale of their media products.

- Unlike traditional publicly or privately owned media organisations, transnational media organisations operate in an increasingly deregulated environment. They face few regulations preventing them from focusing their activities on purely commercial considerations.

- The major transnational organisations, whose main base is in Western societies, dominate the global network of communication. It is the images, music and words of Western societies that are most commonly found in media around the world (Devereux, 2003).

**Media imperialism** Some sociologists argue that the power of transnational media organisations across the world is so great that we are witnessing a new form of *imperialism* – a new type of empire. While the direct political control of one nation by another is no longer very common, media organisations are transmitting Western values and attitudes across the world. 'The global television music of MTV, the global news of CNN, the global box office hits of Hollywood films and the global television soap operas shape the cultures of the global South, ensuring their Westernisation' (Williams, 2003). The media imperialism view claims that the flow of Western media products across the world means that local cultures will be battered into submission and disintegrate.

**Evaluation** Many sociologists reject the view of media imperialism. For example, Giddens (1990) argues that globalisation does not necessarily lead to a Westernised world which watches Hollywood movies, listens to rap music, and takes its lead from Western role models in films and on TV.

Even when the same television programmes are shown around the world, people don't necessarily respond to them in the same way. For example, Dutch viewers enjoyed the glossy US soap opera *Dallas*, but rejected the programme's celebration of the values of American capitalism (Ang, 1985). And even if the rights to

# activity25 media imperialism

Buying pirated videos and DVDs in Shanghai, China. Titles include *Gone With The Wind* and *Disney's Sleeping Beauty.*

Vietnamese edition of 8 Mile

Russian edition of Lord of the Rings

## question

How do these items support the claim that the media are spreading Western tastes and values across the world?

programmes such as *Who wants to be a millionaire?* and *Big Brother* are sold to TV companies across the world, local versions reflecting local cultures are produced.

**Resisting media imperialism** Sreberny-Mohammadi (1996) points to a number of ways in which local cultures resist media imperialism.

- Home-produced programmes can replace imports because they are more attractive to local audiences for cultural reasons. Research in Asia, for example, showed that in seven of nine countries more hours of locally produced television were broadcast than of imported programmes (Gorman & McLean, 2003).

- In some cases, the flow of programmes may be reversed so that local programmes are exported to Western societies. For example, British Asians 'maintain strong ties with their countries of origin through the consumption of popular film and television exported from the Indian sub-continent' (Gillespie, 1995).

- Local producers can create transnational media organisations. For example, ZEE TV, a Hindi-language commercial station, took over TV Asia in Britain.

- In many countries, there are attempts to restrict foreign imports, to block access to foreign web-sites and even ban the sale of satellite dishes.

We should not romanticise these forms of resistance. In some cases, restricting foreign imports and banning the sale of satellite dishes has less to do with seeking to preserve local cultures and more to do with maintaining power. For example, foreign programmes promoting a more liberated image of women may be seen as a threat by men in some societies. At the same time, we need to recognise the global context within which resistance occurs. There may be a two-way flow of media products, but that flow is not an equal one. Richer countries not only have greater access to the new media. They are also the places where the major media organisations are owned and directed.

## key terms

**Globalisation** The process by which the various countries and cultures across the world become more closely intertwined.
**Time-space compression** The process by which time seems to be quickening up and space seems to be getting smaller.
**Global village** The idea that the world seems increasingly like a village.
**Spaceship earth** A view which looks down on the world and sees it like a spaceship populated by all the people on earth.
**Media imperialism** The idea that Western-owned transnational media organisations are like a new type of empire with power over the large sections of the world.

# activity26 ethnic media

*Red Records, Brixton, South London, specialising in African-Caribbean music*

*Radio presenter at Sunrise Radio, an Asian radio station*

*Reading The Voice, an African-Caribbean newspaper*

## question

How do these items demonstrate resistance to media imperialism?

*Indian film poster, Brick Lane. East London*

## summary

1. There are various theories of media effects.

2. The hypodermic syringe theory sees the media having an immediate and direct effect on people's moods and actions.

3. Two-step flow theory argues that attitudes and ideas flow from the media to opinion leaders to the rest of the population.

4. Cultural effects theory sees media effects as a slow, steady, long term build-up of beliefs and attitudes in response to the frequent transmission of similar images and ideas over fairly long periods of time.

5. Researchers are increasingly turning to the audience in order to understand media effects.

6. Audience research shows that people draw on their beliefs, values, knowledge and experience in order to interpret media output.

7. There has been a large amount of research on the effects of media violence. A major concern has been its effect on the more 'vulnerable' and 'impressionable' members of society, particularly children.

8. Research into the effects of media violence is difficult for the following reasons.
   - The problems of defining violence.
   - The context of violent images – audiences give different meanings to similar acts viewed in different contexts.
   - Research methods – every method for studying media effects has its drawbacks.
   - Measuring media effects – it is extremely difficult to separate the effects of media violence from all the other influences on people's behaviour.

9. The following processes have been suggested to explain the possible effects of media violence.
   - Arousal
   - Desensitisation
   - The 'zombie' effect
   - Imitation
   - Catharsis

10. The results of research on the effects of media violence are inconclusive.

11. Whether, and to what extent, media violence is censored depends partly on which viewpoint is taken – the liberal or conservative – and partly on how people view the evidence on the effects of media violence.

12. The media are an important part of the process of globalisation.

13. According to McLuhan, new media technologies encourage people to identify with the 'global village'.

14. Other researchers admit that new media technologies are important, but place more emphasis on the economic and political context in which they operate. For example, the new technologies are used by transnational media organisations for commercial purposes.

15. The dominant position of Western media organisations has led some researchers to see this as media imperialism.

16. However, the flow of ideas and opinions is not simply one way. There are plenty of locally-produced media products, some of which are exported to Western countries.

# 4 Sociological research skills

## Introduction

Are the following statements true or false?

- There has been a steady increase in lone-parent families.
- The higher the class position of a child's parents, the more likely the child is to achieve high grades in school examinations.
- More and more women are taking up paid employment.

According to the 2002 edition of *Social Trends*, published by the Office of National Statistics, all the statements are true.

- In Britain in 1981, 13% of families with dependent children were headed by lone parents. By 2000, this had doubled to 26%.
- In 2000, two-thirds of young people in England and Wales with parents in non-manual occupations achieved 5 or more A* to C grades at GCSE compared to one-third of those with parents in manual occupations.
- In the UK in 1981, 10.9 million women age 16 and over were members of the labour force. By 2001, this number had grown to 13.2 million.

The statements at the beginning of this introduction are not based on opinion or prejudice, they are not based on guesses or gossip. They are based on research.

Research involves systematically collecting and analysing information. The term *data* is often used for information gathered as part of a research project. This chapter looks at sociological research methods – the methods used by sociologists to collect and analyse data.

## chaptersummary

▷ **Unit 1** looks at the reasons for research.

▷ **Unit 2** takes an overview of the research process and considers the ethical issues involved in research.

▷ **Unit 3** looks at the problem of identifying causes and effects.

▷ **Units 4 and 5** outline two types of research – experiments and social surveys.

▷ **Units 6, 7 and 8** examine three methods of data collection – questionnaires, interviews and observation.

▷ **Unit 9** looks at secondary sources of data.

▷ **Unit 10** examines further types of research, including life histories, longitudinal studies and comparative studies.

▷ **Units 11 and 12** look at ways of interpreting and evaluating quantitative and qualitative data.

▷ **Unit 13** outlines how sociologists report research results.

## Unit 1 Reasons for research

### keyissues

1 What's the point of doing research?

2 What are the basic concepts used by researchers?

3 What types of data do sociologists use in their research?

### 1.1 Why do research?

What's the point in doing research? Why not rely on common sense to provide answers?

**Common sense** For hundreds of thousands of years, common sense told us that the world was flat. We now know that this bit of common sense was nonsense. Take another example. What causes illness and death? Common sense has come up with all sorts of weird and wonderful explanations over the years. Research has shown that many of these explanations are no better than fairy stories.

**Experience** Why not rely on people's experience instead of spending large sums of money on research? Older people have 'seen it all', why not ask them for answers? Older people have *not* seen it all, their experience is very limited

– often to a small circle of family, friends and acquaintances.

Some older people talk about the 'good old days' when, for example, there was far less crime and it was safe to walk the streets. But, what evidence can they provide for this view? Not a lot, apart from fond memories which may have been coloured by time.

**Judgements** Why not rely on people's judgement to provide answers? Ask adults in a particular neighbourhood and they might make a judgement that the standards of teaching in their local comprehensive are extremely high. But high compared to what – to the other local comprehensive, to other secondary schools in the county, or in the country as a whole? Or high compared to their experience from their own schooldays? 'High' means nothing unless there is some clearly stated yardstick for measurement.

### What research offers

For many sociologists, research should provide the following.

**Objective knowledge** This is unbiased or value-free knowledge. In other words, it is not influenced by the values, biases and prejudices of the researcher.

**Evidence-based statements** These are statements based on evidence rather than hearsay, gossip, opinion, common sense and unsupported belief.

**Measurement** Data should be available in a form which can be measured. For example, rather than saying 'Most people ...', the data should allow the researcher to state, '85% of people ...'.

Whether research can, or even should, live up to these standards is another question. This question is examined throughout the chapter.

## 1.2 Basic concepts

This section looks at some of the basic concepts which sociologists use to evaluate the quality of data.

**Validity** Data is *valid* if it presents a true and accurate description or measurement. For example, official statistics on crime are valid if they provide an accurate measurement of the extent of crime.

**Reliability** Data is *reliable* when different researchers using the same methods obtain the same results. For example, if a number of researchers observed the same crowd at the same sporting event and produced the same description of crowd behaviour, then their account would be reliable. The method – in this case observation – produces reliable results.

# *activity1 common sense and research evidence*

*The American Soldier* by Samuel A. Stouffer is a detailed study of attitudes of United States' soldiers during World War II. It was strongly criticised by the historian Arthur Schlesinger as stating the obvious and based on little more than common sense.

**Common sense**

1 Better educated soldiers had more psychological problems, eg severe depression, than those with less education. This is because men with less education are more used to dealing with hardship.

2 Soldiers from the warmer southern states were better able to cope with the steamy heat of the South Pacific islands than those from northern states. Southerners were more accustomed to the heat.

3 White soldiers were more eager than Black soldiers to become officers. This is because Black soldiers had been deprived of opportunities before they joined the army and consequently lacked ambition.

4 Men were more eager to return home during the fighting than after the German surrender in 1945. This is understandable as there was a far greater chance of injury or death during the war.

Adapted from Lazarsfeld, 1949

**Research evidence**

1 Less educated soldiers had more psychological problems than those with more education.

2 Men from the northern and southern states showed no difference in adapting to tropical heat.

3 Black soldiers were more eager for promotion than Whites.

4 Men were more eager to return to the USA when the fighting ended than during the war itself.

## questions

1 Read the common sense statements. Do they make sense to you?

2 Read the research evidence. How does it indicate the importance of research?

*US soldiers in Italy during World War II*

However, reliable data may not be valid. Say the crowd was at a baseball match in the USA, and the sociologists were English and knew nothing about baseball. They all produce the same description but they may well fail to understand the crowd's responses to the game. As a result, their description of the crowd's behaviour, while being reliable, may be inaccurate.

**Representativeness** Sociologists cannot study everyone. As a result, they often select a sample from the population they wish to study. For example, the population may be 16-19 year olds in Further Education. The researcher will select a sample which they hope will *represent* the group as a whole. Various ways of selecting a representative sample are outlined on pages 190-191.

**Generalisation** If the sample does indeed represent the larger group, then research findings from the sample can be applied to the larger group. In other words, the findings can be *generalised*.

## 1.3 Types of data

### Primary and secondary data

One of the first questions sociologists ask when starting a research project is 'What kind of data will I use?' There are two main types of data – *primary data* and *secondary data*. Often researchers use both types.

**Primary data** refers to information which was not present before the research began. It is generated by the researcher during the actual process of research. It includes data produced by questionnaires, interviews and observations.

**Secondary data** refers to data which already exists. It includes data from historical records, official statistics, government reports, diaries, autobiographies, novels, newspapers, films and recorded music.

### Quantitative and qualitative data

A second question sociologists ask when starting research is 'What form do I want the data in?' There are two forms of data – *quantitative data* and *qualitative data*. Researchers often use both forms.

**Quantitative data** This is data in the form of numbers. Examples of quantitative data are given in the introduction to this chapter. Here are some more examples from the year 2000. Twenty-six per cent of 16 to 24 year olds in England and Wales had taken cannabis in the past year. In Britain, nine per cent of people with managerial/professional occupations went to the opera in the past year compared to one per cent of people with unskilled manual jobs (*Social Trends*, 2002).

Quantitative data is particularly useful for measuring the strength of relationships between various factors. The above examples would be useful data for measuring relationships between 1) age and illegal drug use and 2) social class and leisure activities.

**Qualitative data** This refers to all types of data that are not in the form of numbers. It includes:

- Descriptive data from observations, eg a description of behaviour in a pub
- Quotes from interviews, eg a woman discussing her marriage
- Written sources, eg diaries, novels and autobiographies
- Pictures, eg photographs, paintings and posters
- Films and recorded music.

Qualitative data can often provide a richer and more in-depth picture of social life than the numbers provided by quantitative data. Many sociologists combine quantitative and qualitative data in their research.

## summary

1. For many sociologists, research should provide:
   - Objective knowledge
   - Evidence-based statements
   - Data in a form that can be measured.

2. Ideally, research data should be valid and reliable. It should be drawn from a representative sample which should provide a basis for generalisation.

3. Sociologists often use both primary and secondary data in their research.

4. Quantitative data is useful for measuring the strength of relationships between various factors.

5. Qualitative data can provide a rich and in-depth picture of social life.

## key terms

**Objective knowledge** Unbiased, value-free knowledge.
**Data** Information collected as part of a research project.
**Validity** Data is valid if it presents a true and accurate description or measurement.
**Reliability** Data is reliable when different researchers using the same methods obtain the same result, ie the same description or measurement.
**Representativeness** A sample is representative if it reflects the characteristics of the larger research population.
**Generalisation** The application of findings from a sample to the research population as a whole.
**Primary data** New data produced by the researcher during the research process.
**Secondary data** Data which already exists, which can then be used by the researcher.
**Quantitative data** Numerical data – data in the form of numbers.
**Qualitative data** All types of data that are not in the form of numbers.

## *activity*2 *types of data*

**Item A** **World War 1 recruiting poster from USA**

These Men Have COME ACROSS
They Are at the Front NOW
JOIN THEM
ENLIST *in the* NAVY

**Item B** **A Hamar woman**

**Item C** **Social class and leisure**

| Great Britain | | | | | Percentages |
| --- | --- | --- | --- | --- | --- |
| | Managerial/ professional | Other non-manual | Skilled manual | Semi-skilled manual | Unskilled manual |
| Sporting events | 24 | 20 | 18 | 15 | 7 |
| Plays | 29 | 17 | 8 | 6 | 5 |
| Opera | 9 | 3 | 2 | 1 | 1 |
| Ballet | 7 | 3 | 1 | 1 | 1 |
| Contemporary dance | 4 | 2 | 1 | 1 | 1 |
| Classical music | 17 | 8 | 4 | 2 | 2 |
| Concerts | 19 | 17 | 13 | 9 | 5 |
| Art galleries/Exhibitions | 30 | 18 | 8 | 6 | 7 |

Adapted from *Social Trends*, 2002

# Unit 2  *The research process*

*keyissues*

1   How do sociologists choose a topic for research?

2   How do they choose research methods?

3   What are the ethical issues involved in research?

Designing a research project, conducting the research, and analysing the results involve a number of decisions. These include choosing a topic and selecting appropriate research methods.

## 2.1 Choosing a topic

Choosing a topic for research is influenced by a range of factors. Some of these will now be briefly examined.

**Values of the researcher** Researchers are likely to study something they consider to be important. And what they see as important is influenced by their values. For example, a sociologist who believes strongly in equality of opportunity may study the relationship between social class and educational attainment, since there is evidence that class inequality prevents equality of educational opportunity. Similarly, a sociologist who believes in gender equality may study the position of women at work and in the home, comparing their workloads and rewards with those of men.

**Values of society** The values of researchers often reflect the values of society. Feminists have criticised mainstream (or 'malestream') society as male-dominated and based on male values. They have made similar criticisms about sociology. For example, sociological research has traditionally focused on male concerns and male interests. As a result, female issues have been seen as unimportant and, until fairly recently, as unworthy of research. For example, Ann Oakley (1974) broke new ground when she chose to research housework, a topic then considered by many male sociologists to be of little significance.

Values in society change and with them the priorities and concerns of researchers. Today, gender inequality is seen as a major issue. And in sociology, it forms the focus of a large number of research projects.

**Funding** Choosing a research project is also influenced by a number of practical issues. For example, is it affordable? Most research projects conducted by professional sociologists require outside funding. Research funds are available from various sources – charitable foundations such as the Joseph Rowntree Foundation and the Runnymede Trust, government organisations such as the Economic and Social Research Council (ESRC), and industry. Each funding body has its own priorities. For example, industrial organisations will tend to fund projects dealing with their own particular concerns, such as solutions to stress in the workplace. The choice of research project is often shaped by the priorities of the funding body.

**Availability of data** It makes little sense to choose a research topic where there is little or no data available and little chance of producing it in the future. For example, there is probably insufficient data to conduct a study of child abuse in Anglo Saxon England. And there is little chance of conducting a systematic study of secret service organisations such as MI5 and MI6.

**Theoretical position** Choosing a research topic is also influenced by the theoretical position of the sociologist. As noted earlier, feminist sociologists will tend to select topics which reflect feminist issues – in particular gender inequalities.

Every theoretical position sees certain aspects of society as particularly important. For example, Marxism sees the class system as the foundation of capitalist society. As a result, Marxists tend to focus on topics such as class inequality, class conflict and class identity.

## 2.2 Choosing research methods

Having selected a topic, the researcher must then choose appropriate methods to collect and analyse data. The

# *activity3 choosing a research topic*

*Vegetable gardening*

*Women's jobs*

## *questions*

1  Choose one of these topics for research.
2  Explain why you have chosen this topic.

*Asian and white rioters in Bradford, 2001*

choice of methods depends on a number of factors. Some of these factors will be introduced briefly in this section and examined in more detail in later sections.

## Practical considerations

Some methods are more suitable than others for conducting particular types of research. Think about the problem of studying a teenage gang whose members sometimes commit illegal acts. They are often hostile to outsiders, particularly those they see as representing authority. Asking gang members for interviews or presenting them with questionnaires is unlikely to produce the required data. However, joining in their activities and gaining their trust can allow the researcher to obtain information by observing their behaviour. This method has been used successfully by a number of sociologists studying gang behaviour.

A researcher can only observe and record the behaviour of a small number of people. What if the research involved

making general statements about the relationship between social class and criminal behaviour? Some sociologists have claimed that members of the working class are more likely to commit crime than members of other social classes. It would take a lifetime of observation to assess this claim. For purely practical reasons, some sociologists have turned to official statistics on crime to investigate the relationship between social class and criminal behaviour. (However, there are problems with the use of official statistics as Section 9.1 shows.)

## 2.3  Ethical issues

Ethical considerations can have an important influence on the research process.

Ethics are moral principles – beliefs about what is right and wrong. In terms of research, ethics are the moral principles which guide research. Sociological associations in many countries have a set of ethical guidelines for

# activity4 choosing methods

### Item A  Casual sex

Laud Humphreys studied casual sex between gay men in public toilets in the USA. His main method of research was observation. He pretended to be a 'voyeur-lookout'. A voyeur doesn't join in but gets pleasure from watching the activities of others. A lookout warns of approaching police.

Adapted from Humphreys, 1970

### Item B  Sex for money

Don Kulick used observation to study transsexual prostitutes in Brazil during 1996. He rented a small room in a house with 13 transsexual prostitutes. The prostitutes are referred to as 'travestis'.

'I associated with travestis pretty much continually during those eight months, eating breakfasts of sweetened coffee and buttered rolls with them when they woke up about midday, chatting with them as they sat in doorsteps, plucking whiskers from their chins in the late afternoon sun, crowding onto mattresses with them as they lay pressed together smoking cigar-sized joints and watching late-night action movies on television. Every night, from about 8pm until 1 or 2am, I walked the streets with them at their various points of prostitution.'

Adapted from Kulick, 1998

### question

Why do you think Humphreys and Kulick chose observation as their main research method?

A transsexual prostitute

conducting research. Sociology departments in universities usually have an ethics committee to ensure that research conducted by members of the department is in line with these guidelines.

There is a growing awareness that those who participate in research have rights and that researchers have responsibilities and obligations. For example, should participants be informed about the purpose of the research and what their participation involves? Should researchers make every effort to ensure that participants come to no physical or psychological harm? Is it ever justifiable to deceive participants about the purpose of the research?

These are some of the ethical questions researchers should consider.

**Informed consent** Many researchers argue that those they are studying should be given the opportunity to agree or refuse to participate in the research. This decision should be 'informed' – information must be made available on which to base a decision to participate or not. Researchers should therefore provide information about the aims of the research, what the conduct of the research involves, and the purposes to which the research will be put.

**Deception** This means that information is withheld from participants and/or they are provided with false information. They may be unaware they are participating in a research study. They may be misled about the purpose of the study and the events that may take place during the research.

Clearly, participants cannot give informed consent if they are deceived. Is deception ever justifiable? Some researchers argue that deception is justified if there is no other way of gathering data. This means using a research method such as *covert (hidden) observation* so that people are unaware they are participating in research. Or, it means misleading participants about aspects of the research. For example, Humphreys (1970) gathered further information about some of the gay men in his research by calling on their homes and pretending to be conducting a health survey.

**Privacy** Researchers generally agree that participants' privacy should be respected. The problem here is that most research intrudes into people's lives. It has been argued that if participants consent to take part in research, then they accept this. However, they may be unaware of the extent of the intrusion. With hindsight, they may see it as an invasion of privacy.

Certain research methods, which are generally considered ethical, may result in an invasion of privacy. Take the case of the informal, unstructured interview – it often develops into a friendly chat between researcher and participant. In this relaxed atmosphere, participants may reveal all sorts of personal and private matters which they may later regret.

**Confidentiality** It is generally agreed that the identity of research participants should be kept secret. According to the British Sociological Association's *Statement of Ethical Practice* (1996), confidentiality must be honoured 'unless there are clear and overriding reasons to do otherwise'. It has been argued that when people in powerful positions misuse their power, then there may be a case for naming names (Homan, 1991).

**Protection from harm** There is general agreement that research participants should be protected from harm. This includes any harmful effects of participating in the actual research process and any harmful consequences of the research.

Publication of research findings may harm those who have been studied. For example, a study by Jason Ditton of workers in a bread factory revealed all sorts of fiddles and petty thefts. As Ditton himself recognised, management may well clamp down on such practices after publication of his book (Ditton, 1977).

**Ethics and the research process** As noted earlier, all researchers have values which define what is right and wrong. To some extent, these ethical values will affect every stage of the research process. If, for example, researchers see poverty, male domination, racial discrimination, or private education as ethically wrong, then they may choose to study these topics in order to reveal the wrongs and discover ways to right them.

## key terms

**Participant observation** A research method where the researcher joins the activities of those they are observing.
**Covert observation** Hidden observation. Participants are unaware that they are being observed as part of a research project.
**Ethics** Moral principles – beliefs about what is right and wrong.

## summary

1. The choice of research topic may be influenced by the
   - values of the researcher
   - values of society
   - type of funding
   - availability of data
   - theoretical position of the researcher.
2. The choice of research methods may be influenced by practical, theoretical and ethical considerations.
3. The research process is influenced by ethical considerations. Most sociologists believe that participation in research should be based on informed consent, that participants should be protected from harm, that their privacy should be respected and their confidentiality assured.

# activity5 ethics and research

## Item A  *The National Front*

Nigel Fielding conducted a study of the National Front, which many, including Fielding, considered to be a vicious, racist organisation concerned with White supremacy. Part of his research involved attending local meetings of the Front, during which he concealed his real reason for being there. In order to avoid suspicion he contributed to discussions, appearing to be sympathetic to the Front's beliefs.

Adapted from Fielding, 1981

## Item B  *Missing lessons*

Val Hey studied friendship between girls. Her research was based on observation in two schools. She would sometimes give the girls small gifts and even excuses to miss lessons in exchange for cooperating in her research.

Adapted from Hey, 1997

## Item C  *Illegal drug use*

In their study of illegal drug use, Howard Parker and his colleagues found that some of the responses to their questionnaires revealed that individuals were not coping with their drug use. The researchers had to decide whether to offer help and advice or maintain the confidentiality they had promised.

Adapted from Parker et al., 1998

*Smoking cannabis*

## questions

1  Why do you think Fielding chose to study the National Front?

2  Discuss the ethical issues involved in his research methods.

3  Do you think Hey (Item B) was justified in helping the girls truant from lessons? Explain your answer.

4  How would you have dealt with the problem faced by Parker in Item C? Give reasons for your decision.

(In the end, the researchers decided to treat each case individually.)

# Unit 3 *Identifying causes and effects*

*keyissues*

1 How do researchers identify causes and effects?

2 What is the difference between correlation and causation?

Sociologists are often concerned with what causes what – for example, what has caused the rise in the divorce rate over the past 100 years. And they are also concerned with effects – for example, what effects have resulted from the rise in the divorce rate.

**Causes come first** How do researchers identify causes and effects? A simple rule is that causes always come first. An effect can only occur as a result of a cause, so the cause must exist before the effect.

**Effects may feed back** The distinction between cause and effect is not as simple as it appears. An effect can become a cause. For example, one effect of the rising divorce rate is a change in attitude towards divorce. As divorce becomes more common, it becomes more acceptable. This change in attitude (an effect) can cause a further rise in the divorce rate. Because divorce is more acceptable, people are more likely to start divorce proceedings.

This example shows how an effect can feed back and reinforce the cause. In this respect, an effect can also be a cause.

## Correlation and causation

If one thing causes another, then they are likely to occur together. If, as is often claimed, poverty causes ill health, then these two factors are likely to be found together. But just because two things tend to occur together does not necessarily mean that one causes the other. Poverty and ill health are often found together but this does not mean there is a causal relationship between them.

**Correlation** Correlational analysis is a statistical technique used to measure the strength of relationships between two or more factors or variables. It requires quantitative data – data in the form of numbers. For example, correlational analysis can be used to measure the relationship between the amount of revision – measured in hours and minutes – and examination performance – measured in the number of marks.

Using correlational analysis, it is possible to obtain a numerical measure of the strength of the relationship between variables. This measure is known as the *correlation coefficient*. Correlation coefficients vary between –1 (perfect negative correlation) to +1 (perfect positive correlation) with 0 showing no correlation at all between the variables.

A positive correlation refers to a relationship where an increase in one variable is accompanied by an increase in another variable. For example, an increase in revision is accompanied by an increase in examination marks. A negative correlation refers to a relationship in which an increase in one variable is accompanied by a decrease in another variable. For example, an increase in visits to the pub is accompanied by a decrease in examination marks. A correlation of zero indicates no relationship between the variables. For example, there may be a zero correlation between hair colour and examination marks.

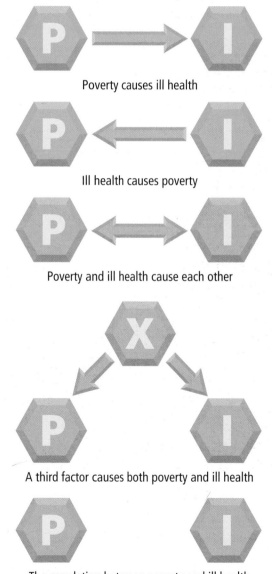

**Figure 1  Correlation and causation**

Poverty causes ill health

Ill health causes poverty

Poverty and ill health cause each other

A third factor causes both poverty and ill health

The correlation between poverty and ill health is due entirely to chance

**Correlation versus causation** If there is a high correlation between two variables, this does not necessarily mean that one causes the other. For example, there is often a high positive correlation between the sales of cold drinks and the yellowness of grass, yet neither of these factors is causing the other. The explanation for this correlation lies in a 'hidden third factor', namely the temperature. On hot summer days the grass tends to turn yellow and everyone wants cold drinks.

**Direction of causation** Even if correlation does indicate causation, it is not clear what causes what. Assume that poverty and ill health are causally related. There are three possible directions of causation as shown in Figure 1. First, poverty causes ill health. Second, ill health causes poverty. Third, each causes the other.

Figure 1 shows two further possibilities to account for the correlation. First, a third factor (x) causes both poverty and ill health. Second, the correlation is due entirely to chance – there is no causal relationship or no third factor involved.

## key terms

**Cause** That which produces an effect. A cause gives rise to an action, event or situation.
**Effect** The result or consequence of a cause. Something that is caused.
**Correlation** A statistical relationship or link between two or more variables.
**Correlation coefficient** A numerical measure of the strength of a correlation.

## summary

1. A simple rule for distinguishing between causes and effects is that causes always come first.
2. A strong correlation between two variables does not necessarily mean that one causes the other.

# activity6 causes and effects

### Item A  TV and aggression

A number of studies have found a positive correlation between the level of children's aggression and the amount of time they spend watching violent TV programmes.

### Item B  Storks and babies

The records of the city of Copenhagen for the 12 years following World War II show a strong positive correlation between a) the annual number of storks nesting in the city and b) the annual number of human babies born in the city.

## questions

1  Read Items A and B.
2  In each case,
   a)  Analyse the correlation using the five possibilities illustrated in Figure 1.

b)  State which possibility seems most reasonable and explain your choice.

# Unit 4 Experiments

## keyissues

1  What are the main types of experiments?
2  Why are experiments rarely used by sociologists?

## 4.1 Laboratory experiments

For most people the word experiment conjures up a picture of white-coated researchers in a laboratory using scientific equipment to prove or disprove something. This is quite a good starting point for understanding the experimental method.

The main aspects of the experimental method can be illustrated by the following example. This experiment was conducted to test the *hypothesis* or supposition that, 'The speed of a boat depends on the shape of its hull'.

**Controlling variables** In order to discover the effect of hull shape on speed it is necessary to identify and control all the variables or factors which might affect speed. This is difficult to do outside a laboratory since variables such as wind strength and temperature cannot be controlled. In a laboratory, it is possible to control such variables and keep them constant so that hull shape is the only factor which varies – from oval, to triangular, to rectangular, etc. In this way it is possible to find out how hull shape affects speed.

**Quantifying results** The results of experiments are usually quantified – presented in the form of numbers. Thus the speed of a model boat in the laboratory can be measured in centimetres per second using a metre rule and a stopwatch. Using a standard objective system of measurement is important as it reduces reliance on the judgement of the investigator and is therefore more likely to produce reliable data. And it allows other researchers to *replicate* or repeat experiments and directly compare the results.

**Correlation and causation** If changes in one variable (eg, the shape of the hull) are matched by changes in another variable (eg, the speed of the boat) then there is a *correlation* between the two variables. But this does not mean that one causes the other. However, being able to control variables in a laboratory does help us to judge whether the correlation is causative rather than coincidental. In the case of the boat, the only apparent change is in hull shape so any change in speed is likely to result from this.

**Laboratory experiments and people** Laboratory experiments have been very successful in the natural sciences such as physics and chemistry. However, many sociologists have serious doubts about their application to human beings. This is partly because people act in terms of their definitions of situations. They are likely to define laboratories as artificial situations and act accordingly. As a result, their actions may be very different from their behaviour in the 'real' world. An attempt to get round this is the *field experiment*, an experiment which takes place in people's everyday situations.

## 4.2 Field experiments

Field experiments are conducted in normal social situations such as the classroom, the factory and the street corner. The following example was devised to test the effect of social class on interaction between strangers (Sissons, 1970). An actor stood outside Paddington Station in London and asked people for directions. The actor, place and request were kept the same but the actor's dress varied from a businessman to a labourer. The experiment indicated that people were more helpful to the 'businessman'. It could therefore be argued that people were responding to what they perceived as the actor's social class. However, there are other possibilities. For example, the actor may behave more confidently in his role as businessman and people might respond to his level of confidence rather than level of class.

**Lack of control** Field experiments are always going to be inexact and 'messy'. It is impossible to identify and control all the variables which might affect the results. For example, it is difficult, if not impossible, to control the social class of the people asked for directions in the above experiment. Most of them may have been middle class. If so, they may have been more helpful to the 'businessman' because he seemed 'more like them'.

**The Hawthorne effect** Whether in the laboratory or in more normal social contexts, people are often aware they are participating in an experiment. And this in itself is likely to affect their behaviour. This particular *experimental effect* is often known as the *Hawthorne effect* since it was first observed during a study at Hawthorne Works of the Western Electric Company in Chicago in the late 1920s. The researchers conducted an experiment to

# *activity*7 *laboratory experiments*

### Item A  *Imitative aggression*

A group of nursery school children watched an adult mistreating a Bobo doll – a large inflatable rubber doll – by punching it, kicking it and hitting it with a mallet. The experimenter, Albert Bandura, then exposed this group and another group who had not watched the violence to the following 'frustrating experience'.

The children were shown a room full of exciting toys and given the impression they could play with them. They were then told they could not play with them. They were then taken, one by one, to a room of unattractive toys which included a Bobo doll and a mallet. As Bandura had predicted, those who had earlier watched the mistreatment of the Bobo doll were more likely to imitate this behaviour and show aggression towards the doll.

Adapted from Bandura, 1973

*Imitating adults – attacking a Bobo doll.*

### Item B  *The real world*

Can the results of laboratory experiments be applied to the real world? For example, does the Bobo doll experiment suggest a link between violence in films and violence in real life? Unlike people, Bobo dolls are designed to be knocked around, they invite violent behaviour. As such they are hardly suitable for an investigation into imitative aggression. Critics of experiments argue that the many differences between the laboratory situation and real life undermine any attempts to apply research findings to the claim that films promote aggressive or violent behaviour by imitation.

Adapted from Williams, 1981

### *questions*

1  What hypothesis is being tested in Item A?

2  Do you agree with the views outlined in Item B? Give reasons for your answer.

*Described as 'sickeningly violent, appallingly funny and arrestingly accomplished', Reservoir Dogs became a cult movie in the mid-1990s (Chronicle of the Cinema, 1995).*

discover whether there was a relationship between the workers' productivity and variables such as levels of lighting and heating and the frequency of rest periods. The researchers were puzzled as the results appeared to make little or no sense. For example, productivity increased whether the temperature in the workplace was turned up or down. The only factor which appeared to explain the increase in productivity was the workers' awareness that they were part of an experiment – hence the term Hawthorne effect.

**Experimenter bias** People act in terms of how they perceive others. They will tend to respond differently if the experimenter is young or old, male or female, Black or White and so on. People also tend to act in terms of how they think others expect them to act. This might explain the results in the experiment involving the actor dressed as a businessman and a labourer. He might be conveying two different expectations and this may affect the responses to his request for directions. For example, he may expect more help in his role as businessman and unintentionally convey this to the participants. The unintended effect of the experimenter on those being studied is known as *experimenter bias.*

**Ethical questions** Is it right to experiment on human beings? This depends partly on the nature of the experiment. Nearly everybody would reject the medical experiments performed on inmates against their will in Nazi concentration camps. However, fewer people would object to the actor asking directions outside Paddington Station. Should people be told they are the subject of an experiment? Yes, according to the British Psychological Society, unless it's absolutely necessary to deceive them, and then they must be told immediately afterwards (British Psychological Society, 1998).

## key terms

**Hypothesis** A statement that can be tested about the relationship between two or more variables.
**Variables** Factors which affect behaviour. Variables can vary or change, eg temperature can increase or decrease.
**Replication** Repeating an experiment or research study under the same conditions.
**Correlation** A measurement of the strength of the relationship between two or more variables.
**Laboratory experiment** An experiment conducted in specially built surroundings.
**Field experiment** An experiment conducted in everyday social settings.
**Experimental effect** Any unintended effect of the experiment on the participants.
**Hawthorne effect** Changes in the behaviour of participants resulting from an awareness that they are taking part in an experiment.
**Experimenter bias** The unintended effect of the experimenter on the participant.

## summary

1. There are two main types of experiments – laboratory experiments and field experiments.

2. Experiments are often designed to test hypotheses.

3. Experiments are usually intended to measure the strength of relationships between two or more variables.

4. Ideally, laboratory experiments allow the researcher to control all the important variables.

5. Laboratory experiments have been criticised for creating artificial situations. Critics argue that as a result, findings from laboratory experiments may not apply to everyday social situations.

6. Field experiments help to avoid artificiality, but they do not provide the same control of variables.

7. Both laboratory and field experiments have been criticised for experimental effects. As a result, their findings may be low in validity.

# activity8 asking directions

*Same man...*

*different response*

## questions

1 Suggest reasons for the different responses pictured above.

2 Using this example, outline some of the problems with field experiments.

# Unit 5 Social surveys

*keyissues*

1 What is a social survey?
2 What types of sample are used for social surveys?

## 5.1 What is a social survey?

**Survey data** The National Readership Survey tells us that in 2000, *The Sun* was the most popular daily newspaper in Britain – read by 20% of adults. The International Passenger Survey tells us that Spain was the most popular overseas holiday destination in 2000 – visited by 28% of UK residents who had a holiday abroad. And the British Gambling Prevalence Survey informs us that the National Lottery Draw was the most popular gambling activity in Britain in 1999, with 65% of people aged 16 and over participating. (All figures from *Social Trends*, 2002.)

**Definition** The above information comes from *social surveys*. A social survey involves the systematic collection of the same type of data from a fairly large number of people. Social surveys are usually designed to gather information on the same variables – eg, age and cinema attendance – from those participating in the survey. This often means asking everybody the same set of questions.

## 5.2 Sampling

Nearly all social surveys are based on a *sample* of the population to be investigated. 'Population' is the term given to everybody in the group to be studied. The population might be adult males, female pensioners, manual workers, 16-19 year old students, parents with dependent children and so on. A sample is a selection of part of the population. Samples are necessary because researchers rarely have the time and money to study everybody in the population. For example, if their research was based on women aged 16 and over in the UK, it would cover over 23 million people.

Most researchers try to select a sample which is *representative* of the population. This means that the sample should have the same characteristics as the population as a whole. Thus, if a researcher is studying the attitudes of British women, the sample should not consist of 1000 nuns, 1000 women over eighty or 1000 divorced women since such groups are hardly representative of British women. With a representative sample, *generalisations* are more likely to be true – findings from the sample are more likely to be applicable to the population as a whole.

## Sample design and composition

**Sampling unit** Who should be included in a sample? In many cases it is fairly easy to define a *sampling unit* – ie, a member of the population to be studied. Dentists, males between 30 and 40 years of age, females who own their own businesses, people with one or more GCE A levels, can be defined without too many problems. However, other groups are not so easy – how would you define a semi-skilled manual worker or a person living in poverty? Who would you include in a population of 'criminals'? Do you limit the population to those convicted of a crime? Or do you include everybody who has ever broken the law, in which case you would include nearly every adult in the UK?

**Sampling frame** Once the research population has been defined, the sample is selected from a *sampling frame* – a list of members of the population to be studied. In some cases an appropriate sampling frame is readily available, eg the Electoral Register for a study of voting behaviour. In other cases researchers may have to rely on listings, such as the Postcode Address File or telephone directories, which may or may not be suitable for their purposes. And all listings have drawbacks – not everyone is included, they are often out of date, certain groups are likely to be over or under-represented, eg the poor are less likely to appear in telephone directories. Sometimes, those who have data needed for a sampling frame are unwilling to release it. This happened to Howard Newby (1977) when the Ministry of Agriculture refused to supply information for his study of Suffolk farmworkers. Newby had to use the *Yellow Pages* for his first sampling frame. Many farmworkers were absent from this directory and those included were probably unrepresentative of the group.

The design and composition of the sample will partly depend on the type of sample used. Some of the more common types will now be outlined.

## Types of sample

**Random samples** A *random sample* gives every member of the sampling frame an equal chance of being selected. Every name is given a number and then a list of random numbers is used to select the sample. This avoids bias in selection. If researchers choose who to include and who to leave out, they may select a sample which supports their hypothesis.

**Systematic samples** This form of sampling systematically selects people from the sampling frame by choosing every 5th, 10th, 20th, or whatever, sampling unit. This method was used by Young and Willmott (1957) in their first study of Bethnal Green (see page 71). They selected every 10th name from the borough's electoral register.

Neither random nor systematic samples necessarily produce representative samples. Few sampling frames cover everybody in the research population. For example, on electoral registers certain groups are unrepresented (those not old enough to vote) or under-represented (the unemployed).

Even if the sampling frame covers the entire research population, a representative sample is not guaranteed. Simply because it *is* random, a random sample may select, for example, a disproportionate number of Labour voters from an electoral register. However, the larger the sample the less likely this will be. Systematic sampling can lead to an unrepresentative sample if the sampling frame is organised systematically. For example, a list of married couples in which husband follows wife would lead to an all male sample if every 10th person was selected.

**Stratified samples** Stratified samples offer a solution to the problem of representativeness. The population is divided into separate *strata* in terms of one of more characteristics, eg age, gender, ethnicity, class. A sample is then drawn which reflects those characteristics. Thus if the aim is to reflect gender divisions in the UK, 51% of the sample will be randomly selected from the female stratum and 49% from the male stratum. In terms of gender, the sample will be representative of the population as a whole.

A stratified sample can only be selected if researchers have sufficient information. In some cases, this is fairly easy to obtain. For example, the distribution of age in the UK population can be obtained from census data and this can then be mirrored in the sampling frame. In other cases, the necessary information is difficult or impossible to obtain. Religion provides an example. How do we get accurate information on the distribution of atheists, agnostics, Catholics, Protestants, Muslims, Hindus and so on in the population as a whole? And even if we can discover this, available sampling frames such as electoral registers may be no use at all since they provide no information about religious belief and practice.

**Quota samples** A market researcher stands on a street corner looking for likely 'victims'. She has to find twenty women between the ages of 30 and 45 to answer a questionnaire on magazine readership. She fills her quota with the first twenty women passing by who a) fit the required age group and b) agree to answer her questions. The sample selection is not random – it is not randomly selected from a sampling frame. The researcher simply fills her quota from the first available bodies. This method is known as *quota sampling*. It is 'a method of stratified sampling in which the selection within strata is non-random' (Moser & Kalton, 1971).

Quota sampling is often used for opinion polls and market research. It has its advantages – it is simpler, quicker and cheaper than stratified random sampling. However, it is less likely to produce a sample which is representative of the research population. For example, where and when a quota is filled can make significant differences to the sample. Stopping people on the street during weekday working hours would exclude many people in paid employment. And the fact that researchers can choose who they interview can bias the sample still further. Faced with two young men one 'smart' and 'pleasant' looking, the other just the opposite, researchers would probably choose the former. In quota sampling, people in the same strata do not have an equal chance of being selected.

**Snowball and volunteer samples** Sometimes researchers have great difficulty obtaining people for their samples. First, lists for a sampling frame might not be available. Second, the research population might be so small that normal sampling methods would not supply the numbers needed. Third, members of the research population might not wish to be identified. Think of the problems in locating the following: burglars, heroin users, collectors of ancient Greek coins, gay men, members of a Masonic Lodge. One possibility is to use a network of like-minded or like-situated individuals. This is the basis of *snowball sampling*, so-called because of its similarity to rolling a snowball.

Snowballing works like this. The researcher finds someone who fits the bill. They are asked to find another person who fits and so on. In this way a network of members of the research population is built up and this forms the basis for the sample.

Snowballing has the obvious advantage of creating a sampling frame where other methods may fail. However, it is unlikely to provide a representative sample since it is not random and relies on personal recommendation.

*Volunteer samples* provide an alternative to snowballing. Advertisements, leaflets, posters, radio or TV broadcasts, newspaper or magazine articles announce the research and request volunteers for the sample. Annette Lawson (1988) wrote a newspaper article about her study of adultery. She used the article to obtain a volunteer sample by asking readers who had experienced adultery to complete a questionnaire. Five hundred and seventy-nine readers responded to her request.

Volunteer sampling has much the same advantages and disadvantages as snowballing. In addition, volunteer samples are *self-selected* which may systematically bias the sample in a particular direction. For example, those who volunteer may have a particular reason for doing so.

## 5.3 Responding to surveys

**Response rates** It's one thing creating a representative sample, it's quite another getting everybody in the sample to participate in the survey. The *response rate* – the percentage of the sample that participates – varies widely. For example, Shere Hite's *The Hite Report on the Family* (1994) based on questionnaires in magazines had a mere 3% response rate, whereas everybody Ann Oakley (1974) asked to take part in her research on housework agreed to do so.

There are many reasons for non-response. They include:

1 Failure to make contact because people have moved, are on holiday, in prison, working away from home or simply out when the researcher calls.

2 Contact is made, but the interview cannot be conducted because the person is ill, deaf, experiencing some personal tragedy or can't speak English.

3 The person refuses to participate. Reasons may include no time, no interest, sees no point in the research, is suspicious of, dislikes, or is embarrassed by the researcher.

**Problems of non-response** Does non-response make the sample unrepresentative? Does it bias the sample and produce systematic error? Often the answer is we don't know since little or nothing is known about those who do not participate. Sometimes information on non-participants does become available. This happened in the surveys attempting to predict the 1992 General Election result. Opinion polls underestimated the Conservative vote by 8.5%. Over half of this underestimate was due to those who refused to participate – they were much more likely to vote Conservative. This produced an unrepresentative sample and in large part accounted for the failure to predict the election result (*Horizon*, BBC TV, 1994).

Evidence such as this suggests that non-response can be a serious problem.

### key terms

**Social surveys** Systematic collection of the same type of data from a particular population.
**Sample** A selection from the research population.
**Sampling unit** A member of the research population.
**Sampling frame** A list of members of the research population.
**Random sample** A sample which gives every member of the sampling frame an equal chance of being selected.
**Systematic sample** A systematic selection of people from the sampling frame, eg every 10th member.
**Stratified sample** A sample which attempts to reflect particular characteristics of the research population. The population is divided into strata in terms of age, gender etc, and the sample is randomly drawn from each stratum.
**Quota sample** A stratified sample in which selection from the strata is not random.
**Snowball sample** Members of the sample select each other.
**Volunteer sample** Members of the sample are self-selected, eg they choose to respond to a questionnaire printed in a magazine.
**Response rate** The percentage of the sample that participates in the research.

### summary

1. Social surveys are designed to provide information about particular populations.

2. They are based on samples which aim to represent the research population as a whole.

3. Whatever type of sample is used, there is no guarantee that it will be representative.

4. A high level of non-response can result in an unrepresentative sample.

## *activity9 sampling*

### Item A  *A stratified random sample*

We wish to study the career plans of university students and have sufficient funds to interview 125. Before selecting the sample, the sampling frame is stratified into departments, eg Physics and Chemistry, and years, eg students in their first year of study. There are 5,000 students in the university and the sample of 125 is one fortieth of this total. The example on the right shows the numbers of students randomly selected from years 1, 2 and 3 in the Physics department.

Adapted from Arber, 1993

**Stratification by department and year**

| Department | Year | Number in year | Number in sample |
|---|---|---|---|
| Physics | 1 | 120 | 3 |
| | 2 | 100 | 3 |
| | 3 | 100 | 2 |
| Total | | 320 | 8 |

## Item B  *A volunteer sample*

Shere Hite's (1994) report on family life in three Western societies received a great deal of publicity. Some of its 'findings' were dramatic. More than one in four women 'have no memory of affection by their father'. Four out of ten fathers frighten their sons with their violent tempers. And 31% of girls and young women 'report sexual harassment or abuse by a male family member'.

Hite's findings were based on 3028 completed questionnaires. Her sample was a self-selected volunteer sample. Hite distributed 100,000 questionnaires, mainly in magazines such as *Penthouse* in America, *Women Against Fundamentalism* in Britain and *Nouvelles Questions Feminists* in France. Her statistics come from the 3% who responded. She claims that self-selected samples are acceptable as long as the study is large enough.

Adapted from Kellner, 1994

### questions

1  Why do you think the researchers in Item A decided to use a stratified random sample?

2  According to one critic, Hite's 'findings' are rubbish (Kellner, 1994). Discuss this claim with reference to a) her sampling procedure and b) the response rate.

*Will the readership of Penthouse provide a representative sample?*

# Unit 6  *Questionnaires*

### keyissues

1  What are questionnaires?

2  What are their advantages and disadvantages?

## 6.1 What are questionnaires?

Questionnaires are lists of questions. They are the main method for gathering data in social surveys. They are sometimes handed to or posted to the respondent – the person answering the questions – and he or she is asked to fill them in. This is known as a *self-completion questionnaire*. They are sometimes read out by an interviewer who records the answers. This is known as an *interview questionnaire* or a *structured interview*.

**Comparable data** In theory questionnaires produce data which can be directly compared. Everybody is answering exactly the same questions and are therefore responding to the same thing. Any differences in the answers will therefore reflect real differences between the respondents.

This is fine in theory. However, it's easier said than done.

As we shall see, the same questions worded in exactly the same way can mean different things to different people. And in the case of the structured interview there is the problem of *interviewer bias* – the effect an interviewer may have on respondents' answers. Imagine how the age, gender and personality of an interviewer might affect your answers on a sensitive subject such as sexual behaviour.

**Quantifiable data** Questionnaires are usually designed to generate data which can be easily quantified – put into

A frank scene in a film shows a man and woman having sex. How would you feel about this being shown on one of the regular television channels?

| | % agreeing |
|---|---|
| Should not be allowed to be shown at all | 23 |
| Only after midnight | 18 |
| Only after 10pm | 35 |
| Only after 9pm | 18 |
| Only after 8pm | 3 |
| Allowed to be shown at any time | 2 |

numbers. The example on the previous page is from *British Social Attitudes: the 17th Report* (Jowell et al., 2000). It shows the percentage of respondents who chose each option. Constructing questions in this way makes it easy to quantify the results.

Numerical data lends itself to statistical techniques. It makes it possible to discover whether or not there is a correlation – a statistical link – between two or more variables.

**Operationalising concepts** Questionnaires are designed to measure things. And to do this, those 'things' must be *operationalised*, ie put in a form which allows them to be measured. How, for example, do you measure the strength of religious belief? The example below is from the 1998 British Social Attitudes Survey. It is an attempt to measure people's belief in God. Respondents were asked to choose the statement which best fits their beliefs.

Operationalising concepts is difficult, especially when sociologists themselves cannot agree on their meaning. For example, how do we operationalise concepts such as poverty and social class? Often concepts are operationalised in different ways in different studies which means the results are difficult, if not impossible, to compare. And the problem of comparability becomes even greater when we attempt to discover what respondents really mean when they answer questions. This problem will be looked at shortly.

**Indicators** Operationalising concepts usually involves breaking them down into categories. These categories are known as *indicators*. Take the concept 'young people'. Who exactly is included in this category? Five-year-olds, 15-year-olds, 30-year-olds? The researcher will need to identify a specific age range that will *indicate* whether or not someone is a 'young person'.

Finding indicators for more complex concepts is more difficult. Take the concept of 'religious person'. Indicators of being a religious person may include 1) a belief in some form of spiritual power 2) praying to that spiritual power 3) regular attendance at a religious institution 4) reading religious texts.

These indicators are then put in a form that can be measured. For instance, in a questionnaire, they are

| Belief in God, Britain, 1998 (%) | |
| --- | --- |
| I don't believe in God. | 10 |
| I don't know whether there is a God and I don't believe there is any way to find out. | 15 |
| I don't believe in a personal God but I do believe in a Higher Power of some kind. | 14 |
| I find myself believing in God some of the time but not at others. | 14 |
| While I have doubts, I feel that I do believe in God. | 23 |
| I know God really exists and I have no doubts about it. | 21 |
| Don't know and no answer. | 3 |

From Jowell et al., 1998

**How often do you attend a religious institution, eg a church, mosque or synagogue?**

- Once a week, or more often
- Once a month
- Once every 6 months
- Once a year

# activity 10 indicators

Many sociologists claim that there has been a move towards *joint conjugal roles*. By this they mean that marital roles – the roles of husband and wife – are becoming increasingly similar and increasingly shared.

## questions

1 Make a list of indicators of joint conjugal roles.
2 Select two of these indicators and put them in the form of questions suitable for a questionnaire.

translated into questions as the following example shows.

Indicators should be valid and reliable. It they are valid, they provide an accurate measurement. Think about the above example. Does regular attendance at a religious institution provide a valid measurement of religious behaviour? Maybe. But, people can go to church for social rather than religious reasons, and non-churchgoers may be deeply religious.

If indicators are reliable, then they are consistent from one measurement to the next. In terms of a questionnaire, this means that everybody who attended a religious institution once a week or more often would tick that box. In order for them all to do this, the question should be clear and unambiguous – it must mean the same thing to everybody.

**Coding answers** Answers to questions are *coded*. This means they are classified into various categories. When concepts, such as belief in God, are operationalised, the questionnaire can be pre-coded. The responses to the Belief in God questionnaire are pre-coded into seven categories. The researcher simply has to count the number of people who choose each category. Quantifying the data is easy.

It is more difficult to code a written answer. Consider the following.

| | |
|---|---|
| *Question* | Do you believe in God? |
| *Answer* | It depends what you mean by God. Do you mean a God that just exists apart from this world? Or, do you mean a God that controls what happens in this world? Sometimes, I think I believe in the first type of God. |

This answer is difficult to code. Researchers usually have a list of categories in terms of which written answers are coded. Often, however, written answers don't fit neatly into a particular category. For example, the above answer would not fit neatly into any of the categories in the Belief in God questionnaire.

Written answers are sometimes difficult to code. As a result, they can be difficult to quantify.

## 6.2 Types of questions

**Closed questions** There are two main types of questions used in questionnaires – closed and open. In *closed questions*, the range of responses is fixed by the researcher. The respondent usually has to select one answer from two or more given alternatives. The questions above on sex on television and belief in God are examples of closed questions. A different example is shown top right in which the respondent is asked to rank the alternatives provided.

Closed questions are relatively easy, quick and cheap to classify and quantify. They are pre-coded in the sense that the categories are set and the respondent simply has to choose one or rank some. However, the researcher has

> Which do you feel are the most important factors in choosing a university? Please rank the following in order of importance to you. Number them from 1 = most important, to 7 = least important.
>
> Closeness to a town or city
> Good academic reputation
> Good chance of getting a job after graduation
> Attractive campus
> Good social facilities
> Good accommodation
> Availability of real ale
>
> From Newell, 1993

chosen the available responses and in this respect is imposing his or her choice of alternatives on the respondent. Look at the question above on choosing a university. Can you think of any 'important factors' not given? There is a way round this problem by adding 'other, please specify' which asks the respondent to add, in this case, any other reasons for choosing a university.

**Open questions** An *open question* asks the respondent to answer a question in their own words. Open questions give the respondent more freedom, but coding the responses can be difficult and time consuming. In many cases it might be difficult to fit responses into a particular category.

Most researchers see closed questions as suitable for simple, factual data such as age, gender and income level. Open questions are usually seen as more suitable for data on attitudes and values where respondents are required to express how they feel. An open question allows them to say things in their own way.

## 6.3 Types of questionnaires

### Self-completion questionnaires

*Self-completion questionnaires* can be left with respondents either to be picked up later or posted back to the researcher. *Postal questionnaires*, as their name suggests, are mailed to respondents with a request to mail them back to the researcher. Usually most of the questions in self-completion questionnaires are closed and pre-coded.

Self-completion questionnaires have the following advantages and disadvantages.

#### Advantages

- Inexpensive – no interviewers to pay, cheap to classify results.
- As a result, often possible to survey a large sample.
- Fast and efficient analysis possible with pre-coded closed questions. Answers can be easily quantified and entered straight on to computers.
- Postal questionnaires allow a geographically dispersed sample to be contacted easily and cheaply.

- No interviewer bias – the interviewer does not influence the respondent's answers.

### Disadvantages

- A relatively low response rate – often well below 50% for postal questionnaires. This may destroy the representativeness of the sample.
- Respondents may not understand the questions or follow the instructions.
- Answers may be incomplete, illegible or incomprehensible.
- Closed questions may seriously limit what respondents want to say.

## Structured interviews

In a structured interview the interviewer reads out the questions and records the responses in writing, on audio-tape or on a portable computer.

### Advantages

- Response rate usually much higher than for postal questionnaires.
- Interviewers can explain the purpose of the research, clarify questions and ask for further details. This can result in more information.
- Respondents who cannot read and write can be included in the survey.

### Disadvantages

- More expensive – interviewers are usually paid.
- Cost increases if sample spread over a wide area.
- Interviewer bias.

# 6.4 Questions and answers

Constructing a questionnaire is not easy. The researcher must make sure that questions are clear and

unambiguous. Where possible, words and phrases should be simple and straightforward. Leading questions, eg 'Don't you agree that ...' should be avoided as they direct the respondent to a particular answer. Questions should be meaningful and relevant – there's not much point in asking people if they've enjoyed their holiday abroad if they've never been out of the country. And, most importantly, the questions must mean the same thing to all respondents. If they mean different things respondents are, for all intents and purposes, answering different questions. And this means that their answers cannot be directly compared.

Researchers sometimes use a *pilot study* to iron out problems with questionnaires. They test the questions on a relatively small number of people who share the characteristics of the main sample. A pilot study can be invaluable for removing ambiguity and misunderstanding. Yet all the preparation in the world cannot completely remove the basic problems of questions and answers.

**What do answers mean?** Are respondents telling the truth? Yes and no. Are they giving the answers they think the researcher wants? Sometimes. Do all respondents understand the questions? Not always. Do the questions mean the same to all respondents? Probably not. Do respondents' answers reflect their behaviour in everyday life? Maybe. Given all this, what appears to be a precise, reliable and efficient research method – the social survey – may be nothing of the sort.

**Creating an impression** Everybody plays the game of 'impression management'. They try to manage the impression of themselves which others form. This can shape their responses to a questionnaire and more particularly to a structured interview. Consider the following example.

Survey after survey has shown a high level of church attendance in the USA, far higher than for any comparable Western industrial society. Yet figures produced by the churches tell a somewhat different story. For example,

## key terms

*Self-completion questionnaire* A questionnaire completed by the respondent.

*Structured interview/interview questionnaire* A questionnaire read out by an interviewer who also records the answers.

*Operationalise* Translating concepts into a form which can be measured.

*Indicators* Specific ways of measuring a concept.

*Coding* Classifying answers into various categories.

*Closed questions* Questions in which the range of responses is fixed by the researcher.

*Open questions* Questions which allow the respondent to answer in their own words.

*Postal questionnaire* A questionnaire mailed to respondents with a request to mail it back after completion.

*Pilot study* A preliminary study designed to identify any problems with the main study.

## summary

1. Questionnaires are the main method for collecting data in social surveys.

2. In theory, questionnaires provide directly comparable data.

3. Closed questions are pre-coded. They produce data which is easy to quantify.

4. Answers to open questions can be difficult to code and quantify.

5. Self-completion questionnaires and structured interviews each have their advantages and disadvantages.

6. It can be difficult to discover what respondents' answers actually mean.

surveys conducted by Gallup suggested that 35% of Episcopalians (a type of Christians) in the USA had been to church in the last 7 days, yet figures from the churches indicated that only 16% actually did so. Why the discrepancy? It appears that many respondents were concerned with giving the 'right' answer to the interviewer – they wished to appear upright, decent and respectable and regular church attendance was, to many, a way of giving this impression (Bruce, 1995).

Examples such as this suggest that researchers must know as much as possible about what questions and answers mean to respondents. Only then can they write appropriate questions and be in a position to interpret the answers.

**Words and meanings** For a questionnaire to do its job, questions have to have the same meaning for all respondents. The following example from the USA illustrates how easy it is for a question to be interpreted differently. A survey of reading habits produced the unexpected result that working-class respondents read more books than middle-class respondents. This result was largely due to the interpretation placed on the word 'book'. Unlike most middle-class respondents, those from the working-class included magazines in their definition of books.

This illustrates that the more researchers know about those they study, the better the questions they ask and the better their interpretation of the answers.

# *activity11 asking questions*

### Item A  **On the toilet**

A study based in Bristol asked nearly 2,000 people to fill out a questionnaire on how many times they went to the toilet during the week and the shape, size, consistency and texture of their faeces. They were required to tick whether it was 'like a sausage or snake but with cracks on its surface' or 'fluffy with ragged edges' and so on.

Adapted from O'Connell Davidson & Layder, 1994

### Item B  **Non-existent videos**

Have you watched this video?

The Video Recording Bill was passed by the Conservative government in 1984. Its aim was to place strict controls on 'video nasties'. Survey evidence was used to support the bill. Children were given a list of video titles and asked to indicate which they had seen. Forty per cent claimed to have seen at least one of the video nasties on the list.

Later, Guy Cumberbatch presented children with a list of fictitious titles such as 'I vomit on your cannibal apocalypse'. Sixty-eight per cent claimed to have seen at least one of these non-existent videos.

Adapted from Harris, 1984

**Item C  Saying one thing, doing another**

In the early 1930s, Richard LaPiere, a social psychologist at Stanford University, travelled 10,000 miles across the USA with a young Chinese-American couple. At the time, there was widespread prejudice against Asians and there were no laws preventing racial discrimination in public accommodation. They visited 250 hotels, restaurants and campsites and only once were they refused service. After the trip, LaPiere sent a letter to all the places they had visited asking, 'Will you accept members of the Chinese race as guests in you establishment?' 92% said 'no', 7% said 'uncertain, depends on the circumstances' and only 1% said 'yes'.

Adapted from LaPiere, 1934

## questions

1 Read Item A. Comment on the accuracy of the data which this questionnaire might produce.

2 What problems do Items B and C raise for interpreting answers to questionnaires?

# Unit 7 Interviews

## keyissues

1 What are the main types of interviews?

2 What are their advantages and disadvantages?

## 7.1 Types of interviews

**Structured interviews** As outlined in the previous unit, structured interviews are simply questionnaires which are read out by the interviewer who then records the respondent's answers. The same questions are read out in the same order to all respondents.

**Semi-structured interviews** Each interview usually has the same set of questions, but in this case the interviewer has the freedom to 'probe'. Respondents can be asked to clarify their answers, to provide examples, and to develop what they've said.

**Unstructured interviews** By comparison, unstructured interviews are more like an everyday conversation. They are more informal, open-ended, flexible and free flowing. Questions are unlikely to be pre-set, though researchers usually have certain topics they wish to cover. This gives the interview some structure and direction.

**Group interviews** The interviews discussed so far involve two people – an interviewer and a respondent or interviewee. Group interviews involve the interviewer and a group of respondents – usually between 8 and 10 people. In some group interviews, the respondents answer questions in turn. In others, known as *focus groups*, participants are encouraged to talk to each other. They are guided rather than led or directed by the interviewer – for example, they are asked to discuss particular questions or topics.

### Structured interviews – advantages and disadvantages

Why use different types of interviews? Each type has its strengths and weaknesses. Structured interviews have many of the advantages and disadvantages of questionnaires. They are particularly suitable for simple, straightforward, 'factual' information such as a respondent's age, gender, educational qualifications and occupation.

Structured interviews are seen as more likely to produce comparable data – since all respondents answer the same questions this should allow researchers to directly compare their responses and identify similarities and differences. Quantifiable data is more likely since questions can be structured to provide yes/no answers or choices between given alternatives. And, as structured interviews are more formal than other types, there may be less chance of interviewer bias.

However, structured interviews can place strict limitations on respondents' answers. This is particularly true of closed questions which force respondents to choose between pre-set alternatives. This prevents respondents from answering in their own words and in their own way.

## Semi-structured interviews – advantages and disadvantages

This type of interview has many of the advantages of the structured interview. In addition, it allows the interviewer to probe – to jog respondents' memories, and ask them to clarify, spell out and give examples of particular points. This can add depth and detail to answers.

However, this gain is accompanied by a loss of standardisation and comparability (May, 2001). Although the basic questions are pre-set, probes are not, which results in non-standard interviews. This means that each interview is somewhat different. As a result, the data is not strictly comparable since, to some extent, interviewees are responding to different questions.

## Group interviews – advantages and disadvantages

Focus groups are becoming increasingly common in sociological research. They have been used to study the effects of long-term imprisonment, victims of crime, conflicts within organisations and changes in working practices among steel workers (May, 2001; Walklate, 2000).

The results of focus group interviews are sometimes different from those of individual interviews. This does not mean that one is 'right' and the other 'wrong'. Interaction within groups affects people's opinions. Since much of our lives is spent in groups, it is important to obtain data from this source (May, 2001).

Some researchers find focus groups provide a rich source of qualitative data. In her study of victims of crime, Sandra Walklate (2000) claims that without the use of focus groups, many of the shades of meaning and subtleties of people's views would be lost.

## Unstructured interviews advantages

Unstructured interviews are often seen to have the following advantages.

**Sensitive groups** Some groups are less likely than others to provide information for researchers. They might be suspicious of outsiders, hostile towards them, afraid of them or simply uncomfortable in their presence. An unstructured interview can allay these feelings as it provides an opportunity for understanding and trust to develop between interviewer and interviewee. This can be seen from the following example. Postal surveys were used in London to find out why people did not apply for welfare

benefits to which they were entitled. The response rate was very low, due partly to fear and suspicion, a reaction often found amongst the frail and the elderly. Research indicated that a one-to-one interview was the most effective way of gaining information, in large part because interviewers were able to put respondents' minds at rest (Fielding, 1993).

**Sensitive topics** Unstructured interviews are also seen as particularly suitable for sensitive topics. Respondents may be more likely to discuss sensitive and painful experiences if they feel that the interviewer is sympathetic and understanding. Unstructured interviews provide the opportunity for developing this kind of relationship. Joan Smith's (1998) study about the family background of homeless young people produced detailed and in-depth information using unstructured interviews.

**Respondent's viewpoint** Structured and semi-structured interviews give respondents few opportunities to develop their answers and direct the interview into areas which interest them. The researcher has constructed the questions and, in the case of closed questions, the range of possible answers. In these respects the researcher has decided what's important.

An unstructured interview offers greater opportunity for respondents to take control, to define priorities and to direct the interview into areas which they see as interesting and significant. In this way, they have a greater chance to express their own viewpoints. And this can lead to new and important insights for the researcher.

**Validity and depth** If respondents feel at ease in an interview situation they will be more likely to open up and say what they really mean. Unstructured interviews can provide this opportunity. They are therefore more likely to produce valid data and to produce richer, more vivid and more colourful data. They also allow interviewers more opportunity to pursue a topic, to probe with further questions, to ask respondents to qualify and develop their answers. Because of this, the resulting data may have more depth.

**Meanings and attitudes** Many researchers see unstructured interviews as particularly suited to discovering meanings, values, attitudes, opinions and beliefs. People often take these for granted and find it difficult to spell them out. For example, what exactly are people's religious beliefs; what does music really mean to them; what do they really think about the welfare state? Unstructured interviews can explore such areas without the limitations of pre-set questions.

Meanings and opinions are not simple and clear-cut. There are shades of meaning. Opinions are not cut and dried, they are hedged with qualification. A skilled interviewer can encourage and enable people to spell out this complexity. Structured interviews with pre-set questions are unlikely to capture this range of meaning. However, not everybody agrees with this view. The British Social Attitudes Survey uses a very detailed structured interview and a self-completion questionnaire to discover attitudes on a range of issues.

### Unstructured interviews – disadvantages

**Interviewer bias** Interviewer bias is unavoidable. To some extent the interviewer will affect the responses of the interviewee.

Interviewers are people with social characteristics – they have a nationality, ethnicity, gender, social class, age group and so on. They also have particular personalities – they may be shy or outgoing, caring or uncaring, aggressive or unaggressive. These social and psychological characteristics will be perceived in certain ways by interviewees and will have some effect on their responses. In some cases this may systematically bias the results.

A number of American studies have examined the effect of the social characteristics of interviewers and respondents. J. Allan Williams Jr (1971) claims that the greater the status difference between interviewer and respondent, the less likely respondents are to express their true feelings. He found that African-Americans in the 1960s were more likely to say they approved of civil rights demonstrations if the interviewer was Black rather than White.

**Social desirability** In general, people like to present themselves in a favourable light. This can result in respondents emphasising socially desirable aspects of their behaviour and attitudes in the presence of interviewers. As noted in the previous unit, Episcopalians in the USA tend to exaggerate the frequency of their attendance at church in order to appear upright and respectable (see pages 196-197).

Respondents tend to be open about and even exaggerate aspects of their behaviour which they see as socially desirable, and to conceal or minimise aspects seen as undesirable.

**Validity** Do respondents lies? Is their memory hazy or faulty? Is what they say in interviews different from what they have done or will do? In some cases the answer is yes to all these questions. An instance has been given above in the case of church attendance. Voting intention is a case where people's intentions expressed in interviews and their actions at a later date are sometimes different. And there is evidence that some people tell downright lies, for example when recounting their sexual activity to an interviewer (O'Connell Davidson & Layder, 1994).

**Comparability** Interviews, particularly those at the unstructured end of the continuum, can develop in all sorts of directions. As a result, data from one interview to the next can vary considerably. This makes comparisons between data from different interviews difficult. It also means that generalisations should be treated with caution.

**Coding and quantifying** It is difficult to code and quantify much of the qualitative data produced by unstructured interviews.

## 7.2 The interview process

Books on research methods are full of advice on how to conduct effective interviews and how to avoid pitfalls and problems.

**Non-directive interviewing** The standard advice is to be *non-directive*, to avoid leading respondents and to allow them to express themselves in their own way. The idea is

### key terms

**Structured interview** A questionnaire which is read out and filled in by the interviewer.
**Semi-structured interview** Similar to a structured interview, but the interviewer is allowed to probe with additional questions.
**Unstructured interview** Few, if any, pre-set questions, though researchers usually have certain topics they wish to cover.
**Group interviews** Interviews which involve an interviewer and a group of respondents.
**Focus groups** Group interviews in which the interviewer encourages respondents to discuss topics with each other.
**Interviewer bias** The effect that the interviewer has on the respondent's answers.
**Non-directive interviewing** An interviewing technique which seeks to avoid leading or directing respondents to answer in particular ways.
**Rapport** A friendly, trusting and understanding relationship.

### summary

1. There are four main types of interview – structured, semi-structured, unstructured and group interviews.

2. Structured interviews are seen as more likely to produce comparable data.

3. The probes available with semi-structured interviews can add depth and detail to answers.

4. Unstructured interviews provide an opportunity to develop trust and understanding. This is important with sensitive groups and sensitive topics. It can add validity and depth to respondents' answers.

5. Unstructured interviews are more prone to interviewer bias and social desirability effects, both of which will reduce validity.

6. Focus groups provide an opportunity to obtain people's views in a group situation. They can be a rich source of qualitative data.

7. The standard advice to interviewers is to avoid direction and develop rapport. However, on occasion, more active approaches may produce better results.

to minimise interviewer bias. It is important to establish *rapport* – a friendly and understanding relationship – while at the same time appearing sensible and businesslike. Interviewers should not be too familiar, they must maintain a certain distance or respondents will be unduly influenced. Probing is allowed, in order to get respondents to clarify or develop their answers, but it must be used with care as it can easily lead to bias (Fielding, 1993).

**Active approaches** Non-directive interviewing can result in an artificial situation which makes respondents feel uneasy. Some sociologists have found that non-directive approaches can be frustrating for both parties. Platt (1976) notes that respondents 'would have liked guidance on what I regarded as relevant, but I was anxious not to mould the data to my preconceptions by giving them any. This produced a few tortured interviews in which an unhappy respondent spoke at length on aspects of the research which it was probably clear were not of interest to me.'

There is some evidence that more direct and aggressive interviewing techniques can produce more information. Howard Becker (1971) used this approach with some success in his interviews with Chicago schoolteachers. He found that many of the teachers were prejudiced against working class and ethnic minority pupils, information they would not normally volunteer. However, by adopting an aggressive approach Becker states, 'I coerced many interviewees into being considerably more frank than they had originally intended'.

# activity 12 interviewing

## Item A  *Interviewers*

## Item B  *Three interviews*

**Interview 1** An eight-year-old Black boy from Harlem in New York is interviewed by a 'friendly' White interviewer who presents him with a toy jet plane and asks him to describe it. The setting is formal. There are long silences followed by short two or three word answers, which hardly provide an adequate description of the plane.

**Interview 2** Another Black boy from Harlem is interviewed. Again the setting is formal but this time the interviewer is Black and raised in Harlem. The boy responds in much the same way as the boy in the first interview.

**Interview 3** The boy and the interviewer are the same as in the second interview. This time the interviewer sits on the floor, the boy is provided with a supply of crisps and his best friend is invited along. The change is dramatic. The boy is enthusiastic, talkative, and gives a detailed description of the toy plane.

Adapted from Labov, 1973

## questions

1  You are being interviewed on a) your sexual behaviour and b) your views on race relations. Choose an interviewer for each interview from Item A. Explain your choices.

2  Explain the idea of interviewer bias using your answers to Question 1.

3  Suggest reasons for the similarities and differences between the three interviews in Item B.

# Unit 8 *Observation*

*keyissues*

1  What are the main types of observation?

2  What are their advantages and disadvantages?

## 8.1 Participant observation

How do we really find out about the way of life of a group of people? One way is to join them – to participate in their daily activities and observe what they say and do. This research method is known as *participant observation.*

It was used by John Howard Griffin (1960) a White journalist who dyed his skin black in order to discover what it was like to live as a Black man in the southern states of America in the late 1950s. It was used by the anthropologist Bronislaw Malinowski who spent many years studying the Trobriand Islanders of New Guinea. He observed the most intimate details of their lives as he peered into grass huts gathering data for *Sex and Repression in Savage Society* (1927). And it was used by the sociologist Erving Goffman (1968) when he adopted the role of assistant to the athletics director in order to study the experience of patients in a mental hospital in Washington DC.

### Ethnography

Participant observation is one of the main research methods used in *ethnography*. Ethnography is the study of the way of life of a group of people – their culture and the structure of their society. Often researchers attempt to 'walk a mile in their shoes' – to see the world from their perspective, discover their meanings and appreciate their experiences. Many argue that participant observation is the most effective method of doing this.

Participant observation gives researchers the opportunity to observe people in their natural setting as opposed to the more artificial contexts of the laboratory or the interview. It allows researchers to see what people do as opposed to what they say they do.

Participant observation has produced a number of classic ethnographies – Elliot Liebow's (1967) study of Black 'streetcorner' men in Washington DC; William F. Whyte's (1955) account of an Italian-American gang in Boston – and a range of anthropological studies of small scale non-Western societies from the Yanomamo of Amazonia (Chagnon, 1968) to the Mbuti of Zaire (Turnbull, 1961).

### Gaining entry

Participant observation cannot work unless the researcher gains entry into the group and some degree of acceptance from its members. This can be difficult. Many groups don't want to be studied, especially those whose activities are seen as deviant or criminal by the wider society. However, as the following examples indicate, it is often possible to enter even closed groups.

For his research into casual sex between men in public toilets – the 'tearoom trade' – Humphreys (1970) acted as a lookout. By performing this useful and accepted role, he gained the trust of those he observed without having to join their sexual activities.

On other occasions, researchers have to participate more directly in order to gain entry. Dick Hobbs (1988) wanted to research the relationship between criminals and detectives in the East End of London. He agreed to coach a local soccer team when he discovered that Simon, a detective, was the father of one of the players. He developed a friendship with Simon who provided him with introductions and vouched for him (said he was OK). Hobbs also drank in *The Pump*, a local pub that was frequented by several detectives. These contacts enabled Hobbs to gain entry into the world of the detectives – he joined their conversations and observed their activities.

Sometimes researchers are forced into even greater participation to gain entry. Festinger (1964) found that the only way to observe a small religious sect was to pretend to be a believer and become a member of the sect.

The above examples are of *covert* research where the identity and purpose of the researcher are kept hidden. *Overt* research, where those being studied are aware of the researcher's role and purpose, has its own problems of access and acceptance. People often reject what they see as nosy, interfering outsiders, unless they are sponsored by a trusted member of the group who grants the researcher entry. This happened in Judith Okely's (1983) study of traveller-gypsies. Entry was a long and difficult process until she gained the friendship and trust of a family who had recently suffered a tragic death. The sympathetic and understanding relationship she developed with members of this family provided entry to the rest of the group.

### Conducting research

**Looking and listening** Participant observation involves looking and listening. The general rule is to 'go with the flow' rather than forcing the pace and influencing people's behaviour. Since the aim is to observe people in their normal setting, the researcher must not disturb that setting. Blending into the background is usually recommended, though this is not always possible. For example, a participant observer in a classroom can stand out like a sore thumb. This can result in an 'artificial' lesson. However, it's surprising how soon he or she becomes invisible and taken for granted. In his study of a secondary school, Walford (1993) found that it took four weeks of observation before any class misbehaved. However, the situation changed rapidly after this time and Walford was soon watching 'mock wrestling' and chairs flying around the classroom!

**Asking questions** Watching and listening are not always adequate for the researcher's purposes. Sometimes a participant observer must take a more active role in order to obtain information. This usually involves asking questions. In such cases, the dividing line between participant observation and unstructured interviews is blurred. For example, William Whyte (1955) discussed his observations with Doc, the leader of the gang Whyte was studying, to the point where Doc became 'a collaborator in the research'.

**The key informant** Doc became a *key informant* – a member of the group who has a special relationship with the researcher and provides vital information. As noted earlier, Dick Hobbs developed a friendship with a detective called Simon. In Hobbs' (1988) words, Simon 'emerged as my principal police informant, granting me formal and informal interviews, access to documents, and introductions to individuals and settings that would otherwise be inaccessible'.

**Hanging around** A good deal of participant observation is informal, unplanned and unstructured – it consists of 'hanging around'. In his study of pilferage from the docks in St Johns, Newfoundland, Mars (1982) wandered round the wharves and sheds chatting to the dockers, and hung round bars drinking with them in the evening.

**Recording observations** Recording the findings of participant observation can be a problem, especially when the research is covert. Researchers usually write up the day's findings each evening whilst events are still fresh in their mind. In some cases the toilet has proved a useful place to make brief notes, which are written up in a more detailed form later (Festinger, 1964; Ditton, 1977). However, a lot relies on the researcher's memory which is inevitably selective.

**In the field** Participant observation can be a long process with a year or more being spent 'in the field'. It can require dedication, stamina and courage. Researchers are often cut off from the normal supports of family and friends, sometimes living a double life in an alien setting. And participant observation can be dangerous. For example, Haralambos (1994) was threatened with guns on more than one occasion during his research into African-American music on the south side of Chicago.

Many of the advantages and disadvantages of participant observation have been mentioned already. Some of the more important will now be summarised.

## Advantages of participant observation

**Validity** What people say and what they do are sometimes very different, as indicated earlier in the units on questionnaires and interviews. Participant observation offers the chance to discover what people actually do, the chance to obtain valid data. For example, Haralambos (1994) observed African-Americans who a few hours earlier had said they disliked blues, singing and dancing to blues music and quite obviously enjoying themselves.

**Insight** Looking back on his observation of a streetcorner gang in Boston, William Whyte noted, 'As I sat and listened, I learned the answers to questions that I would not have had the sense to ask if I had been getting my information solely on an interviewing basis'. This comment has been echoed by many participant observers. For example, during her observation of the Moonies, a religious movement, Eileen Barker (1984) handed out leaflets advertising a concert organised by the Moonies at the Royal Albert Hall. She found that trying to convince members of the public to take an interest actually helped to convince her that the concert was a worthwhile activity. Barker's participation provided an insight into the workings of religious sects – by selling the group's beliefs to others they are actually selling those beliefs to themselves.

Other research methods rely to a greater extent on prior knowledge. For example, to ask relevant questions in an interview you must already know something about the group under investigation. Participant observation can provide the kind of insight, fresh information and new directions for research which are less likely to come from other methods.

**Insider's view** Many supporters of participant observation argue that it offers the best opportunity to discover how people see the world in which they live. Other research methods are more likely to reflect the priorities of the researcher to the exclusion of those of the researched. For example, the designer of a questionnaire has decided what is relevant and significant and this may bear little relationship to the lives of those being studied.

By watching and listening, a participant observer has the chance to discover the priorities and concerns, the meanings and definitions of people in their everyday situations. There may therefore be less likelihood of distorting people's view of the world.

**Practicality** Sometimes participant observation may be the only method with any chance of success. Some groups are closed to outsiders – their members reject requests for information. Such groups may include those involved in criminal activity, those whose behaviour is regarded as deviant by the wider society (eg, certain religious sects) and those who are hostile to the wider society (eg, some members of ethnic minority groups). Under these circumstances, joining the group, participating in its members' activities, obtaining their cooperation and even their trust, may be the only way of obtaining information.

## Disadvantages of participant observation

**Time, money and personal cost** As already noted, participant observation can involve personal cost – stress and even danger. And costs in terms of time and money can be considerable – some researchers spend years in the field. However, given the quality of information that participant observation can produce, many would see these costs as reasonable.

**Loss of objectivity** The personal involvement which participant observation demands can reduce objectivity. An observer can identify so strongly with a group, that the behaviour of its members is invariably seen in a positive light. In rare cases, this identification is carried to its extreme – observers 'go native', join the group and never return to their former lives.

Conversely, researchers can view those they observe in a negative light. Something of this can be seen from the Policy Studies Institute study of policing in London. At times researchers had to walk away from situations when they found the behaviour of the police racist and offensive. This does not necessarily result in a biased view, but it does little to encourage objectivity.

**Changing behaviour** Would you change your behaviour if a participant observer joined your social circle? The answer is yes, even if you weren't aware you were being observed. This is how 'Doc', William Whyte's main informant in the streetcorner gang, saw the effect of participant observation on his own behaviour. In Doc's words, 'You've slowed me up plenty since you've been down here. Now, when I do something, I have to think what Bill Whyte would want to know about it and how I can explain it. Before, I used to do things by instinct' (Whyte, 1955).

Given the importance of observing everyday life in its normal setting, do comments like this invalidate the findings of participant observation? While recognising the problem, many researchers would say no. After a while most people get used to an observer and carry on more or less as normal. This is how David Hargreaves (1967) saw his effect as a participant observer in a boys' secondary school. 'Initially my presence caused changes in the boys' behaviour though once they became accustomed to me, they behaved normally.'

**Replication** Participant observation studies are difficult, if not impossible, to replicate – repeat under the same or very similar conditions. There are various reasons for this. Participant observation is often unsystematic – there are no fixed procedures; things happen and the observer tags along.

Participant observation relies heavily on the personal qualities of the researcher. To some degree, these qualities will affect how well they get on with those they observe, what they see and how they interpret it. And this reduces the chance of replication, as the following example suggests. In the late 1920s, Robert Redfield (1930) studied the village of Tepoztlan in Mexico. He found a close-knit society characterised by cooperation and a strong sense of belonging. Seventeen years later, Oscar Lewis (1951) studied the same village. He pictured a society divided by fear, envy and distrust. Maybe the differences were due to changes during the intervening years but, more probably, they reflect differences between the two observers.

**Generalisation** Sample sizes in participant observation studies are small. The researcher can't be everywhere observing large numbers of people. In view of the small numbers, it is not possible to generalise from the findings of participant observation. However, these findings can be used to refute or support generalisations from larger studies. Or they can produce fresh insights which can then be investigated on a larger scale.

**Ethical questions** All research involves ethical issues – questions of right and wrong. Participant observation, particularly when it is covert (hidden), brings these issues centre stage. According to the British Sociological Association, sociologists should explain the purpose of their research to those they study. However, these are guidelines rather than hard and fast rules (Hornsby-Smith, 1993).

Many sociologists would justify covert research under particular circumstances. For example, Nigel Fielding (1993) justified his covert observation of the National Front 'on the basis that this racist group was particularly hostile to sociology'. Laud Humphreys (1970) argues that covert participant observation is the only practical way to observe the 'tearoom trade' – casual sexual encounters between gay men in public toilets. He justifies his research because it destroys various harmful myths – for example, straight people are *not* drawn into gay sex – and it shows that gays are not a threat to society and that extensive police surveillance is therefore unnecessary.

## 8.2 Non-participant observation

The researcher need not participate to observe people's behaviour. A *non-participant observer* is like a birdwatcher in a hide, observing behaviour without joining in. For example, a researcher may secretly observe children's behaviour in a school playground from an upstairs room in the school. They may use a *behaviour schedule* – a checklist of activities which are noted as and when they occur.

Compared to participant observation, non-participant observation has a number of advantages and disadvantages.

### Advantages
- The observer is less likely to influence the group, especially if group members are completely unaware of his or her presence.
- Researchers have more opportunities for using research aids such as behaviour schedules and notebooks.

## Disadvantages

- As non-participants, researchers have fewer opportunities for discovering the meanings which direct the actions of those they observe.
- As a result, researchers are more likely to impose their own interpretations and meanings onto behaviour they observe (O'Connell Davidson & Layder, 1994).

### key terms

**Participant observation** The researcher participates in the activities of those he or she is observing.

**Ethnography** The study of the way of life of a group of people. It often involves an attempt to see the world from their point of view.

**Covert research** The identity of the researcher and purpose of the research are hidden from those being studied.

**Overt research** The identity of the researcher and purpose of the research are made clear to those being studied.

**Key informant** A member of a group being observed who develops a close relationship with the researcher and helps them by answering questions, introducing them to other members, and so on.

**Non-participant observation** The researcher observes, but does not participate in the activities of those being studied.

**Behaviour schedule** A checklist of activities which are noted on the schedule when they occur.

### summary

1. Many researchers argue that participant observation is the most effective method of seeing the world from the perspective of those being studied.

2. Participant observation involves looking and listening.

3. The advantages of participant observation include:
   - The chance to discover what people actually do
   - The chance to gain new insights
   - The opportunity to take the insider's view
   - Practicality – it may be the only method with a chance of success.

4. The disadvantages of participant observation include:
   - Time, money and personal costs
   - A possible loss of objectivity
   - The possibility of changing the behaviour of those observed
   - Difficulties in replicating research
   - Small samples, therefore not possible to generalise
   - Ethical problems, particularly with covert observation.

5. Non-participant observation is less likely to affect the behaviour of those observed. But, it provides fewer opportunities for discovering the meanings which direct their actions.

# *activity*13 *participant observation*

### Item A  *Just hang around*

*The following extract is taken from William Whyte's participant observation study of an Italian-American gang.*

Sometimes I wondered whether just hanging on the street corner was an active enough process to be dignified by the term 'research'. Perhaps I should be asking these men questions. However, one has to learn when to question and when not to question as well as what questions to ask.

I learned this lesson one night in the early months when I was with Doc (the gang leader) in Chichi's gambling joint. A man from another part of the city was regaling us with a tale of the organisation of gambling activity. I had been told that he had once been a very big gambling operator, and he talked knowingly about many interesting matters. He did most of the talking, but the others asked questions and threw in comments, so

*Whyte's research was carried out in the Italian-American community of South Boston. Many east coast American cities have large Italian communities. This picture shows 'Little Italy' in New York.*

at length I began to feel that I must say something in order to be part of the group. I said: 'I suppose the cops were all paid off?'

The gambler's jaw dropped. He glared at me. Then he denied vehemently that any policemen had been paid off and immediately switched the conversation to another subject. For the rest of that evening I felt very uncomfortable.

The next day Doc explained the lesson of the previous evening. 'Go easy on that "who", "what", "why", "when", stuff, Bill. You ask those questions, and people will clam up on you. If people accept you, you can just hang around, and you'll learn the answers in the long run without even having to ask the questions.'

Adapted from Whyte, 1955

## Item B  *In the classroom*

The following extract is taken from David Hargreaves's study of an all-boys secondary school in England. He sat at the back of the classroom to observe lessons. Later, he talked to some of the boys about the behaviour of the teachers. This is what they said.

'When you're in he tries to act calmly as though he's a little angel and all that.'

'They put on a show for you. They put the good act on, smiles and all that.'

'Like if Mr O's getting mad 'cos someone's ripped a book or something, but if you're in he seems to drop it. If you weren't there, he'd get real mad.'

Adapted from Hargreaves, 1967

## Item C  *In the pub*

Dick Hobbs's research involved much heavy drinking in pubs and he experienced some of the dangers of 'going native'. He writes: 'I often had to remind myself that I was not in a pub to enjoy myself but to conduct an enquiry and repeatedly woke up the following morning with an incredible hangover facing the dilemma of whether to bring it up or write it up'.

Adapted from Hobbs, 1988

## Item D  *Backstage*

As part of his research, Rubenstein completed police training and rode as an 'armed observer' in patrol cars in Philadelphia – and perhaps that degree of involvement has helped to produce what will surely become a classic. His *City Police* is an insider's view of backstage police behaviour. In microscopic detail, Rubenstein takes us into the policeman's world. The information he collected on violence and corruption could only have been gained by a trained observer who was accepted by the policemen.

Adapted from Punch, 1979

## *questions*

1  Item A points to one of the main problems of participant observation. What is this problem and how is it usually dealt with?

2  What are the advantages and disadvantages of participant observation indicated by Items B, C and D?

# Unit 9 *Secondary sources*

## *keyissues*

1  What are the main secondary sources of data?

2  What are the advantages and disadvantages of using these sources?

**Primary data** So far, this chapter has been mainly concerned with *primary data* – data produced by researchers using methods such as questionnaires, interviews and observation. Primary data is new data that did not exist before the research began.

**Secondary data** There is a vast range of existing information which is available for sociological research. It includes letters, diaries, novels, autobiographies, legal documents, parish records, official statistics, newspapers, magazines, television and radio programmes, recorded music, films, photographs and paintings. These sources of information are known as *secondary sources* and the data itself as *secondary data*.

This unit looks at a number of secondary sources and assesses the usefulness of secondary data.

# 9.1 Official statistics

## Sources of official statistics

Official statistics are numerical data produced by national and local government bodies. They may be a by-product of the normal workings of a government department. For example, the claimant count measure of unemployment – a measure of unemployment based on the number of people who claim unemployment-related benefit – is a by-product of administering the benefit system. Or official statistics may result from research designed to produce them – for example, the Labour Force Survey collects information on unemployment from a quarterly survey of 60,000 households.

Official statistics cover a wide range of behaviour including births, deaths, marriage and divorce, the distribution of income and wealth, crime and sentencing and work and leisure. The following are among the main sources of official statistics.

1  **Government departments** Departments such as Education and Skills and the Home Office regularly request information from organisations such as local tax offices, social services departments, hospitals, job centres and police stations. This information is then processed and much of it published.

2  **Surveys** The Office for National Statistics is the government agency responsible for compiling and analysing many of the UK's economic, social and population statistics. Surveys are a major source of statistical data. Every ten years the Office for National Statistics carries out the Census of the Population which covers every household in the UK. Each head of household must, by law, complete a questionnaire that deals with family composition, housing, occupation, transport and leisure. Other large scale surveys include the annual General Household Survey based on a detailed questionnaire given to a sample of nearly 12,000 people and the New Earnings Survey based on a 1% sample of employees drawn from Inland Revenue PAYE records.

## Using official statistics

Official statistics provide a vast array of quantitative data. However, sociologists cannot accept them at face value – they must use them only with care and caution. It is essential to bear the following points in mind.

How are official statistics constructed? Sociologists must know how official statistics are constructed in order to assess the quality of the data they provide. The example of unemployment statistics shows why.

As noted earlier, there are two main sources of data for unemployment statistics – the benefit system and social surveys. And there are two main definitions of unemployment – the claimant count definition which uses data from the benefit system, and the International Labour Organisation definition which uses data from the Labour Force Survey. Although both measures show broadly the same levels of and trends in unemployment, there are differences.

Sociologists using official statistics on unemployment should be aware of how these statistics have been constructed. This applies to all official statistics, no matter what the topic.

**Who decides what statistics are collected and published?** Official statistics are government statistics. Elected representatives and government officials decide what information is important and useful and, on this basis, what data to collect and publish. And, maybe more importantly, they decide what *not* to collect and publish.

These decisions may be 'political'. They may reflect the concerns and priorities of government rather than a desire to provide sound and reliable information. For example, Muriel Nissel, the first editor of *Social Trends*, an annual publication of the Office for National Statistics has written, 'From time to time, there has been great pressure on directors of statistics in departments to withhold or modify statistics, particularly in relation to employment and health, and professional integrity has forced some to threaten resignation' (Nissel, 1995).

**Are official statistics politically biased?** Does the actual construction of statistics reflect government interests? Are they shaped to present the government of the day in a favourable light? The following evidence suggests that in some cases this might happen.

According to the Labour Party, Conservative governments changed the method used to count unemployment over 30 times between 1982 and 1992. And in practically every case, these changes resulted in a drop in the official level of unemployment (Denscombe, 1994). At best, some would argue, this is politically convenient, at worst it is outright fiddling to present the government in a better light.

## Do official statistics provide valid measures?

Do official statistics really measure what they claim to measure? For example, do the annual crime statistics produced by the Home Office provide an accurate measurement of crime? Even the Home Office accepts that the answer is no. Similar criticisms can be made for a range of official statistics from unemployment and suicide to the distribution of income and wealth.

The problem of validity is looked at in terms of crime statistics in Activity 14.

**Advantages of official statistics** Despite the above warnings, official statistics can be very useful for sociological research. They have the following advantages.

- Published statistics are readily available and cost little or nothing to use.
- Care is taken to select representative samples and sample sizes are often large. Surveys as large as the General Household Survey are usually outside sociologists' research budgets.
- Many government surveys are well planned and organised with detailed questionnaires or interview schedules. As such, they meet the standards of sociological research.
- Surveys are often conducted regularly, for example on a fortnightly, monthly, annual or ten yearly basis. This can allow for comparisons over time and the identification of trends.
- Sometimes official statistics are the only major source of information on a particular topic.

## key term

**Official statistics** Statistics produced by local and national government, government agencies and organisations funded by government.

## summary

1. Sociologists using official statistics should be aware of how those statistics have been constructed.

2. Decisions on what statistics to collect and publish may be politically biased.

3. In some cases, official statistics fail to produce valid measures.

4. Official statistics can provide valuable data for sociological research.

5. Positivists see official statistics as a potentially valuable source of quantitative data. Interpretivists see official statistics as meanings in terms of which people construct their social reality. Marxists see official statistics as an aspect of ruling class ideology.

# activity14 crime statistics

### Item A  Ethnicity and crime

Stop and search

African Caribbeans make up around 1.5% of the UK population. In the mid-1990s, they formed nearly 12% of the prison population.

The police rely on the public to report crimes to them. Evidence indicates that White people are more likely to report Black rather than White suspects. In London, Black males aged 16 to 24 were ten times more likely to be stopped by police under stop and search powers. If arrested for the same offence, young Black males were more likely to be charged than their White counterparts. And if found guilty of the same offence, Black people were more likely to be sent to prison.

Research indicates that statistics which link ethnicity and crime result from a series of decisions based on prejudice and discrimination. This is why so many Black people end up in prison.

Adapted from May, 2001

### Item B  The social construction of crime statistics

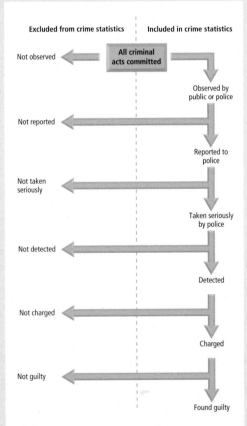

*questions*

1 a) What are the statistics in Item A actually measuring?

  b) Do they indicate a link between ethnicity and crime?

2 Look at Item B. Why does it suggest that crime statistics must be treated with caution?

# 9.2 Documents

The term documents covers a wide range of written and recorded material. It includes letters, diaries, memoirs, autobiographies, novels, newspapers, advertisements, posters, photographs and radio and television broadcasts.

This section looks at some of the ways sociologists have analysed documents. Ray Pawson (1995) distinguishes three main types of analysis, 1) formal content analysis 2) thematic analysis 3) textual analysis.

## Formal content analysis

This method attempts to classify and quantify the content of a document in an objective manner. Say you were interested in the portrayal of gender roles in children's fiction published during the last five years. You could take a sample of the books and analyse each in terms of the same pre-set categories. For example, which activities are shared by girls and boys and which are limited to one or the other. The results are then quantified and interpreted. If, for example, preparing food and taking care of younger brothers and sisters is limited to girls, then it could be argued that gender roles remain distinct.

Critics accept that formal content analysis can often effectively measure simple straightforward aspects of content – see the example in Activity 15, Item A. However, they argue that it says little about the meaning of a document, either in terms of its meaning to the audience or the meaning the producer intends to communicate.

## Thematic analysis

This approach looks for the motives and ideologies which are seen to underlie documents. For example, a news broadcast may reflect the interests of powerful groups in society. The job of the researcher is to uncover this underlying ideology. The Glasgow University Media Group combined content and thematic analysis in their analysis of TV news broadcasts in the 1970s and 80s. They made a strong case that there is a pro-management, anti-union bias in the reporting of industrial disputes.

However, there are a number of problems with thematic analysis. Who is to say that the sociologist's interpretation of the underlying ideology is correct? And if it is correct, does the existence of such ideology matter? Readers of *The Sun*, for instance, may see through or ignore or be unaware of its right-wing views. This may well explain why a significant minority of *Sun* readers regularly vote Labour.

## Textual analysis

Rather than looking for underlying ideologies, this method involves a close examination of the 'text' of a document to see how it encourages a particular reading and creates a particular impression. Ray Pawson (1995) gives the following example from a newspaper headline, GIRL GUIDE, 14, RAPED AT HELLS ANGELS CONVENTION. This is an example of the 'innocent victim'/'wicked perpetrator' pair which creates the impression of two extremes, one good, the other evil. It is one of the many tricks of the trade used to convey particular messages.

As with thematic analysis, the problem with textual analysis is reading things into the text which may have little or nothing to do with the intentions of the producers or the interpretations of the audience.

## Audience research

Some researchers argue that the focus of document research should be the audience. From this viewpoint, the audience is not made up of passive consumers who are brainwashed by underlying ideologies or swayed by textual 'tricks of the trade'. Instead, it sees audiences actively negotiating the meaning of messages with the outcome of negotiation ranging from acceptance to indifference to opposition (Pawson, 1995).

**The news game** But finding out how audiences respond is far from easy. Jenny Kitzinger's use of the 'news game' provides a novel and interesting alternative to the methods examined so far. Small 'audience groups' averaging three people from different social backgrounds were given a set of 13 photographs taken from TV news items and documentaries about AIDS. The groups were asked to select pictures and use them to write a news report on AIDS. Kitzinger (1993) concluded from this exercise that audiences are selective in their interpretation of news. They highlight certain views and modify or oppose others. They are able to 'read between the lines' of news reports, to uncover dominant themes and to construct alternative accounts which draw on their personal experience and political beliefs. This gives some indication of the variety and complexity of audience responses.

The 'news game' was first used by Greg Philo to study audience response to the media and the miners' strike of 1984/85. It represents an important change of direction – from the document, to the document in relation to the audience.

**Audience understandings** In more recent research, Greg Philo and David Miller (2002) examined BBC and ITN TV news broadcasts of the Israeli/Palestinian conflict. The broadcasts focused on images of violence and the bleak prospects for peace. The researchers' audience sample included 300 young people aged 17-22. The responses of this sample show how TV news affected their knowledge and understanding of the conflict.

News broadcasts made little reference to the history and background of the Israeli/Palestinian conflict. Broadcasts referred to 'occupied territories' but provided no explanation of what they were. Only 9% of the young people sampled knew it was Israelis occupying Palestinian land, 71% had no idea what the term meant, and 11% actually thought it was the Palestinians occupying Israeli land. Broadcasts showed Palestinians burning the American flag and mentioned their distrust of American peace proposals. There was little or no mention of why. For example, there was hardly a reference to the fact that the USA supplied some three billion dollars of aid to Israel each year, much of it in military hardware. When asked to explain Palestinian distrust of the Americans, 66% of the sample had no idea, 24% thought America 'supported' Israel and only 10% mentioned money and arms (Philo & Miller, 2002).

This study shows the importance of audience research.

Sociology is the study of people in society. When researchers examine 'documents' such as TV news, a major concern is how they affect members of society. And this requires researchers to discover the meanings people give to those documents and the understandings they draw from them. To do this they must 'ask the audience'.

## key terms

**Formal content analysis** A method which seeks to classify and quantify the content of a document.
**Thematic analysis** A method which seeks to identify the themes, motives and ideologies which underlie a document.
**Textual analysis** A method which closely examines the 'text' of a document to see how it encourages a particular reading and creates a particular impression.
**Audience research** An investigation of audience understanding of and response to documents.

### Historical documents

For studying the past, historical documents are often the major and sometimes the only source of information. Max Weber's classic study *The Protestant Ethic and the Spirit of Capitalism* could not have been written without a range of

# activity 15 analysing documents

## Item A Content analysis

Television programmes containing reference to or depiction of disability

| Genre | Number of programmes | Percentage of total programmes | Number with disability | Percentage of total with disability |
|---|---|---|---|---|
| News | 221 | 27 | 54 | 42 |
| Current affairs | 28 | 4 | 0 | 0 |
| Documentary | 155 | 19 | 21 | 16 |
| Magazine | 70 | 9 | 20 | 16 |
| Informational | 59 | 7 | 4 | 3 |
| Debate | 15 | 2 | 2 | 2 |
| Religious | 9 | 1 | 2 | 2 |
| Quiz | 24 | 3 | 3 | 2 |
| Music/dance | 38 | 5 | 0 | 0 |
| Educational | 5 | 0.6 | 2 | 2 |
| Game show | 44 | 5 | 0 | 0 |
| Chat show | 24 | 3 | 4 | 3 |
| Sport | 36 | 4 | 1 | 1 |
| Special broadcast | 46 | 6 | 12 | 9 |
| Special interest programme | 3 | 0.4 | 3 | 2 |
| Other | 27 | 3 | 0 | 0 |
| Total | 804 | 99 | 128 | 100 |

From Cumberbatch & Negrine, 1992

## Item B The Israeli/Palestinian conflict

Palestinian boy with a slingshot hurling stones at a Jewish settlement in the occupied territories

**Item C** *First World War posters*

## questions

1 a) What does Item A tell us?

  b) What further information might be useful?

2 a) What additional information would you need in order to understand what's going on in Item B?

  b) Do you think most young people in the UK have this information? Explain your answer.

3 What use might a sociologist studying gender make of the posters in Item C?

---

historical documents. For example, he illustrates the spirit of capitalism with quotes from two books by Benjamin Franklin, *Necessary Hints to Those that would be Rich* (1736) and *Advice to a Young Tradesman* (1748). Weber builds a strong case for the religious basis of the capitalist work ethic by quoting from the speeches and writings of ministers such as John Calvin (1509-1564).

Geoffrey Pearson's *Hooligan: A History of Respectable Fears* (1983) provides a more recent example of the use of historical documents. Pearson looks back to Victorian England and forward to today to show that 'for generations Britain has been plagued by the same fears and problems'. He looks at 'hooliganism' – street crime and violence – the moral panics it generates and its 'discovery' time and time again as something new, in contrast to the 'good old days'. Pearson builds up a substantial case for this argument with a range of historical documents which include newspapers, magazines such as *Punch* and *The Teacher's World*, contemporary novels and government reports.

**Using historical documents** Historical documents are often a long way from the objectivity which sociologists strive for. They are usually biased, prejudiced, one-sided and concerned with putting over a particular point of view. However, as long as researchers take them for what they are, historical documents provide a rich and valuable source of data. Thus Lord Ashley's announcement in the House of Commons in 1843 that, 'the morals of the children are tenfold worse than formerly' (quoted in Pearson, 1983) cannot be seen as a balanced assessment of juvenile morality. However, for Pearson's study of 'respectable fears', it is a very useful piece of data since it exemplifies a fear that has recurred throughout the past two centuries.

Historical documents bring their own problems of interpretation because they are from a different era, a different culture, and those who produced them are often dead. Add to this the fact that interpretation relies heavily on the researcher's viewpoint and background and it is clear that there is plenty of room for disagreement. For example, J. Berger argued that a number of paintings from the 17th and 18th centuries showed how art patrons at the time were very concerned with material possessions. He saw this concern as linked to the rise of capitalism. However, as Berger himself notes, this interpretation was hotly disputed by an art critic (discussed in Macdonald & Tipton, 1993).

**Assessing historical documents** John Scott (1990) provides four 'quality control criteria' for assessing documents which are particularly applicable to historical documents.

**Authenticity** The first refers to authenticity. Is the document genuine or a forgery? As the famous 60 volume *Hitler Diaries* which surfaced in 1983 showed, forgeries can fool even top historians. Or, is the document an original or a copy? For example, the writings of Roman historians have been copied and recopied by hand. How true to the originals are the copies?

**Credibility** Is the author of the document 'sincere' or does he or she distort the evidence in order to mislead the reader? There are plenty of examples of distortion, deceit and outright lies in documents. Former US President Nixon denied all knowledge of the illegal break-in at the Democratic Party's headquarters which became known as the Watergate Affair. This lie appeared in TV and radio broadcasts by Nixon and his officials, and in White House press releases.

**Representativeness** To what extent is the document representative? For example, is a newspaper article typical of the articles which appear in that particular newspaper? The question of representativeness is particularly important in the case of historical documents as many have been lost or destroyed. Those that remain may be untypical. For example, a study of witchcraft in 17th century New England was based on court records relating to 114 suspects. The researcher believes that these surviving records are only the 'tip of the iceberg', a 'tip' which may well be unrepresentative (discussed in O'Connell Davidson & Layder, 1994).

**Meaning** What does a document mean? This ranges from the literal meaning of the text – can the researcher 'literally' understand it, eg can the researcher read a text in Anglo Saxon English – to higher level interpretations of meaning and significance. As the previous section on analysing documents has indicated, questions of meaning will never be settled.

## summary

1.   There are three main methods for the analysis of documents – formal content analysis, thematic analysis and textual analysis. In each case, the analysis is conducted by the researcher.

2.   In recent years, the focus has moved towards audience research. The emphasis here is on how audiences interpret documents.

3.   For studying the past, historical documents are often the major and sometimes the only source of information.

4.   Historical documents are usually biased and one-sided but this does not necessarily detract from their usefulness.

5.   Historical documents can be assessed in terms of their authenticity, credibility, representativeness and meaning.

# activity 16 historical documents

### Item A   The diaries of a cabinet minister

*Richard Crossman was an MP and cabinet minister in the Labour government of 1964-1970. His political diaries were published after his death in 1975.*

Memory is a terrible improver – even with a diary to check the tendency. And it is this which makes a politician's autobiography so wildly unreliable. But if I could publish a diary of my years as a minister without any editorial improvements, as a true record of how one minister thought and felt, I would have done something towards lighting up the secret places of British politics and enabling any intelligent elector to have a picture of what went on behind the scenes between 1964 and 1970.

Of course the picture which this diary provides is neither objective nor fair – although as a lifelong political scientist I have tried to discipline myself to objectivity. In particular, I have tried to avoid self-deception, especially about my own motives; the tendency to attribute to others my own worst failings; and the temptation to omit what might make me look silly in print. I have been urged by many to remove all the wounding passages about colleagues or officials. I have not done so because it would make the book untrue, and I hope that when some of them find me intolerably unfair, they will recall the follies and illusions I faithfully record about myself. A day-by-day account of a Government at work, as seen by one participant, is bound to be one-sided and immensely partisan. If it isn't, it too would fail to be true to life.

Adapted from Crossman, 1975

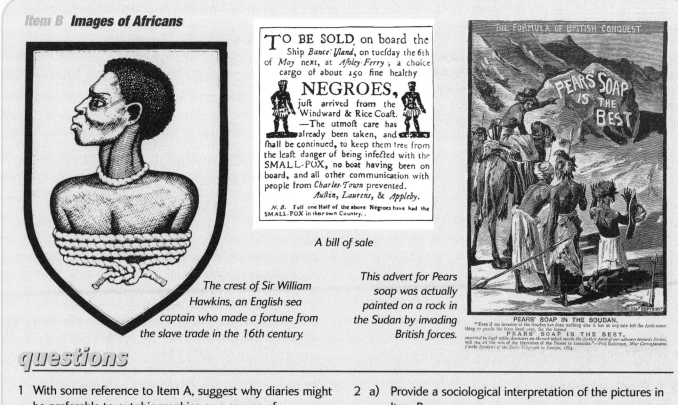

Item B  **Images of Africans**

THE FORMULA OF BRITISH CONQUEST

TO BE SOLD, on board the Ship *Bance-Island*, on tuesday the 6th of *May* next, at *Ashley-Ferry*; a choice cargo of about 250 fine healthy

NEGROES,

just arrived from the Windward & Rice Coast. —The utmost care has already been taken, and shall be continued, to keep them free from the least danger of being infected with the SMALL-POX, no boat having been on board, and all other communication with people from *Charles-Town* prevented.

*Austin, Laurens, & Appleby.*

N. B. Full one Half of the above Negroes have had the SMALL-POX in their own Country.

*A bill of sale*

The crest of Sir William Hawkins, an English sea captain who made a fortune from the slave trade in the 16th century.

This advert for Pears soap was actually painted on a rock in the Sudan by invading British forces.

PEARS' SOAP IN THE SOUDAN.

*questions*

1  With some reference to Item A, suggest why diaries might be preferable to autobiographies as a source of information.

2  a)  Provide a sociological interpretation of the pictures in Item B.

   b)  Critically assess your interpretation.

# Unit 10  *Types of research*

*keyissues*

1  Why use different types of research?

2  What are their strengths and weaknesses?

This chapter has already looked at three types of research – experiments, social surveys and ethnography. This unit looks at several more.

## 10.1 Life histories

As their name suggests, *life histories* are accounts of people's lives which they tell to researchers.

Something of the flavour and significance of life histories can be obtained from a brief discussion of *Cheyenne Memories*, the life history of John Stands In Timber (1884-1967) as told to the anthropologist Margot Liberty. He was a member of the last generation who experienced the traditional way of life of the Cheyenne Indians during the 19th century.

The Cheyenne were a non-literate society, so oral accounts are particularly important. Stands In Timber's

account of his life and the history and culture of his people is given from the Cheyenne point of view. In Margot Liberty's words, 'John has given us the history of the Cheyennes as they themselves recall and interpret it' (1967). Much of the material is new, that which isn't confirms, complements and amplifies 19th century ethnographic accounts.

**Advantages** Life histories have illuminated many areas of social life. For example, *The Polish Peasant in Europe and America*, a five volume work first published from 1918 to 1920, included an extensive life history of a Polish peasant which provided many valuable insights into the experience of migration from Poland to the USA (Thomas & Znaniecki, 1958). *The Jack Roller* (Shaw, 1930) is a story, written in his own words and from his own point of view, of a young American 'jack roller', the 1930s equivalent of today's 'mugger'. It is this first-hand account of people's experience of their life as they see it which many researchers regard as the main value of the life history. It can provide insights and information which are not obtainable from any other source, as Stands In Timber's life history shows. It can give a picture of the process and development of social life over time. It can also serve as a basis for confirming or questioning other interpretations and accounts. And it can direct researchers into new areas and encourage them to ask new questions.

**Disadvantages** However, as the title *Cheyenne Memories* suggests, the life history is heavily dependent on people's memory which is inevitably patchy and selective. To some extent, it will also reflect their attitudes and opinions. Some would see this as a serious criticism of the life history. For example, Stands In Timber has been criticised by other members of his tribe for being too pro-Crow – the Crow are traditional enemies of the Cheyenne.

A further criticism concerns the researcher. There is a temptation for researchers to lead as life histories are recounted, particularly when areas of interest to them are touched upon. For example, Margot Liberty (1967) writes, 'My tendency was at first to press him for stories. I soon found it far better to trust his own instinct. Where he did not volunteer material freely he usually had little to say'.

While accepting many of the criticisms of life histories, supporters argue that they are far outweighed by the valuable information that a good life history can provide.

## 10.2 Case studies

A case study is a study of one particular case or instance of something. It may be a study of a particular school, factory or hospital, or a study of a single individual such as a manual worker, a mother with dependent children, or a retired person. The life history is an example of a case study. Using examples from the previous section, it is the study of one Cheyenne Indian or one Polish peasant.

Case studies have a number of advantages.

- By focusing on a particular case, they can provide a richer and more detailed picture than research based on large samples.
- This may result in new insights and fresh ideas.
- Case studies can provide useful information for a larger research project. For example, the experiences of one retired person could be used in a questionnaire in order to discover how far they apply to other retired people.
- There is a better chance of a questionnaire or interview being relevant and meaningful if it is based, at least in part, on a case study.
- Theories can be tested to see whether they apply in particular situations. Sociologists at Lancaster University tested the theory of secularisation (the idea that religion is becoming less important in modern societies) by conducting a case study of religion in a single town – Kendal in the Lake District.

Some of the advantages of case studies can be seen from Macbeath and Mortimore's (2001) study of school effectiveness. They used case studies of a small number of schools in addition to a large-scale social survey. The case studies helped them identify key themes to explore in their survey, allowed them to check that their survey findings held true in particular schools, and added depth to their quantitative data.

## *activity* 17 *bullying – a case study*

The only thing that prevented me from enjoying my first year at high school was one person in my class who started to bully me. This led to several other people following his example and my life became sheer misery. At first, I was upset but able to cope with it, then I became angry and distressed. I couldn't sleep for worrying about the next day. It would be name-calling, stone-throwing and threatening. It all got too much and I decided to tell my Mum and Dad. We all agreed that I had to tell the teacher. The next day, though worried, I did.

The teacher was very sympathetic and said it must stop. We had lunch meetings to discuss the problems. The bullies were very surprised that they were included instead of being punished. We discussed my feelings at being bullied and we would agree on some plan of action so that I would get support from my friends. Once the bullies realised that they were being included, the bullying ceased.

Adapted from Donnellan, 1994

### *question*

Using examples from this activity, suggest some advantages of the case study approach.

Case studies have sometimes been criticised as limited and unrepresentative. Since they are one-off instances, they cannot be used as a basis for generalisation. However, this is their strength. They are a valuable warning against rash and sweeping generalisations. A single case study can call into question the findings of a much larger study.

## 10.3 Longitudinal studies

How can you show what a person looks like? One way is to produce a photograph. This is similar to most sociological research which consists of a snapshot, a one-off investigation of an aspect of social life. Another way of showing what a person looks like is to produce a series of photographs taken at different points in their lifetime. This shows how their appearance changes and develops. The equivalent in sociology is the longitudinal study which examines the same group of people over a fairly long period of time.

As the following example shows, longitudinal studies can provide important insights. Each year from 1991 to 1995, 1125 young people in Merseyside and Greater Manchester filled in a confidential questionnaire about their attitudes to and use of illegal drugs. At the start of the research, members of the sample were aged 14, by the end, aged 18. The study was carried out by a team of sociologists led by Howard Parker (1998). Parker was interested in the extent of illegal drug use within this age group and whether sensational media reports about widespread drug abuse were accurate. The questionnaire was concerned with the types of drugs taken, reasons for the first use of drugs, how drug use changed over time and why some people refused to take drugs.

Parker's team found that cannabis was the most frequently used illegal drug. It was also the first drug that most of the sample experimented with. Working-class young people were more likely to experiment at an early age, though by 18 the middle class had caught up. There were few differences between boys and girls. By aged 18, 20-25% of the sample were regular users.

**Advantages** As these findings suggest, the strength of the longitudinal study is its ability to examine developments over time. By studying the same group, ie by keeping the same sample, the researcher can be sure that any changes in attitudes and behaviour are not simply due to changes in the makeup of the sample.

**Disadvantages** But keeping the same group is one of the main difficulties with longitudinal studies. The National Child Development Study has attempted to follow the lives of every child born in Britain between 3rd and 9th March 1958. Follow-up surveys were conducted in 1965, 1969, 1974, 1981, 1991 and 1999 to trace developments in health, education, family life, career and so on, and to try to establish links between these changes and factors such as class, gender and ethnicity. The survey began with

17,400 children but by 1999 researchers were able to contact only 11,400 members of the original sample. Reasons for this *sample attrition* included death, emigration, refusal to participate and failure to trace. The result is not just a smaller sample but, in all probability, a less representative one.

Researchers are aware of this and attempt to minimise the problem of sample attrition. This can be seen from the lengths that some go to in order to trace members of an original sample. Parker's team sent letters, follow-up letters, further reminders and even Christmas cards to their sample. If none of these worked, they actually went from door to door tracking their 'lost' respondents. The National Child Development Study has adopted a similar approach, contacting relatives, visiting workplaces and searching telephone directories and electoral registers. As this suggests, longitudinal studies can cost a great deal of time and money. Few organisations have the resources to fund an investigation which continues for twenty years or more.

## 10.4 The comparative method

Comparative studies make comparisons between different societies, between different groups within the same society, and between societies and groups over time.

Durkheim's study of suicide, first published in 1895, is an example of a comparative study. He compared suicide rates in different European societies, eg Italy, England, France and Denmark, at different time periods, eg 1866-70, 1871-75, 1874-78. He also compared suicide rates for different groups within society, eg rates for Protestants compared to Catholics, city dwellers compared to rural dwellers, and married compared to unmarried people.

The comparative method helps sociologists to investigate what causes what. For example, Durkheim's study suggested that religion may be a factor affecting the suicide rate. His figures indicated that the suicide rate for Protestants *within* particular societies was higher than the rate for Catholics. The same applied to comparisons *between* societies – the suicide rate for Protestant countries was significantly higher than the rate for Catholic societies.

**A natural laboratory** The comparative method is the nearest most sociologists get to the laboratory method of the natural sciences. Unlike laboratory experiments, variables in the real world cannot be systematically manipulated and controlled. However, it is possible to find 'natural' laboratories which allow the influence of variables to be estimated.

Europe provided a natural laboratory for Durkheim. He found a statistical link between suicide rates and religion between European societies, within those societies, and over different time periods.

**Cross-cultural studies** Is social inequality universal – ie, is it found in every society? Is a division of labour based on gender natural – ie, is it natural to have male jobs and female jobs? These are important questions, particularly for those concerned about social inequality. Cross-cultural studies – studies based on a number of different cultures – help to answer this type of question. For instance, if cross-cultural evidence indicated that, in some societies, gender has little or no influence on job allocation, then this suggests that any influence of gender on the division of labour is based on culture rather than nature.

**Evaluation** The comparative method has some obvious strengths. It provides a natural laboratory for researchers to estimate the influence of variables. It allows researchers to look at the effect of culture on behaviour.

But cross-cultural research has inbuilt problems. How, for example, can a Western researcher understand non-Western cultures? When he or she compares marriage in various cultures, are they comparing like with like? Does marriage mean the same thing in different societies, does it involve the same rights and responsibilities? Despite these problems, the comparative method holds considerable promise (May, 2001).

## 10.5 Triangulation and methodological pluralism

The types of research outlined in this unit may draw data from various research methods and various sources. For example, a case study might be based on participant observation or interviews, on primary or secondary data, on quantitative or qualitative data. Sometimes, different kinds of data and research methods are combined within a single study.

**Triangulation** Some researchers combine different research methods and different types of data in order to check the validity and reliability of their findings. This is known as

# activity18 Britain and France

**Item A  Similarity – production technology**

Fawley oil refinery, Hampshire

**Item B  Difference - nationality**

Britain and France

Duncan Gallie compared workers in oil refineries in Britain and France. Would the same kind of production technology – in this case the technology used in oil refineries – lead to the same kind of behaviour at work? Gallie found important differences between British and French workers, for example there were far more strikes in the French refineries.

Adapted from Gallie, 1978

## question

How might the comparative method be useful for explaining behaviour at work?

*triangulation.* For example, if participant observation and interviews produce conflicting findings, this raises questions about the validity of the data. This often leads to further research to re-examine the original findings.

**Methodological pluralism** Other researchers combine different research methods and different types of data in order to build up a fuller picture of social life. This approach is known as *methodological pluralism.*

It recognises that each method and type of data has its particular strengths and weaknesses. Combined they are seen to produce a more comprehensive and rounder picture of social reality. And their combination can also provide new insights and new directions for research.

Some of the strengths of methodological pluralism can be seen from Eileen Barker's (1984) study of the Moonies – the Unification Church. She conducted in-depth interviews, each lasting 6-8 hours, with a number of Moonies. The interviews dealt with their background, why they became a Moonie, their life in the church and the meaning of religion as they saw it. Barker also lived as a participant observer in several centres with the Moonies at various times during the six years of her research. This enabled her to gain the trust of many members of the church, resulting in information which would not have been given to an outsider. Two years after the start of her research, she constructed a large (41 page) questionnaire based on her findings from interviews and observation. This provided information from a larger

sample and was intended to reveal 'social patterns, trends and tendencies and gain a more reliable understanding of regularities between variables – of "what goes with what" '.

Barker claims that combining different methods of investigation gave her a much fuller picture than any one method or data source could have provided.

# *activity 19 methodological pluralism*

Our research on victims of crime was based on methodological pluralism. This approach favours neither qualitative or quantitative research methods. It is a position which recognises that different research techniques can uncover different layers of social reality and that the role of the researcher is to look for confirmations and contradictions between those different layers of information.

So, for example, for the first stage of our data-gathering process we walked our two research areas with police officers, we frequented the public houses, and we engaged in in-depth interviews with a variety of people working in the localities.

Then, on the basis of this information, we produced a criminal victimisation survey questionnaire and conducted a survey in each area, and, on the basis of this experience, moved into focus group discussions with survey participants. So, as a research process, we were always moving between quantitative and qualitative data looking for ways of making sense of the different layers of social reality which were being revealed to us.

Adapted from Walklate, 2000

*Victims of crime - burgled during their wedding*

## question

According to this extract, what are the main advantages of methodological pluralism?

## summary

1. Life histories provide a first-hand account of people's life experience as they see it. This can result in valuable insights. However, life histories are dependent on people's memory which is often patchy and selective.

2. Case studies focus on a particular case. This can provide a rich and detailed picture. A single case study can call into question the findings of a much larger study.

3. The main strength of the longitudinal study is its ability to examine developments over time. The main problem is sample attrition – the steady loss of sample members.

4. The comparative method provides a 'natural laboratory' within which the influence of variables can be estimated. It allows researchers to examine the effect of culture on behaviour. The main difficulty for researchers is understanding different cultures.

5. Triangulation provides a check on the validity and reliability of research findings.

6. Methodological pluralism builds up a fuller picture of social life.

# Unit 11 Interpreting and evaluating quantitative data

## keyissues

1 How is quantitative data presented?

2 How is quantitative data interpreted, analysed and evaluated?

Your survey is complete. The questionnaires have been collected and the responses have been coded and quantified. What happens next?

Researchers then:

- describe
- present
- interpret
- analyse and
- evaluate the data.

These steps are interconnected. For example, presenting data in a bar chart involves describing and analysing the data.

## 11.1 Describing and presenting quantitative data

Quantitative data can be described and presented in various ways. The following examples are taken from *Social Trends*.

**Tables** A table of numbers is a set of numbers arranged and displayed in a logical and systematic way. As the following example shows, a table can pack a large amount of information into a small space.

Table 1 contains the following categories or variables – male, female, full time, part time, undergraduate, postgraduate and year. The data is systematically organised in terms of these categories. The population from which the data is drawn is noted – in this case all students in higher education in the United Kingdom – and the meaning of the numbers is stated – they represent thousands of people.

### Table 1 Students in higher education: by type of course and gender

**United Kingdom** *Thousands*

| | Undergraduate | | Postgraduate | | All higher education |
|---|---|---|---|---|---|
| | **Full time** | **Part time** | **Full time** | **Part time** | |
| **Males** | | | | | |
| 1970/71 | 241 | 127 | 33 | 15 | 416 |
| 1980/81 | 277 | 176 | 41 | 32 | 526 |
| 1990/91 | 345 | 193 | 50 | 50 | 638 |
| 2000/01 | 511 | 228 | 82 | 118 | 940 |
| **Females** | | | | | |
| 1970/71 | 173 | 19 | 10 | 3 | 205 |
| 1980/81 | 196 | 71 | 21 | 13 | 301 |
| 1990/91 | 319 | 148 | 34 | 36 | 537 |
| 2000/01 | 602 | 320 | 81 | 124 | 1,128 |

Adapted from *Social Trends*, 2002

The table allows certain trends to be identified at a glance – for example, the rapid growth in the numbers of students in higher education, particularly the numbers of female students.

**Line graphs** These are useful for presenting a visual display of trends over time. The following example clearly illustrates a steady increase in video purchases from 1986 to 2000. The vertical axis (on the left) shows numbers in millions for the UK. The horizontal axis (along the bottom) shows time in years.

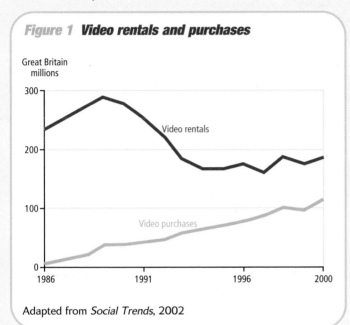

**Figure 1** *Video rentals and purchases*

Adapted from *Social Trends*, 2002

**Bar charts** These are particularly useful for comparing the behaviour of different groups. In the example below, different age and gender groups are compared in terms of their use of the Internet.

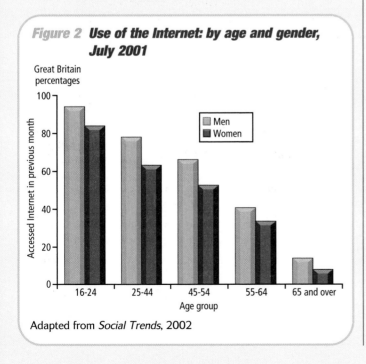

**Figure 2** *Use of the Internet: by age and gender, July 2001*

Adapted from *Social Trends*, 2002

Each bar shows the percentage of men and women for each of the five age groups who had used the Internet at least once during the month before the survey. For example, over 90% of men and over 80% of women in the 16-24 age group had accessed the Internet during the month before the survey. This drops to under 20% of men and 10% of women in the 65 and over age group.

The bar chart clearly shows that age is a major factor affecting Internet use, though gender is also important.

Bar charts are a useful method of organising and presenting data. They provide a simple visual summary of the main points.

**Pie charts** These are a useful visual aid when illustrating the proportion of each type that makes up the whole category. The pie chart below shows the percentage of each type of household in Britain in 2000. For example, one-person households make up 32% of all households. (Note that the data must be shown as a percentage of 360 in order to work out the angles – eg, the angle for the 32% segment is 32% of 360 which is just over 115°.)

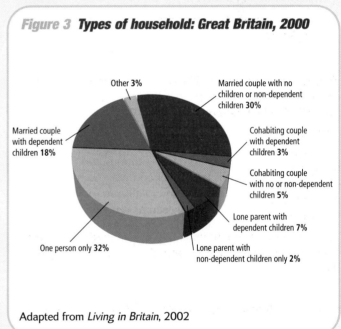

**Figure 3** *Types of household: Great Britain, 2000*

Adapted from *Living in Britain*, 2002

# 11.2 Interpreting, analysing and evaluating quantitative data

What does the data mean? What does it indicate? How can it be used? How good is it? These are some of the questions researchers ask when interpreting, analysing and evaluating quantitative data.

## Patterns and trends

Interpreting and analysing data involves looking for patterns and trends. Often these 'jump out' once the data has been described and presented in tables, graphs and charts.

Look at the table on page 218. It shows a steady increase

# activity20 reading the data

**TABLES**   Look at the table on page 218.

1   How many full-time male undergraduates were there in 2000/01?

2   Compare the growth in the numbers of male and female undergraduates from 1970/71 to 2000/01.

**LINE GRAPHS**   Look at the line graph on page 219.

3   Briefly summarise the rentals and purchases of videos from 1986 to 2000.

4   Suggest possible trends in rentals and purchases.

**BAR CHARTS**   Look at the bar chart on page 219.

5   Both age and gender appear to affect Internet use, with age being the most important factor. How does the bar chart show this?

**PIE CHARTS**   Look at the pie chart on page 219.

6   Work out the angle needed to draw the segment representing married couples with no children or non-dependent children.

---

in participation in higher education. This increase is particularly marked for females. From 1970/71 to 2000/01, the number of enrolments for men on undergraduate courses more than doubled, for women the increase was nearly fivefold.

## The wider context

Interpretation and analysis can go beyond the figures themselves. If patterns and trends have been identified, the next questions are 'What do they show?' 'What do they mean?' Answering such questions involves looking at the data in a wider context and comparing it with additional data.

What does the increased participation of women in higher education indicate? This trend may be interpreted as evidence of greater female participation in mainstream society. This, in turn, may be seen as reflecting a change in women's values – an increasing concern with paid employment outside the home and with career advancement.

Further information can be used to support this interpretation. Official statistics show that employment rates for women have risen from 52% to 70% between 1970 and 2000 (*Social Trends*, 2002). Sociological research indicates that working-class London schoolgirls in the 1970s saw their future mainly in terms of love, marriage and children. By the 1990s, a similar sample attached much more importance than their 1970s counterparts to education, having a job or career, and being able to support themselves (Sharpe, 1976 and 1994).

Interpreting and analysing quantitative data involves:

● looking for patterns and trends in the data
● interpreting these in a wider social context
● bringing in further information to provide a broader picture.

## Correlational analysis

Quantitative data is data in numbers. As such, it lends itself to correlational analysis – see pages 185-186. Correlational analysis is a statistical technique which measures the strength of the relationship between two or more variables. As noted earlier, a strong correlation does not in itself show a cause and effect relationship. However, it indicates the possibility of a causal relationship. Further analysis may strengthen this possibility, especially if additional data points to a causal relationship.

## Validity

All the interpretation and analysis in the world is a waste of time if the data is not valid. For example, some researchers have found a high positive correlation between unemployment and crime. But, if the measures of unemployment and crime are not valid, then any correlation is meaningless. Put another way, the analysis is worthless if the data fails to present a true and accurate measurement of unemployment and crime.

The problem of validity is highlighted by a recent Home Office Research Study entitled *Rape and Sexual Assault of Women: The extent and nature of the problem* (Myhill & Allen, 2002). The study was based on a nationally representative sample of 6,944 women aged 16 to 59. It estimated that nearly one in twenty women in England and Wales have been raped since they were 16 – an appalling 754,000 victims.

The operational definition (see page 194) of rape used in this study is the use of violence, threats or intimidation to force a woman to have sexual intercourse against her will. Is this a valid definition of rape? It seems reasonable. But, only 60% of the women classified as rape victims in terms of this definition were prepared to classify their experience as rape or to see it as a crime. They tended to be women who had been raped by their partner or by a 'date'.

In an article in the *Daily Mail* (July 24, 2002), Melanie Phillips presents a scathing attack on the Home Office research, describing it as 'a load of manipulative, malevolent rubbish'. She claims that the researchers have 'muddied' the concept of rape. A flavour of her argument can be seen from the following quotation.

# activity21 *validity*

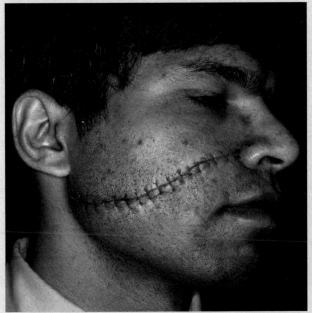

*Teacher in Tower Hamlets, London, after being attacked outside an anti-racist concert*

*Synagogue in Finsbury Park, London, after being vandalised and desecrated*

## question

With some reference to the pictures, briefly discuss the problems of obtaining valid quantitative data on racial attacks.

---

'Although the study claims the word "forced" implies an assault, it does nothing of the kind. A woman might feel forced to have sex against her will, for example, if her lover tells her that otherwise he will leave her for another woman. Or she might be an unwilling participant because he is drunk, hasn't had a bath for a week, or she doesn't love him.

The crucial point is that in such circumstances she is participating in sex even though she could choose not to do so. She is therefore not the victim of violence. By any fair-minded or common-sense definition, this is not rape.'

Whether or not the Home Office researchers have produced a valid measure of rape is a matter of judgement. This applies to some extent to every operational definition – from crime to unemployment to marital satisfaction to leisure activity.

### Official statistics

Official statistics are quantitative data produced by official bodies such as local and national government. As with all research producing quantitative data, official statistics are as good as the operational definition on which they are based. Are they measuring what they are intended to measure? Is the data valid? These issues are examined in detail on pages 207-208, along with an evaluation of official statistics.

## summary

1. Quantitative data can be described and presented in terms of:
   - Tables
   - Line graphs
   - Bar charts
   - Pie charts.
2. Interpreting and analysing quantitative data involves looking for patterns and trends.
3. Quantitative data lends itself to correlational analysis.
4. Assessing validity is one of the main ways of evaluating quantitative data.

# Unit 12 Interpreting and evaluating qualitative data

## key issues

1 What is content analysis and how is it used?

2 How do sociologists interpret and evaluate data from observations and unstructured interviews?

## 12.1 Interpreting and evaluating documents

### Content analysis

Various forms of content analysis were introduced in Unit 9, pages 209-210. This section looks at an example of content analysis in practice. It is based on an analysis of gender roles in six reading schemes, including the *Janet and John* and *Ladybird* series, which were widely used in primary schools during the 1960s and 1970s (Lobban, 1974).

- First, a sample of the materials to be analysed is examined. In terms of the above example, three books from each of the series might be selected.
- Second, categories are created in terms of which the data can be classified and organised. The categories reflect the purpose of the research – in this case an analysis of gender roles. Categories developed from the reading schemes included objects, activities and roles that are linked to girls, those that are linked to boys, and those that are linked to both.
- Third, a larger sample is selected and the researcher classifies data from the books in terms of the various categories. Table 2 presents the results of this analysis for the six reading schemes.

**Themes** The classification of data into categories is usually only a first step. Once this has been done, further analysis can take place. For example, the researcher might look for themes which are common to many of the categories in Table 2. The following themes might be identified from the way boys and girls are presented in the reading schemes.

- Boys are presented as more adventurous than girls
- As physically stronger
- As having more choices.
- Girls are presented as more caring than boys
- As more interested in domestic matters
- As followers rather than leaders.

The researcher may then widen the focus and, for example, relate these themes to adult roles such as the mother-housewife role and gender divisions in the labour market. For instance, women are concentrated in the caring professions – nursing, social work and primary

*Illustrations from The Ladybird Key Words Reading Scheme (1972)*

school teaching. Men outnumber women in leadership roles such as managers. The researcher may then ask how the themes identified in the reading schemes form a part of gender socialisation – the way boys learn to be men and girls learn to be women. For example, how do these themes steer men and women into 'men's jobs' and 'women's jobs'?

**Summary** This example shows content analysis at work. Data from the reading schemes is coded into various categories such as toys and pets and activities. These categories are then related to gender roles as shown in Table 2. This is a preliminary stage – it is concerned with sifting and sorting the data. Further interpretation and analysis take place when the researcher identifies themes which cut across many of the categories. The researcher may then relate findings from the content analysis to broader issues such as gender roles in adult society.

**Table 2** *Gender roles that occurred in three or more of the six schemes*

| Gender for which role was allocated | Toys and Pets | Activities | Taking the lead in activities that both boys and girls take part in | Learning a new skill | Adult roles presented |
|---|---|---|---|---|---|
| **Girls only** | 1 Doll<br>2 Skipping rope<br>3 Doll's pram | 1 Preparing the tea<br>2 Playing with dolls<br>3 Taking care of younger siblings | 1 Hopping<br>2 Shopping with parents<br>3 Skipping | 1 Taking care of younger siblings | 1 Mother<br>2 Aunt<br>3 Grandmother |
| **Boys only** | 1 Car<br>2 Train<br>3 Aeroplane<br>4 Boat<br>5 Football | 1 Playing with cars<br>2 Playing with trains<br>3 Playing football<br>4 Lifting or pulling heavy objects<br>5 Playing cricket<br>6 Watching adult males in occupational roles<br>7 Heavy gardening | 1 Going exploring alone<br>2 Climbing trees<br>3 Building things<br>4 Taking care of pets<br>5 Sailing boats<br>6 Flying kites<br>7 Washing and polishing Dad's car | 1 Taking care of pets<br>2 Making/building<br>3 Saving/rescuing people or pets<br>4 Playing sports | 1 Father<br>2 Uncle<br>3 Grandfather<br>4 Postman<br>5 Farmer<br>6 Fisherman<br>7 Business owner<br>8 Policeman<br>9 Builder<br>10 Bus driver<br>11 Bus conductor<br>12 Train driver<br>13 Railway porter |
| **Girls and boys** | 1 Book<br>2 Ball<br>3 Paints<br>4 Bucket and spade<br>5 Dog<br>6 Cat<br>7 Shop | 1 Playing with pets<br>2 Writing<br>3 Reading<br>4 Going to the seaside<br>5 Going on a family outing | | | 1 Teacher<br>2 Shop assistant |

Adapted from Lobban, 1974

# activity22 *content analysis*

## Item A **Men looking for women**

Professional male 43 articulate, sincere, successful, own business, flat/car, of varied interests seeks intelligent lady companion.

*Scotsman*, May 1996

Gentleman company director 6ft tall, 54 wishes to meet lady for company and conversation. I am in good health and enjoy life to the full. I smoke and drink in moderation.

*Scotsman*, May 1996

**Analysis** About one third of men described themselves in terms of their occupational, educational and economic status. They represented themselves as hard-working, industrious, ambitious, successful achievers, consistent with traditional gender stereotypes of masculinity.

Adapted from Jagger, 2001

## Item B **Women looking for men**

Caring, easy-going, warm, attractive F seeks tall M for walking, talking and cuddles.

*Guardian*, March 1996

Woman warmth and affection in abundance. Petite, attractive, dark brown hair, eyes that reflect great capacity for kindness, fun, giving and receiving at many levels. Deep understanding of humanity. Act one has ended with lots completed. Act two is to begin. Looking for male companion, 40s plus.

*Independent*, May 1996

Adapted from Jagger, 2001

Item C **Men's magazines**

## questions

1 Item A presents a textual analysis of dating adverts placed by men. Try to analyse the adverts (placed by women) in Item B in a similar way.

2 Suggest ways of using content analysis to analyse the covers of the men's magazines in Item C. What conclusions might you draw?

## Discovering meanings

The analysis of qualitative data often aims to discover the meanings which underlie what people say and do. There is no simple recipe for doing this. It relies heavily on the interpretative skills of the researcher, and is best illustrated by example.

**Newspaper headlines** Look at the newspaper headlines in Figure 4. They refer to men and women infected with AIDS through blood transfusions, and mother to child transmission of AIDS in the womb.

What meanings lie behind these headlines? One interpretation runs as follows. The word 'innocent' crops up again and again. This suggests that the people concerned do not deserve to be infected – it is not their fault. As one headline states, they come from 'ordinary families', and this kind of thing does not, and should not, happen to 'ordinary people'. This implies that unlike 'ordinary people', 'typical' AIDS victims are not so 'innocent' – in some way they deserve their fate, in some way they are guilty for what happens to them.

**Television news** Here is another example of interpreting meanings, from the Glasgow University Media Group's (1976) analysis of the reporting of industrial disputes on television news. Trade unionists were typically asked, 'What are you doing to end the strike?' whereas the typical question put to managers was, 'How much production or

Figure 4 **Newspaper headlines**

Adapted from *Kitzinger*, 1993

exports have you lost?' The assumption appears to be that unions cause strikes which result in lost production and lost export markets. Shop stewards were often accused by TV interviewers of 'acting irresponsibly', 'destroying the company' and 'cutting their own throats'. The implication is that the blame for strikes lies with workers and trade unions. Other factors which may have caused the strike, such as bad management, low wages despite high profits, or high inflation, were largely ignored.

This type of content analysis looks closely at the words and phrases people use and the assumptions that lie behind them. In this case, the researchers concluded that the view that unions cause industrial problems

underpinned television news coverage.

Interpreting meanings is not simple and straightforward. Researchers may provide evidence to support the meanings they claim to have discovered. But, in many cases, they are a long way from demonstrating that their interpretations are correct. Despite this, the search for meanings is important. Meanings guide and direct human action. And the analysis of meanings that underlie qualitative data is often convincing and insightful.

# *activity*23 *music and meaning*

## Item A  **Gospel**

*Gospel singers – The Five Blind Boys of Alabama*

### Prayer changes things
I've traveled through sorrow valley,
So many times my heart's been made to bleed.
By some friends whom I thought were with me,
Through disappointment, I was knocked down to my knees.
But I rose with faith and grace,
I found nobody to take God's place
I know, yes I know, prayer changes things.

### God shall wipe all tears away
When we reach that blessed homeland,
Where 'tis ever lasting day.
On that bright, eternal morning,
God shall wipe all tears away.

## Item B  **Blues**

*Blues singer Albert King who recorded these songs.*

### I've been down so long
I've been down so long,
That down don't bother me,
I'm gonna take all of my troubles,
And toss them in the deep blue sea.

### Born under a bad sign
Born under a bad sign,
Been down since I began to crawl,
If it wasn't for bad luck,
You know I wouldn't have no luck at all.

## Item C  **Rap**

*Tupac Shakur*

### I don't give a fuck
How much shit can a nigga take,
I ain't goin' nowhere no how,
Folks wanna throw down,
Better bring your gun, pal,
Cos this is the day we make 'em pay.
Fuck bailin' hay,
I'm bailin' straight with a A-K,
And even if they shoot me down,
There be another nigga,
Bigger from the motherfuckin' underground
I've had enough,
And I just don't give a fuck.

*question*

Interpret and compare the meanings underlying the songs in Items A, B and C.

## 12.2 Interpreting and evaluating observational data

Participant observation can be a lengthy process – it can go on for a year or more. Often the researcher has only a vague idea of what they're looking for. As Ken Pryce (1979) said about his study of the African-Caribbean community in Bristol, one of his problems was to 'work out a focus for the research … I only knew that I wanted to study lifestyles'. This focus often comes as the participant observer looks, listens and *interprets* what they see and hear. And the focus sharpens when they finish their research and sit down to interpret and analyse their findings. How does this process of interpretation and analysis work? The following example offers some indication.

**Behaviour in a mental hospital** Erving Goffman's classic participant observation study, *Asylums* (1968), is an investigation of the behaviour of inmates in a mental hospital in Washington DC. Goffman spent a year in the hospital in the role of a member of staff. As a participant observer, he watched and listened, and amassed a vast quantity of data. How could he make sense of it all?

Goffman did not decide in advance what was relevant. He did not start with pre-set categories in which to classify the data. Instead, he simply watched and listened. Categories, themes and patterns gradually emerged from his observations. Here is an example of how he organised and made sense of his data.

Goffman identified a pattern of behaviour which he called the *mortification process*. He recognised this process time and time again during his stay at the mental hospital. It consisted of 'a series of abasements, degradations, humiliations, and profanities of self' in terms of which inmates were stripped of their former identities and treated as 'mental cases' who had little social significance and 'were hardly capable of acting like a fully-fledged person at all'. The idea of a mortification process connected a range of apparently unconnected behaviours, it identified a common theme underlying those behaviours, and made sense of them.

On entry to mental hospitals, inmates are often stripped of various supports which help them to maintain their former self-concepts. Their clothes, an important symbol of identity, are sometimes removed. Their possessions, a further symbol of identity, may be taken away and stored for the duration of their stay. They may be washed, disinfected and have their hair cut. They may be issued with a new 'identity kit' such as regulation clothes and toilet articles. Such standardised articles tend to remove individuality.

Once the entry phase is over, the inmate settles down to a range of 'mortifying experiences'. Each day is strictly timetabled into a set of compulsory activities controlled by the staff. Inmates are allowed little freedom of movement, few opportunities for self-expression, and little chance to show initiative or take decisions. Their actions are scrutinised and assessed by the staff in terms of the rules and regulations of the institution. A demeaning system of rewards and privileges is administered to encourage obedience and 'appropriate behaviour'. Watching TV, an extra cup of coffee or a cigarette are awarded for 'good behaviour', or withheld from those who don't 'toe the line'. Many of the behaviours demanded from inmates are degrading – for example, in some mental hospitals, a spoon is the only utensil provided for them to eat with.

Goffman found that his idea of a mortification process identified a theme running through a large number of apparently differing behaviours. It connected those behaviours and made sense of them. Time and time again the mortification process told inmates they were less than human.

**Evaluation** Goffman's study is generally regarded as a classic. However, it relies heavily on his interpretation of the behaviour he observed. Did he get it right? Here are Goffman's thoughts about this question.

'I want to warn that my view is probably too much that of a middle-class male; perhaps I suffered vicariously about conditions that lower-class patients handled with little pain. Also, unlike some patients, I came to the hospital with no great respect for the discipline of psychiatry' (Goffman, 1968).

Here Goffman is admitting that his interpretation relies in part on his own background and experiences. He tried to put himself in the shoes of the lower-class patients and to imagine the suffering they experienced. But Goffman's sensitivities were those of a middle-class male. As a result, he may have misinterpreted the meanings patients gave to their situation. In addition, Goffman didn't think much of psychiatry. This would encourage a negative view of the way patients were treated.

Goffman's interpretation and analysis to some degree reflects his own background and values. Yet, for many, his research is convincing.

## 12.3 Interpreting and evaluating interview data

Interpreting and analysing data from unstructured interviews involves much the same processes as the

# activity24 *interpreting behaviour*

## question

With some reference to the pictures, briefly discuss the problems that an adult observer might have in interpreting the behaviour of young children in a school playground.

interpretation and analysis of other sources of qualitative data. Researchers look for themes and patterns. Sometimes these 'jump out' from the data – they are obvious. Other times, they are not immediately apparent – the researcher has to search them out. The following study provides an example of the interpretation of interview data.

### Becoming a carer

Patricia Taraborrelli (1993) studied 'informal carers' – people without formal training who cared for family members or friends. She was concerned with carers who looked after people with Alzheimer's disease which involves a steady deterioration of the brain. In its severe form, sufferers may fail to recognise family members, have difficulty walking, and become confused about time and place – for example, they may go shopping at night.

Taraborrelli's study involved in-depth unstructured interviews with twenty-three carers. She wanted to understand the process of becoming a carer. Two concepts or ideas immediately evident from the data were 'initial innocence' and 'the carer's perspective'. Initial innocence refers to the fact that most carers had little idea about what was involved in caring for someone with Alzheimer's disease. Comments like, 'I never thought it would turn into a 24 hour a day commitment' were frequent. Eventually, initial innocence developed into the carer's perspective –

## summary

1. Content analysis identifies themes that run through qualitative data.

2. The analysis of qualitative data aims to discover the meanings which underlie what people say and do.

3. Participant observers interpret what they see and hear. They look for patterns of behaviour – aspects of behaviour which fall into a similar pattern.

4. Data from unstructured interviews is analysed in much the same way as other sources of qualitative data. Researchers look for themes and patterns.

5. The analysis of qualitative data relies heavily on the interpretative skills of the researcher. To some extent, this analysis will be influenced by the researcher's values and beliefs.

carers lost their 'innocence' and adopted a realistic view of what the illness involved and the demands of caring.

Classifying and analysing qualitative data from interviews involves interpretation and judgement. Has the researcher got it right? There is no certain answer to this question. Others can only make their own judgement from data the researcher presents to support their interpretation and analysis.

# activity25 talking about families

In the book *Family Understandings* (2001) the researchers used semi-structured interviews to find out what members of families with teenage children thought about family life. One question asked about the importance of family life. The most common themes in the answers were identified and 'representative quotations' used to illustrate each theme. Below are examples of two of the themes or categories identified, followed by representative quotations.

| Category | Meaning of category |
|---|---|
| Positive attributes | ● The family as a source of positive ideals, particularly the giving and receiving of care, help and love. |
| Taken-for-granted | ● The family is taken for granted and 'natural'.<br>● Its importance is hard to describe.<br>● However, respondents are able to say that they would be lost without a family. |

*Happy families*

'It just grows with you and grows round you and you are there and you'd hate to be without it.' (Roger Hutchinson, father)

'I wouldn't like not to have the kids and I wouldn't like not to have Stan.' (Linda Barnes, mother)

'Um, you've got people around you who love and care about you.' (Leanne Field, 11)

'It's the caring isn't it, and the love that's there in your family.' (Mandy Lawson, mother)

'I just think it's the right way to be.' (Carol Brook, mother)

'The love that I get from them.' (Kate Baxter, 14)

'I'm not sure really. I don't really know, just – I'm not sure'. (Jayne Towers, mother)

'I wouldn't be the same if I didn't have my family. If I was put up for adoption I would have been an emotional wreck really.' (Andrew Corner, 16)

Adapted from Langford et al., 2001

## questions

1 Which quotations illustrate each of the four bullet points in the table?

2 Do you think it would be possible to interpret any of the quotations in a different way? Explain your answer.

3 To what extent do you think the selection of quotations and the analysis of interview data relies on the judgement of the researcher?

# Unit 13 | Reporting research results

## keyissues

1 How is a typical research report organised?

2 What ethical issues are involved in writing and publishing research?

The final part of the research process is reporting the findings of your research. This is crucial. It makes the research available to other sociologists and to anyone else who is interested.

This unit looks at what sociologists have said about writing a research report. The following chapter contains specific advice about writing up *your* research report for OCR coursework.

Good writing is essential for reporting research results. It should be clear, direct and to the point. The researcher's job is to present the evidence and develop an argument based on that evidence. The researcher should persuade and convince the reader – persuade them that the argument is reasonable and convince them that the findings are valid (Gilbert, 1993; Bryman, 2001).

Table 3 presents a typical example of the way a sociological research report is organised.

### Table 3  **A sociological research report**

Title

Author

Abstract

Introduction

Theory

Data and methods

Results

Conclusions

References

From Gilbert, 1993

**Title and author** Research reports begin with the title and the name of the author or authors.

**Abstract** This is a short summary of the content of the report and of the argument the author will develop.

**Introduction** This presents the abstract in a more detailed form. It spells out the researcher's aims or hypothesis, states what the research is looking at and why it is important.

The introduction reviews what has already been written about the topic, shows how the research relates to past studies and how it develops existing findings.

The introduction should grab the reader's attention and indicate why the report is interesting and significant.

**Theory** In this section, the author outlines the concepts and theories used in the research. For example, if the study is looking at how young people form groups, concepts might include peer group, identity and subculture. These may be some of the concepts used to organise and explain the findings.

**Data and methods** In this section, the researcher describes the research methods used to collect the data. Table 4 provides an example of points which might be covered.

This section should be fairly detailed. It's not enough to say that the study was based on 6 months participant observation or a number of semi-structured interviews. As

### Table 4  **Data and methods**

Sample size

Sample design

Sampling frame

Date of data collection

How settings selected for observation were chosen

Response rate achieved

Limitations of and possible biases in the data

Sources of secondary data
(eg, statistics from government surveys)

Basic demographic characteristics of the sample
(eg, age, gender, ethnicity)

Explanation of any special data analysis techniques used

From Gilbert, 1993

Table 4 indicates, a lot more information is required.

This section has two main aims.

- First, to present sufficient details about the research methods for another researcher to repeat the study.

- Second, to allow the reader to evaluate the methods and the results. For example, data from a questionnaire given to a sample of five people hardly provides a sound basis for generalisation.

**Results** This section outlines the main findings of the research. Quantitative data is presented in tables along with statistical analyses. Qualitative data is used for illustration and flavour. For example, typical statements from unstructured interviews are quoted or descriptions from observations provided.

This section assesses the degree to which the results support the hypothesis or meet the aims of the research.

**Conclusion** This section brings everything together. It relates the results to the questions and issues raised in the introduction. It attempts to explain the results and relates them to various theories. It looks at the implications of the findings for future research. For example, what questions are raised which require further research?

**References** Throughout the research report, publications have been referred to by author/s and date, eg (Smith, 2003). The references provide full details of the books and articles noted in the text – these include title, author and year of publication. See the references at the back of this book for an illustration.

The following activity gives examples of reporting research results taken from actual studies. They are based on examples given by Bryman (2001).

# activity 26 reporting results

## Item A An introduction

Religion remains a central element of modern life, shaping people's world-views, moral standards, family lives, and in many nations, their politics. But in many Western nations, modernisation and secularisation may be eroding Christian beliefs, with profound consequences that have intrigued sociologists since Durkheim. Yet this much touted secularisation may be overstated – certainly it varies widely among nations and is absent in the United States (Benson, Donahue, and Erickson, 1989; Felling, Peters, and Schreuder, 1991; Firebaugh and Harley, 1991; Stark and Iannaccone, 1994). We explore the degree to which religious beliefs are passed on from generation to generation in different nations.

Kelley & De Graaf, 1997

St John the Divine, London

## Item B Research methods

The following is a summary of some of the main research methods used in a study of vegetarianism by Beardsworth and Keil (1992).

- Semi-structured interviews and the reasons for using this method
- The number of people interviewed and the context in which the interviews took place
- How the interview data was analysed – this mainly involved identifying themes.

Adapted from Bryman, 2001

## Item C Conclusion

The following is an excerpt from the conclusion to the research report on vegetarianism referred to in Item B.

Just as meat tended to imply strongly negative connotations for respondents, concepts like 'fruit' and 'vegetable' tended to elicit positive reactions, although less frequently and in a more muted form than might have been anticipated on the basis of the analysis of the ideological underpinnings of 'wholefoods' consumption put forward by Atkinson (1980, 1983), or on the basis of the analysis of vegetarian food symbolism advanced by Twigg (1983).

Beardsworth & Keil, 1992

Promoting vegetarianism at the Earth Summit in Johannesburg, 2002

## questions

1 Look at Item A.
   a) What are the authors trying to do in this introduction?
   b) How well are they doing it?
2 Judging from Item B, does the methods section in this research report do the job?
3 What are the authors doing in Item C?

## Ethical issues

Writing and publishing research reports raises a number of ethical questions. Authors have to ask: Am I protecting the welfare and interests of those who participated in the research? Am I respecting their privacy and maintaining their anonymity? Am I telling the truth? Do I have a duty to publish my results?

**Protecting participants** When research reports are published anybody can read them, anybody can comment on them – in the press, on radio and on TV. Those who participate in the research may gain or lose as a result of publication. They may be affected as individuals in terms of their job security and promotion prospects – they may lose their jobs, or their career may grind to a halt. They may also be affected collectively. For example, the organisation they work for may be presented in a good or a bad light. Similarly, groups such as teachers, doctors, police, bakery workers and others may gain or lose in terms of the standing of their professions. For example, the publication of a research report critical of teachers may have a negative effect on the whole profession.

The same applies to various social groups – women, ethnic minorities, older people, gays and so on. A research report may present them in a positive light or, often unwittingly, provide a negative view – for example, by reinforcing stereotypes of older people.

Clearly, researchers must consider these issues carefully before publication. They have responsibilities to those who take part in their research.

**Telling the truth** There is general agreement that researchers must do their best to tell the truth as they see it. This can produce a conflict of interest – telling the truth may harm research participants. There is no easy way out of this dilemma.

Telling the truth 'as they see it' inevitably involves bias – all researchers are influenced to some extent by their values and beliefs. There is no such thing as a totally objective research report. To guard against extreme bias and to check 'the truth', some researchers argue that research participants should be shown the data and asked to comment on it before publication (Simons, 1984).

**Confidentiality and anonymity** Codes of conduct for researchers in sociology and other social sciences stress the need for confidentiality and anonymity. Participants are told that anything they say is confidential – that there is no way it can be linked to them when published. One obvious way of doing this is ensuring anonymity – making sure their identities are not disclosed. For example, questionnaire respondents are often identified by number rather than name and sometimes given a false name in the published report. Similarly, places of employment and residence are not mentioned by name or given invented names.

Researchers are aware of the harm that can be caused by naming names. For example, Holdaway (1982) in his participant observation study of police behaviour disguised people's identities, their place of work, and where events occurred. His reasons? The behaviour he observed could result in disciplinary action, it could ruin careers, or lead to dismissal from the force.

**Obligation to publish** Some sociologists argue that researchers have a duty to publish for the following reasons.

- To advance knowledge
- To inform government policy
- Because the public has a right to know (Homan, 1991).

Apart from the difficulty of getting a professional journal or book publisher to publish research, there are other barriers to publication. Many organisations who fund research issue contracts with the right to veto (prevent) publication. This can be used, for example, by governments to prevent publication of views critical of their policy (Willmott, 1980). Similarly, researchers have been prevented from continuing research within organisations because their findings have been critical of the management and/or staff (Platt, 1976).

**Conclusion** There is growing recognition by researchers that they have duties and obligations to those who participate in their research and to the groups to which the participants belong. The ethical codes which govern sociological research now cover the entire research process – which includes the writing and publication of research.

## summary

1.  When writing a research report, the author's job is to present the evidence and develop an argument based on that evidence.

2.  A typical research report contains the following:

    | | |
    |---|---|
    | Title | Data and methods |
    | Author | Results |
    | Abstract | Conclusions |
    | Introduction | References. |
    | Theory | |

3.  Writing and publishing a research report raises ethical issues. Authors should:

    - Protect participants
    - Tell the truth (as they see it)
    - Maintain confidentiality and make sure participants remain anonymous.

# 5 Coursework – the Research Report

## Introduction

Sociologists collect information about society by conducting research. You will have come across many references to sociological research in this book. Much of this research provides fascinating insights into society and is well worth a closer look. The OCR AS coursework task – the *Research Report* – provides exactly this opportunity.

The Research Report asks you to examine one piece of research in depth. By applying your knowledge of sociological research methods to a particular study you will be able to focus on the methodological choices that the sociologist made and the practical and ethical issues that arose in carrying out the research. You will need to consider whether the research really achieved its aims and discuss the accuracy of the data collected.

The Research Report should be no more than 1000 words and is worth 30% of your AS marks. If you go on to A2, it makes up 15% of the final A-level grade.

*A study of the construction of masculine identities in a secondary school. It was based on observation, informal discussions and semi-structured interviews.*

THE MAKING OF MEN
MASCULINITIES, SEXUALITIES AND SCHOOLING

MÁIRTÍN MAC AN GHAILL

## chaptersummary

▶ **Unit 1** is an overview of the requirements of the Research Report.

▶ **Unit 2** looks at the first part of the coursework: the outline of the research design.

▶ **Unit 3** explains how to identify the reasons for the selection of research methods.

▶ **Unit 4** explains how to outline and evaluate the findings of the research.

## Unit 1 General advice

The last chapter closed with a look at the views of sociologists on writing a research report. Some of this will be useful for your coursework.

This chapter gives specific advice on writing the OCR Research Report.

### 1.1 The specification

The exam board specification spells out the concepts and issues you need to be familiar with. These can be summarised as follows.

- Key concepts of reliability, validity, representativeness and generalisation
- The role of ethics in research
- Sampling issues
- Interpreting, evaluating and reporting data
- Methods of primary data collection such as questionnaires, interviews and observation
- Sources of secondary data such as official statistics and

historical documents.

Every Research Report will need to display knowledge of the first four points. Other material needs to be used selectively, depending on its relevance to your particular study. Detailed information on the above points can be found in Chapter 4.

### 1.2 The Answer Book

The exam board has produced an *Answer Book* that you must use for your Report. You will either be given the Answer Book by your teacher or you can download it from the OCR website. There are four sections in the Answer Book and they must all be completed. At the start of each section there is a prompt to tell you what needs to be covered. There is also a suggested word length. You are strongly advised to keep to these word lengths since each section requires something different. And if the word limit is exceeded in one section you will not have enough words left to meet the requirements of another.

## 1.3 Selecting a study

There are many possible sources for Research Reports, ranging from whole books, to articles, to summaries of studies. Your teacher will be able to advise in more detail. However, there are certain factors that you need to take into account when making a choice.

The study you choose must be sociological and provide some detail about the aims of the research, the methods employed and the results obtained. It is also helpful if sampling and piloting are discussed, although this is not always appropriate in some ethnographic studies. Check all this by skimming through the study before you begin.

The research you choose can have other uses. Using a study directly related to other AS (or A2) topics will allow you to use the research as evidence in exam answers. If you are doing your own Personal Study as A2 coursework then you could select a piece of research that would be relevant to the topic you are going to investigate.

It is also worth reflecting on your strengths and weaknesses as a student. Perhaps you want to choose something as short and simple as possible. Alternatively,

you may have ambitions to follow a social science course at university. In this case, it is worth having a go at an entire book – great practice for the sort of demands a university course will make.

## 1.4 Source

The first section of the Answer Book asks you to provide full details of the source of the research. This includes the author, title, publisher and date. If you have used a summary or extract, make sure you include the source of the summary or extract as well as the original research itself.

### key terms

**Research Report** The OCR AS coursework task. An examination of one piece of sociological research.
**Answer Book** A booklet provided by the exam board. You must use it for your Research Report.

### summary

1. You will need to show that you know, understand and can apply relevant material from the Sociological Research Skills module – see Chapter 4.
2. An Answer Book is provided by the exam board which you must use.
3. Make sure the study you choose provides detailed information on its:
   - Aims
   - Sampling
   - Methods
   - Results.
4. You need to provide details of the study you choose including its title, author, date and publisher.

## Unit 2 *Outline of the research design*

This makes up section (b) of the Answer Book. It is suggested that you use approximately 210-300 words.

You are required to do two things in this section. First, summarise the aims of the research and second, describe the research design and methodology. The prompt at the start of this section in the Answer Book provides guidance on what to include.

The first part of the prompt is a general statement:

*You should state the objective of your chosen piece of research, and use this section to outline how the researcher/s carried out their research.*

The second part of the prompt provides further detail and some specific suggestions:

*You should describe the aims of the research and the research methods that were used. (You may wish to consider methods, sample size, access to sample, ethics etc.)*

Note that the prompt uses the words 'objective' and 'aims' to mean the same thing.

## 2.1 The objective/aims of the research

Try to keep the summary of aims short and to the point. Your ability to identify the aims is extremely important as a clear idea of what the sociologist set out to achieve is essential when you come to write later sections. Your analysis of the research design, evaluation of its effectiveness and description of the findings all need to be linked to the aims of the study.

The aims then, act as a reference point for you throughout the rest of the Research Report.

Don't expect all sociologists to set out specific aims at the start of their research. Some do set them out clearly in an introduction, some refer to them throughout the text, and some spell them out in the concluding chapter. Some sociologists do present a number of specific aims, others give only a very general aim. For example, Adler (1993) in a study of drug dealing wanted to '...present an ethnographic description and analysis of a deviant social scene and the illicit activities of its members'. This is very broad and you would try to show in section (c) why such a general aim might be appropriate for this kind of qualitative research.

Other research may have very detailed aims which will require you to work hard to produce a short and clear summary. In *The Growth of Lone Parenthood* by Karen Rowlingson and Stephen McKay (1998) there are a number of aims that are identified at the start of each chapter. In this case you would need to select the key ones.

If there are several aims you may decide to list them using numbers or bullet-points. This makes it easier to refer to them later. If the researcher has already done this, then you will need to make sure that your summary of the aims is in your own words.

This is the only part of the Research Report that you can present as a list, the rest should be in continuous writing.

## 2.2  Description of the research design

The remainder of section (b) should be a detailed description of the research design. Provide as much detail as possible within the word limits. This will give you enough material on which to base an analysis and evaluation of the design in sections (c) and (d).

The second part of the prompt reminds you that describing a research design involves talking about the sample, the sample size, access to the sample, the methods used by the researcher and any ethical issues that arise.

### key term

*Plagiarism* Copying someone else's words and passing them off as your own.

Whether or not all of these issues are relevant will depend on the nature of the research.

In this section you are *not* asked to say why the researcher used the methods or set the research up in the way that they did. The emphasis is on *description* of the research.

You might want to ask yourself some questions based on the prompt as guidance.

What methods were used? Who made up the target population? What size was the sample? What sampling frame, if any, did the researcher use? What was the sampling technique? How long did the research take? If interviews were used, what type were they and how long did they last? If observation was the main method, how long did that take? How did the researcher obtain access to the group or groups? Were there any ethical issues involved?

Finally, remember to write entirely in your own words, however strong the temptation to copy passages. Copying is known as *plagiarism* and you can only be awarded marks for your own work. In order to help you use your own words you could work with a friend. Try telling them about the research. Explaining to someone else will help you develop your summary skills and your friend will be able to tell you what makes sense and what doesn't.

### summary

1.  The recommended length of section (b) is 210 – 300 words.
2.  It requires you to:
    - Summarise the aims of the research
    - Describe the research design of the study.
3.  Be careful to use your own words.

## *activity1 section (b)*

### questions

1. A sociologist is conducting research on football fans. With some reference to the picture, develop one possible general aim and three specific aims for this research.

2. Briefly describe the methods which might be used for this research.

# Unit 3 *Reasons for the selection of methodology*

This makes up section (c) of the Answer Book. The word length suggested is 250-300.

## 3.1 Reasons for choice of methods

The prompt at the start of section (c) of the Answer Book says that

*You should use the section to outline the reasons why the researcher/s chose the methodology outlined above (in section (b)).* It goes on to say that *you should explain why the methodology was thought to be suitable for achieving the kind of data required by the researchers.*

This section is where you apply your knowledge and understanding of research methods and methodology. There are two aspects to this section but they are interrelated. The first is to explain why the researcher chose their research design and methods. The second is to analyse why the researcher saw the design and methods as appropriate for this particular research. You can do these together. This will demonstrate your understanding of the relationship between them.

One way to tackle this section is put yourself in the shoes of the researcher and try to look at the research process from their point of view. Try to use your own knowledge and understanding of research methods and not rely entirely on what the researcher has to say. They will have their own view of why they did the research as they did, but you may well be able to think of other reasons.

## 3.2 Questions to ask

Think about what you have just written in section (b) and, without repeating yourself, ask the question 'why?' about every aspect of the research design and methodology. For example, why did the researcher use a particular method? Was the researcher looking for in-depth qualitative data or were they looking for quantitative data that would enable them to make comparisons and identify trends?

Asking yourself questions about the study will help you maximise your marks. Questions such as: Does the sociologist appear to have a particular view of the world that might lead them to choose a particular method? Did they use more than one method? If so, why?

For example, feminists often use unstructured interviews because they believe this type of interview helps to break down the hierarchical relationship between the researcher and the researched. In her study *Managing Money*, Vivienne Elizabeth (2001) conducted 20 in-depth interviews to find out how heterosexual cohabiting couples organised their finances. You should ask why she chose to use this type of interview.

You might ask yourself whether the researcher needed to build up a rapport in order to gain respondents' trust.

Hanmer and Saunders (1993), in their research on women in Leeds, returned to the same households three times. By the third time they had built up a relationship with the women. Compared to previous visits, the information they received was more detailed and personal. In this instance, you might want to ask whether any interviewer bias may have occurred. Had the women presented their experiences in a particular way in order to please the researchers?

Other questions might be: Were the participants aware they were being researched? If not, what are the ethical implications? Was the research set up ethically? Was everyone's consent gained at the start?

As you write this section, think back to the aims of the research and explain why you think the researcher made their decisions in the light of their stated aims. Perhaps the sociologist might have chosen to do a large quantitative study because their aim was to identify trends and make comparisons. Alternatively, a qualitative approach would be more suited to aims which focus on the feelings and experiences of the sample.

Finally, avoid writing generally about the advantages and disadvantages of various methods. Examiners are not looking for a general essay on research methods. They want you to consider the methods and design of this *particular* study.

### summary

1. Section (c) of the Research Report asks for reasons for the choice of methodology.
2. The recommended length is 250-300 words.
3. This section requires you to explain the researcher's choice of methodology.
4. You need to analyse their choices in the light of the aims of their study.

# activity2 choosing methods

**Item A** Representation of females

**Item B** Vandalism

**Aim of research** To examine the representation of females in girls' magazines

**Method** Content analysis

**Aim of research** To test the hypothesis that young people vandalise property because they feel cut off from society.

**Method** Unstructured interviews

## questions

1. Suggest reasons for the choice of methods in Items A and B.
2. In each case, suggest one additional method. Give reasons for your choices.

# Unit 4 Outline and evaluation of the findings of the research

This makes up section (d) of the Answer Book. The word guideline for this section is 350-400.

## 4.1 Outline of the findings

You need to summarise the findings of the research in approximately 100 words. Think about the original aims of the study and try to link the findings back to the aims. This will show that you understand the relationship between the two and give your Research Report a sense of continuity.

The prompt at the start of this section begins by telling you that:

*You should use this section to outline briefly the main findings of the study, making reference to a limited sample of the research data to illustrate particular points.*

It is important to pay attention to the instruction to make reference to a limited sample of the research data. By including quotations, tables, graphs and so on from the study, you demonstrate your understanding of how the

research data informs and illustrates the findings. However, since you are limited to 400 words you should take the opportunity offered to place the sample of data in an appendix:

*(The sample may be attached to the Report as an appendix and may take the form of a graph, table, text quotations etc. It will not be included in the word count.)*

The appendix should only be used for samples of the research data. The examiner will take account of your skills of interpreting the data in relation to the findings and of selecting relevant extracts whether they are statistical or text quotations. Anything else that you include will be ignored.

## 4.2 Evaluation of the findings

The second task in this section, and the one that will enable you to pick up marks for evaluation as well as knowledge and understanding and interpretation and analysis, is the one that requires you to *identify the parts of* the research that have worked well and those that have not.

Once again you will need to use your knowledge and understanding of research methods and methodology to discuss what worked well in the study and what did not. There are a number of key concepts that you should use here. The prompt says:

*You will need to show that you are aware of ways in which the methods selected have affected the quality of the data collected and produced, using the concepts of reliability, validity, representativeness and generalisability.*

When using these concepts you will need to let the examiner know that you understand them. That does not necessarily mean providing a definition – using them accurately will make it clear that you understand them.

You must, as the prompt says, discuss the research in terms of all of the key concepts above. You will not get into the top levels of the Mark Scheme unless you do so. There are other concepts which may also aid your discussion. If you are discussing the validity of the research, you may want to use concepts such as interviewer bias. If on the other hand, you are discussing the extent to which a piece of research might be representative of the target population you need to discuss

the sampling techniques that were used and the size of the sample.

In addition, you should discuss the ethics of the research if that is appropriate.

Finally, revisit the aims of the study and think about the researcher. Is there any chance that their particular view of the world has influenced the quality of the data collected? If they are a feminist, for example, has that affected their aims, the methods used, or the way the data was interpreted?

## summary

1. Section (d) of the Research Report asks you to outline and evaluate the findings.
2. The recommended length is 350 - 400 words.
3. The findings of the study need to be summarised in about 100 words.
4. An appendix can be used to include a sample of the findings. This does not form part of the word count.
5. The concepts of validity, reliability, representativeness and generalisability must be used to evaluate the findings.

# activity3 section (d)

The picture shows an in-depth, unstructured interview. The interviewer takes notes from time to time. The repondent/interviewee is being asked about his attitudes towards women and ethnic minorities.

## questions

1 Answer the following questions with reference to validity and reliability.

a) What difference might it make to the respondent's answers if the interviewer was male?

b) What difference might it make to the respondent's answers if the interviewer was Black?

2. The research was based on 20 male respondents in a college of further education.

Discuss this sample with reference to representativeness and generalisability.

# References

Abbott, D. (2000). Identity and new masculinities. *Sociology Review, 10*, no. 1.

Abercrombie, N. (1996). *Television and society*. Cambridge: Polity.

Acheson, Sir D. (1998). *Inequalities in health report*. London: HMSO.

Adler, P. & Adler, P. (1998). *Peer power*. New Jersey: Rutgers University Press.

Adler, P. (1993). *Wheeling and dealing: An ethnography of an upper-level drug dealing and smuggling community*. New York: Columbia University Press.

Adonis, A. & Pollard, S. (1997). *A class act*. London: Hamish Hamilton.

Alexander, C. (1996). *The art of being Black*. Oxford: Clarendon Press.

Allan, G. & Crow, G. (2001). *Families, households and society*. Basingstoke: Palgrave.

Allan, G. (1985). *Family life*. Oxford: Blackwell.

Allan, S. (1999). *News culture*. Buckingham: Open University Press.

Allen, I. & Dowling, S.B. (1999). Teenage mothers: Decisions and outcomes. In S. McRae (Ed.), *Changing Britain: Families and households in the 1990s*. Oxford: Oxford University Press.

Allen, T. (1992). Taking culture seriously. In T. Allen & A. Thomas (Eds.), *Poverty and development in the 1990s*. Oxford: Oxford University Press.

Allport, G.W. & Postman, L. (1947). *The psychology of rumor*. New York: H. Holt & Company.

Anderson, D. (1997). They don't whistle while they work. *Spectator*, July 26.

Anderson, M. (1971). Family, household and the industrial revolution. In M. Anderson (Ed.), *Sociology of the family*. Harmondsworth: Penguin.

Ang, I. (1985). *Watching 'Dallas': Soap opera and the melodramatic imagination*. London: Methuen.

Appleyard, D. (2002). *Out of love*. London: Black Swan.

Arber, S. (1993). Designing samples. In N. Gilbert (Ed.), *Researching social life*. London: Sage.

Archer, J. & Lloyd, B. (1985). *Sex and gender*. Cambridge: Cambridge University Press.

Ariès, P. (1962). *Centuries of childhood*. London: Jonathan Cape.

Atkinson, J.M. (1978). *Discovering suicide*. London: Macmillan.

Back, L. (1996). *New ethnicities and urban culture*. London: UCL Press.

Baker, A. & Duncan, S. (1985). Child sexual abuse: A study of prevalence in Great Britain. *Child Abuse and Neglect, 9*, 457-467.

Ballard, R. (Ed.) (1994). *Desh pradesh*. London: Hurst & Co.

Bandura, A. (1973). *Aggression: A social learning analysis*. Englewood Cliffs, NJ: Prentice Hall.

Barker, C. (1999). *Television, globalisation and cultural identities*. Buckingham: Open University Press.

Barker, E. (1984). *The making of a Moonie*. Oxford: Blackwell.

Barker, M. & Petley, J. (Eds.) (2001). *Ill effects*. London: Routledge.

Barley, N. (1995). *Dancing on the grave*. London: Abacus.

Bathurst, B. (2002). It isn't clever and it isn't fun. *The Guardian*, September 30.

Baxter, J. & Western, M. (1998). Satisfaction with housework: Examining the paradox. *Sociology, 32*, 101-120.

Beardsworth, A. & Keil, T. (1992). The vegetarian option: Varieties, conversions, motives and careers, *Sociological Review, 40*, 253-293.

Beattie, J. (1964). *Other cultures: Aims, methods and achievements in social anthropology*. London: Routledge & Kegan Paul.

Beck, U. (1997). *The reinvention of politics*. Cambridge: Polity Press.

Beck, U. (1992). *Risk society: Towards a new modernity*. London: Sage.

Beck-Gernsheim, E. (2002). *Reinventing the family*. Cambridge: Polity.

Bedell, G. (2002). One step beyond. *OM*, October 6.

Belson, W.A. (1978). *Television violence and the adolescent boy*. Westmead: Saxon.

Benston, M. (1972). The political economy of women's liberation. In N. Glazer-Malbin & H. Y. Waehrer (Eds.), *Woman in a man-made world*. Chicago: Rand McNally.

Ben-Tovim, A., Elton, A., Hildebrand, J., Tranter, M. & Vizard, E. (Eds.) (1988). *Child sexual abuse within the family: Assessment and treatment: The Work of the Great Ormond Street Team*. London: Wright.

Beresford, P., Green, D., Lister, R. & Woodard, K. (1999). *Poverty first hand: Poor people speak for themselves*. London: CPAG.

Berger, P. (1966). *Invitation to sociology*. Harmondsworth: Penguin.

Bernades, J. (1997). *Family studies: An introduction*. London: Routledge.

Berthoud, R. & Beishon, S. (1997). People, families and households, In Modood, T. et al. (Eds.), *Ethnic minorities in Britain: Diversity and disadvantage*. London: Policy Studies Institute.

Berthoud, R. & Gershuny, J. (2000). *Seven years in the lives of British families*. Bristol: Policy Press.

Berthoud, R., McKay, S. & Rowlingson, K. (1999). Becoming a single mother. In S. McRae (Ed.), *Changing Britain: Families and households in the 1990s*. Oxford: Oxford University Press.

Billig, M. (1995). *Banal nationalism*. London: Sage.

Blackmore, S. (1999). *The meme machine*. Oxford: Oxford University Press.

Bourdieu, P. (1984). *Distinction*. London: Routledge & Kegan Paul.

Bowie, F. (1993).Wales from within. In S. MacDonald (Ed.), *Inside European identities*. Oxford: Berg.

Brazier, C. (1995). African village. *New Internationalist*, June.

British Psychological Society. (1998). *Code of conduct, ethical principles and guidelines*. Leicester: British Psychological Society.

British Sociological Association. (1996). *Statement of ethical practice*. Durham: British Sociological Association.

Bruce, S. (1995). Religion and the sociology of religion. In M. Haralambos (Ed.), *Developments in Sociology, Volume 11*. Ormskirk: Causeway Press.

Bryant, J. & Zillmann, D. (Eds.) (1994). *Media effects: Advances in theory and research*. Hove: Erlbaum.

Bryman, A. (2001). *Social research methods*. Oxford: Oxford University Press.

Buckingham, A. (1999). Is there an underclass in Britain? *British Journal of Sociology, 50*, no. 1.

Buckingham, D. (1996). *Moving images: Understanding children's emotional responses to television*. Manchester: Manchester University Press.

Buckingham, D. (2000). *After the death of childhood: Growing up in the age of electronic media*. Cambridge: Polity.

Bukatko, D. & Daehler, M.W. (2001). *Child development: A thematic approach* (4th ed.). Boston: Houghton Mifflin Company.

Butler, C. (1995). Religion and gender. *Sociology review*, February.

Calam, R., Horn, L., Glasgow, D. & Cox, A. (1998). Psychological disturbance and child sexual abuse: A follow-up study, *Child Abuse and Neglect, 22*, 901-913.

Cantril, H. (1940). *The invasion from Mars: A study in the psychology of panic*. New York: Harper & Row.

Carter, C. & Weaver, C. (2003). *Violence and the media*. Buckingham: Open University Press.

Castells, M. (1996). *The rise of network society*. Oxford: Blackwell.

Cecil, R. (1993). The marching season in Northern Ireland. In S. MacDonald (Ed.), *Inside European identities*. Oxford: Berg.

Chagnon, N. (1968). *Yanomamo*. New York: Holt, Rinehart & Winston.

Charles, N. & Kerr, M. (1988). *Women, food and families*. Manchester: Manchester University Press.

Charles, N. (1990). Food and family ideology. In C.C. Harris (Ed.), *Family, economy and community*. Cardiff: University of Wales Press.

Cheal, D. (1999). The one and the many: Modernity and postmodernity. In G. Allan (Ed.), *The sociology of the family: A reader*. Oxford: Blackwell.

Cherlin, A. (1992). *Marriage, divorce, remarriage*. Cambridge MA: Harvard University Press.

Chester, R. (1984). Divorce. In E. Butterworth & D. Weir (Eds.), *The new sociology of modern Britain*. Glasgow: Fontana.

Cicourel, A.V. (1976). *The social organisation of juvenile justice*. London: Heinemann.

Clarke, J. & Saunders, C. (1991). Who are you and so what? *Sociology Review, 1*, no. 1.

Cockburn, A. (1993). Class of 93. *Observer Life*, December 12.

Cockett, M. & Tripp, J. (1994). *The Exeter family study: Family breakdown and its impact on children*. Exeter: Exeter University Press.

Cohen, S. (1987). *Folk devils and moral panics*. Oxford: Blackwell.

Coleman, D. & Chandola, T. (1999). Britain's place in Europe's population. In S. McRae (Ed.), *Changing Britain: Families and households in the 1990s*. Oxford University Press.

Collins, R. & Murroni, C. (1996). *New media, new politics*. Oxford: Polity Press.

Connell, R.W. (1995). *Masculinities*. Cambridge: Polity Press.

Coote, A. & Campbell, B. (1982). *Sweet freedom*. London: Pan.

Corby, B. (2000). *Child abuse: Towards a knowledge base* (2nd ed.). Buckingham: Open University Press.

Cottle, S. (Ed.) (2000). *Ethnic minorities and the media*. Buckingham: Open University Press.

Creighton, S. & Noyes, P. (1989). *Child abuse trends in England and Wales 1983-1987*. London: NSPCC.

Critcher, C. (2003). *Moral panics and the media*. Buckingham: Open University Press.

Crompton, R. (1998). *Class and stratification: An introduction*. Cambridge: Polity.

Crossman, R.H.S. (1975). *The diaries of a cabinet minister*. London: Jonathan Cape.

Croteau, D. & Hoynes, W. (1997). *Media/society*. London: Forge Pine Press.

Crow, G. & Hardy, M. (1992). Diversity and ambiguity among lone-parent households in modern Britain. In C. Marsh & S. Arber (Eds.), *Families and households*. London: Macmillan.

Cumberbatch, G. & Negrine, R. (1992). *Images of disability on television*. London: Routledge.

Cumberbatch, G. (1987). *The portrayal of violence on British television: A content analysis*. London: BBC Publications.

Curran, J. & Seaton, J. (1997). *Power without responsibility*. London: Routledge.

Daniels, T. (1996). Programmes for Black audiences. In J. Corner & S. Harvey (Eds.), *Television times*. London: Arnold.

Daniels, T. (1998). Television studies and race. In C. Geraghty & D. Lusted (Eds.), *The television studies book*. London: Arnold.

Davies, N. (1997). *Dark heart*. London: Chatto & Windus.

Dean, H. & Taylor-Gooby, P. (1992). *Dependency culture*. Hemel Hempstead: Harvester Wheatsheaf.

DeAngelis, T. (1993). *APA Monitor*, August.

Delphy, C. & Leonard, D. (1992). *Familiar exploitation*. Cambridge: Polity.

Dennis, N. & Erdos, G. (2000). *Families without fatherhood* (3rd ed.). London: Institute for the Study of Civil Society.

Dennis, N., Henriques, F. & Slaughter, C. (1956). *Coal is our life*. London: Eyre & Spottiswoode.

Denscombe, M. (1994). *Sociology update 1994*. Leicester: Olympus Books.

Department of Health (1995). *Child protection: Messages from research*. London: HMSO.

Department of Health (2000). *Working together to safeguard children: A guide to inter-agency working to safeguard and promote the welfare of children*. London: The Stationery Office.

Devereux, E. (2003). *Understanding the media*. London: Sage.

Devine, F. (1992). *Affluent workers revisited: Privatisation and the working class*. Edinburgh: Edinburgh University Press.

Devine, F. (1997). *Social class in America and Britain*. Edinburgh: Edinburgh University Press.

Diamond, J. (1998). *C: Because cowards get cancer*. London: Vermillion.

Ditton, J. (1977). *Part-time crime*. London: Macmillan.

Dobash, R. & Dobash, R. (1992). *Women, violence and social change*. London: Routledge.

Dodd, K. & Dodd, P. (1992). From the East End to *EastEnders*. In D. Strinati & S. Wagg (Eds.), *Come on down: Popular media culture*. London: Routledge.

Donnellan, C. (Ed.) (1994). *The rights of the child*. Cambridge: Independence.

Douglas, M. (Ed.), (1964). *Man in society: Patterns of human organisation*. London: Macdonald & Co.

Dowds, L. & Young, K. (1996). National Identity. In R. Jowell, J. Curtice, A. Park, L. Brook & K. Thomson (Eds.), *British social attitudes 13th report*. Aldershot: Dartmouth Publishing Company.

Duncombe, J. & Marsden, D. (1993). Love and intimacy. *Sociology, 27*, 221-241.

Duncombe, J. & Marsden, D. (1995). 'Workaholics and whingeing women': Theorising intimacy. *Sociological Review, 43*, 150-169.

Dunham, C. (1992). Brotherly love. *Observer Magazine*, October 18.

Dunne, G. (1997). *Lesbian lifestyles: Women's work and the politics of sexuality*. London: Macmillan.

Durkheim, E. (1970). *Suicide: A study in sociology*. London: Routledge.

Dykstra, P.A. & Knipscheer, C.P.M. (1995). The availability and intergenerational structure of family relationships. In C.P.M. Knipscheer, J. de Jong Gierveld, T.G. van Tilburg & P.A. Dykstra (Eds.), *Living arrangements and social networks of older adults*. Amsterdam: VU University Press.

Edgell, S. (1980). *Middle-class couples*. London: George Allen & Unwin.

Edholm, F. (1982). The unnatural family. In E. Whitelegg et al. (Eds.), *The changing experience of women*. London: Martin Robertson/Open University.

Eldridge, J., Kitzinger, J. & Williams, K. (1997). *The mass media and power in modern Britain*. Oxford: Oxford University Press.

Elias, N. (1978). T*he civilising process, volume 1*. Oxford: Basil Blackwell.

Elliot, F.R. (1996). *Gender, family and society*. Basingstoke: Macmilan.

Engels, F. (1972). *The origin of the family, private property and the state*. London: Lawrence & Wishart.

Eversley, D. & Bonnerjea, L. (1982). Social change and indications of diversity. In R.N. Rapoport, M.P. Fogarty & R. Rapoport (Eds.), *Families in Britain*. London: Routledge & Kegan Paul.

Fein, E. & Schneider, S. (2000). *The rules*. London: Harper Collins.

Ferguson, M. (1983). *Forever feminine*. London: Heinemann.

Feshbach, S. & Singer, R.D. (1971). *Television and aggression: An experimental field study*. San Francisco, CA: Jossey-Bass.

Festinger, L. et al. (1964). *When prophecy fails*. New York: Harper Torchbooks.

Fielding, N. (1981). *The National Front*. London: Routledge & Kegan Paul.

Fielding, N. (1993). Qualitative interviewing. In N. Gilbert (Ed.), *Researching social life*. London: Sage.

Finch, J. & Mason, J. (1993). *Negotiating family responsibilities*. London: Routledge.

Firth, R. (1963). *We the Tikopia: A sociological study of kinship in primitive Polynesia*. Palo Alto: Stanford University Press.

Fiske, J. (1987). *Television culture*. London: Methuen.

Fiske, J. (1989). *Reading the popular*. London: Unwin Hyman.

Fitzgerald, B. (1999). Children of lesbian and gay parents: A review of the literature. *Marriage & Family Reviews, 29*, 57-75.

Fletcher, R. (1966). *The family and marriage in Britain*. Harmondsworth: Penguin.

Folk, K. (1994). For love or money: Costs of child care by relatives. *Journal of Family and Economic Issues, 15*, 243-260.

Fortes, M. (1950). Kinship and marriage among the Ashanti. In A.R. Radcliffe Brown & D. Forde (Eds.), *African systems of kinship and marriage*. London: Oxford University Press.

Frankenberg, R. (1966). *Communities in Britain*. Harmondsworth: Penguin.

Franklin, B. (1997). *Newszak and news media*. London: Arnold.

Furedi F. (2001). *Paranoid parenting*. London: Penguin.

Gallie, D. (1978). *In search of the new working class*. Cambridge: Cambridge University Press.

Garey, A. (1995). Constructing motherhood on the night shift: 'Working mothers' as 'stay at home moms'. *Qualitative Sociology, 18*, 415-437.

Gauntlett, D. (1995). *Moving experiences: Understanding television's influences and effects.* London: John Libbey.

Gauntlett, D. (2002). *Media, gender and identity.* London: Routledge.

Geraghty, C. (1992). British soaps in the 1980s. In D. Strinati & S. Wagg (Eds.), *Come on down: Popular media culture.* London: Routledge.

Gerbner, G. & Gross, L. (1976). Living with television: The violence profile. *Journal of Communication, 26*, 173-199.

Gershuny, J. (1992). Change in the domestic division of labour in the UK, 1975-1987: Dependent labour versus adaptive partnership. In W. Abercrombie & A. Warde (Eds.), *Social change in contemporary Britain.* Cambridge: Polity Press.

Ghee, C. (2001). Population review of 2000: England and Wales. *Population Trends, 106*, 7-14.

Giddens, A. (1990). *The consequences of modernity.* Cambridge: Polity Press.

Giddens, A. (1991). *Modernity and self-identity.* Cambridge: Polity Press.

Giddens, A. (1992). *The transformation of intimacy: Sexuality, love and eroticism in modern societies.* Cambridge: Polity Press.

Giddens, A. (2001). *Sociology* (4th ed.). Cambridge: Polity Press.

Gilbert, G.M. (1951). Stereotype persistence and change among college students. *Journal of Abnormal and Social Psychology, 46*, 245-254.

Gilbert, N. (1993). Writing about social research. In N. Gilbert (Ed.), *Researching social life.* London: Sage.

Gillespie, M. (1993). Technology and tradition. In A. Gray & J. McGuigan (Eds.), *Studying culture.* London: Edward Arnold.

Gillespie, M. (1995). *Television, ethnicity and cultural change.* London: Routledge.

Gilroy, P. (1987). *There ain't no black in the Union Jack.* London: Hutchinson.

Gittins, D. (1993). *The family in question* (2nd ed.). Basingstoke: Macmillan.

Glasgow Media Group (1976). *Bad news.* London: Routledge & Kegan Paul.

Glasgow Media Group (1980). *More bad news.* London: Routledge.

Glasgow Media Group (1982). *Really bad news.* London: Writers & Readers.

Glasgow Media Group (1997). *Ethnic minorities in television advertising.* Glasgow: GMG.

Goffman, E. (1968). *Asylums.* Harmondsworth: Penguin.

Goffman, E. (1969). *The presentation of self in everyday life.* Harmondsworth: Penguin.

Goldberg, S. (1979). *Male dominance.* London: Abacus.

Golding, P. & Middleton, S. (1982). *Images of welfare: Press and public attitudes to poverty.* Oxford: Blackwell.

Golding, P. & Murdock, G. (2000). Culture, communication and political economy. In J. Curran. & M. Gurevitch. (Eds.), *Mass media and society.* London: Arnold.

Goldscheider, F.K. & Waite, L.J. (1991). *New families, no families?* Berkeley CA: University of California Press.

Goldthorpe, J.H., Lockwood, D., Bechofer, F. & Platt, J. (1969). *The affluent worker in the class structure.* Cambridge: Cambridge University Press.

Goode, E. & Ben-Yehuda, N. (1994). *Moral panics: The social construction of deviance.* Oxford: Blackwell.

Gordon, P. & Rosenberg, D. (1989). *The press and Black people in Britain.* London: Runnymede Trust.

Gorman, L. & McLean, D. (2003). *Media and society in the twentieth century.* Oxford: Blackwell.

Goulborne, H. (1999). The transnational character of Caribbean kinship in Britain. In S. McRae (Ed.), *Changing Britain: Families and households in the 1990s.* Oxford: Oxford University Press.

Gowler, D. & Legge, K. (1978). Hidden and open contracts in marriage. In R. Rapoport, R. & R.N. Rapoport with J.M. Bumstead, J.M. (Eds.), *Working couples.*

Graham, H. (1987). Being poor: Perceptions and coping strategies of lone mothers. In J. Brannen & G. Wilson (Eds.), *Give and take in families.* London: Allen & Unwin.

Gray, A. (1992). *Video playtime: The gendering of a leisure technology.* London: Routledge.

Grenier, J. (2002). *Playing safe.* Spiked-online.com.

Griffin, J.H. (1960). *Black like me.* New York: Signet.

Habermas, J. (1992). Further reflections on the public sphere. In C. Calhoun (Ed.), *Habermas and the public sphere.* Cambridge, MA: MIT Press.

Halfpenny, P. (1984). *Principles of method.* York: Longman.

Hall, E.T. (1973). *The silent language.* New York: Doubleday.

Hall, R., Ogden, P.E. & Hill, C. (1999). Living alone: Evidence from England and Wales and France for the last two decades. In S. McRae (Ed.), *Changing Britain: Families and households in the 1990s.* Oxford: Oxford University Press.

Hall, S. (1980). Encoding/Decoding. In S. Hall, D. Hobson, A. Lowe & P. Willis (Eds.), *Culture, media, language.* London: Hutchinson.

Hall, S. (1992). The question of cultural identity. In S. Hall, D. Held & T. McGrew (Eds.), *Modernity and its futures.* Cambridge: Polity Press.

Hall, S. (1995). The whites of their eyes. In G. Dines & J. Humez (Eds.), *Gender, race and class in media.* London: Sage.

Hall, S. (1997). *Representations: Cultural representations and signifying practices.* London: Sage Publications with Open University.

Hall, S. (1997). The spectacle of the 'other'. In S. Hall (Ed.), *Representation: Cultural representations and signifying practices.* London: Sage.

Hall, S., Critcher, C., Jefferson, T., Clarke, J. & Roberts, B. (1978). *Policing the crisis.* London: Macmillan.

Hanmer, J. & Saunders, S. (1993). *Women, violence and crime prevention.* Aldershot: Avebury.

Haralambos, M. (1994). *Right on: From blues to soul in Black America.* Ormskirk: Causeway Press.

Hargreaves, D.H. (1967). *Social relations in a secondary school.* London: Routledge and Kegan Paul.

Harris, M. (1984). The strange saga of the Video Bill. *New Society*, 26 April, 140-142.

Hartmann, P. & Husband, C. (1984). *Racism and the mass media.* London: Davis Poynter.

Harvey, D. (1989). *The condition of post modernity.* Oxford: Oxford University Press.

Haskey, J. (1994). Stepfamilies and stepchildren in Great Britain. *Population Trends, 76*, 17-28.

Haskey, J. (2001). Cohabitation in Great Britain: Past, present and future trends – and attitudes. *Population Trends, 103*, 4-19.

Haskey, J. (2002). One-parent families – and the dependent children living in them – in Great Britain. *Population Trends, 109*, 46-57.

Help the Aged (1995). *Topic sheets.* London: Help the Aged.

Herman, E. & Chomsky, N. (1988). *The political economy of the mass media.* New York: Pantheon Books.

Hetherington, A. (1985). *News, newspapers and television.* London: Macmillan.

Hetherington, E.M. (2002). *For better or for worse: Divorce reconsidered.* New York: Harper & Brothers.

Hewitt, R. (1996). *Routes of racism.* Stoke-on-Trent: Trentham Books.

Hey, V. (1997). *The company she keeps.* Milton Keynes: Open University Press.

Higson, A. (1998). National identity and the media. In A. Briggs & P. Cobley (Eds.), *The media: An introduction.* Harlow: Longman.

Hill, A. (2002). Who needs you, baby? *The Observer*, July 21.

Hill, G. (1995). The American Dream. *The Guardian*, February 15.

Hobbs, D. (1988). *Doing the business.* Oxford: Oxford University Press.

Hochschild, A. (1990). *The second shift.* London: Piatkus.

Hoebel, E.A. (1960). *The Cheyennes.* New York: Holt, Rinehart & Winston.

Hoggart, R. (1957). *Uses of literacy.* London: Chatto and Windus.

Holdaway, S. (1982). An inside job: A case study of covert research on the police. In M. Bulmer (Ed.), *Social research ethics.* London: Macmillan

Homan, R. (1991). *The ethics of social research.* Harlow: Longman.

Hopkins, N. (2000). Tide of violence in the home: Domestic attacks occur every six seconds. *The Guardian*, October 26.

Hornsby-Smith, M. (1993). *Gaining access.* In N. Gilbert (Ed.), *Researching social life.* London: Sage.

Humphreys, L. (1970). *Tearoom trade: Impersonal sex in public places.* Chicago: Aldine.

Iannucci, A. (1995). Play your card right. *The Guardian,* May 2.

Jagger, E. (2001). Marketing Molly and Melville. *Sociology, 35,* 639-659.

James, O. (2003). *They f*** you up: How to survive family life.* London: Bloomsbury.

Johnson, M. (1995). Patriarchal terrorism and common couple violence. *Journal of Marriage and the Family, 57,* 283-294.

Jowell, R., Curtice, J., Park, A., Brook, L., Thomson, K. & Bryson, C. (Eds.), (1998). *British and European social attitudes in the 15th report: How Britain differs.* Aldershot: Ashgate.

Jowell, R., Curtice, J., Park, A., Thomson, K., Jarvis, L., Bromley, C. & Stratford, N. (Eds.), (2000). *British social attitudes the 17th report: Focusing on diversity.* London: Sage.

Karlins, M., Coffman, T.L. & Walters, G. (1969). On the fading of social stereotypes: Studies in three generations of college students. *Journal of Personality and Social Psychology, 13,* 1-16.

Kassam, N. (1997). *Telling it like it is.* London: Women's Press.

Katz, D. & Braly, K.W. (1933). Racial stereotypes of 100 college students. *Journal of Abnormal and Social Psychology, 28,* 280-290.

Katz, E. & Lazarsfeld, P. (1955). *Personal influence.* New York: Free Press.

Kellner, P. (1994). The figures are Shere Nonsense. *The Sunday Times,* February 27.

Kelly, L., Regan, L. & Burton, S. (1991). *An exploratory study of the prevalence of sexual abuse in a sample of 16-21 year olds.* London: Child Abuse Studies Unit, University of North London.

Kerr, M. (1958). *The people of Ship Street.* London: Routledge & Kegan Paul.

Kiernan, K. & Mueller, G. (1999). Who divorces? In S. McRae (Ed.), *Changing Britain: Families and households in the 1990s.* Oxford: Oxford University Press.

Kitzinger, J. (1993). Understanding AIDS. In J. Eldridge (Ed.), *Getting the message: News, truth and power.* London: Routledge.

Kitzinger, J. (1997). Resisting the message: The extent and limits of media influence. In D. Miller, J. Kitzinger, J. Williams & P. Beharrel (Eds.), *The circuit of mass communication.* London: Sage.

Kluckhohn, C. (1951).The study of culture. In D. Lerner & H. Lassweell (Eds.), *The policy sciences.* Stanford: Stanford University Press.

Korbin, J. (Ed.) (1981). *Child abuse and neglect: Cross-cultural perspectives.* Berkeley CA: University of California Press.

Kulick, D. (1998). *Travesti – Sex, gender and culture among Brazilian transgendered prostitutes.* Chicago: University of Chicago Press.

Kurz, D. (1995). *For richer, for poorer: Mothers confront divorce.* London: Routledge.

Labour Force Survey. (Spring 2002). Office of National Statistics.

Laing, R.D. (1976). *The politics of the family.* Harmondsworth: Penguin.

Langford, W., Lewis, C., Soloman, Y. & Warin, J. (2001). *Family understandings.* London: Joseph Rowntree Foundation.

LaPiere, R.T. (1934). Attitudes vs. actions. *Social Forces, 13,* 230-237.

Law, I. (1997). *Privilege and silence: 'Race' in the British news during the general election campaign, 1997.* Leeds: University of Leeds.

Lawson, A. (1988). *Adultery: an analysis of love and betrayal.* Oxford: Blackwell.

Lazarsfeld, P.F. (1949). The American Soldier: An expository review. *Public Opinion Quarterly, 13,* 377-404.

Leach, E.R. (1967). *A runaway world?* London: BBC publications.

Lee, D. & Newby, H. (1983). *The problem of sociology.* London: Hutchinson.

Lee, N. (2001). *Childhood and society: Growing up in an age of uncertainty.* Buckingham: Open University Press.

Lees, S. (1986). *Losing out: Sexuality and adolescent girls.* London: Hutchinson.

Lees, S. (1993). *Sugar and spice.* Harmondsworth: Penguin.

Leonard, M. (2000). Back to the future? The domestic division of labour. *Sociology Review 9,* no. 2.

Lévi-Strauss, C. (1956). The family. In H. L. Shapiro (Ed.), *Man, culture and society.* London: Oxford.

Lewis, J. (2001). Women, men and the family. In A. Sheldon (Ed.), *The Blair effect: The Blair government 1997-2001.* London: Little, Brown and Company.

Lewis, O. (1951). *Life in a Mexican village: Tepoztlan restudied.* Urbana IL: University of Illinois Press.

Liebert, R.M. & Baron, R.A. (1972). Some immediate effects of televised violence on children's behavior. *Developmental Psychology, 6,* 469-475.

Liebow, E. (1967). *Tally's Corner.* Boston: Little Brown.

Lister, R. (1996). Back to the family: Family policies and politics under the Major government. In H. Jones & J. Millar (Eds.), *The politics of the family.* Aldershot: Avebury.

*Living in Britain: Results from the 2000 General Household Survey* (2002). London: The Stationery Office.

Livingstone, S. (1997). *Making sense of television: The psychology of audience interpretation.* London: Routledge.

Lobban, G. (1974). Data report on British reading schemes. *Times Educational Supplement,* March 1.

Long Lance, Chief Buffalo Child (1956). *Long Lance.* London: Corgi Books.

Lynch, M. & Roberts, J. (1982). *The consequences of child abuse.* London: Academic Press.

Mac an Ghaill, M. (1992). Coming of age in 1980s England: Reconceptualising Black students' schooling experience. In D. Gill, B. Mayor & M. Blair (Eds.). *Racism and education: Structures and strategies.* London: Sage.

Mac an Ghaill, M. (1994). *The making of men: Masculinities, sexualities and schooling.* Buckingham: Open University Press.

Macbeath, J. & Mortimore, P. (2001). *Improving school effectiveness.* Buckingham: Open University Press.

Macdonald, K. & Tipton, D. (1993). Using documents. In N. Gilbert (Ed.), *Researching social life.* London: Sage.

MacInnes, J. (1998). Manly virtues and masculine vices. *Living Marxism,* November.

Mair, L. (1971). *Marriage.* Harmondsworth: Penguin.

Malinowski, B. (1927). *Sex and repression in savage society.* London: Routledge.

Mann, M. (1986). *The sources of social power.* Cambridge: Cambridge University Press.

Mansfield, P. & Collard, J. (1988). *The beginning of the rest of your life?* Basingstoke: Macmillan.

Marcuse, H. (1964). *One dimensional man.* London: Routledge & Kegan Paul.

Mars, G. (1982). *Cheats at work: An anthropology of workplace crime.* London: Allen & Unwin.

Marshall, G., Rose, D., Newby, H. & Vogler, C. (1989). *Social class in modern Britain.* London: Unwin Hyman.

May, T. (2001). *Social research: Issues, methods and process* (3rd ed.). Buckingham: Open University Press.

McCrone, D. & Surridge, P. (1998). National identity and national pride. In R. Jowell et al. (Eds.), *British and European social attitudes.* Aldershot: Ashgate.

McCullagh, C. (2002). *Media power.* Basingstoke: Palgrave.

McDonough, F. (1997). Class and politics. In Storry, M. and Childs, P. (Eds.), *British cultural identities.* London: Routledge.

McGlone, F., Park, A. & Roberts, C. (1999). Kinship and friendship: Attitudes and behaviour in Britain, 1986-1995. In S. McRae (Ed.), *Changing Britain: Families and households in the 1990s.* Oxford: Oxford University Press.

McGrew, A. (1992). A global society. In S. Hall et al. (Eds.), *Modernity and its futures.* Cambridge: Polity.

McLuhan, M. (1994). *Understanding media: The extensions of man.* London: Routledge.

McMahon, A. (1999). *Taking care of men: Sexual politics in the public mind.* Cambridge: Cambridge University Press.

McNair, B. (1996). *News and journalism in the UK.* London: Routledge.

McQuail, D., Blumler, J. & Brown, R. (1972). The television audience: A revised perspective. In D. McQuail (Ed.), *Sociology of mass communication.* Harmondsworth: Penguin.

McRae, S. (1999). Introduction: Family and household change in Britain. In S. McRae (Ed.), *Changing Britain: Families and households in the 1990s.* Oxford: Oxford University Press.

McRobbie, A. (1991). *Feminism and youth culture: From Jackie to Just Seventeen.* London: Macmillan.

McRobbie, A. (1999). *In the culture society: Art, fashion and popular music.* London: Routledge.

McVeigh, T. (2001). Games stunt teen brains. *Observer*, September 19.

Mead, M. (1935). *Sex and temperament in three primitive societies.* New York: Morrow.

Mead, M. (1949). *Male and female.* London: Gollanz.

Mead, M. (1962). *Male and female.* Harmondsworth: Penguin.

Miliband, R. (1973). *The state in capitalist society.* London: Quartet Books.

Modood, T., Beishan, S. & Virdee, S. (1994). *Changing ethnic identities.* London: Policy Studies Institute.

Modood, T., Berthoud, R. et al. (1997). *Ethnic minorities in Britain: Diversity and disadvantage.* London: Policy Studies Institute.

Morgan, P. (1999). *Farewell to the family: Public policy and family breakdown in Britain and the USA.* London: The IEA Health and Welfare Unit.

Morgan, P. (2003). The family today. In M. Holborn (Ed.), *Developments in Sociology, Volume 19.* Ormskirk: Causeway Press.

Morley, D. (1980). *The 'nationwide' audience.* British Film Institute.

Mosco, V. (1996). *The political economy of communication.* London: Sage.

Moser, C.A. & Kalton, G. (1971). *Survey methods in social investigation* (2nd ed.). London: Heinemann.

Moss, P.G., Brannen, J. & Mooney, A. (2001). *An inter-generational study of employment and care.* London: University of London, Institute of Education.

Mullender, A. (1996). *Rethinking domestic violence: The social work and probation response.* London: Routledge.

Mulvey, L. (1975). Visual pleasure and narrative cinema. *Screen, 16*, (3).

Murdock, G. (1992). Embedded persuasions: The fall and rise of integrated advertising. In D. Strinati & S. Wagg (Eds.), *Come on down: Popular media culture.* London: Routledge.

Murdock, G.P. (1949). *Social structure.* New York: Macmillan.

Murray, C. (1990). *The emerging British underclass.* London: Institute of Economic Affairs.

Murray, C. (1994). The new Victorians and the new rabble. *Sunday Times*, May 29.

Murray, C. (2001). *Underclass + 10: Charles Murray and the British underclass, 1990-2000.* London: Civitas.

Myhill, A. & Allen, J. (2002). *Rape and sexual assault of women: The extent and nature of the problem.* London: Home Office Research, Development and Statistics Directorate.

Nazroo, J. (1999). Uncovering gender differences in the use of marital violence. In G. Allan (Ed.), *The sociology of the family: A reader.* Oxford: Blackwell.

Neale, B. & Smart, C. (1997). Experiments with parenthood? *Sociology, 31*, 201-219.

Negrine, R. (1994). *Politics and the mass media in Britain.* London: Routledge.

Neuman, S.B. (1991). *Literacy in the television age.* Norwood, NJ: Ablex.

Newbold, C., Boyd-Barrett, O. & Van Den Bulk, H. (Eds.) (2002). *The Media Book.* London: Arnold.

Newburn, T. & Hagell, A. (1995). Violence on the screen. *Sociology Review*, February.

Newby, H. (1977). In the field: Reflections on a study of Suffolk farm workers. In C. Bell & H. Newby (Eds.), *Doing sociological research.* London: Allen & Unwin.

Newell, R. (1993). Questionnaires. In N. Gilbert (Ed.), *Researching social life.* London: Sage.

Newson, J. & Newson, E. (1980). Parental punishment strategies with eleven-year-old children. In N. Frude (Ed.), *Psychological approaches to child abuse.* London: Batsford.

Nissel, M. (1995). Vital statistics. *New Statesman*, January 27.

O'Brien, M. (2000). Family life. In M. Haralambos (Ed.), *Developments in Sociology Volume 16.* Ormskirk: Causeway Press.

O'Connell Davidson, J. & Layder, D. (1994). *Methods, sex and madness.* London: Routledge.

O'Hagan, A. (1995). *The missing.* London: Picador.

O'Hagan, S. (2003). From sinner to saint. *The Observer*, January 12.

Oakley, A, (1972). *Sex, gender and society.* London: Temple Smith.

Oakley, A. (1974). *The sociology of housework.* London: Martin Robertson.

Okely, J. (1983). *The traveller-gypsies.* Cambridge: Cambridge University Press.

Page, R. (2002). New Labour and the welfare state. In M. Holborn (Ed.), *Developments in Sociology, Volume 18.* Ormskirk: Causeway Press.

Pahl, J. (1989). *Money and marriage.* Basingstoke: Macmillan.

Pakulski, J. & Waters, M. (1996). *The death of class.* London: Sage.

Parke, R.D., Berkowitz, L., Leyens, J.P., Wet, S. & Sebastian, R.J. (1977). Some effects of violent and nonviolent movies on the behaviour of juvenile delinquents. In I. Berkowitz (Ed.), *Advances in experimental psychology, 10.* New York: Academic Press.

Parker, H., Aldridge, J. & Measham, F. (1998). *Illegal leisure: The normalisation of adolescent recreational drug use.* London: Routledge.

Parsons, T. & Bales, R.F. (1955). *Family, socialisation and interaction process.* New York: The Free Press.

Pawson, R. (1995). Methodology. In M. Haralambos (Ed.), *Developments in Sociology, Volume 5.* Ormskirk: Causeway Press.

Peake, S. (2002). *The Guardian media guide 2003.* London: Atlantic Books.

Pearson, G. (1983). *Hooligan: A history of respectable fears.* London: Macmillan.

Pence, E. (1987). *In our best interest: A process for personal and social change.* Duluth MN: Minnesota Program Development, Inc.

Perrons, D. (2003). The new economy and the work life balance: Conceptual explorations and a case study of new media. *Gender Work and Organisation, 10*, 65-93.

Phillips, M. (1995). Whatever happened to the middle classes? *Observer*, July 2.

Phillipson, C., Bernard, M., Phillips, J. & Ogg, J. (1999). Older people in three urban areas: Household composition, kinship and social networks. In S. McRae (Ed.), *Changing Britain: Families and households in the 1990s.* Oxford: Oxford University Press.

Philo, G. (1993). Getting the message: Audience research in the Glasgow University Media Group. In J. Eldridge (Ed.), *Getting the message: News, truth and power.* London: Routledge.

Philo, G. & Miller, D. (2002). Circuits of communication and power: Recent developments in media sociology. In M. Holborn (Ed.), *Developments in Sociology, Volume 18.* Ormskirk: Causeway Press.

Platt, J. (1976). *Realities of social research: An empirical study of British sociologists.* London: Chatto and Windus.

Pleck, J. (1985). *Working wives, working husbands.* London: Sage.

Postman, N. (1983). *The disappearance of childhood.* London: W.H. Allen.

Pryce, K. (1979). Endless pressure. Harmondsworth: Penguin.

Punch, M. (1979). Observation and the police. In M. Hammersley (Ed.), *Social research: Philosophy, politics and practice.* London: Sage.

Radway, J. (1984). *Reading the romance: Women, patriarchy and popular literature.* Chapel Hill: University of North Carolina Press.

Rapoport, R. & Rapoport, R.N. (1971). *Dual career families.* Harmondsworth: Penguin.

Reay, D. (1998). *Class work: Mothers' involvement in their children's primary schooling.* London: UCL Press.

Redfield, R. (1930). *Tepoztlan: A Mexican village.* Chicago: University of Chicago Press.

Reid, I. (1998). *Class in Britain.* Cambridge: Polity Press.

Reynold, E. (2001). Learning the hard way. *British Journal of Sociology of Education, 22*, no. 3.

Ritzer, G. (2002). *McDonaldization: The reader.* Thousand Oaks: Pine Forge Press.

Roberts, K. (2001). *Class in modern Britain.* Basingstoke: Palgrave.

Rodgers, B. & Pryor, J. (1998). *Divorce and separation: The outcomes for children.* York: Joseph Rowntree Foundation.

Rojek, C. (2000). Leisure and the rich today. *Leisure Studies, 19*, no. 1.

Ross, K. (1996). *Black and White media.* Cambridge: Polity Press.

Rowlingson, K. & McKay, S. (1998). *The growth of lone parenthood.* London: Policy Studies Institute.

Saunders, P. (1990). *Social class and stratification*. London: Routledge.

Saunders, P. (2000). Afterward: Family research and family policy since 1992. In N. Dennis & G. Erdos, *Families without fatherhood* (3rd ed.). London: Institute for the Study of Civil Society.

Savage, M., Bagnall, G. & Longhurst, B. (2001). Ordinary, ambivalent and defensive. *Sociology, 35*, no. 2.

Savage, M., Barlow, J., Dickens P. & Fielding, T. (1992). *Property bureaucracy and culture*. London: Routledge.

Scanzoni, J., Polonko, K., Teachman, J. & Thompson, L. (1989). *The sexual bond*. Newbury Park: Sage.

Scase, R. (2000). *Britain in 2010*. Oxford: Capstone Publishing.

Schlesinger, P. & Tumber, H. (1994). *Reporting crime: The media politics of criminal justice*. Oxford: Clarendon.

Schlesinger, P. (1991). Media, state and nation. London: Sage.

Schudson, M. (2000). The sociology of news production revisited – again. In J. Curran & M. Gurevitch (Eds.), *Mass media and society*. London: Arnold.

Sclater, S.D. (2001). Domestic violence: Private troubles or social problems? *Sociology Review*, April.

Scott, J. (1982). *The upper classes: Property and privilege in Britain*. London: Macmillan.

Scott, J. (1990). *A matter of record*. Cambridge: Polity Press.

Scruton, R. (1986). The myth of cultural relativism. In F. Palmer (Ed.), *Anti-racism*. London: Sherwood Press.

Sharpe, S. (1976). *Just like a girl: How girls learn to be women*. Harmondsworth: Penguin.

Sharpe, S. (1984). *Double identity*. Harmondsworth: Penguin.

Sharpe, S. (1994). *Just like a girl: How girls learn to be women: The 70s to the 90s*. Harmondsworth: Penguin.

Shaw, C. (1930). *The Jack Roller*. Chicago: University of Chicago Press.

Simons, H. (1984). Guidelines for the conduct of an independent evaluation. In C. Adelman (Ed.), *The politics and ethics of evaluation*. London: Croom Helm.

Sissons, M. (1970). T*he psychology of social class*. Milton Keynes: Open University Press.

Skelton, C. (2001). *Schooling the boys*. Buckingham: Open University Press.

Smith, J., Gilford, S. & O'Sullivan, A. (1998). *The family background of homeless young people*. London: Family Policy Studies Centre (now available through the Joseph Rowntree Foundation).

Social Exclusion Unit (1998). *Bringing Britain together*.

*Social Trends* (2002). London: The Stationery Office.

*Social Trends* (2003). London: The Stationery Office.

Solomos, J. & Back, L. (1996). *Racism and society*. London: Macmillan.

Sreberny-Mohammadi, A. (1996). The global and local in international communication. In J. Curran & M. Gurevitch (Eds.), *Mass media and society*. London: Arnold.

Stacey, J. (1996). *In the name of the family: Rethinking family values in the postmodern age*. Boston MA: Beacon Press.

Stainton Rogers, W. & Stainton Rogers, R. (2001). *The psychology of gender and sexuality*. Buckingham: Open University Press.

Stainton Rogers, W. (2001). Constructing childhood, constructing child concern. In P. Foley, J. Roche & S. Turner (Eds.), *Children in society: Contemporary theory, policy and practice*. Basingstoke: Palgrave.

Stands In Timber, J. & Liberty, M. (1967). *Cheyenne memories*. New Haven, Yale University Press.

Stanko, E. (2003). *The day to count ...* www.domesticviolencedata.org/5

Stevenson, N. (1995). U*nderstanding media cultures*. London: Sage.

Strinati, D. (1992). Postmodernism and popular culture. *Sociology Review*, April.

Sugrue, B. & Taylor, C. (1996). Cultures and identities. *Sociology Review, 5*, no. 3.

Tam, M. (1997). *Part-time employment*. Aldershot: Avebury.

Taraborrelli, P. (1993). Becoming a carer. In N. Gilbert (Ed.), *Researching social life*. London: Sage.

Tebbit, N. (1990). Fanfare on being British. *The Field*, May.

Thomas, W.I. & Znaniecki, F. (1958). *The Polish peasant in Europe and America*. New York: Dover.

Thompson, J. (1990). *Ideology and modern culture*. Oxford: Polity Press.

Thompson, J. (1995). *The media and modernity*. Oxford: Polity Press.

Tizard, B. & Phoenix, A. (1993). *Black, White or Mixed race*. London: Routledge.

Tuchman, G. (1978). *Making news*. New York: Free Press.

Tuchman, G. (1981). The symbolic annihilation of women by the mass media. In S. Cohen & J. Young (Eds.). *The manufacture of news*. London: Constable.

Tunstall, J. (1983). *The media in Britain*. London: Constable.

Turnbull, C. (1961). *The forest people*. London: Jonathan Cape.

Van Dijk, T. (1991). *Racism and the press*. London: Routledge.

Van Dijk, T. (1993). Denying racism: Elite discourse and racism. In J. Wrench & J. Solomos (Eds.), *Racism and migration in Western Europe*. Oxford: Berg.

Vogler, C. & Pahl, J. (1994). Money, power and inequality within marriage. *Sociological Review, 42*, 263-288.

Waddington, P.A.J. (1999). Police (canteen) sub culture. *British Journal of Criminology, 39*, no. 2.

Walford, G. (1993). Researching the City Technology College Kingshurst. In R. Burgess (Ed.), *Research Methods*. London: Nelson.

Walkerdine, V., Lucey, H. & Melody, J. (2001). *Growing up girl*. Basingstoke: Palgrave.

Walklate, S. (2000). Researching victims. In R.D. King & E. Wincup (Eds.), *Doing research on crime and justice*. Oxford: Oxford University Press.

Weale, S. (2002). The right to choose. *The Guardian*, December 2.

Weber, M. (1958). *The Protestant ethic and the spirit of capitalism*. New York: Charles Scribner's Sons.

Weeks, J., Heaphy, B. & Donovan, C. (1999a). Partners by choice: Equality, power and commitment in non-heterosexual relationships. In G. Allan (Ed.), *The sociology of the family: A reader*. Oxford: Blackwell.

Weeks, J., Heaphy, B. & Donovan, C. (1999b). Families of choice: Autonomy and mutuality in non-heterosexual relationships. In S. McRae (Ed.), *Changing Britain: Families and households in the 1990s*. Oxford: Oxford University Press.

Westwood S. & Bhachu, P. (1988). Images and realities. *New Society*, May 6.

Whyte, W.F. (1955). *Street corner society* (2nd ed.). Chicago: University of Chicago Press.

Wilkinson, H. (1997). The androgynous generation. In G. Dench (Ed.), *Rewriting the sexual contract*. London: Institute of Community Studies.

Williams, B. (1981). *Obscenity and film censorship*. Cambridge: Cambridge University Press.

Williams, J.A. Jr. (1971). Interviewer-respondent interaction. In B.J. Franklin & H.W. Osborne (Eds.), *Research Methods*. Belmont: Wadsworth.

Williams, K. (2003). *Understanding media theory*. London: Arnold.

Willmott, P. (1980). A view from an independent research institute. In M. Cross (Ed.), *Social research and public policy: Three perspectives*. Social Research Association.

Willmott, P. (1986). *Social networks, informal care and public policy*. London: Policy Studies Institute.

Women's Aid (2001). *About Women's Aid*. Bristol: Women's Aid.

Wood, W., Wong, F.Y. & Chachere, J.G. (1991). Effects of media violence on viewers' aggression in unconstrained social interaction. *Psychological Bulletin, 109*, 371-383.

Woodward, K. (Ed.), (1997). *Identity and difference*. London, Sage.

Young, M. & Willmott, P. (1957). *Family and kinship in East London*. London: Routledge & Kegan Paul.

Young, M. & Willmott, P. (1973). *The symmetrical family*. London: Routledge & Kegan Paul.

Zillmann, D. & Bryant, J. (1984). Effects of massive exposure to pornography. In M.N. Malamuth & E. Donnerstein (Eds.), *Pornography and sexual aggression*. New York: Academic Press.

# Author index

# Subject index